Forms of Thinking in Leopardi's *Zibaldone*
Religion, Science and Everyday Life in an
Age of Disenchantment

LEGENDA

LEGENDA is the Modern Humanities Research Association's book imprint for new research in the Humanities. Founded in 1995 by Malcolm Bowie and others within the University of Oxford, Legenda has always been a collaborative publishing enterprise, directly governed by scholars. The Modern Humanities Research Association (MHRA) joined this collaboration in 1998, became half-owner in 2004, in partnership with Maney Publishing and then Routledge, and has since 2016 been sole owner. Titles range from medieval texts to contemporary cinema and form a widely comparative view of the modern humanities, including works on Arabic, Catalan, English, French, German, Greek, Italian, Portuguese, Russian, Spanish, and Yiddish literature. Editorial boards and committees of more than 60 leading academic specialists work in collaboration with bodies such as the Society for French Studies, the British Comparative Literature Association and the Association of Hispanists of Great Britain & Ireland.

The MHRA encourages and promotes advanced study and research in the field of the modern humanities, especially modern European languages and literature, including English, and also cinema. It aims to break down the barriers between scholars working in different disciplines and to maintain the unity of humanistic scholarship. The Association fulfils this purpose through the publication of journals, bibliographies, monographs, critical editions, and the MHRA Style Guide, and by making grants in support of research. Membership is open to all who work in the Humanities, whether independent or in a University post, and the participation of younger colleagues entering the field is especially welcomed.

ALSO PUBLISHED BY THE ASSOCIATION

Critical Texts
Tudor and Stuart Translations • *New Translations* • *European Translations*
MHRA Library of Medieval Welsh Literature

MHRA Bibliographies
Publications of the Modern Humanities Research Association

The Annual Bibliography of English Language & Literature
Austrian Studies
Modern Language Review
Portuguese Studies
The Slavonic and East European Review
Working Papers in the Humanities
The Yearbook of English Studies

www.mhra.org.uk
www.legendabooks.com

ITALIAN PERSPECTIVES

Editorial-Committee
Professor Simon Gilson, University of Warwick (General Editor)
Dr Francesca Billiani, University of Manchester
Professor Manuele Gragnolati, Université Paris-Sorbonne
Dr Catherine Keen, University College London
Professor Martin McLaughlin, Magdalen College, Oxford

Founding Editors
Professor Zygmunt Barański and Professor Anna Laura Lepschy

In the light of growing academic interest in Italy and the reorganization of many university courses in Italian along interdisciplinary lines, this book series, founded by Maney Publishing under the imprint of the Northern Universities Press and now continuing under the Legenda imprint, aims to bring together different scholarly perspectives on Italy and its culture. *Italian Perspectives* publishes books and collections of essays on any period of Italian literature, language, history, culture, politics, art, and media, as well as studies which take an interdisciplinary approach and are methodologically innovative.

APPEARING IN THIS SERIES

20. *Ugo Foscolo and English Culture*, by Sandra Parmegiani
21. *The Printed Media in Fin-de-siècle Italy: Publishers, Writers, and Readers*, ed. by Ann Hallamore Caesar, Gabriella Romani, and Jennifer Burns
22. *Giraffes in the Garden of Italian Literature: Modernist Embodiment in Italo Svevo, Federigo Tozzi and Carlo Emilio Gadda*, by Deborah Amberson
23. *Remembering Aldo Moro: The Cultural Legacy of the 1978 Kidnapping and Murder*, ed. by Ruth Glynn and Giancarlo Lombardi
24. *Disrupted Narratives: Illness, Silence and Identity in Svevo, Pressburger and Morandini*, by Emma Bond
25. *Dante and Epicurus: A Dualistic Vision of Secular and Spiritual Fulfilment*, by George Corbett
26. *Edoardo Sanguineti: Literature, Ideology and the Avant-Garde*, ed. by Paolo Chirumbolo and John Picchione
27. *The Tradition of the Actor-Author in Italian Theatre*, ed. by Donatella Fischer
28. *Leopardi's Nymphs: Grace, Melancholy, and the Uncanny*, by Fabio A. Camilletti
29. *Gadda and Beckett: Storytelling, Subjectivity and Fracture*, by Katrin Wehling-Giorgi
30. *Caravaggio in Film and Literature: Popular Culture's Appropriation of a Baroque Genius*, by Laura Rorato
31. *The Italian Academies 1525-1700: Networks of Culture, Innovation and Dissent*, ed. by Jane E. Everson, Denis V. Reidy and Lisa Sampson
32. *Rome Eternal: The City As Fatherland*, by Guy Lanoue
33. *The Somali Within: Language, Race and Belonging in 'Minor' Italian Literature*, by Simone Brioni
34. *Laughter from Realism to Modernism: Misfits and Humorists in Pirandello, Svevo, Palazzeschi, and Gadda*, by Alberto Godioli
35. *Pasolini after Dante: The 'Divine Mimesis' and the Politics of Representation*, by Emanuela Patti

Managing Editor
Dr Graham Nelson, 41 Wellington Square, Oxford OX1 2JF, UK
www.legendabooks.com

Forms of Thinking in Leopardi's *Zibaldone*

Religion, Science and Everyday Life in an Age of Disenchantment

Paola Cori

Italian Perspectives 43
Modern Humanities Research Association
2019

*Published by Legenda
an imprint of the Modern Humanities Research Association
Salisbury House, Station Road, Cambridge CB1 2LA*

*ISBN 978-1-78188-863-6 (HB)
ISBN 978-1-78188-864-3 (PB)*

*First published 2019
Paperback edition 2021*

All rights reserved. No part of this publication may be reproduced or disseminated or transmitted in any form or by any means, electronic, mechanical, photocopying, recording or otherwise, or stored in any retrieval system, or otherwise used in any manner whatsoever without written permission of the copyright owner, except in accordance with the provisions of the Copyright, Designs and Patents Act 1988, or under the terms of a licence permitting restricted copying issued in the UK by the Copyright Licensing Agency Ltd, Saffron House, 6–10 Kirby Street, London EC1N 8TS, England, or in the USA by the Copyright Clearance Center, 222 Rosewood Drive, Danvers MA 01923. Application for the written permission of the copyright owner to reproduce any part of this publication must be made by email to legenda@mhra.org.uk.

Disclaimer: Statements of fact and opinion contained in this book are those of the author and not of the editors or the Modern Humanities Research Association. The publisher makes no representation, express or implied, in respect of the accuracy of the material in this book and cannot accept any legal responsibility or liability for any errors or omissions that may be made.

Trademark notice: Product or corporate names may be trademarks or registered trademarks, and are used only for identification and explanation without intent to infringe.

© *Modern Humanities Research Association 2019*

Copy-Editor: Charlotte Brown

CONTENTS

❖

Abbreviations		ix
Acknowledgments		x
Introduction		1

PART I: MATHEMATICS AND RELIGION

1	The Conscious and the Unconscious	39
2	The Continuum and the Discrete	49
3	The Psychology of Clarity	53
4	'ec. ec. ec.': The Determinate and the Indeterminate	63
5	Clarity and Confession	77
6	Naturalness and Natural Law	87
7	Naturalization of Religion	94
8	Messianic Inclinations	101
9	Naturalness as the Style of Grace	105

PART II: PHYSICAL SCIENCES

10	Towards a Philosophy of Life and Technique	117
11	The Heading 'Vitalità, Sensibilità' (I): Leopardi's Elastic Writing	121
12	Swarms of Birds: The Heading 'Vitalità, Sensibilità' (II) and Leopardi's Self-adjusting Thought	134
13	Electric Thought	150
14	Disenchanted Mnemotechnics	164
15	The Hypnotic Image: A Preliminary Contextualization	172
16	Leopardi's Philosophy of Exposure and Attenuation	187

PART III: EVERYDAY LIFE

17	The Practice of Everyday Life	207
18	Leopardi as Master and Student in the *Zibaldone*	214
19	Metropolitan Encounters: Quotations and the *Zibaldone* 'Index'	227
20	The End of the *Zibaldone*: Conclusions	245
	Bibliography	248
	Index	262

ABBREVIATIONS

C   Giacomo Leopardi, *Canti*, trans. by Jonathan Galassi (New York: Farrar, Straus & Giroux, 2010)

E   Giacomo Leopardi, *Epistolario*, ed. by Franco Brioschi and Patrizia Landi, 2 vols (Turin: Bollati Boringhieri, 1998)

EZ   Giacomo Leopardi, *Zibaldone: The Notebooks of Leopardi*, ed. by Michael Caesar and Franco D'Intino, trans. by Kathleen Baldwin and others (London: Penguin, 2013); all page numbers are the same as those for *Zib* and so are not be given separately

MT   Giacomo Leopardi, *Moral Tales*, trans. by Patrick Creagh (Manchester: Carcanet New Press, 1983)

TPP   Giacomo Leopardi, *Tutte le poesie e tutte le prose*, ed. by Lucio Felici and Emanuele Trevi (Rome: Newton Compton, 2007)

Zib.   Giacomo Leopardi, *Zibaldone di pensieri*, ed. by Fiorenza Ceragioli and Monica Ballerini (Bologna: Zanichelli, 2009) (CD-ROM); this abbreviation followed by the original manuscript page number

Unless otherwise stated, all translations are my own.

ACKNOWLEDGEMENTS

This book could not have been completed without the help of my most attentive reader, Alan Suter. I am also grateful to my family and to the friends who, in the course of the years, have always offered encouragement and had faith in what I was doing: Michela Centioni, Simona Conversi, Luca Malici, Alessandra Marini, Angela Matheson, Diego Panzini, Patrizia Perrotti, Ilaria Serafini, George Turvey, Cosetta Veronese, and Francesca Zoppi. Among them, I would also like to thank Alessandra Aloisi for the many precious conversations which have inspired me and motivated me in many ways.

I am grateful to Fabio Camilletti for his advice and his very useful comments on an advanced draft and to Sophie Bouvier for some helpful linguistic tips. The first part of this book was possible also thanks to a Small Research Grant from the Cesare Barbieri Endowment (Trinity College, Hartford, USA); I am very grateful to the Barbieri Executive Committee for their support, and in particular to John Alcorn for his constant advice and his careful reading and comments, which I treasure, especially for my chapter 'Leopardi as Master and Student in the *Zibaldone*'.

Many initiatives and collaborations hosted by the Leopardi Centre at Birmingham were beneficial to the early development of this book. At Birmingham special thanks also go to Clelia Boscolo and Paolo De Ventura. The Dante Society at Birmingham offered me many chances to present and discuss my research in a very welcoming and stimulating atmosphere, and I wish to thank Rosalia Beccarelli for her kindness. The time I spent as Lecturer at Cardiff University in the academic year 2016–17 helped me finalize my project, and the supportive approach of the Department of Italian has been crucial in creating an ideal environment for my studies. My many conversations with Peter Coss have helped me to clarify my ideas, and among the *leopardisti*, I wish to thank Novella Bellucci, Michael Caesar, Emanuela Cervato, Franco D'Intino, and Pamela Williams for their advice over the years. I would also like to thank Simon Gilson and the editorial board of the Legenda 'Italian Perspectives' series for having evaluated and accepted my manuscript, as well as Graham Nelson and Charlotte Wathey for their patient support in the production process.

Some chapters of this study, now extensively revised, have appeared previously in the following publications: '"ec. ec. ec.": The Determinate and the Indeterminate' appeared as '"ec. ec. ec.": modi e forme della sospensione nello *Zibaldone*', in *Lo 'Zibaldone' di Leopardi come ipertesto*, ed. by Maria de las Nieves Muñiz Muñiz (Florence: Olschki, 2013), pp. 93–107; 'Electric Thought' develops ideas expounded in '"Tensione" nello *Zibaldone*', in *Per un lessico leopardiano*, ed. by Novella Bellucci and Franco D'Intino (Rome: Palombi, 2011), pp. 133–49; 'Leopardi's Philosophy of Exposure and Attenuation' was first published as 'L'attenuazione in Leopardi: lingua, diritto e storia delle idee', in *La metafora da Leopardi ai contemporanei*, ed. by Antonella Del Gatto, special issue of *Studi Medievali e Moderni*, 1 (2016), 43–62; and 'Leopardi as Master and Student in the *Zibaldone*' derives from 'The *Zibaldone* as Leopardi's Self-education', *Italica*, 93.1 (2016), 77–91. I thank all the editors for their permission to elaborate on these studies.

This book is for my mother, Rosaria Serafini, in memory of her.

> I've been waiting for a guide to come
> And take me by the hand
> Could these sensations make me feel
> The pleasures of a normal man?
> These sensations barely interest me
> For another day
> I've got the spirit, lose the feeling
> Take the shock away.
>
> — Joy Division, 'Disorder'

Trovatomi intieramente solo e nudo [...], l'essere esposto al di fuori [...] estingue tutte le mie facoltà, in modo ch'io [...] voglio parlare e non so che diavolo mi dire, non sento più me stesso, e son fatto in tutto e per tutto una statua.

[I found myself entirely alone and naked. Being exposed in the open extinguishes all my faculties, to the point that I want to speak and I don't know what the hell to say, I do not feel myself anymore and I am entirely reduced to stone.]

— Giacomo Leopardi, letter to Carlo, Rome, 23 November 1822

With what awful fear he had deprecated the success of his pursuit, and prayed that the Unpardonable Sin might never be revealed to him. Then he ensued that vast intellectual development, which, in its progress, disturbed the counterpoise between his mind and heart.

— Nathaniel Hawthorne, *Ethan Brand*

The great simulacra constructed by man evolve from a universe of natural laws to one of forces and tensions, and finally, today, to a universe of structures and binary oppositions.

— Jean Baudrillard, *Symbolic Exchange and Death*

Light is not only glorious and sacred, it is voracious, carnivorous, unsparing. It devours impartially, without distinction, the whole living world.

— Lawrence Gowing, *Turner: Imagination and Reality*

INTRODUCTION

In the *Protagoras*, Plato narrates the myth of the creation of man and other animals. Once the gods had formed the species by moulding the natural elements, Protagoras explains, the moment arrived when they were destined to come to life. Epimetheus, the brother of Prometheus, was charged with equipping all species with prerogatives and tools essential for their preservation. Thus he distributed strength to some animals and swiftness to others; some he armed, some he provided with a considerable size that protected them, and to others who were weaker he gave the ability to fly, so that they could escape danger. But when it came to human beings, Epimetheus realized that he had forgotten about them, and having already used all the available skills for other species, he had no faculties or tools to spare. Human beings were thus destined to come to life naked and exposed. It was only thanks to the intervention of Prometheus, who stole fire from Athena and Hephaestus (and the knowledge of the mechanical technique necessary to use it), that human beings were eventually able to acquire for themselves clothing and food, as well as develop other means of survival such as language. This intellectual and technical approach, however, made them the only creatures aware of their bareness and exposed state. What distinguished man from the other creatures was precisely this self-reflexive gaze which pushed them to elaborate strategies to overcome their exposure.[1]

This myth inaugurated a long philosophical and theological tradition that conceives of nudity as a condition which can (and/or should) be repaired. At the same time, because unawareness prevented nakedness from becoming a problem for the other animals, the consideration of nakedness itself has been somehow obscured as a shared state and often treated as an exclusive domain of anthropocentric perspectives. This has also created an overlap between the idea of 'being' and that of 'oneness'.[2] However, as Jean-Luc Nancy explains, the idea of singularity should not be separated from that of plurality, as some forms of contiguity and contagion constantly occur between individual entities. The idea of 'being' is always linked to that of 'being in the other' and what exists can be thought of as an ensemble of bodies whose primary constituent characteristic is that of *touching* other bodies. In performing touch each body discovers its own extension and limits, and finds its own identity as part of a co-existing plurality: 'all of being is in touch with all of being, but the law of touching is separation'; the philosophy of exposure thus conceives of humanity as 'the exposing of the world' while 'the world is the exposure of humanity'.[3] There is a sense of permeation, porosity, and malleability in this conception, which I believe could be fruitfully transposed into the field of textual analysis.

My book proposes a reading of Leopardi's 4526-page notebook, the *Zibaldone*, through the idea of exposure in order to explore the influence of three main areas of inquiry — religion, science, and everyday life — which permeate Leopardi's thought and shape the formal nature of the text. The *Zibaldone* has inspired a variety of metaphors and models to represent its character,[4] while resisting classification within a specific literary genre.[5] This is a work containing reflections on all possible aspects of human understanding (from autobiographical notes to considerations on literature, philosophy, social and political sciences, and anthropology), hosting a variety of forms (from fragments to essays, including Leopardi's own poetry as well as quotations from other authors, in various languages, both European and ancient). Although private in character, it switches constantly from more intimate and self-addressed reflections to dialogical constructions implying a virtual reader, and is motivated by a strong propensity for the systematic and encyclopaedic while at the same time nourishing the recreational function of un-programmatic creative impulses, unpredictable, renewable, and surprising to the author himself. What I wish to argue is that the variety of themes and forms hosted, despite their different scopes and motivations, can be thought of and analyzed as an *informing response* to a reality which constantly urges the mind that approaches it to act (sometimes unconsciously), and to stay alert. The *Zibaldone* writing can be conceived in general as the materialization of a *boundary of touch*, or the liminal territory where contact takes place between the inner emotional and intellectual existence and the external reality on which the mind operates. On the one hand there is Leopardi's attempt to grasp the universe of possible knowledge by pushing his reflections towards new topics, and by applying new points of focus to old themes. Creating connections and comparisons between different areas of knowledge is the way in which Leopardi's research instinct projects, within the textual universe of the *Zibaldone*, the complex and infinite domain of possibilities for what constitutes the thinkable and the imaginable. In this respect, and with reference to Leopardi's encyclopaedic inclination, it is certainly possible to speak of his hierarchical and horizontal approaches to systemization, which have been the object of interest of recent critical works devoted to the *Zibaldone* as an autonomous text.[6]

At the same time, however, there is a strong element of *passivity* that the text necessarily sustains in face of the reality with which it communicates. Leopardi's empiricist philosophy of reference taught him about a self whose senses are constantly hit by sensations awaiting the intervention of the intellect for analysis. However, Leopardi also intuited by his own means what certain sensationalist and *idéologue* philosophers had theorized (often unbeknown to him), namely that these sensations can be overwhelming, thus escaping the control of the mind.[7] Leopardi voices (in different ways and modalities of expression) the 'perils of imagination' and the fragmentation typical of the 'post-revolutionary self', which replaces Cartesian self-evidence with an identity shaped by unreachable layers of emotions and fissures of unconsciousness.[8] Leopardi engages with the ethical aspects of an imagination which might lead one to confuse imaginary objects for the real, and shows interest in conditions of automatic responses of attention which would later be fully theorized by the physiological philosophy of the nerves in the course of the nineteenth century. His thought is also concerned with issues of authenticity of the self, which are brought about by certain daring uses of language, and this directs his reflection also onto our way of acting in the world rather than exclusively onto our own knowledge of ourselves.[9] In the *Zibaldone* there is a realm of opaque and latent currents of feelings and understanding which runs below the surface of Leopardi's lucid organizational strategies and that is characteristic of the very complex and articulated *longue durée* towards the discovery of the unconscious, which took place from the second half of the eighteenth century to the end of the nineteenth century.[10]

Critical approaches emphasizing the systematic nature of the *Zibaldone* have tended to neglect this universe of subterranean forces and this study attempts to provide an interpretation of how religion, science, and everyday life influenced Leopardi's thought at both conscious and unconscious levels and determined specific configurations of writing. These three central categories are *generative forms*, or, in other words, *themes which have become forms*, external objects of observation of a certain cultural, literary, or scientific significance which *affect* or stimulate Leopardi's intellect and imagination to the point of becoming internalized and so activating their truest essence as an influence over words. These forms behave towards the text in the same way that a stone does with respect to the human organism in Nancy's thought:

> A stone is the exteriority of singularity in what would have to be called its mineral or mechanical actuality [*litteralité*]. But I would no longer be a 'human' if I did not have this exteriority 'in me', in the form of the quasi-minerality of bone.[11]

Domenico Secondulfo defines a 'generative form' as 'lo stampo, la matrice che in un determinato momento storico-sociale, organizza, informa ed orienta la costruzione sociale della realtà o di suoi pezzi rilevanti' [the imprint, the matrix which in a certain historical-social moment organizes, informs, and orientates the social construction of reality, or of its relevant parts].[12] Secondulfo refers to generative models of the real which filter the process of constructing reality by channelling it within certain relational schemes and particular characteristics, which are specific to the form itself.[13] Generative forms flow into different cultural products which can be very distant from the original area to which a generative form belongs and their existence is more visible in moments of crisis and transformation. In these cases, new historical and social formations become dominant over older formations and start to consolidate new generative forms which replicate themselves and exercise hegemony over previous social structures thus modifying them. Generative forms originate, among the various social aspects in which they operate, 'una armonia ed una similitudine che, seppure nella diversa fenomenologia del loro essere, permettono di riconoscerli come simili e sostanzialmente uguali' [a harmony and a similitude which, despite the different phenomenology of their being, make it possible to recognize them as similar and substantially equal].[14] Their influence can be synchronic, or in other words exercised by more than one single dominant generative form. They often share similar characteristics and reproduce themselves in other areas, objects, or social incarnations, through latent processes of poïesis. It is important to note how Leopardi perceives the generative function of dominant structures when he states that 'la morale è un detto, e la politica un fatto: la vita domestica, la società privata, qualunque cosa umana prende la sua forma dalla natura generale dello stato pubblico di un popolo' ('ethics is a word, politics a fact. Domestic life, private society, every human thing takes its form from the general nature of the public condition of a people') (*Zib.* 311).[15] He is indeed insisting on homologies between macro- and micro-structures which recur in all aspects and at all levels of human life.

In this book the idea of generative forms is adapted to explain the textual dimension of the *Zibaldone*, bearing in mind, as I have already pointed out, that my focus is not only on the content of Leopardi's notes, but also on their mutual interactions, shape, and disposition, which often suggests a surplus of meaning that is perceived in the most material and sensorial dimension possible by the reader. There is a dimension of praxis and performance in language which extends beyond discourse. Moving from this concrete and embodied effect that language exercises, it is possible to build an analogy between certain textual configurations and specific aspects of the real to which religious, scientific, and everyday-life generative forms refer. My primary objective is not to reconstruct only what Leopardi *says* regarding the themes of religion, science, and everyday life over the course of the years, although in-depth awareness of Leopardi's ideas is essential in order to link his reflections to the broader context of Western thought, spanning from antiquity to contemporary philosophy. Rather, I am interested in investigating, for example, why religious preoccupations converge with an almost obsessive attention to clarity; how far it is possible to assert that Leopardi's ornithological interest generates symbols for antiquity and modernity that influence the way in which he corrects his own thought; and to what extent Leopardi's conception of walking, dialectically linking ancient dialogical philosophy to the chaotic encounters of modern city life, transforms the actual text into a territory to be traversed.

Needless to say, the forms that I propose in this study do not pretend to cover all the lenses through which it would be possible to investigate Leopardi's writing. The three core categories do however represent the primary centres of irradiation and inter-connectedness in Leopardi's thought, as they act as the most essential *touching* macro-structures that were absorbed and transformed into micro-textual harmonies in the *Zibaldone*. This means that specific religious, scientific, or everyday values or concerns which occupy a relevant thematic place in Leopardi's gnoseology also influence the way in which the text is moulded: syntactical and lexical patterns, recursion, modes of revision, rote learning, and dialogical structures, among others, reproduce within the zibaldonic organism the same laws, preoccupations, and rapports which are responsible for a particular sensitivity in the author's external — extra-textual, 'real', biological — world. They constitute the foundational forms for the organization of thought in Leopardi's daily relationship with his notebook, as shown for example by the fact that some of the most important reflections in the *Zibaldone*, such as for instance those on grace, pertain to more than one of these structuring forms at the same time; they are polymorphic and multi-layered, provoking in the reader a switch of attention between coexistent and alternating points of focus on different cultural and symbolical systems, similar to multi-stable images which provide alternate visualizations of different figures appearing from the same lineaments, or to stereoscopic images revealing objects advancing from depth onto a two-dimensional surface.

This book is organized into three parts each with an autonomous focus but at the same time open to recursive analysis of specific philosophical motifs in which the core generative forms are closely interconnected. Certain entries in the *Zibaldone* are subject to synchronic formative generation, and they are therefore investigated more than once from different perspectives. Mathematics and religion in its naturalized form are the generative forms discussed in Part I. They constitute the pillars of Leopardi's writing, in that they are closely linked with certain cognitive structures and drives which lend themselves to metaphorical transformation in other realms of knowledge. These forms are significant because they shape both the trajectory of writing and Leopardi's deepest, most intimate relationship with the text. As far as mathematics is concerned, the idea of the limits and the divisibility of the real corresponds to Leopardi's at times obsessive tendency to atomize analytical thought and deconstruct his speculations in all their possible aspects, variations, and components. There is an almost manic obsession with divisibility in which abstract theorization meets Leopardi's most personal need for spiritual clarity. Religion, instead, is the atavistic filter through which knowledge of the world is introduced by means of Jesuit instruction to the young Leopardi, and his later atheistic thought would never completely escape the influence of religious prescription. Rather, Leopardi prefers to conceal religion under the cloak of his system of nature while progressing in his disenchanted unveiling of truth. The second part of the volume, on science, provides models to interpret in detail the ways in which the *Zibaldone* notes develop and interact. Electric and magnetic imagery are the core lenses used to detect the diachronic development of writing as well as isolated apparitions of images, while at the same time revealing Leopardi's sensibility towards scientific models which would become fully operative only in the later decades of the nineteenth century. The third part, on everyday life, addresses Leopardi's view on the importance of a praxis of living, and the way morality as praxis applies to the notebook as a whole. In discussing how the late *Zibaldone* resolves a tension between antiquity and modernity, I also attempt to explain how and why the *Zibaldone* ends.

These three parts and their respective chapters do not follow a strict chronological order, and in this the structure of my book reflects the non-linear character of the *Zibaldone*. However, there is a logic which presides over the order of the three sections and a macro-chronological development is discernible. In addressing religious structures, Part I necessarily focuses mostly on the *Zibaldone*'s early life, corresponding to the more general process of naturalization of religion mentioned before, which was already effective in 1820 and can be considered to have been completed by 1824. The formation of Leopardi's religious and philosophical understanding in these years — in 1819, the year of the 'mutazione totale' ('total transformation') and 'passaggio dallo stato antico al moderno' ('my passing from ancient to modern') (*Zib.* 144), Leopardi had already envisioned his ultra-philosophy (cf. *Zib.* 115) — provides both his thought and the *Zibaldone* with the flexible structure capable of receiving and moulding a variety of other generative forms which will continue to interact and overlap with the religious system in the course of the years. Part II, in dealing with different manifestations of Leopardi's scientific interest, provides specific textual analysis and progresses towards the mature pre-'Index' phase of the *Zibaldone*. The notebook is here scrutinized in both its demonstrative speculations — particularly dominant in the years 1821–23, representing the most intense period of writing, as Leopardi in those two years wrote about two thirds of the whole notebook — and its creative imagery. Crucial entries from 1825 are analyzed by focusing on forms deriving from the physical world, so as also to discuss the change in Leopardi's attitude towards his notebook. The year 1825 is the moment at which clarity, the pillar of Leopardi's naturalized religion, philosophy of language, and phenomenology of the mind, assumes a more radical connotation. Together with the limits of philosophical inquiry, Leopardi also discovers a new philosophical posture 'in expansion' rather than in profundity, and with this, new risks of unfiltered exposure to truth on behalf of a mind that seems to have lost the protection of the senses which had once allowed it to judge the external world from a distance. Part III aims to provide an interpretation of the final post-'Index' period of the intellectual diary (1827–32) through a focus on Leopardi's practice of everyday life. This is the part of the notebook in which it is possible to detect a shift which affects the intrinsic dialogical and Socratic character of the work. In the next paragraphs of this Introduction I will expand on the significance of key concepts which inform this study, namely *exposure* and *creaturality*. The concept of *form* will also be discussed further, while the formal and substantive characteristics of the *Zibaldone* will be highlighted with reference to the tradition of notebook writing.

Exposure and Creatureliness

Leopardi's thought is deeply concerned with the condition of exposure, which he perceives from a perspective of creatureliness, that is, from the awareness that the *touch* with the real places any sentient being, the more sensitive it is, in a state of vulnerability.[16] Eric L. Santner, in his book *On Creaturely Life*, defines the idea of creatureliness as that type of 'signifier of an ongoing exposure, of being caught up in the process of becoming creature through the dictates of divine alterity'.[17] Similarly in Leopardi there is the sense that the sentient being is constantly under the effect of a Nature which manifests otherness and resists understanding. As Julia Lupton observes by commenting on Franz Rosenzweig's conception of creaturely life, 'creature' means 'everlastingly creature', that is, a 'continuously subjected subjectivity in relation to a Creator who remains sublimely other from it', as the suffix '-ura' from the Latin *creatura* suggests by implying the sense of something in a state of emergence, 'always in the process of undergoing creation' or 'perpetually becoming created', that is, formed, informed, and even deformed.[18] Beneath the external layer of systematic progress and under the effect of disruptive forces emanating from the constitutional disharmony perceived to exist between the human beings' aims and those of Nature, the *Zibaldone* is constantly decentred, shifted, and shattered. For Leopardi, if on the one hand experience, or the moment of becoming part of the reality which is approached, is necessary to keep our sensorial and intellectual activity in motion, at the same time there are risks of annihilation intrinsic to facing Nature directly. It is not by chance that the Icelander protagonist of the 'Dialogo della Natura e di un Islandese' [Dialogue Between an Icelander and Nature] finds death at the same time as finding Nature, or that the eyes contemplating an apparently blooming garden become witness to a process of the advancement of death (cf. *Zib.*. 4175–77). The botanical system, flourishing when seen from a distance, on closer scrutiny turns into vegetation besieged by illness and decay.[19] Approaching nature too closely means to unveil an engine of death.

This understanding informs Leopardi's philosophy at least from 1819, when, with his 'mutazione totale', he suffered for the first time the burns caused by extreme vicinity to Nature. The latter is meant here as absolute truth, as an ordeal indifferent and 'other' to being human, whose supreme logic and scopes are hidden to man, but whose destructive effects are nevertheless fully operative even if only by means of momentary contact. Looking closely at the way Leopardi describes his first *direct witnessing* of Nature ('cominciai a sentire [...] l'infelicità certa del mondo, in luogo di conoscerla' ('I began [...] to feel the incontrovertible unhappiness of the world, rather than knowing about it'), *Zib.* 144), one realizes that Leopardi is not only recalling the moment in which, for the first time, he experienced first-hand something of which before he had only possessed abstract knowledge.[20] He is also describing an overwhelming experience, namely his first uncanny intellectual shock, a trauma which cannot be reabsorbed back into the level of understanding. Despite the fact that as a consequence of that event Leopardi started to 'riflettere profondamente sopra le cose' ('to reflect deeply on things'), the feeling of his transformation does not pertain to the framework of knowledge, nor to an albeit unsuccessful process of sense-making. Leopardi is not telling us that he had attempted to understand what happened to him but could not. He is actually excluding any rational approach to that state; he is stating a condition of absolute foreignness in which a certain indeterminate feeling has *replaced* rationality ('cominciai a sentire [...] *in luogo di* conoscer[e]'). Here begins for Leopardi the long journey of resistance to a personal and cultural shock which constantly threatens to re-emerge during the *Zibaldone*, and which Leopardi tries to restrain by creative means through notebook writing.

We could conceive of the *Zibaldone* entry on the 'mutazione totale' as the first example of an (exposed) witnessing sensitivity which Leopardi would fully theorize after the journey to Rome (1823). This reflection is closely linked to his parallel understanding of the state of exception which the immature thinker believes he possesses, while the mature and disillusioned person rationally denies but tries to recreate in his imagination as a form of survival.²¹ By 'feeling' rather than only 'knowing about' unhappiness Leopardi has activated the process which will allow him to understand rationally that there are no exceptions to the natural (mechanistic) rule, but that if one wants to survive the ordeal and keep the natural living essence alive, one needs to *forget* this truth or *pretend* that exception does indeed apply. This, as we shall see, is the vital logic that nourishes the *Zibaldone*.

It is essential to remark that in Leopardi's thought exposure is necessary as a poetic and intellectual means of discovery, but only as a relative and partial experience, while on the contrary integral exposure coincides with nothingness and immobility. Any area of knowledge with which Leopardi engages is exposed to, or in open communication with, other thematic fields in which crossings and leaps of thought often occur suddenly. The same can be said in relation to its form, the position and frequency of words, the length of passages, and the correspondences between entries, as well as Leopardi's engagement with his own writing and with other authors he quotes; all these prerogatives assume specific forms which strictly depend on and vary according to the 'pressure' that certain cultural instances evoked by the text itself or leaning on it from the depth of a non-verbal dimension, be it conscious or unconscious, exercise on Leopardi's thought. Peter Gratton and Marie-Eve Morin define Nancy's writing (for what in particular concerns his practice of using catalogued lists) as 'exscriptive': 'at the heart of his texts is an attempt to rethink the very act of "writing" as "exscription", a movement of sense always in excess of the inscribed meaning that allows writing to touch the thing'.²² We shall see how the use and significance of enumeration methods find an equivalent value in Leopardi, although the notebook writing carries within itself not only the trace of its launch towards the 'open', but also the imprint or the wound that the 'open' leaves when 'leaning' on the text (Chapter 4).

From a general overview of the lifespan of the *Zibaldone* (from 1817 to 1832) it is possible to gather that the notebook remains active inasmuch as exposure is partial and discontinuous (Chapters 10 to 14), until the point when, in 1827, Leopardi prepares an index of the *Zibaldone* which organizes all the entries under specific thematic headings, thus attempting a totalizing experience of knowledge which progressively immobilizes writing and reduces it to silence (Chapter 19). Through the 'Index' operation Leopardi reorganizes his thought into a set of continuous patterns in which disparate entries converge, somehow losing or flattening out, under the levelling influence of a common thematic class, their discontinuous specificities (namely the original motivations and curiosity which stimulated the author to take certain notes at a specific moment). Notwithstanding the movement of thought elicited by the network of newly detected inter-connections between entries noted at the moment of revision in the body of the text, once the indexing process was terminated, the routes traced by Leopardi functioned as a map covering the entirety of the territory, and as in any other map, coordinates are fixed, and they crystalize thought into permanent static collocations. As we shall see, it is not by chance that in this integral clarification of thought Leopardi discovers his affinity with the atavistic predecessor of illumination and first informed being, Adam (Chapter 20).

Formation, Operative Memory, and Simulacra

In constructing the hypothesis that Leopardi's thought is permeated by a concern with exposure and that his writing develops as a form of touch or contagion between different areas of knowledge, I insist on the primary necessity to investigate the formal value of the notebook and its openness to being informed by different cultural impulses, as well as its intrinsic textual logic. This formal value can take the shape of recurrent, recognizable shapes in the disposition of single words, images, and passages of texts, or of isolated textual events assuming specific configurations which correspond to or signal the presence of specific lines of thought or unconscious drives which directly influence the appearance of the text. In other cases, by change of form I mean Leopardi's revisiting of the entire history of the notebook, a moment of fracture and change which leads him to 'treat' his own entries and the relationship with the authors that animate his daily writing with a different degree of familiarity (Chapter 19). These changes of form respond and are strictly connected to specific problems and interests in Leopardi's multifaceted literary, historical, religious, and scientific culture, including, on the one hand, his classical heritage, and, on the other, philosophical intuitions which project his thought towards the twentieth century. Thus, the way I conceive of 'form' has nothing to do with an idea of a 'fixed' shell or container in which contents are stored. Form is meant instead as a continuous process of thinking and creation which can require specific interventions of memory or which stimulates repeated unconscious textual performances. Forms vary according to the different degrees of engagement with or detachment from the content (Chapter 14), and writing can also assume the form of automatism (Chapter 4). For this reason three main concepts characterize the conception of form in this study: *formation, operative memory*, and *simulacrum*.

The first could be explained through the aid of reflections drawn by another author of notebooks, and one of the most interesting theorists and practitioners of form of the twentieth century, Paul Klee. This artist conceives of art as 'the world of qualities which opens out the more one descends into the unconscious depths', that is, 'not the world of forms already dead and established, but the world of nascent form, of formation, of *Gestaltung*'.[23] The world of the image, Klee believes, should not be considered as separate from the world of real objects because the former is able to generate and emanate the same physical vitality as the latter. According to Klee, who shares with Leopardi a strong attachment to the power of communal values and to shared lived experience as the carrier of concrete and true beliefs, the work of an individual artist is never the product of isolation but always the concentration of common roots and history pertaining to a specific stage of human civilization. He pays attention to what he calls the 'analysis of genesis' of an image, or morphogenesis, a discipline born with Goethe, who, in his *Metamorphosis of Plants* (1790), went in search of common formal principles acting as an underlying unity for different botanical species. According to Klee:

> Before the first line is drawn, there lies a whole pre-history: not only man's longing, his desire to express himself, his outward need, but also a general state

of mind (whose directions we call philosophy), which drives him from inside to manifest his spirit in one place or another.[24]

The artist is therefore not one who imitates the forms made by nature but rather one who is able to reproduce the genetic process of formation, the morphogenetic principles from which they derive; he does not imitate nature as a created thing but as *naturans*, as a set of processes of creation.[25] This is what Leopardi also meant when he stated that 'non imita la nat. [natura] chi non la imita con naturalezza' ('he who does not imitate nature naturally does not imitate nature') (*Zib.* 21), and that:

> Per molto che uno abbia letto, è ben difficile che al concepire un pensiero, lo creda suo, essendo d'altri; lo attribuisca all'intelletto, all'immaginazione propria, non appartenendo che alla memoria [...]; e quel pensiero che porta seco la sensazione [...] dell'originalità, [...] sarà [...] nuovo; [...] non quanto alla sostanza, ma quanto alla forma.
>
> [No matter how much a person has read, it is very unlikely when he conceives a thought that he will believe it to be his own, when it is someone else's; that he will attribute it to his own intellect, his own imagination, when it actually belongs to his memory [...]; and the thought that bears with it the sensation [...] of originality [...] will be new [...]; not, I should say, as to the substance, but as to the form.] (*Zib.* 4503)

This implies that creative activity should go beyond treating nature as an object, and the creator should reiterate its essential vital force, in an attempt to grasp the generative invariant principles which activate any process of formation into differentiated forms, and which transmit themselves through a kind of 'operative memory'.

At the origin of natural life and form, among the possible explanations, Giuseppe Di Napoli identifies a:

> Fortuita condizione in cui elementi diversi si sono trovati a interagire tra loro, scatenando-sprigionando una reazione che si è tradotta in un impulso organizzativo, nel senso che ha conferito una particolare disposizione spaziale a tutto l'insieme, generando, casualmente, una *struttura che connette*.[26]
>
> [A fortuitous condition, the elements of which have found themselves interacting, triggering a reaction which was translated into an organizational impulse, in the sense that it conferred a particular spatial disposition on the ensemble, thus generating, casually, *a structure that connects*].

The 'risvegli morfologici' [morphological awakenings], or recurrence of morphogenetic processes in the course of time, in different spatial conditions, and for different natural species, are not the result of chance, as reiterative structures recur when certain conditions and elements are found together.[27] Thus one needs to presuppose the existence of 'una memoria operativa, di un programma che in qualche modo si avvia se queste condizioni si combinano in modo tale da funzionare come impulso formativo che avvia il processo morfogenetico' [an operative memory of a programme which somehow starts if these conditions combine, thus functioning as a formative impulse which starts the morphogenetic process].[28] These prerogatives, Di Napoli believes, pertain as much to the physical and biological world as to the psychical and perceptive world, that is, to the way we approach experience and form our ideas. Similar to the natural formation discussed by Di Napoli, there is an 'operative memory' in Leopardi's writing which reiterates specific formal and thematic patterns according to the presence or absence of certain creative conditions. The way 'electric thought' — that is, a configuration of writing that assumes the shape of currents, circuits, and sudden sparks — transmits itself in the surrounding areas of the text is one of the most interesting examples of this process (Chapter 13).

In applying the idea of generative forms to the *Zibaldone* I am implying a further level of formation to that presumed by generative forms imprinted in material objects. The text is in itself a form capable of absorbing the harmonies deriving from non-textual generative forms and emitting them within the textual reality at a further sub-level of generation. Certain forms assumed by the text generate, in turn, sets of textual relations which recur in other parts of the text, so that writing itself becomes a replica of the generative essence of the living world. In this sense, the text can also be considered as a generator of simulacra, that is, a matrix of self-generative forms reproducing dominant — but also insurgent and soon-to-be-dominant — models. Leopardi's modern mnemotechnics and the semantic 'monopoly' of certain recurring images which continue to be associated with specific meanings in the course of the years is revealing of this value (Chapter 14). Any process of sense-making, in more general semiotic terms, can be considered a result of both a morphogenetic activity and a textual activity; the former performs the function of projecting and *integrating* within a certain textual context various synchronic trajectories of sense that a given concept possesses, whereas the latter is a *discrete* process which diachronically constructs propositional relationships between signs according to the syntactical, semantic, and pragmatic features of language.[29] Thus, from the combination of these two perspectives the notes of the *Zibaldone*'s 'semiosphere' can also be considered as forms which affect the surrounding areas and generate relationships of continuity and discontinuity, temporality and tensions between subject and alterity:[30] 'each time a form is constituted as an ongoing closed gestalt, it also exerts effects in the field, and this generates a never ending circle of tension between the figure and the background'.[31] Certain textual markers act as inducers of transformation within the text, as '*threshold-like signs*, which are able to perturb the semiotic field, to make it unstable and lead *subject-environment form* toward a catastrophe', that is, stages of transition which are more or less abrupt.[32]

In order to reconstruct these dynamics of generation, production, and crises (or passages between different formative matrixes), I will conduct genetic reconstructions linking specific motifs of interest for Leopardi with their value in the history of Western literature and thought, and analyze whether and how far they generate resonances in specific linguistic, thematic, and formal configurations in the *Zibaldone*.

The Un-Programmatic Character of the *Zibaldone*

In opening this study by discussing the way Leopardi's thought is *exposed*, and by considering theories of formation, my aim is to introduce approaches that can help us to grasp significant, recurrent processes of generation intrinsic to the intricate, fragmented, and diffracted nature of Leopardi's notebook.[33] Indeed, my objective is not to reconstruct a thematic map of the notebook, nor to provide a history of the development of the most important topics over the years, and nor is it to discuss the creative projects that are linked to the *Zibaldone*,[34] as they were listed in 'separate slips' of the *Zibaldone* apparatus — the so called 'polizzine non richiamate'.[35] Rather, I believe that while a strong impulse for project-planning certainly animates Leopardi's daily notebook writing, it is however a fact that these projects remained as such and were never accomplished. One of the reasons for this, I argue, is that the attraction of un-programmatic creations in Leopardi's everyday note-taking was equally if not more powerful than that exercised by the perspective of his imagined corpus of works yet to be completed. This is a question of the difference between the long term and abstract prospect of accomplishment on the one hand, and, on the other, daily satisfaction, sudden attraction, curiosity, and research temptations to be fulfilled in the short term by exploring sudden ideas which might not turn into an organized work but which offer the author at least distraction, if not also momentary aesthetic beatitude. Writing had primarily a salvific function for Leopardi and some of this beatific power resided in its unpredictability, the sudden emergence of images, and the possibility to renew this experience every day and in a different way, not knowing where writing would lead.

I therefore believe that while significant advances have been made in assessing the systematic character of the *Zibaldone* (which can be summarized as a work in expansion and at the same time in search of horizontal connections and relationships of cause and effect, as well as connected by organizational aims for project-planning also linked to the indexing operation), this focus explores one side only of Leopardi's twofold approach to knowledge. In the same way that Leopardi's conception of nature hosts paradoxes and contradiction, Leopardi's own attitude towards knowledge and note-taking in general is also *bipolar* and driven by antithetical impulses, of which systematic approach and project-planning are only one. To Cervato's rigorous interpretation of the impossibility of Leopardi realizing his creative designs, which is based on the primary importance assigned by Cervato to Leopardi's project-planning objectives, should be added, in my view, a more general consideration of the role of the *Zibaldone* as a companion from which Leopardi expects to draw daily intellectual satisfaction, emotional pleasure, and relief. For this reason, as we shall see, Leopardi valued the performative character of his notebook, because this allowed him to be exposed (partially) to the beneficial impact of the moment of creation. The text was capable of *responding* to its writer as if it were another person. This could not happen if Leopardi had to approach his entire text on a daily basis with the a priori aim of modelling his notes on pre-devised projects. And indeed, when a rigid organizational habit imposes itself in the post-'Index' phase, the vital energy of the *Zibaldone* begins to fade.

Bearing in mind the contrasting impulses at play in Leopardi's mind (which my study also explores), it is essential to investigate the dominant mechanisms through which Leopardi's thought emerges and informs his writing, often thanks to casual and un-programmatic conditions in the text. There is an intrinsic level of generation which depends on specific chronological or recursive textual dynamics typical of the *Zibaldone*'s diaristic structure, and there is an influence of generative forms deriving from unconscious, subliminal, and subtle motivations which require explanation according to the specific textual environment out of which they grow. What a reading exclusively focused on project-planning cannot provide, for instance, is an insight into the nature and weight of forces of broad religious, scientific, and material provenance which influence the text also in the form of the unsaid (Chapter 4). Moreover, I aim to explore how even a thematic approach based on one of the most demonstrative and philosophically focused 'Index' headings ('Vitalità, Sensibilità' [Vitality, Sensibility]) can reveal a certain capacity of the text to be moulded into elastic and cohesive configurations which are not directly addressed in the notes in question, but which pertain to deeper cultural and historical palimpsests of the Leopardian universe. The entries grouped under this heading possess a strong relational and systematic character, but the forms that they assume in their interaction are not explained or presumed in the heading discourse. Instead, they reflect a thought in excess which is grounded in the depth of Leopardi's understanding of the physical world (Chapters 11 and 12).

There are of course developments in Leopardi's thought which trace a partial history of the self, but it is essential to recognize that in the same way that the story of any growing individual is creaturely and exposed, because it '[aspetta] la forma che [riceverà] dalle circostanze' ('await[s] the form [he or she] will receive from circumstances') (*Zib.* 1905), so the same applies to the *Zibaldone* as Leopardi's work in progress. It is precisely the importance of the textual 'circumstances' that my study also aims to bring to light.

The *Zibaldone* as the 'cutting off of Infinity'

The start of the *Zibaldone* in the summer of 1817 was primarily driven by Leopardi's mnemonic aim, namely his wish to collect thoughts for future retrieval and possible further development. The Alsatian priest Joseph Anton Vogel, who was a friend of the Leopardi family, might have suggested to Giacomo that he keep an updated notebook in the first instance,[36] although in his 27 November 1807 letter to Filippo Solari he did not fail to emphasize the limitations of note-taking by referring in general to the 'zibaldoni' notebooks as 'caos scritto' [written chaos].[37] However, collections of notes are not always characterized by a negative connotation of disorder by theorists. The entry 'Ricordi' in the Italian translation of Ephraim Chambers's *Universal Dictionary of Arts and Science*, which is present in the Leopardi library, speaks about 'adversaria', or 'common-place-books', as:

> Un registro, o raccolta ordinata di quanto occorre degno d'esser notato, e ritenuto nel corso della lettura, o studio di un'uomo [*sic*]; così disposta, che tra una moltiplicità di capi, e di cose d'ogni sorta ciascheduna di queste possa ivi facilmente ritrovarsi, mettervisi, rimandarvisi a piacere.[38]

[A Register, or orderly Collection of what things occur worthy to be noted, and retain'd in the Course of a Man's reading, or Study; so dispos'd, as that among a Multiplicity of Heads, and Things of all Kinds, any one may be found, and turn'd to at pleasure.][39]

Collections of commonplaces existed even when writing involved materials less durable than paper, and when the *ars memoriae* and its visual techniques were still very strongly practiced as the privileged means of non-writerly collection and recollection.[40] Ann Blair remarks how 'note-taking manuals and treatises on the art of memory formed two quite distinct traditions that made no explicit reference to one another', and while the visual aids of the *ars memoriae* were employed mainly for short-term remembering, the practice of note-taking was a more effective aid for long-term retention.[41] Already in antiquity there are remarkable examples of the practice of noting quotations, one of which was Pliny the Elder, who believed, as his younger nephew recalled, that 'there was no book so bad that some good could not be got out of it', while in the Middle Ages the *ars excerpendi* was at the root of the compilation of *florilegia*, comprising quotations from model sources which served the purpose of both a portable library to be consulted for example while travelling, and that of a synthetic selection of remarkable passages to be passed on to different generations of students.[42] They could thus save time in their study by having all relevant passages already at hand. In commonplace books, by the very same casual nature of recording, striking encounters with noteworthy passages from exemplar authors often result in sequences of quotations which are unrelated and diverse, only following the chronological order of reading. Of course, in early modern times the character of the notebooks was un-programmatic only to a certain extent, given that the reading patterns inspiring notebook-writing were often regimented by moral and religious parameters functioning within specific educational programmes. In any case the very same act of recording presupposed the possibility of a subsequent retrieval in which unconnected juxtapositions of quotations could be revisited and reordered in new thematic classes. It was in order to emphasize the importance of this second phase of systematization that manuals on commonplace notebooks often recommended the use of headings, the employment of one or more indexes, and the support of multiple notebooks with different criteria of classification through which to organize the extracts. It was very common to copy the same text more than once into different notebooks, in the same way as merchants used to do with their data banks, recording certain commercial transitions both in chronological order and according to the specific nature of their content.

The practice of notebook-writing found its propellant force in the diffusion of print because together with the expanding circulation of paper as a preferred material for writing, there was also an increasing circulation of printed pedagogical manuals instructing learners on strategies for note-taking.[43] In Renaissance pedagogy the practice of repetition and copying became more and more important also because artificial memory started to be criticized as a set of procedures which were too complex and which prevented, rather than facilitated, knowledge and understanding. The practice of copying extracts from books and learning

materials continued to maintain this function among learners over the course of
the centuries, and the theory and practice of collecting notes played a conspicuous
role in various courses of study. A relevant example is the work of the two most
authoritative Jesuit pedagogues of the time, Francesco Sacchini (1570–1625) and
Jeremias Drexel (1581–1638), whose precepts were the basis of the Jesuit instruction
underpinning Leopardi's formation as a pupil.[44] These two instructors insisted on
the importance of note-taking as an aid for memory not only for its storage capacity,
but also as way of fixing ideas in the mind. In the act of copying, the mind would
reflect on the line copied in a more effective way than it would do in a reading-
only process. They envisioned the function of notebook-writing primarily as a form
of mental gymnastics which should constantly be repeated. In their view it was a
waste of time and resources to read without noting. Setting aside the specificities
and the differences of Sacchini's and of Drexel's methodologies, it is precisely this
mental exercise, reiterated at large by all Jesuit instruction, which remains very
effective in Leopardi's own study habits and which underpins the writing of the
Zibaldone. Of course, we are dealing here with a level of complexity and profundity
of thought which was unimaginable in the pedagogy of the two theorists, but the
strong and unbreakable bond between mind and pen, and the latter's function
almost as a material extension of the former are constant elements in the evolution
of the 'immenso volume ms. o scartafaccio' [immense manuscript volume, or
notebooks].[45] Independently of the formal or content specificities of each treatise,
Leopardi shares with these Jesuit instructors a conception of the notebook as a
training ground for mental activity, for experimenting with thought in the same
way as one would challenge the limits of the body during physical exercise.

However, Leopardi's rigour was also the product of the scientific revolution, which,
by enlarging the understanding of the horizon of the universe, and by favouring a
new attitude towards science in which evidence and mathematical exactness should
be the basis of any acceptable investigation, influenced the individual's approach
to knowledge. Note-taking became an exercise in precision, and as the attention
to the infinitely small structured the fundamentals of calculus, so philosophers and
writers started to rethink their relationship with the text through metaphorical
constellations alluding to key scientific concepts. Approximation, infinity, and
the discrete emerged as different images for the textual dimension. One example
of this renewed attitude can be found already in Francis Bacon, whom Leopardi
defines as 'quasi il primo filosofo moderno: e quindi il primo vide assai più che
non saprebbero vedere infiniti suoi successori, con tutti i lumi in seguito acquistati'
('virtually the first modern philosopher, and so the first saw much further than
his countless successors would be able to see, despite all the enlightenment later
acquired') (*Zib.* 1349). While discussing and promoting the inclusion of a wide
range of contents which the notes should address, from literary to philosophical
quotations and observations deriving from experience, Bacon referred to memory
strategies such as 'Constitutive Instances' (that is, 'order or distribution'), places, and
verses as modes of 'cutting off of Infinity' through a careful allocation of ideas:

> For when we try to recollect or call a thing to mind, if we have no prenotion
> or perception of what we are seeking, we seek and toil and wander here and

there, as if in infinite space. Whereas if we have any sure prenotion, infinity is at once cut off, and the memory has not so far to range.[46]

The written text functions as a microcosm of the universe, or as the sample world that emerges from the circumscribing of a vast reality whose laws and mechanisms it preserves and replicates.

The *Zibaldone* can also be read in this way, as an organism condensing within its parts the same vital relationships upon which life is based. Like Bacon, Leopardi was also very well aware of the importance of finding a balance between, on the one hand, accumulation and excess of information, typical of his encyclopaedic inclination, and, on the other, the necessity to limit and sacrifice knowledge in order to make it expressible to the mind. In his attempt to organize the materials of the *Zibaldone* in an index,[47] Leopardi had faced the same problems that, as Michael Caesar observes, the indexer normally shares with the translator, namely that of finding himself 'trapped as it is between the hammer of ready comprehensibility and the anvil of absolute accuracy — the temptation, or the inclination, to rewrite the original, however gently and discreetly'.[48] Leopardi's initial attempts to construct an index as accurately and comprehensively as possible turned into almost a replica of the diary itself.[49] Orienting oneself in the detailed headlines, often partially reproducing the content of specific passages, was almost as difficult an operation as that of extracting specific themes from the notebook itself. Having learnt the importance of the art of circumscribing, in 1827 Leopardi's aim was to balance the need for clarity and completeness with an urge for agility and synthesis. It is perhaps thanks to his need to orientate himself in the *Zibaldone*'s forest of possible intersecting pathways that Leopardi treasured the methodology of Jesuit instruction and tended to advance in his philosophical exploration by initially retrieving the key ideas of a specific point so as to illuminate the exact direction of a specific path. Many reflections indeed present the methodical repetition of previously discussed points before expanding the discourse towards new points of focus (Chapter 11).

As noted by Cervato in an observation related to George Landow's theorization of the hypertext, centrality in the *Zibaldone* has to be constantly defined by the reader, it 'risiede negli occhi di chi guarda' [resides in the eye of the beholder].[50] Much like the use of hyperlinks in the world wide web, textual elements which in a certain moment of reading hold a central position in the reader's mind, can later pass on their prominence to related peripheral elements:

> Ciascun brano dell'ipertesto diventa centrale nel momento in cui viene letto, mentre i brani ad esso collegati assumono un ruolo temporaneamente marginale, seppure sono pronti a reclamare centralità nel momento in cui il lettore sposti su di loro la sua attenzione.[51]

> [Each passage of text becomes central in the moment in which it is read, while the passages connected to it assume a temporary, marginal role, although they are ready to claim back their centrality at the moment in which the reader shifts their attention back to them.]

The reader who is looking for something specific in the *Zibaldone* must set up their own reading strategies and methodologies in order to make progress in gathering the information needed. Unlike any standard linear text, the sequence of reading is not given from the outset, and proceeding chronologically is only one of many possible reading patterns. Thus Cervato concludes that the *Zibaldone* could be defined according to Michael Joyce's model of 'explorative hypertexts', namely as a text which naturally invites its readers to assume a critical approach and to advance constant interpretative moves when arranging the entries for editorial purposes, although the matrix on which this operation takes place is still Leopardi's own writing and so cannot be changed.[52] Differently to what happens with the 'constructive hypertexts', the reader moves within a set of directions established by the author and is not allowed to contribute new textual additions which modify the substance of the original.

If this is certainly valid for the common reader when confronting the *Zibaldone* as an existing text, in the case of Leopardi as the first reader and reviewer of his own pages *in fieri*, subsequent interventions modify not only the specific content of a particular discourse, but also its conceptual and formal nature. When a reflection is suspended, and thus enters a state of indeterminacy, or vice versa when a suspended thought is retrieved and refocused, it is not so much the thematic nature of a particular reflection that changes, but its status in Leopardi's cognitive dimension. We are dealing here with subsequent treatments of thought and processes of writing which alter the place that this very same idea occupies in Leopardi's conscious or unconscious mind, and writing reflects oscillations in attentiveness. Sometimes certain entries trigger the reappearance of past thought and function as a gateway to entire speculative worlds. These can be activated by the overall message of a particular reflection as much as by individual words. At the same time, the accumulation of thoughts related to specific themes can cause switches and deviations in the direction of thinking that necessarily lead Leopardi to correct or abandon specific pathways (Chapter 12). Returning to a previous speculation often means, for Leopardi, changing the status that a specific memory holds in his mind in a constant process of differentiation and reappropriation. Thus from the perspective of Leopardi as the first user of his notebook, the text can assume the form of not only an 'explorative' but also a 'constructive hypertext', and even a 'broken hypertext', the latter manifesting itself when Leopardi cannot restore a previous train of thought and needs to personalize his ideas once again in a new specific textual contingency; as we shall see, the case of subsequent additions of et ceteras to pre-existing ones is an example of this process (Chapter 4). In these cases, we could compare Leopardi's speculative navigation to message error 'http 404' or 'page not found' in web surfing, which appears when the internet user is able to communicate with the server but the server cannot find the requested page. This can happen, among other reasons, because the link is either dead (that is, the page has been removed), or it has not been updated (the URL and its contents have been moved to another domain but appropriate links to the new domain have not been created). Through additional 'etc.' Leopardi signals to himself that something has occurred while reconnecting with past thought: either an error of connection, meaning that he cannot find all the information which was present in his mind at the time of writing, or, alternatively, a new unregistered 'update' regarding this information, when the passing of time has given him the chance to deepen or expand his focus further. The *Zibaldone*, like the web, is an almost infinite world in which movement of thought is at the same time a necessary element and at risk of getting lost.

The parallel between the *Zibaldone* and the web is certainly an interpretative tool which extends beyond Leopardi's own possibility of conceptualization. Nevertheless, I argue in Part II, the roots of an idea of virtuality can be found in his own relationship with his images, which in certain cases activate a system of self-generation that can be considered as a forerunner of the world of simulation later theorized by Baudrillard (Chapter 14). Tracing an archaeology of scientific impulses which merge with a variety of cultural concerns requires attention to indirect or subtle channels of communication and metamorphoses of images. This approach serves both to explain localized modes of interaction between entries and to highlight specific recurrent practices through which both demonstrative thought and images are formed. In the next section I will introduce a further interpretative tool which focuses on urban models and the practice of wandering to describe the progress of notebook writing as a whole and to understand how Leopardi's own way of conceiving of his notebook mutated in the post-'Index' phase.

Wandering and Everyday Life

In the course of the eighteenth century, when the practice of notebook-writing began to allow more room for personal notes and thoughts, notebooks were also the privileged companions of travellers and explorers who would use them to record their experiences and to document the new horizons. Here the notebook pages were a testament to different degrees and stages of both immersion in and detachment from the world that for the first time came into view. They belonged 'both to the field and to the cabinet', and while they attempted to register the immediacy and vividness of the adventure, they were necessarily subject to a certain delay between the actual lived experience and its transcription.[53] Even the most promptly kept records would necessarily require recollection in a moment of calm and rest subsequent to the actual activity of the traveller. Although, strictly speaking, the *Zibaldone* is the antithesis of a travel notebook in the sense that it was physically written mostly in Recanati, during times when Leopardi was not travelling, and is therefore the product of a static condition, nevertheless the idea of discovery can be adopted to describe Leopardi's purpose. What Leopardi could not fulfil in factual terms, namely his desire to 'vedere il mondo' [see the world], he achieved intellectually in the constant expansion of his search for knowledge and his revisiting and correcting his notes, which may be compared to the activity of the traveller who adjusts and reorders the sketches jotted down in haste during the exploration.[54] The use of small cards was part of the set of recommendations given to travellers, who were advised to 'take notes in pocket-sized paperbooks, or erasable table books, and later transfer the material to larger notebooks'.[55] More generally, the practice of using small cards as a mnemonic support was widespread in the tradition of notebook-compiling, and was meant to register findings produced in the actual moment of reading, so as not to slow down the reading process. These notes on loose cards could then be organized under appropriate headings at a later stage.

The apparatus of the *Zibaldone* also presents a strong relationship between macro-text and portable texts.[56] It consists of the 1827 'Index' of the *Zibaldone*, the catalogue (*schedario*) and the *polizzine* ('separate slips'). The catalogue comprises 555 small filing cards (*cedoline*) which were prepared by Leopardi in different phases (from 1820 to 1827) to organize his 'Index'.[57] The thirty-eight so-called 'polizzine richiamate' (separate slips 'referred to in the 1827 Index', *EZ*, p. 2073) are cards related to the catalogue in which many entries were later also listed under various headings of the 'Index', while the 'polizzine non richiamate', noted previously, comprise cards which do not relate to specific headings but list seven titles of treatises which are followed by relevant numbers corresponding to pages and paragraphs of the *Zibaldone*.[58] They refer to contents useful for creative plans which Leopardi did not pursue. It is true that the relation between notebook and card files for Leopardi follows a reverse order to that of travel diaries, in that the starting-point is the huge bulk of notes from which material is selected and organized on small cards (even if this occurred without significant delay),[59] and not vice versa as in travel notebooks, where notes that are jotted down on cards first are later reorganized to form a narrative. However, the parallel with travel notes is helpful once the diary pages already written are compared to a mental landscape in which the author constantly moves, and which is retraced, reaccessed, and reorganized through additions, corrections, and searches for thematic pathways, in a constant re-exploration of the intricate vegetation of thought. Leopardi's journeys constantly approach the notebook as a world to be re-experienced.

The chronological sequence of the *Zibaldone* pages and the relationships between passages written within a certain close timeframe could be compared to a journey 'on foot', as it were, which allows the explorer or passenger to appreciate the details in his immediate sight, the spatial and temporal plasticity of physical objects. Trees, buildings, or other wanderers on the way that are part of the environment in which the traveller is physically immersed become embodied sensorial experiences. The wanderer's gaze is drawn to particular objects that are encountered and switches between the external space and his personal position. Similarly, and like a camera framing, Leopardi's diachronic writing expands under the influence of what surrounds present writing and through constant movement between close-ups of constituent existential and individual features and a deep focus on general natural and historical truths. Much like taking a walk, thinking here often progresses through adjacencies, associations, and purposes of inquiry which, as the wandering proceeds, become apparent to the viewer/writer step by step.

In contrast, the large-scale reviewing operation of the 1827 'Index', as well as the numerous internal cross-references in the manuscript which derive from this rereading, result from the *purpose of finding* homologies and itineraries rather than *incursion into* singularities and side paths.[60] By overviewing and covering the extension of and fractures between reflections distant in time, these intra-textual cross-references allow bird-like flights between the pages, conjoining disparate fragments and requiring Leopardi's attention to produce synchronic connections between entries originally positioned in different temporal and physical 'spaces' in the manuscript. The cross-references and the 'Index' can be read as an attempt to create waymarkers between glimpses of experiences in order to form patterns in a landscape of thought, almost like routes on a map that has been drawn from aerial photography.

I therefore propose as one of the possible conceptual models of reference to interpret Leopardi's text the praxis of movement as wandering and traversing mentioned above, which in his 'real' life Leopardi experienced as a wanderer — there are many references to walks and strolls he enjoyed in Recanati and the other cities he visited, with attention to both their most striking physical and psychological effects — and as an observer.[61] One should not forget how walking also informed Leopardi's imagined life in a bygone culture, when in ancient times thinkers, in solitude or in the company of others, would combine philosophical reflection with physical exercise. The third section of this volume explores the importance of this ancient philosophical point of reference (Chapter 18). It is however necessary to clarify from the outset how in focusing on the *Zibaldone* as a landscape which hosts wanderings, views, and encounters with other travellers, which are all conceived in the most physical way possible so creating the closest link possible between physical and mental space, I am providing a reading in harmony with Leopardi's own vision of writing as a *path* or a *road* to be taken, to which he refers in some of his letters and in the *Zibaldone* itself. These wandering practices are more than images employed by the interpreter to understand metaphorically the author's relationship with his notebook, but rather they are effective configurations of a textual replica of the real, which influence Leopardi's thinking processes and the way thought is expressed. This wandering imagery confers on the text certain prerogatives of the physical world.

There is a moment in 1827 at which the notebook mutates its form, and after first resembling the enclosed space of a small village — the *Zibaldone* indeed begins with a reference to a nocturnal view of the familiar town-scape of Recanati by a traveller ('Palazzo bello. Cane di notte dal casolare, al passar del viandante [...]. Nella (dalla) maestra via s'udiva il carro/ Del passegger' ('Palazzo Bello. Dog in the night from the farmhouse, as the wayfarer goes by [...]. On (from) the highway you could hear/ The traveller's carriage'), *Zib.* 1) — it starts to assume the shape of a bigger city.[62] Leopardi's own way of approaching the notes in these two separate phases changes in the same way as social relations change between the two distinct urban environments (Chapter 19). His notes reflect both the development of Leopardi's own relationship with the humanist tradition of reference, and his awareness of socio-cultural changes between the pre-modern and the modern world which he is the first Italian thinker to fully perceive.

It is primarily a shift in attention which towards the end of the *Zibaldone* leads Leopardi to engage with other authors and texts in a more somnambulistic way, similarly to a city dweller who is exposed to a 'concentrated and exaggerated type of social life'.[63] Modern city life constantly bombards the wanderer with a variety of impulses, leading him first to an extreme effort of attention, and then, precisely because of this excess, into a stupefied state of distraction and abstention from intellectual effort. Leopardi's relationship with the *Zibaldone* before, during, and after the indexing process can be read through this urban lens. In the final period of the notebook's life, Leopardi experiences in his writing the same psychological effects of shock as the city wanderer which would later be fully theorized by Baudelaire and Benjamin but also by other theorists of somnambulism and hypnotism in the late nineteenth century, and inspire a new, more direct and at the same time subjectivized relationship with the real in early Modernist artists.

We are dealing with experiences of modernity (the ephemeral, the simulacrum, and the replicability of the real) which would mature in Western thought only after Leopardi's lifetime, but which materialize in the *Zibaldone* often with no theoretical support, from an author who lived in largely pre-modern conditions in the backward papal province of Recanati, with limited travelling opportunities and lack of first-hand experience of the modern international world. This makes the reading of the *Zibaldone* an extraordinary performance that reveals surprising and fascinating embodiments of cultural phenomena often new to Italy and which find a place in Leopardi's acute sensitivity alongside established classical constructs. However, here also resides the challenge posed by a text, extremely complex in content and form, in which different and at times clashing cultural impulses operate simultaneously and at different levels of awareness, often revealing flashes of a latent sensitivity.

Leopardi's Scientific Thought

Leopardi's scientific frame of reference is Newtonian and Galilean, based on projective geometry and mechanical physics. His *Dissertazioni filosofiche* [Philosophical Dissertations] testify to his early interest in the main scientific theories of the physical world elaborated in the previous two centuries.[64] Also in the *Zibaldone* Leopardi often reflects on topics and adopts a certain terminology which testify to his keen interest in the scientific achievements of his day especially concerning gravity and the theory of fluids, which was associated in particular with the recently established science of electricity and magnetism. In addition to this area of inquiry, although Leopardi did not know the principles of thermodynamics, he was concerned with processes of conservation and dissipation, applied broadly to a variety of philosophical issues rather than specifically to theories of heat. The essential idea of a continuum of forces in which contrasting and even antithetical manifestations of a certain phenomenon take place in the same body or environment, or are part of the same physical or moral law, recurs in a variety of speculative settings. Certain forces are able to assume different forms while continuing to be part of the same substance or process: they are merely different ways of being of a given entity. When Leopardi states that excess of sensitivity leads to insensitivity, or, more generally, that 'il troppo [...] è padre del nulla' ('Too much [...] is [...] the father of nothing') (*Zib.* 714), he is applying to his philosophy the idea in thermodynamics that a certain amount of work transforms productive energy into a dissipated, no longer usable form, and that these forms are part of the same physical spectrum. It is a philosophy of exposure, excess, and adjacency, also implying the idea of a co-habitation with an intangible 'other' reality which occupies the same 'space' as the factual reality, but without offering clear or visible clues as to the nature of its presence.

This idea also informs more broadly Leopardi's vision of the irreversible path towards modernity. In the *Zibaldone* he states that the individual carries within himself the more general conditions of his civilization 'come una camera oscura ricopia un [*sic*] piccoliss.o una vasta prospettiva' ('much as a camera obscura copies a vast prospect on a miniature scale'), and that the direction of this process is one of progressive immobility:

> L'animo e il corpo dell'uomo civile si rende appoco appoco immobile in ragione de' progressi della civiltà: e si va quasi distruggendo (gran perfezionamento dell' uomo!) la principal distinzione che la natura ha posto fra le cose animate e inanimate, fra la vita e la morte, cioè la facoltà del movimento.
>
> [The mind and body of civilized man is gradually rendered immobile by reason of the advances of civilization, and (what a great thing this perfecting of man is!) we are almost on our way to destroying the principal distinction that nature has put between animate and inanimate things, between life and death, namely, the faculty of movement.] (*Zib.* 1608)

Although, because of his Galilean formation, motion and not heat is here conceived by Leopardi as the parameter of individuation of uniformity, it is evident that he suggests the presence of a continuum of states between the organic and the inorganic, which also governs the relationship between the production of heat and entropic waste. A more latent idea of a progressive 'cooling' affecting civilization is implicit in Leopardi's idea of modernity as a condition of increasing indifference and insensitivity, as opposed to the warm and heated passions of the ancients. However, the entry on pages 1607–08 is interesting also because it provides an example of the overlapping of different cultural and conceptual models in Leopardi's thought which are only partially based on a fully systematic and coherent theoretical knowledge. The passage in question employs the image of the camera obscura which, since Locke and Newton, had not only constituted the optical paradigm, but was also a model to describe the inner activities of the mind as well as the relationship between mind and senses ('the *understanding* is not much unlike a closet wholly shut from light, with only some little opening left, to let in external visible resemblances, or *ideas of things without*').[65] It is a rapport which maintains separation of what is 'outside' the individual's mind from what is 'inside'. The mind processes impulses received from the senses into the enclosed space of its subjective dominion in the same way that images from the external reality are projected onto the walls of the device. The latter can be occupied by a spectator who thence experiences a vision of the real in a separate and enclosed environment. Although the images projected onto the walls of the camera obscura are identical to the real, and mirror the movements of the outside reality, nevertheless 'the movement and temporality so evident in the camera obscura were always prior to the act of representation; movement and time could be seen and experienced, but never represented'.[66] This is the principle around which the general sensationalist philosophy which is the basis of Leopardi's philosophical context of reference builds its various theorizations of the formation of ideas. However, as discussed earlier, already in the second half of the eighteenth century and at the beginning of the nineteenth century, certain sensationalist and *idéologique* constructs of the mind conceived of sensations bombarding the subject in a continuous flow, or as apparitions which the mind could not grasp, recall, or interpret. The dynamic principles of fluid movement promoted by the Newtonian revolution, the circulation and release of electric and magnetic power, and experiments in somnambulism and hypnotism were important stimuli for an interest in the explanation for unconscious intellectual faculties. In the course of the nineteenth century the camera obscura model gave way to different models of physiological optics based on the discovery of the function of the retina, which started to propose a different regime of visuality. Representation started to be seen as subjective, as it depended on nerve responses that were progressively activated by the body. In the space of a few lines of a single entry, Leopardi condenses the essence of this paradigm shift: while on the one hand he employs the traditional model of the camera obscura, which suggests an idea of a distinct environment in which a corresponding image of the real is projected, in stating how organic matter progressively resembles the inorganic, he also implies a certain exposure of the subject's point of interaction to the real. Much like the retina, which, compared to the mind as a 'closet wholly shut from light', is more 'forthcoming' to the light, exposed and actively implicated in the elaboration of perception, so the subject 'advances' towards the condition of the inorganic, and his point of interaction with the real little by little merges with the limit (inconceivable to the mind) at which non-homogenous entities meet. This reflection provides a more general image for Leopardi's universe of thought, in which the human and nature, the organic and the inorganic, as well as the informed world circumscribed by the writing of the *Zibaldone* and the formless possibilities of the unsaid, face each other in extreme and uncanny vicinity.

The psychology of the modern wanderer, whose attention is shattered and diffracted by a multiplicity of external stimuli, is affected by dissipation and thus shares significant aspects with entropic imagery. In this overlapping, modern everyday life and science become synchronic generative forms which are a source of recognizable harmonies and relationships within the fabric of the text.

Religious Frameworks

Generative formation takes place in the *Zibaldone* not only with respect to physical reality but also symbolic reality. Here, the concepts of civil and natural laws, with which Leopardi draws parallels to clarity and naturalness in writing, are crucial elements of a 'threshold' alluding to unconscious and latent drives replicating antithetical impulses towards temptation and liberation from sin (Chapter 6). Adam, the symbol for modernity as a whole, is a constant presence haunting the *Zibaldone* through both direct and indirect references. Leopardi feels an ineluctable identification with him while at the same time striving to differentiate his own experience from that of the predecessor. Already in December 1820, in an entry to which I shall refer on more than one occasion in this study (*Zib.* 434), Leopardi associates with the Fall an image of incendiary rationality, defining the outcomes of Adam's sin as the integral fulfilment of gnoseological impulses. Similarly, Leopardi attributes to the pattern of modernity an analogous tendency towards the rational explanation of causes that had persisted in a state of mystery in antiquity, and which modernity instead desires to disclose completely. Modernity has burned down the pathos which would lead the ancient poet to believe in the power of illusions, dissipated imaginative energy, and imposed a state of face-to-face exposure to the real, much like Adam, whose mind, in Leopardi's representation, after eating the apple became still, fixedly contemplating a reality of arid uniformity. Cesare Beccaria intuited the risks intrinsic in 'too much presence' of thought, when he speculated on the importance of not expressing all accessory ideas present in the mind because in so doing some ideas would be awakened but others would remain inactive and dampen the general meaning.[67] A certain lacuna or positive negligence capable of granting secondary ideas their latency would instead stimulate the mind actively to fill the gaps between ideas with additional creations and maintain a sense of motion. Leopardi's understanding of the effect of beliefs and determinations, that is, the importance of constant new illusions and objectives towards which we can orient our drives, revolves around the same preoccupations. As we shall see in the third part of this book, a proto-entropic sensitivity acts as a generative form for the way Leopardi represents Adam and modernity (Chapter 20). This philosophical, literary, and cultural entropic risk is operative in Leopardi's thought already in the early life of the *Zibaldone* (the entry *Zib.* 434, was made on 19 December 1820). All subsequent writing, I argue, is profoundly motivated by an attempt to avoid the same fate that awaited Adam, and which modern culture has already triggered by progressively endorsing a state of complete indifference and emotionlessness.

The key concept, in this respect, is clarity. In Leopardi's view this is a principle by which the student should always abide, but as we shall see in Part I, it also performs a certain confessional function which in the deepest recesses of Leopardi's psyche propels a daily purge of the sinful drives embodied in writing (Chapters 3 and 5). Deep philosophical inquiry is a dangerous and daring operation which requires constant assessment, and Leopardi's ideal and practice of clarity serves this purpose. However, the surveilling function of methodical, confessional clarity coexists alongside the sudden emergence of poetic images which embody an alternative to the rational propensity to dig into the causes. They represent the state and the style of grace, that is, a concept permeated by both an aesthetic and a religious meaning within the framework of Leopardi's naturalized religion (Chapters 8 and 9). While in its religious form grace confers the most sublime state of redemption on writing, seen with respect to its meaning in the sphere of law, grace is the tool of praxis and adjustment, the means for harmonizing the gap between abstract absolutes and circumstantial experience. As Monica Stronati writes:

> La iustitia è interpretazione, mediazione, non è essa stessa diritto; per secoli s'è posta in funzione della ricerca della soluzione giuridica equa, rispondente al diritto, ha mediato tra l'idea assoluta di giustizia e la concreta imperfetta condotta umana. La grazia sembra collocarsi al confine delle due nozioni, legge e diritto, per colmare lo iato tra la legge ed il suo contenuto, ma anche tra legge e morale.[68]

> [Justice is interpretation, mediation; it is not right in itself; for centuries it has been a function of the search for a fair and just juridical solution and it has mediated between the absolute idea of justice and concrete and imperfect human conduct. Grace seems to be located on the boundary between the two notions of law and right in order to fill the hiatus between the law and its content, but also between law and ethics].

There is an intrinsic value to mediation between abstract generalities and an un-programmatic praxis of living, which makes grace the tool of flexibility and pragmatic assessment. As a state of exception, grace is the 'no-man's land between public law and political fact, and between the juridical order and life'.[69] This is the approach that Leopardi's ultra-philosophy also adopts by stepping back from direct exposure to philosophical truth in the attempt to return to a primordial state of forgetfulness and practical cultivation of illusions. As with grace, this is an operation of distancing, resistance, and exception from the attraction exercised by reason.

The *Zibaldone* and the Icelander

It is necessary to note that 1827, the year that signals a transformation in the landscape of the *Zibaldone* brought about by religious and philosophical tensions (as we shall see in Part III), is not only the year of the compilation of the 'Index', that is, Leopardi's final effort to revisit his research through a full network of connections, but it is also the year of the publication of the *Operette morali* [Moral Tales], the most intellectually radical book in modern Italian literature. It is precisely the comparison with a crucial *dialogo* of the *Operette* which might here help us to put into context the ending of the *Zibaldone*, which will be discussed in the final part of this book. Leopardi's position in the *Zibaldone* until 1827 is similar to that of the Icelander (in the 'Dialogo della Natura e di un Islandese') who wanders around the world trying to embody a state of exception by attempting to escape Nature, or unhappiness. Likewise, Leopardi once again explores the whole territory of the *Zibaldone* and tries to gain, through the 'Index', a comprehensive vision of his work that embraces all horizons of possible knowledge. This Adamic move, however, comes at a price, and instead of finding creative satisfaction as a form of renewable hope, Leopardi finds intellectual stasis. From this moment on, the *Zibaldone* is no longer the same.

Like the Icelander, Leopardi's notebook also suffers two kinds of deaths (or two different aspects of the same death). In the same way as his character is eventually devoured by two lions, Leopardi's writing also finds a predator at the end of its journey in the form of real and pure lived life, the desire for which progressively emerges through the pages of the notebook finally to annihilate writing. The fissure created by the advancement of the real is irreversibly opened from 1831 onwards. I shall refer to 'philosophical predation' — the condensation of Leopardi's philosophy of exposure and creatureliness — on more than one occasion in the course of this study to emphasize how in general in the *Zibaldone* there is a constant sense of a *danger* awaiting thought outside or between words which are clearly and precisely noted (Chapters 4 and 12). If evocation, allusion, and the unsaid are powerful poetic tools for Leopardi, there is however a constant fear of the loss of identity which requires absolute balance in any philosophical and expressive choice. At the same time, like the Icelander who (in the second finale of the *dialogo*) might have found death by exhaustion and paralysis ('un fierissimo vento, levatosi mentre che l'Islandese parlava, lo stese a terra, e sopra gli edificò un superbissimo mausoleo di sabbia' (*TPP*, p. 536) ('a might wind arose while the Icelander was speaking and bowled him over and covered him with a most superb mausoleum of sand', *MT*, p. 104), Leopardi's writing impulses are also overwhelmed by the excess of rationality brought about by the 'Index'.

Vento [wind, or current of air] is an image charged with metaphoric polyphony, alluding often and at the same time in Leopardi to both the semantics of air and that of electricity. In the world literature of the magnetic age, many examples could be drawn of magnetizers and magnetized victims perishing under the effect of either magnetic influence or electric fulguration and reduced to ash, sand, or withered matter.[70] The second tragic end of the Icelander could also be read through this lens. Because of the metaphorical potential of the 'wind' in Leopardi's writing, it is possible to interpret the image of the 'fierissimo vento' — etymologically subtly conjoined with the 'lions', which are, invoking Dante, *fiere* [beasts] — that rises to bury the Icelander under a pile of sand, as an electric or magnetic wind which kills him after excessive exposure (Nature 'guardavalo fissamente' (*TPP*, p. 533) ('stared intently at him', *MT*, p. 99) and reduces him to the state of dry matter ('diseccato perfettamente, e divenuto una bella mummia', *TPP*, p. 536 ('perfectly dried out, and turned into a fine mummy', *MT*, p. 104)). The Icelander succumbs to the effect of an incendiary influence which kills him in the same way that hyper-clarity, or excess of reason, reduces Adam to a condition of stupefied and insensitive contemplation. The same happens to the *Zibaldone*, devoured by the real and ending in shock, that is a fate awaiting any form in expansion which has acquired full awareness and total vision of its own working mechanisms: '*Steriliscono* le facoltà ridotte ad arte, vale a dire gli uomini non trovano altro che le *amplifichi*, come trovavano quando ell'erano ancora informi, e senza nome e senza leggi propri' ('Faculties reduced to art *become sterile*, in other words people find no way of *enlarging* them, as they did when the faculties were still formless and nameless and without their own laws') (*Zib.* 39; my emphasis). However, since Leopardi's reflection on the 'total transformation', in which not by chance he states that his 'fantasia era quasi disseccata' ('imagination had almost dried up') (*Zib.* 144), and then during and after his first trip to Rome, in which he discovers himself to be more 'social' than he had expected, the writing of the *Zibaldone* represents the constant striving against this ineluctable end. In this he is similar to the Icelander, who confesses that he has been trying to escape Nature (that is, to except himself from an unavoidable fate), but finds her eventually at the end of his life. In fact, the Icelander's journey, like the journey of the *Zibaldone*, is the response to a discovery which has already been made.[71] Both the Icelander and the writer of the *Zibaldone* had *already* met Nature when they embarked on their adventure, and actually their pre-knowledge of Nature is the reason why they set out to wander in the first place in a search for survival. When they both find Nature in the deserts of Africa and in 1832 in Florence respectively, they are only re-encountering her, this time in a final extreme act of exposure. At this point Leopardi's performative inclinations will have to find a way to pursue the truest essence of his practical philosophy beyond the notebook, in life.

The *Zibaldone* Today

The *Zibaldone* successfully appeals to scholars and thinkers from different disciplines and with various points of focus not merely thanks to its incredibly rich and finely articulated content, but also because of its malleable form which intrinsically lends itself to different mind frames and conceptual lenses. These range, in this study, from linguistics (lexicographical analysis, study of forms of suspension and mitigation, as well as etymology) to literary and philosophical interests (from parallels with Plato and classical authors, to the Renaissance, European Enlightenment, and post-Romantic writers, as well as more contemporary philosophical approaches deriving from post-Structuralism and so-called Italian Theory), and including incursions into the history of science and cultural history. If through its strong textual approach my study helps even partially to demonstrate the importance of detailed textual analysis in shedding light on the writing praxis of one of the most significant Western thinkers and, above all, in so doing reveals how this creative praxis is both symptomatic of cultural transformation and capable of perceiving the approach of broader cultural shifts, then I will consider my aims to have been accomplished. This, however, does not mean restricting the study of the *Zibaldone* to merely stylistic or aesthetic questions, for it involves a more general rethinking of the interactions between scientific sensitivity, ethics, and self-hood in the post-revolutionary years and beyond.

The way the first English translation of the *Zibaldone* (first published in 2013) was received immediately after its publication is telling of the work's capacity to speak to thinkers across a broad spectrum, both geographical and intellectual, and to fields of interest much broader than just the literary.[72] The English *Zibaldone* was reviewed enthusiastically in newspapers and magazines ranging from the *Financial*

Times to the *New York Review of Books* to *The New Republic*, and leading writers and intellectuals in the history of ideas have expressed their marvel at their first reading of the notebook; for instance the British philosopher John Gray, the Romanian literary theorist Thomas Pavel, the Indian novelist Vikram Seth, and the American historians of ideas Robert Pogue Harrison and Hayden White among others, have all shown interest in the *Zibaldone* or included the notebook in their most recent studies.[73]

The *Zibaldone* has now been freed from the persistent tendency in Italian culture to manipulate Leopardi's thought (since the first publication of the *Zibaldone* by Giosuè Carducci between 1898 and 1900) to make it adhere to the dictamens of either idealism or political materialism, and to subordinate Leopardi's philosophy to his poetic activity.[74] This impeded a proper dissemination of Leopardi's creative work as a whole. He was certainly well received and appreciated in Italy and abroad during the nineteenth and the twentieth centuries, but mainly as a poet, with the lack of circulation of his thought and of consideration of the *Zibaldone* as an autonomous work often resulting in reducing Leopardi's writing to mere sentimentalism.[75] Unlike other canonical authors and poets, from Goethe to Coleridge to Baudelaire, Leopardi's poetry could not be considered in conjunction with his equally original philosophy until at least the 1980s,[76] when a new critical reflection placed greater value on the consideration of the strong links between the poetic and the philosophical.[77] There were thinkers such as Nietzsche and Benjamin who, sharing an intellectual affinity with Leopardi, before knowing the *Zibaldone* but through his creative work, were able to understand the powerful radicalism of his thought; a thought that allows ontological and practical contradiction, but not compromise, when faced with an acceptance of the hopelessness and meaninglessness of man's biological nature, while at the same time striving to construct a praxis of living which keeps the values of illusion and vitality alive, if only for a short time.[78] However, these thinkers were, understandably, exceptions and it is now time to rethink the canon of Western thought by including Leopardi among its original figures.

Shedding light on the forms of thinking in the *Zibaldone* means adding a chapter to intellectual history, as it provides a kind of 'case study' of how large-scale cultural and historical dynamics have an impact on the craft of thought in the creative process of exceptional thinkers. Sometimes it is microscopical linguistic details which reveal these shifts, and Leopardi's writing becomes the ideal seismograph for registering the different ways in which the writerly mind operates when approaching knowledge in a new age of disenchantment and ephemerality.

Notes to the Introduction

1. On self-reflexivity as a way to distinguish the human from *what it is not* (the animal), see Giorgio Agamben, *The Open: Man and Animal*, trans. by Kevin Attell (Stanford, CA: Stanford University Press, 2004), pp. 23–27.
2. See Tommaso Ariemma, 'Dell'esposizione: contro l'integralismo', *Kainos*, 8 (2008), <http://www.kainos.it/numero8/ricerche/ariemma-esposizione.html> [accessed 3 August 2017]. Ariemma discusses the philosophy of exposure and nudity also in *Il nudo e l'animale: filosofia*

dell'esposizione (Rome: Editori Riuniti, 2006) and *Il senso del nudo* (Milan: Mimesis, 2007).
3. Jean-Luc Nancy, *Being Singular Plural*, trans. by Robert D. Richardson and Anne E. O'Byrne (Stanford, CA: Stanford University Press, 2000), pp. 5, 18.
4. Carlo Ferrucci, for instance, reflects on the appropriateness of associating with the *Zibaldone* a textile metaphor rather than conceiving of it as an 'edifice'. He refers to the development of Leopardi's discourse as a fabric of threads capable of articulating themselves into other threads, 'Leopardi e l'esperienza estetica della verità', in *Leopardi e il pensiero moderno*, ed. by Carlo Ferrucci (Milan: Feltrinelli, 1989), pp. 199–213 (p. 199). See also, by the same author, 'Il "sistema" dello *Zibaldone*', in *Leopardi e la cultura europea*, ed. by Franco Musarra and Serge Vanvolsem (Rome: Bulzoni, 1989), pp. 227–34 (p. 230). The *Zibaldone* has also been compared to a labyrinth, for which see Fabiana Cacciapuoti, *Dentro lo 'Zibaldone': il tempo circolare della scrittura di Leopardi* (Rome: Donzelli, 2010), p. 44. The *Zibaldone* as a hypertext is also a very productive conceptualization, which was proposed for the first time by Mark Hebsgaard, 'Giacomo Leopardi's "Zibaldone" and Hypertext', in *Storia e multimedia*, ed. by Francesca Bocchi and Peter Denley (Bologna: Grafis, 1994), pp. 647–53. See also Marco Riccini, 'Lo *Zibaldone di pensieri*: progettualità e organizzazione del testo', in *Leopardi e il libro nell'età romantica*, ed. by Michael Caesar and Franco D'Intino (Rome: Bulzoni, 2000), pp. 81–104. The 2013 international conference of Leopardi Studies in Barcelona was dedicated to the hypertextual character of the *Zibaldone*; see *Lo 'Zibaldone' di Leopardi come ipertesto*, ed. by Maria de las Nieves Muñiz Muñiz (Florence: Olschki, 2013). In this volume, see in particular the essays by Emanuela Cervato, 'Lo *Zibaldone* come ipertesto: limiti e possibilità' (pp. 313–32), and Silvia Stoyanova, 'Lo *Zibaldone di pensieri* di Leopardi: un'edizione ipertestuale e una piattaforma di ricerca (http://zibaldone. princeton.edu)', pp. 333–42 (p. 338). The Hypertext Research Platform elaborated by Stoyanova at Princeton University allows the user to navigate through the different constellations of the 'Index' entries and visualize for each heading the degree of centrality of each entry-component, its relations with other co-entry-components as well as their possible participation with other headings. This interactive tool is partly capable of recreating and modelizing the experience of the actual encounter with the text because in the lack of linearity typical of a traditionally printed book with a specific leading narrative, the digital user, like the *Zibaldone* reader, is constantly forced to approach the text in a more active and personalized way. See <http://digitalzibaldone. net/entry> [accessed 7 February 2017]. The *Zibaldone* has also been considered as a rhizome, for which see my 'Reflections on Leopardi, Borges, Deleuze and the Rhizome', *Appunti leopardiani*, 1.1 (2011), 20–25, <http://www.appuntileopardiani.cce.ufsc.br/edition012011/artigosphp/paola. php> [accessed 23 August 2017]. The three models, the labyrinth, the hypertext, and the rhizome, are also discussed by Emanuela Cervato, *A System that Excludes All Systems: Giacomo Leopardi's 'Zibaldone di Pensieri'* (Bern: Peter Lang, 2017), pp. 60–97. Pietro Citati uses the metaphor of the solar system to represent the interaction between key words and other words in the notebook (Pietro Citati, 'Così Leopardi ha scritto il libro infinito', *La Repubblica*, 6 August 2009, <http://ricerca.repubblica.it/repubblica/archivio/repubblica/2009/08/06/zibaldone-cosi-leopardi-ha-scritto-il-libro.html> [accessed 9 August 2018]). Cervato discusses this reflection in pp. xxii–xxiii of her book. The image of the spiral has also been adopted (see María de las Nieves Muñiz Muñiz, 'Introduzione', in *Lo 'Zibaldone' di Leopardi come ipertesto*, ed. by Muñiz Muñiz, pp. v–x).
5. On the relationship between the *Zibaldone* and specific genres and writing structures see Franco D'Intino and Luca Maccioni, *Leopardi: guida allo 'Zibaldone'* (Rome: Carocci, 2016), pp. 28–38. See also Joanna Ugniewska, 'Strutture saggistiche e strutture diaristiche nello *Zibaldone* leopardiano', *La rassegna della letteratura italiana*, 91.1 (1987), 325–38; Antonio Prete, 'Sulla scrittura dello *Zibaldone*: la forma dell'essai e i modi del preludio', in *Lo 'Zibaldone' cento anni dopo: composizione, edizioni, temi*, ed. by Ronaldo Garbuglia (Florence: Olschki, 2001), pp. 387–93; and Anna Dolfi, 'Da l'"intime" al "philosophique": le strutture cognitive dello *Zibaldone*', in *'Journal intime' e letteratura moderna*, ed. by Anna Dolfi (Rome: Bulzoni, 1989), pp. 109–39.
6. I refer here to Cervato's *A System that Excludes All Systems*. Cervato remarks how the critical debate on the philosophical character of the *Zibaldone* has often depended on the variety of meanings attributed to the concept of 'philosophy' as well as the inevitable influence exercised

by individual philosophical postures in approaching the *Zibaldone*. The *Zibaldone* has now been recognized as a text with philosophical characteristics, also given the fact that since the 1990s a philosophical character has been attributed also to works which lack logical-formal coherence and present reflections which are fragmentary in nature. On the systematic and combinatorial character of the *Zibaldone* see also Cacciapuoti, *Dentro lo 'Zibaldone'*.

7. Already Locke, for whom the self is the result of self-reflexivity and memory, had admitted the presence of experiences which the mind cannot recall and that are forever lost from the grasp of one's mind. Cabanis presupposed the presence of a 'vertical fragmentation' of the self, in which certain sensations are operative but not consciously controlled by the *moi* [self]. Maine de Biran discusses the presence of a certain 'mollesse' [softness] constituting our identity which allows impulses to modify and shape our selves beyond our awareness of the process. Leopardi's reflections on the child's character, which in his view can be likened to a soft dough (as we shall see in Chapter 14), shares many similarities with Biran's 'mollesse'. These and other positions pertaining to an anti-Cartesian line of thought interested in unconscious and fragmented psychological dynamics are discussed, with respect to the French context, by Jan Goldstein, *The Post-revolutionary Self: Politics and Psyche in France, 1750–1850* (Cambridge, MA, & London: Harvard University Press, 2008), particularly pp. 103–38.
8. See the chapter 'The Perils of Imagination' in Goldstein, *The Post-revolutionary Self*, pp. 21–59.
9. Cf. Goldstein's definition of 'segmentation' in *The Post-revolutionary Self*, p. 3.
10. Goldstein believes that the innovations brought about by the Freudian unconscious should be reconfigured not as a break or a cultural shock, but as the mature outcome of a certain sensitivity already operative since the eighteenth century. See her 'The Advent of Psychological Modernism in France: An Alternate Narrative', in *Modernist Impulses in the Human Sciences, 1870–1930*, ed. by Dorothy Ross (Baltimore, MD: John Hopkins University Press, 1994), pp. 190–209.
11. Nancy, *Being Singular Plural*, p. 18.
12. Domenico Secondulfo, 'Introduzione', in *I volti del simulacro: realtà della finzione e finzione della realtà*, ed. by Domenico Secondulfo (Verona: Quiedit, 2007), pp. 9–34 (p. 17). The idea of generative forms appears in thinkers of different intellectual postures such as Herbert Spencer, *Principles of Sociology* (London: Macmillan, 1969); Max Weber, *Economy and Society: An Outline of Interpretive Sociology*, ed. by Guenther Roth and Claus Wittich (Berkeley: University of California Press, 1978); David Riesman, *The Lonely Crowd: A Study of the Changing American Character* (New Haven, CT, & London: Yale University Press, 2001); Charles Wright Mills, *White Collar: The American Middle Classes* (New York: Oxford University Press, 1956).
13. Secondulfo, 'Introduzione', p. 17.
14. Ibid., p. 23.
15. See also *Zib.* 143: 'Nella carriera poetica il mio spirito ha percorso lo stesso stadio che lo spirito umano in generale' ('In its poetic career, my spirit has followed the same course as the human spirit in general'); and *Zib.* 3029–30: 'l'andamento, il progresso, le vicende, la storia del genere umano è simile a quella di ciascuno individuo poco meno che una figura in grande somigli alla medesima figura fatta in piccolo' ('In many other things the course, progress, events, history of the human race is similar to that of each individual, very like the way in which a figure drawn large resembles the same figure drawn small').
16. See for instance *Zib.* 4198–99: 'se tanti [...] trovati moderni, come quei della navigazione a vapore, dei telegrafi ec. riceveranno applicazioni e perfezionamenti tali da cangiare in gran parte la faccia della vita civile [...]; certamente gli uomini che verranno di qua a mille anni [...] diranno che noi vivevamo in continui ed estremi timori e difficoltà, [...] essendo di continuo esposti ai pericoli delle tempeste, dei fulmini ec., navigare con tanto rischio di sommergersi' ('if so many [...] modern discoveries, like those of steam navigation, telegraphs, etc., find applications and improvements so as to change the face of civilized life [...]; then certainly men in a thousand years' time [...] will say that we were living in continual and extreme fear and hardship, [...] being continually exposed to the danger of storms, lightning, etc., navigate at sea with such risk of sinking').
17. Eric L. Santner, *On Creaturely Life: Rilke, Benjamin, Sebald* (Chicago, IL, & London: Chicago University Press, 2006), p. 28.

18. Julia Reinhard Lupton, 'Creature Caliban', *Shakespeare Quarterly*, 51.1 (2000), 1–23 (pp. 4, 1). The work by Franz Rosenzweig that started the twentieth-century reflection on creation and the creature from a critical perspective is *Der Stern der Erlösung* (1921); *The Star of Redemption*, trans. by William W. Hallo (New York: Holt, Rinehart and Winston, 1971).
19. For a reading of this passage see Luigi Blasucci, 'Su una famosa pagina dello *Zibaldone*: il giardino malato (4174–77)', in *Lo 'Zibaldone' di Leopardi come ipertesto*, ed. by Muñiz Muñiz, pp. 41–53.
20. The concept of a 'double' nature, as a benign source for poetic inspiration, illusion, and ancient vitality, on the one hand, and, on the other, an indifferent mechanism of production and destruction, and origin of unhappiness, has occupied the interest of critics since the publication of the *Zibaldone*. The distinction between 'historical' and 'cosmic' pessimism appeared in Bonaventura Zumbini, *Studi sul Leopardi*, 2 vols (Florence: Le Monnier, 1902–04). The debate between Sebastiano Timpanaro and Sergio Solmi which took place between 1967 and 1976 rekindled the discussion on Leopardi's concept of nature as either twofold but not contradictory (Solmi) or evolving in time and divided into two different phases (Timpanaro). See: Sebastiano Timpanaro, *Classicismo e illuminismo nell'ottocento italiano* (Pisa: Nistri-Lischi, 1969), pp. 379–407; Sergio Solmi, *La vita e il pensiero di Leopardi* (1967) and *Le due 'ideologie' di Leopardi* (1967), now in Sergio Solmi, *Studi leopardiani* (Milan: Adelphi, 1987), pp. 39–84 and 99–112. The core aspects of their debate were again discussed by Emilio Bigi, 'La teoria del piacere e la poetica del Leopardi', in *Lo 'Zibaldone' cento anni dopo*, ed. by Garbuglia, pp. 1–15, and, more recently, by Cosetta Veronese, 'Il sistema dello *Zibaldone* e i suoi lettori: Solmi e Timpanaro a confronto', in *Lo 'Zibaldone' di Leopardi come ipertesto,* ed. by Muñiz Muñiz, pp. 451–60. Marco Moneta has recently reassessed the clashing connotations of nature in Leopardi's thought. He argues that rather than being a passage from a limited (historical) to a more extended (cosmic) pessimism, Leopardi's conception of nature should be conceived of as intrinsically twofold and based on the difference between existence and life. The first type of manifestation, or nature as existence, is a pure mechanical cycle of production and destruction; the second is nature as the essence of all living beings, that is, a more or less refined capacity to feel. These two qualities are complementary and contradictory, and unhappiness derives from the *witnessing*, on behalf of living nature, of the persecution and besieging activity of the non-sensitive mechanistic counterpart. Since 1823, in Leopardi's reflection man is discharged of his responsibility for having detached himself from the vital natural naivety and having thus suffered the consequences of the advent of arid truth. The process of distancing is now considered by Leopardi inevitable and intrinsic to nature itself. See Marco Moneta, *L'officina della aporie: Leopardi e la riflessione sul male negli anni dello 'Zibaldone'* (Milan: Franco Angeli, 2006), pp. 149–55. On the relation between Leopardi's ideas of nature and guilt see also my ' "Di temenza è sciolto": pensiero e poesia della soglia', *Rivista Internazionale di Studi Leopardiani*, 7 (2011), 41–68.
21. See this passage in the entry on the 'total transformation' where Leopardi refers to 'quella solita illusione che noi ci facciamo, cioè che nel mondo e nella vita ci debba esser sempre un'eccezione a favor nostro' ('our customary delusion, that in life and the world there must always be an exception in our favour') (*Zib.* 143). For an interpretation of this passage see Claudio Colaiacomo, '*Zibaldone di pensieri* di Giacomo Leopardi', in *Letteratura italiana*, ed. by Alberto Asor Rosa, 16 vols (Turin: Einaudi, 1995), III, 217–301 (pp. 228–31).
22. Peter Gratton and Marie-Eve Morin, 'Introduction', in *Jean-Luc Nancy and Plural Thinking: Expositions of World, Ontology, Politics and Sense*, ed. by Peter Gratton and Marie-Eve Morin (Albany: State University of New York Press, 2012), pp. 1–10 (p. 5).
23. Giulio Carlo Argan, 'Preface', in Paul Klee, *Notebooks. Vol. 1. The Thinking Eye*, trans. by Ralph Manheim (London: Lund Humphries, 1973), pp. 11–18 (p. 16).
24. Klee, *Notebooks*, pp. 99–100.
25. See Giuseppe Di Napoli, *I principi della forma: natura, percezione e arte* (Turin: Einaudi, 2011), p. xvi.
26. Ibid., p. 7.
27. Ibid., p. xvii.
28. Ibid., p. 8.
29. Cf. Raffaele De Luca Picione, *La mente come forma, la mente come testo: una indagine semiotico-psicologica dei processi di significazione* (Milan: Mimesis, 2015), pp. 169–70.

30. The definition of 'semiosphere' belongs to Juri Lotman: 'in reality, clear and functionally mono-semantic systems do not exist in isolation. Their articulation is conditioned by heuristic necessity. Neither, taken individually, is in fact, effective. They function only by being immersed in a specific semiotic continuum, which is filled with multi-variant semiotic models situated at a range of hierarchical levels. Such a continuum we, by analogy with the concept of "biosphere" introduced by V. I. Vernadsky, will call the "semiosphere"' (Juri Lotman, 'On the Semiosphere' [1984], trans. by Wilma Clark, *Sign Systems Studies*, 33.1 (2005), 205–29 (p. 206).
31. Raffaele De Luca Picione and Maria Francesca Freda, 'The Processes of Meaning Making, Starting from the Morphogenetic Theories of René Thom', *Culture & Psychology*, 22.1 (2016), 139–57 (p. 151).
32. Ibid., p. 151.
33. The concept of diffraction, as elaborated by Karen Barad in *Meeting the Universe Half-way: Quantum Physics and the Entanglement of Matter and Meaning* (Durham, NC: Duke University Press, 2007), Donna Haraway in *Modest_Witness@Second_Millennium: FemaleMan©_Meets_OncoMouse™* (New York & London: Routledge, 1997), and Iris Van Der Tuin in 'A Different Starting Point, a Different Metaphysics: Reading Bergson and Barad Diffractively', *Hypatia*, 26.1 (2001), 22–42, serves to conceptualize phenomena of productive interference in heterogenous and non-linear history. On how this theoretical framework can be helpful for an understanding of Vico and Leopardi, see Martina Piperno's 'Introduction' to her *Rebuilding Post-revolutionary Italy: Leopardi and Vico's 'New Science'* (Oxford: Voltaire Foundation, 2018), pp. 15–21.
34. In addition to Cervato's *A System that Excludes All Systems*, which reconstructs the development of the themes of knowledge and ethics, recent monographs dedicated to the *Zibaldone* which correspond to these approaches are: Angela Bianchi, *Pensieri sull'etimo: riflessioni linguistiche nello 'Zibaldone' di Giacomo Leopardi* (Rome: Carocci, 2012); Maria Donata Di Stefano, *Per ragionar da poeta: il linguaggio poetico nello 'Zibaldone' di Giacomo Leopardi* (Florence: Atheneum, 2007); Anna Dolfi, *Le verità necessarie: Leopardi e lo 'Zibaldone'* (Modena: Mucchi, 1995); Patrizia Girolami, *L'antiteodicea: Dio, dei, religione nello 'Zibaldone' di Giacomo Leopardi* (Florence: Olschki, 1995); Loretta Marcon, *Vita ed esistenza nello 'Zibaldone' di Giacomo Leopardi* (Rome: Stango, 2001); Giulio Rosa, *Gli infiniti disordini delle cose: sullo 'Zibaldone' di Leopardi* (Salerno: Edisud, 2012); and Malgorzata Ewa Trzeciak, *L'esperienza estetica nello 'Zibaldone' di Giacomo Leopardi* (Rome: Aracne, 2013). In addition to *Dentro lo 'Zibaldone'*, Fabiana Cacciapuoti's other works devoted to the notebook propose a thematic reading with the aim of demonstrating project-planning as Leopardi's most incisive productive drive with respect to note-taking: 'La scrittura dello "Zibaldone" tra sistema filosofico ed opera aperta', in *Lo 'Zibaldone' cento anni dopo*, ed. by Garbuglia, pp. 249–56; and 'La forma della scrittura nello *Zibaldone* di Giacomo Leopardi: dalla circolarità al progetto', in *Lo 'Zibaldone' di Leopardi come ipertesto*, ed. by Muñiz Muñiz, pp. 73–85. Cacciapuoti is also the editor of a thematic edition of the *Zibaldone* based on the 'Index': Giacomo Leopardi, *Zibaldone di pensieri: nuova edizione tematica condotta sugli indici leopardiani*, ed. by Fabiana Cacciapuoti (Rome: Donzelli, 2014). Although I recognize project-planning as a strong motivation for Leopardi's writing, my study proposes an alternative analysis of Leopardi's daily relationship with his notes. I insist on the twofold character of Leopardi's approach to the text, and I stress the importance of un-programmatic impulses which co-exist with — and are antithetical but also preponderant to — project-planning.
35. Leopardi's planned projects to be drawn from the *Zibaldone* were the seven treatises listed in the 'polizzine non richiamate' (separate slips 'not referred to in the 1827 Index' (*EZ*, p. 2073) which are part of the external apparatus of the *Zibaldone*): 'Lingue'; 'Manuale di filosofia pratica'; 'Trattato delle passioni, qualità umane ec'; 'Memorie della mia vita'; 'Latino volgare'; 'Della natura degli uomini e delle cose, Teorica delle arti, lettere ec. Parte pratica, storica ec'; 'Teorica delle arti, lettere ec. Parte speculativa ec'. Leopardi also planned a 'Dizionario filosofico' (discussed for the first time in a letter to Antonio Fortunato Stella of 13 September 1826) and an 'Enciclopedia delle cognizioni inutili, e delle cose che non si sanno; o Supplemento a tutte le Enciclopedie', to which Leopardi refers with various titles in his *Disegni letterari* (and, for the last time with the above-mentioned title, in the eleventh list of planned projects which dates back to 1829). The indexing operation of 1827 was motivated by the need to orientate himself in the

zibaldonic labyrinth, organize his materials and inter-connection also in view of his project for a 'Dizionario filosofico'. See Cervato, *A System that Excludes All Systems*, pp. 91–97.
36. See Marcello Verdenelli, 'Cronistoria dell'idea leopardiana di Zibaldone', *Il Veltro*, 5–6.31 (1987), 591–621.
37. Joseph Anton Vogel, 'Lettera al marchese Filippo Solari di Loreto', in *Epistolario*, ed. by Marcello Verdenelli (Ancona: Transeuropa, 1993), pp. 92–98 (p. 92). However, as Emilio Peruzzi observes, it is unlikely that Leopardi started his notebook under the direct influence of Vogel's advice; see Emilio Peruzzi, 'Presunti antecedenti', in Giacomo Leopardi, *Zibaldone di pensieri*, photographic edition of the *Zibaldone*, ed. by Emilio Peruzzi, 10 vols (Pisa: Scuola Normale Superiore, 1989–94), I, XIX–XXIII.
38. Ephraim Chambers, *Dizionario universale delle arti e delle scienze di Efraimo Chambers*, 9 vols (Venice: Pasquali, 1747), VII, 185. The edition present in the Leopardi library was published in Genoa in 1770.
39. Ephraim Chambers, 'Common-Place-Books' in *Cyclopaedia: or, An Universal Dictionary of Arts and Sciences*, 2 vols (London: J. & J. Knapton, 1741), I.
40. On the tradition of the art of memory I refer to the essential classic bibliography: Frances A. Yates, *The Art of Memory* (London: Routledge & Kegan Paul, 1966); Mary Carruthers, *The Book of Memory: A Study of Memory in Medieval Culture* (Cambridge & New York: Cambridge University Press, 1990), and *The Craft of Thought: Meditation, Rhetoric, and the Making of Images, 400–1200* (Cambridge: Cambridge University Press, 1998); Paolo Rossi, *Clavis universalis: arti della memoria e logica combinatoria da Lullo a Leibniz* (Bologna: Il Mulino, 2000), and *Il passato, la memoria, l'oblio: otto saggi di storia delle idee* (Bologna: Il Mulino, 2013); Lina Bolzoni, *Il teatro della memoria: studi su Giulio Camillo* (Padua: Liviana, 1984), *La stanza della memoria* (Turin: Einaudi, 1995), and *La rete delle immagini: predicazione in volgare dalle origini a Bernardino da Siena* (Turin: Einaudi, 2009).
41. Ann M. Blair, *Too Much to Know: Managing Scholarly Information Before the Modern Age* (New Haven, CT, & London: Yale University Press, 2010), p. 76.
42. Pliny the Younger, *The Letters of the Younger Pliny*, trans. by Betty Radice (Harmondsworth: Penguin, 1969), p. 89.
43. See Richard Yeo, *Notebook, English Virtuosi, and Early Modern Science* (Chicago, IL, & London: University of Chicago Press, 2014), and *Encyclopaedic Visions: Scientific Dictionaries and Enlightenment Culture* (Cambridge: Cambridge University Press, 2001), especially pp. 101–92.
44. The following works by Drexel are present in the Leopardi library: *Opera omnia* (Lyon: Huguetan, 1658), tom. 2; *Considerazioni dell'eternità dell'inferno e del giudizio* (Rome: n. pub., 1739–43), tom. 3; *Il zodiaco cristiano, segni e simboli della predestinazione* (Rome: Grignani, 1645).
45. This is how Leopardi defines his notebook in a letter to Antonio Fortunato Stella of 22 November 1826 (*E*, II, 1268).
46. Francis Bacon, *Novum Organum*, in *The Works of Francis Bacon*, IV, *Translations of the Philosophical Works 1* (1858), ed. by James Spedding, Robert Leslie Ellis, and Douglas Denon Heath (Cambridge: Cambridge University Press, 2011), p. 162.
47. Cacciapuoti identifies three different stages of thematization of the *Zibaldone* in the apparatus constituted by the catalogue and the 'Index', namely a first stage between 1820 and 1823, a second stage between 1823 and 1824, and the general revision of the text in 1827 in preparation for the 'Index' ('La forma della scrittura nello *Zibaldone* di Giacomo Leopardi', p. 77).
48. Michael Caesar, 'On the Indexing of the *Zibaldone*', in *Lo 'Zibaldone' di Leopardi come ipertesto*, ed. by Muñiz Muñiz, pp. 287–300 (p. 287).
49. See Silvana Gallifuoco, 'Pensieri di varia filosofia e di bella letteratura', in Leopardi, *Zibaldone di pensieri*, ed. by Peruzzi, x, 9–18. See also Paola Zito, 'Danno del conoscere la propria età', in Leopardi, *Zibaldone di pensieri*, ed. by Peruzzi, x, 31–42.
50. Cervato, 'Lo *Zibaldone* come ipertesto', p. 330.
51. Ibid.
52. Ibid., p. 331. Michael Joyce's model is discussed in *Of Two Minds: Hypertext Pedagogy and Poetics* (Ann Arbor: University of Michigan Press, 1995).
53. Marie-Noëlle Bourguet, 'A Portable World: The Notebooks of European Travellers (Eighteenth to Nineteenth Centuries)', *Intellectual History Review*, 20.3 (2010), 377–400 (p. 378).

54. Giacomo Leopardi, 'Vita abbozzata di Silvio Sarno', in *Scritti e frammenti autobiografici*, ed. by Franco D'Intino (Rome: Salerno, 1995), p. 65.
55. Yeo, *Notebook, English Virtuosi, and Early Modern Science*, p. 46.
56. See Cacciapuoti, *Dentro lo 'Zibaldone'*, pp. 159–79.
57. See Marcello Andria, 'Dallo schedario all'indice', in Leopardi, *Zibaldone di pensieri*, ed. by Peruzzi, x, 49–61.
58. See Fabiana Cacciapuoti, 'Polizzine richiamate e non richiamate', in Leopardi, *Zibaldone di pensieri*, ed. by Peruzzi, x, 63–68.
59. Cacciapuoti argues that unlike the 1827 'Index', which implied a later revision of earlier notes, the compilation of the cards of the catalogue, which took place between 1820 and 1827, proceeded in parallel with the writing of the notebook (see *Dentro lo 'Zibaldone'*, pp. 159–79). This idea of catalogue cards which serve as orientating markers reinforces the parallel between the writing of the *Zibaldone* and exploration, as they record the movements of the noting traveller. The 'Index', instead, is the charting of a topographical map from above which is 'less involved' with the actual experience of wandering, as I will explain in the third part of this study.
60. Stoyanova has identified five different typologies of cross-references in the *Zibaldone*. The first degree of semantic relationship is represented by those references of the type 'Alla p. [#]' [For page [#]], located at the beginning of an entry, connecting it to topics already discussed. The second category comprises those references which Leopardi added as notes in the margin, at the end (after the date) or in the middle of an entry during the composition of the 1827 'Index'. To the third category belong all those references alluding to previous reflections but without specifying their exact textual location. They are often characterized by expressions such as 'come ho detto altrove' [as I have said elsewhere]. The fourth degree of referencing comprises all the entries grouped together under specific thematic headings in the 'Index'. These four typologies of referencing are specifically intrinsic to the writing of the *Zibaldone*, while the fifth level of referencing constituted by the partial index of the 'polizzine non richiamate' has the primary aim of serving as the basic structure for creative projects external to the notebook ('Lo Zibaldone di pensieri di Leopardi', p. 338).
61. See for instance the letter of 3 December 1822 to his sister Paolina from Rome: 'queste strade [...] interminabili, sono tanti spazi gittati fra gli uomini, invece d'essere spazi che contengano uomini. Io non vedo che bellezza vi sia nel porre i pezzi degli scacchi della grandezza ordinaria, sopra uno scacchiere largo e lungo quanto cotesta piazza della Madonna' [these streets that [...] are never-ending, are so many spaces thrown between men, instead of being spaces that contain men. I can't see what is so attractive about putting chess pieces of normal size on a chess board as long and wide as the piazza of the Madonna in Recanati] (Giacomo Leopardi, *The Letters of Giacomo Leopardi 1817–1837*, trans. by Prue Shaw (Leeds: Northern Universities Press), p. 122)]. See also the letter of 23 November 1825 to his brother Carlo from Bologna: 'sospiro ogni giorno più di rivedere voi altri miei cari, e in certe passeggiate solitarie che vo facendo per queste campagne bellissime, non cerco altro che rimembranze di Recanati' [I yearn more and more as the days go by to see you again. In some of the solitary walks that I take in this beautiful countryside, I seek nothing but remembrances of Recanati] (*E*, I, 1004), and that of 5 August 1828 to Monaldo from Florence: 'Io ho riprese le mie passeggiate prima di pranzo, che avea tralasciate da più mesi per timor del caldo. Queste passeggiate sono la mia salute, mentre quelle dopo pranzo non mi fanno altro che male' [I have restored the habit of walking just before lunch, which I had discontinued for months in fear of the heat. These walks are very beneficial to my health, while the ones that I take after lunch only have ill effects on me] (*E*, II, 1542).
62. On the first page of the *Zibaldone* see the interpretation provided by Fabio A. Camilletti, *Leopardi's Nymphs: Grace, Melancholy, and the Uncanny* (Oxford: Legenda, 2013), pp. 131–44.
63. Gabriel Tarde, *The Laws of Imitation* [1890], trans. by E. C. Parsons (New York: Henry Holt, 1903), p. 84. Jonathan Crary refers to this passage in *Suspension of Perception: Attention, Spectacle and Modern Culture* (Cambridge, MA, & London: MIT Press, 2001), p. 240.
64. The work of Catholic apologists, which was the main source for the *Dissertazioni*, was the means by which Leopardi came into contact for the first time with eighteenth-century materialism.

See Sebastiano Timpanaro, *Classicismo e illuminismo*, p. 145, n. 29, and Tatiana Crivelli's 'Introduction', in Giacomo Leopardi, *Dissertazioni filosofiche*, ed. by Tatiana Crivelli (Padua: Antenore, 1995), pp. 5–8.
65. John Locke, *An Essay Concerning Human Understanding*, ed. by Kenneth P. Winkler (Indianapolis, IN: Hackett, 1996), p. 65 (II, 11).
66. Jonathan Crary, *Techniques of the Observer: On Vision and Modernity in the Nineteenth Century* (Cambridge, MA, & London: MIT Press, 1992), p. 34.
67. Cf. Cesare Beccaria, *Ricerche intorno alla natura dello stile* (Milan: Galeazzi, 1770), p. 41.
68. Monica Stronati, *Il governo della 'grazia': giustizia sovrana e ordine giuridico nell'esperienza italiana (1848–1943)* (Macerata: Giuffrè, 2009), p. 205.
69. Giorgio Agamben, *State of Exception*, trans. by Kevin Attell (Chicago, IL, & London: University of Chicago Press, 2005), p. 1.
70. A short tale by Thomas Hardy where hypnotic gaze plays a central narrative function is entitled 'The Withered Arm' (1887) (with reference to one of the main characters' (Gertrude) physical deterioration due to evil influence), while in the novella *Ethan Brand* (1850), Hawthorne defines the heart of the magnetizer protagonist as 'withered', 'contracted', and 'hardened' (in Nathaniel Hawthorne, *Selected Stories*, ed. by Brenda Wineapple (Cambridge, MA, & London: Harvard University Press, 2011), p. 331). Frankenstein's oak 'had disappeared, and nothing remained but a blasted stump'; the tree was 'shattered in a singular manner. It was not splintered by the shock, but entirely reduced to thin ribbons of wood' (Mary Shelley, *Frankenstein* [1818], ed. by David H. Guston, Ed Finn, and Jason Scott Robert (Cambridge, MA, & London: MIT Press, 2017), p. 23).
71. On the contradictory position of the Icelander, and the relations between this and the diarist form of the *Zibaldone*, see Colaiacomo, '*Zibaldone di pensieri* di Giacomo Leopardi', pp. 246–50.
72. Giacomo Leopardi, *Zibaldone: The Notebooks of Leopardi*, ed. by Michael Caesar and Franco D'Intino, trans. by Kathleen Baldwin and others (London: Penguin, 2013).
73. For an account of the press releases see 'Lo Zibaldone parla l'inglese', Sapienza Università di Roma, 29 July 2013, <http://www.uniroma1.it/archivionotizie/lo-zibaldone-parla-inglese>, and 'Promoting the Zibaldone', University of Birmingham, 2013, <http://www.birmingham.ac.uk/research/activity/leopardi/projects/promoting.aspx> [accessed 7 August 2018]
74. The *Zibaldone* published by Giosuè Carducci appeared with the title *Pensieri di filosofia e di bella letteratura*, which is the title given by Leopardi to one of the partial indexes of the *Zibaldone* which indexed the first one hundred pages of the notebook.
75. Cf. Cosetta Veronese, *The Reception of Giacomo Leopardi in the Nineteenth Century: Italy's Greatest Poet After Dante?* (Lewiston, NY: Edwin Mellen Press, 2008), and 'Leopardi and the "Zibaldone" into the New Millennium', in *Ten Steps: Critical Inquiries on Leopardi*, ed. by Fabio A. Camilletti and Paola Cori (Oxford: Peter Lang, 2015), pp. 57–83.
76. On this issue see Michael Caesar and Franco D'Intino, 'Introduction', in *Zibaldone: The Notebooks of Leopardi*, ed. by Caesar and D'Intino, pp. xi–lxviii (pp. xiii–xvi).
77. The seminal works for this perspective are Antonio Prete, *Il pensiero poetante* (Milan: Feltrinelli, 1980) and Carlo Ferrucci, *Leopardi filosofo e le ragioni della poesia* (Venice: Marsilio, 1987).
78. Nietzsche was influenced by Leopardi's thought in his unfinished essay 'Über Wahrheit und Lüge im aussermoralischen Sinn' [On Truth and Lies in a Nonmoral Sense] (1873) and in the second of his *Unzeitgemässe Betrachtungen* [Untimely Meditations], 'Vom Nutzen und Nachteil der Historie für das Leben' [On the Use and Abuse of History for Life] (1874); see Camilletti, *Leopardi's Nymphs*, p. 13. Benjamin refers to Leopardi various times in his *Arcades Projects*, especially his 'Dialogo della moda e della morte' [The Dialogue of Fashion and Death]; Benjamin is also the author of a review of a German translation of Leopardi's *Pensieri* [Thoughts], see Walter Benjamin, 'G. Leopardi, *Gedanken*', in *Critiche e recensioni*, ed. by Giorgio Agamben (Turin: Einaudi, 1979).

PART I

Mathematics and Religion

CHAPTER 1

The Conscious and the Unconscious

Among the various forms of Leopardi's writing, ranging from isolated fragments, anecdotes, and sketches to articulate reflections and long demonstrative expositions of philosophical concepts, pairs of antithetical forces mirroring the operation of a twofold mind seem to coexist and interact. On the one hand, there is the search for systematic thinking, in which each component of a certain reflection seeks to find a coherent position and function among other parts of the intellectual ensemble. This includes the constant expansion of previously annotated thought, the subsequent revision and correction of ideas taking place at a second moment of rereading of the manuscript, as well as the 1827 *Index* and the intra-textual cross-references linking thoughts written at distant moments in time. On the other hand, the growing mass of the *Zibaldone* does not appear to lend itself to constrictions of homogeneity of form and shape. The insertion of newly created links to Leopardi's own thinking and the constant dialogue with geographically and temporally distant sources and authors constantly threatens the search for cohesion and at times even disrupts the coherence of the existing whole.[1] Often the subsequent inclusion of additional notes, instead of securing and reinforcing the hold between entries, introduces fragmentariness and dispersion. At times, the passage from one idea to the other is as abrupt as an electric shock; at other times, it runs so smoothly and imperceptibly that one finds oneself unexpectedly docked at semantic ports so far from the departure point that the idea which originally launched the speculative journey becomes almost completely invisible on the horizon of memory. The effort to register and collect ideas with the aim of remembering, therefore, often also becomes a function of variation and change. Because of this, the *Zibaldone* seems to give voice to what Richard Terdiman has defined the 'memory crisis' or the 'uncanny ambiguity' of memory, typical of the post-revolutionary years. This definition is rooted in a sense that 'recollection had ceased to integrate with consciousness', and on both an individual level and on a general historical level, memory fails to provide one with the reassurance of continuity that reinforces one's sense of identity.[2] By failing to recognize sameness between past and present, the post-revolutionary subject experiences discontinuity, and the rupture of a linear connection between past, present, and future generates, at psychological and socio-political levels, a new notion of memory as 'both preserving and destroying'.[3] 'Memory crisis' thus coincides with identity and representational crisis because the past that recurs in recollection is primarily recognized as a form of representation rather than re-enactment, and the incongruity between the past lived and the past reimagined makes us doubt the function and reliability of our faculty of retrieval.[4] There is, in other words, a temporal disjunction, in which the presentation of an event, idea, or image cannot coincide anymore with its representation.

It is essential to insist on contradiction and internal conflicts as the matrix for different forms of writing in the *Zibaldone*. These tensions take place within a general configuration of Leopardi's own mind which could be called, as I have already stated, twofold. Leopardi's mode of thinking is ambivalent because on the one hand it is regulated by a strong, almost obsessive will to control, to measure, and weigh every idea, all the details comprising an idea, as well as their relation with other parts of the system. For this purpose of control and vigilance over thinking and writing, self-examination and self-control play an essential role. But on the other hand, Leopardi's writing mirrors an equally strong impulse to evade the constraints of order, harmony, and cohesion to give expression to more spontaneous sparks of imagination, which sometimes seem to emerge suddenly from a subconscious dimension and which often manifest themselves through subtle, implicit associations or recurrences of words or images that are not obviously recognizable as part of a linear discourse. In the attempt to remain clear and present to himself, a constant feature of the *Zibaldone*, Leopardi's notes draw a thin line between two opposite, adjacent cognitive planes, that of the lucid awareness of the most minuscule movements of thought, and that of the indeterminate abyss of the pre-verbal and the unconscious, which Leopardi acknowledges as an equally powerful, but at the same time dangerous, tool for imagination and knowledge.

Some terminological clarification is necessary at this point. As discussed in the Introduction, by referring to Leopardi's unconscious, I generally have in mind a multifaceted pre-Freudian conception of the term.[5] I assume that an interest in psychological dynamics which escape the control of reason, as well as in modalities of performance in everyday life which pose problems to the integrity and authenticity of the self, was fully present in Leopardi's philosophical frame of reference, as demonstrated by Jan Goldstein with respect to France. Leopardi's intuitions of a fragmentary and decentred selfhood are more visible in the actual creative praxis than in any explicitly articulated 'theory'. In referring to unconscious states I am considering those components of Leopardi's thought which he analyzes with a general (often second-hand) philosophical context in mind and according to Cartesian, sensationalist, and *idéologique* terminology. It is at times extremely difficult if not impossible to determine exactly what Leopardi knew about that frame of reference, and therefore, in examining the presence in Leopardi of a certain philosophical sensitivity, I believe that it is often more productive to attempt an investigation into the history of ideas rather than a discourse on possible sources and influences.[6] At the same time, my pre-Freudian focus should not imply that a psychoanalytical reading of his work would not bring fruitful results,[7] nor is it meant to undermine the recognition that there are elements of Leopardi's reflections which could lend themselves to comparison with certain aspects of Freud's interpretations of latent drives and processes of transference.[8]

Günter Gödde has proposed another useful classification of the pre-Freudian unconscious with regards to eighteenth- and nineteenth-century German philosophers interested in explaining the functioning of a mind not present to itself.[9] Although the majority of the thinkers who elaborated a view on the unconscious were unknown to Leopardi, there are elements of commonality and in certain cases it is possible to reconstruct a dialogue, albeit an indirect one, with some of their core positions. Gödde individuates a classification of three main traditions in German thought: the 'cognitive unconscious' which can be found in Leibniz, Wolff, and Platner; the post-Kantian 'romantic' and 'vitalist' unconscious present in German Romanticism and Idealism; and the 'drive-related' and 'irrational' unconscious of Schopenhauer, Hartmann, and Nietzsche.[10] In the 'cognitive unconscious' approach, 'perceptions only enter consciousness when they are characterized by sufficient levels of attention and intensity'.[11] The Leibnizian tradition provided a re-evaluation of states alternative to clarity and distinctness which had been dismissed by Descartes, for whom the *cogito* could only be self-aware. The interest fell on obscure states of mind, namely on ideas which the mind cannot distinguish from other ideas or of which the mind is not aware. Nevertheless, contrary to Freud's unconscious as a permanent 'hidden' condition of the psyche, in Leibniz's system nothing impedes an obscure idea from being retrieved, under certain conditions, and returned to a clear presence of mind. From this perspective Leibniz's unconscious is still a function of clarity and distinctness. As we shall see, Leopardi's analytical speculation is in harmony with this vision. But there are other elements of his aesthetic thought and praxis of writing which share certain features with the second and third philosophical approaches. The second began with Kant, who reached revolutionary conclusions on the unconscious between 1781 and 1787, that is, the time between the first and the second versions of the 'Transcendental Deduction' of the first *Critique*.[12] In this transition he progressively abandoned an initial Leibnizian view of obscure ideas as latent ideas which have been overwhelmed by more powerful, clear ideas, to embrace a conception of the split subject (as at the same time subject of understanding and object of intuition). For Kant it is not possible to grasp one's self because the 'I' as subject, or the faculty of understanding, does not possess an intuition capable of directing itself 'up into itself', and 'as far as inner intuition is concerned we cognize our own subject only as appearance but not in accordance with what it is in itself'.[13] Kant's thought influenced German Romanticism and Idealism by envisioning the unconscious as the result of a disjunction between sensibility and understanding. Despite the fact that even with respect to this second approach it is not possible to prove any concrete knowledge on Leopardi's behalf of its main representatives (Goethe, Herder, and Schelling), nevertheless Leopardi's work also presents an analogous view, as an alternative to the rationalistic approach of the philosophers of the Enlightenment, and which focuses on the 'dark' sides of nature and the soul by taking into consideration leaps of consciousness in the field of emotions.[14] Furthermore, between Kant and Leopardi there is a shared view on the limits of intellectual speculation in seeking to understand nature, and the necessity to integrate rationality with imaginative thinking. This, even if it does not bring us to the knowledge of the truest essence of things, at least allows us to feel nature's purposes and tendencies.[15]

With regard to the third 'drive-related' perspective, already an early reader of Leopardi's poetry such as Nietzsche had understood the possibility of virtual dialogue between Hartmann's 'philosophy of the unconscious', which was influenced by Schopenhauer, and Leopardi's theory of illusions.[16] In this regard, and in addition to quoting Leopardi in both his second ('On the Uses and Disadvantages of History for Life') and fourth ('Richard Wagner in Bayreuth') *Untimely meditations*,[17] Nietzsche mentions Leopardi in a note written in preparation for his *On the Uses and Disadvantages of History for Life*.[18] Here Hartmann's idea of a senile age to come for humanity, in which all illusions will be unmasked, is in parallel to the figure of Leopardi as the symbol par excellence of intellectual radicalness, although in fact Nietzsche rejects the possibility that a total disappearance of illusions would ever come into effect. In addition to the many contributions which have already established parallels between Leopardi and Nietzsche,[19] recent studies have demonstrated the importance of latent forms of desire in Leopardi's work, thus further proving the necessity to investigate the presence of creative as well as destructive impulses of the psyche for which Leopardi did not possess a theoretical formulation but which are present in the fabric of the text.[20]

In referring to Leopardi's reflection on or creative manifestations of an unconscious condition, I will bear in mind these different perspectives and the way Leopardi touches on them, even if only tangentially, but I will not attempt to include Leopardi in any specific tradition. This would be improper given that his philosophy, together with the entire Italian eighteenth- and nineteenth-century tradition of thought, lacks the systematic character — meant here as abstract and based on logical and formal terminology — of other European philosophical traditions. Roberto Esposito writes of a:

> Singolare propensione, da parte della filosofia italiana, nei confronti del non filosofico. Sia l'impegno civile che la contaminazione con altri stili di espressione determinano un effetto di rottura nei confronti del lessico, specializzato e autoreferenziale, che caratterizza, invece, il discorso filosofico in altre tradizioni.[21]

> [Unique propensity of Italian philosophy for the nonphilosophical. Both its civil commitment and its contamination from other styles of expression result in a rupture with the specialized, self-referential lexicon that characterizes the philosophical discourses of other traditions.][22]

Leopardi himself reaches the same conclusion when he defines the Italian philosophical tradition as 'practical' rather than 'intellectual', describing the other European nations (France, England, and Germany) as 'più filosofe degl'Italiani nell'intelletto' [more philosophical than the Italians as far as intellect is concerned], while the Italians 'nella pratica sono mille volte più filosofi del maggior filosofo che si trovi in qualunque delle dette nazioni' [are thousands of times more philosophical in practice than the greatest philosophers who are found in those above mentioned nations].[23]

I aim to explore Leopardi's particular contribution to the development of a Western conceptualization of the unconscious by following creative traces which offer themselves for virtual and circumstantial comparisons. However, from a strictly theoretical point of view, and in light of the scope of the present section of the book, which is to explore the influence of mathematics and religion as generative forms, of the three traditions proposed by Gödde, it is the 'cognitive unconscious' approach that lends itself here for a dialogue with Leopardi's philosophy of the mind, given the attention devoted by Leopardi during his education to a broader tradition of thought which, from Locke and Condillac to the French Idéologues, aimed to configure the mental processes that led to the formation of language, its relations to ideas, as well as the role of signs in eliciting thought. Here dynamics of emergence and suppression of ideas and the search for clear and distinct expression always seem to work against a psychological background which is constantly assessed according to the possibility or impossibility of verbalization.

Clarity of expression is the cognitive and stylistic category that Leopardi elects as a means to come to terms with the effect of the two different contrasting impulses in the mind, namely the will to bring thought to light in a distinct and circumscribed form and the restless hidden remoulding activity of the psyche, manifesting itself on the surface of consciousness only as fugitive glimpses. Because of the importance attributed to what in the mind is obscure and confused, Leopardi's reflection on and praxis of clarity seems comparable more to the Leibnizian tradition of thought than to the Cartesian. As in Leibniz, clarity is the dynamic process in the search for the definition of specific properties typical of a certain object, but clear and distinct ideas are never extrapolated in a pure absolute form; rather, they are seen as what emerges from and continues to interact with the indistinct and the indeterminate. Unlike in Descartes, clarity and distinction are not the starting-point of analysis, the solid and unquestionable premise mirroring the undisputable truths of the *cogito*. Clarity, instead, is for Leopardi a never-resting process hosting antithesis and contradiction. For Leopardi, as for Leibniz, the two states of mind, that of clarity and that of non-conscious perception, are coexistent, and even the most determined ideas do not exclude a further presence of thought which, while waiting to be comprehended, continues to affect our understanding and regulate our perceptions. Of course, both the eighteenth-century encyclopaedic ideal, and the post-Kantian 'will to system' — borrowing from Philippe Lacoue-Labarthe and Jean-Luc Nancy's definition of a response to the crisis of the subject inaugurated by Kant, and determined by 'the absence of a subject whose self-presence is guaranteed by originary intuition' — strongly animate Leopardi's thinking.[24] Leopardi's attempt to reconnect with his past self tends towards an over-arching structure, but rather than accomplishing identity in a circular pattern of thought, every return to the subject, as in a spiral-shaped structure, implies the inclusion of a further and deeper order of observation. This also involves the sense that what presents itself to the mind as expressible through language — and language is the only means for Leopardi to 'materialize' thinking — is always the result of an extraction of thought and the framing of it into forms drawing from a profound, unspeakable, undifferentiated cognitive matter.[25] The latter, on the other hand, never ceases to exercise force 'from below' on the signifier. At the same time, this tendency for reconnection and reactivation always has to come to terms with the inhibiting sense of a surplus of meaning which writing cannot register fully, with a sense of entropic and irreversible dispersion of thought which projects Leopardi beyond Romanticism and towards modernity.[26]

My hypothesis is that although the presence of subterranean ideas or of spontaneous poetic interactions between words represent a perilous, difficult, and uncomfortable presence for one half, so to speak, of the poet's psyche — for the half obsessed with avoiding errors, with monitoring and documenting his own rational and emotional processes — nevertheless Leopardi was also very well aware of the creative potential of the indeterminate, of the sudden emergence of images and words that might arrive as isolated imaginative sparks but that could find their *raison d'être* and their connection with other parts of the system only at a later stage, in the process of further writing and rereading.

It is the entire conception of history and civilization which in Leopardi disassociates itself from trust in the idea of cumulative and progressive augmentation, be it of knowledge, skills, or technology as vehicles of happiness, and enters the realm of the unexpected emergence of phenomena and their return 'in difference', which is reflected in Leopardi's recursive mode of thinking. The origin of this conception lies first of all in his observation of the functioning of our cognitive and communicative faculties, which are intrinsically characterized by leaps and discontinuity. Moving from the observation of the self as the most immediate object of inquiry, Leopardi detects contradiction, displacement, and event-based development as common factors for both intellectual (and emotional) manifestations and the structure of wide-ranging social and cultural circumstances.

In the same way as Benjamin, Leopardi observes how a particular recollection or event in the past suddenly gains meaning in a new historical context (or new condition in the history of the self). Whenever a new sensitivity to cultural and historical impulses causes norms and tastes to be assessed differently, images and meanings which might for a long time have been in front of our eyes but remained unnoticed, unexpectedly appear and acquire significance. Unpremeditated events often link apparently unrelated human manifestations through subsequent revelations of meaning. Not only does the *Zibaldone* leave traces of this awareness at the level of reflection, but it is also primarily the praxis of notebook-writing itself which is fruitfully exposed to the 'now of a particular recognizability'.[27] According to this idea, the relationship between past and present is not one of explanation of one of the two temporalities by means of the other. The past is not relevant as it helps to understand the present through a genealogical reconstruction, nor, vice versa, is the present considered as a provider of cultural categories to illuminate the past by virtue of additionally gained experience. The following reflection is a clear example of this view:

> Or come ho potuto io povero ingegno, [...] trovar da me solo queste profondissime, e quasi ultime verità, che ignorate p. 60. secoli, hanno poi mutato faccia alla metafisica, e quasi al sapere umano? [...]

Non è dunque vero in se stesso, che lo spirito umano progredisce, graduatamente, e giovandosi principalmente dei lumi proccuratigli dal tempo [...], e adoprando i materiali già preparati. Se noi potessimo interrogare i sommi scopritori delle più sublimi, profonde ed estese verità, sapremmo quante poche di queste scoperte si debbano ai lumi somministrati dalle età precedenti; quanti di detti geni, per l'ordinario intolleranti degli studi, abbiano ignorate le verità già scoperte ec.; quanti abbiano ritrovate le grandi verità che hanno manifestate al mondo, non prevalendosi delle cognizioni altrui, ma da loro stessi, e in seguito de' soli loro pensieri; e piuttosto dopo ritrovate, si siano accorti ch'elle erano conseguenze delle già conosciute.

[How ever could I, with my meager intelligence, [...] find these very profound and all but ultimate truths on my own, which, though unknown for 60 centuries, have changed the face of metaphysics, and human knowledge itself almost? [...]

It is therefore not true of itself that the human mind progresses by degrees, by availing itself chiefly of the enlightenment procured for it by time, [...] and employing the materials already prepared. If we could question the supreme discoverers of the most sublime, profound, and far-reaching truths, we would know how few of these discoveries are due to the enlightenment provided by the previous ages, how many of those geniuses, as a rule allergic to study, may have been unaware of truths that had already been discovered, etc., how many may have discovered the great truths which they have revealed to the world not by availing themselves of the knowledge of others but for themselves and following only their own thoughts, and that it was after they had made their discoveries that they realized they were the consequences of already known truths.] (*Zib.* 1348–49)

If Leopardi insists on the lack of linearity intrinsic even to our own intellectual faculties ('pochi fra gli stessi più dotti, sono capaci di rintracciare [...] le origini, i progressi, il modo dello sviluppo, insomma la storia delle loro proprie cognizioni e pensieri, del loro sapere, del loro intelletto' ('few of the most learned are capable of retracing in detail [...] the origins, progress, mode of development, in short, the history of their own notions and thoughts, their knowledge and their intellect', *Zib.* 1376), similarly Benjamin's conception of time is bound to an idea of intermittence and sudden flashes of synchronic activations: 'image is that wherein what has been comes together in a flash with the now to form a constellation'.[28] Thus the *Zibaldone* is always a playground for unexpected possibilities. Images recur after hundreds of pages and new meanings, not visible from the outset, are discovered, not only by the reader but also by Leopardi himself, who is constantly renewing his own personal relationship with his text.

In the following chapters we shall explore, through a preliminary parallel with the philosophy of Leibniz (which Leopardi knew of only indirectly) and Pascal, but also first and foremost through the reading of religious texts devoted to the practice of confession, how Leopardi valorizes the power of the obscure, the pre-verbal, and not-yet-framed cognitive substratum, as sources for unexpected recreative images. The concept of 'naturalness', which condenses senses of spontaneity and immediacy also permeated by religious reverberations, corresponds to a 'purified' and legitimized version of the emergence of non-conscious states, and, together with clarity, functions as the principle foundation of Leopardi's writing.

Notes to Chapter 1

1. On Leopardi's syntactical strategies to maintain cohesion see Alessio Ricci, 'Sintassi e testualità dello "Zibaldone di pensieri" di Giacomo Leopardi, parte II', *Studi linguistici italiani*, 28.1 (2002), 33–59, and the following article highlighting syntactical disagreements which result from a semantic memory linking *ad sensum* different elements of the discourse, 'Sintassi e testualità dello "Zibaldone di pensieri" di Giacomo Leopardi, parte I', *Studi linguistici italiani*, 27, 2 (2001), 172–213.
2. Richard Terdiman, *Present Past: Modernity and the Memory Crisis* (New York: Cornell University Press, 1993), pp. 3–4.
3. Laurie Ruth Johnson, *The Art of Recollection in Jena Romanticism: Memory, History, Fiction, and Fragmentation in Texts by Friedrich Schlegel and Novalis* (Tübingen: Max Niemeyer, 2002), p. 9.
4. Cf. Ibid. pp. 15–16.
5. On the origin and development of the term 'unconscious' see David Armando, 'Ignaro, ignoto, inconoscibile... metamorfosi di una parola', in *L'Africa interiore: l'inconscio nella cultura tedesca dell'Ottocento*, ed. by Ludger Lütkehaus, trans. by Antonio Marinelli (Rome: L'asino d'oro, 2015), pp. 271–316.
6. For instance, Leopardi knew Locke's *Essay Concerning Human Understanding* through the Italian translation of Winne's abridged version of the essay by Francesco Soave, *Saggio filosofico di Gio. Locke su l'umano intelletto, compendiato dal Dr. Winne, tradotto, e commentato* (Venice: Baglioni, 1801); this book also served as a channel for the knowledge of Condillac, given that Soave had included, as a premise to the second section on 'Ideas', a small essay 'Analisi dell'umano intelletto' in which Condillac's essential ideas were introduced and commented. The Leopardi library also hosts the unabridged French translation of Locke, *Essai philosophique concernant l'Entendement humain traduit de l'anglais par Pierre Costet* (Amsterdam: Henri Schelte, 1723), and, by the same author, *Della educazione de' fanciulli* (Venice: Pitteri, 1735). As for Leopardi's knowledge of the philosophy of the Idéologues, his sources were mainly indirect and the issue of Leopardi's bibliography of reference is still a matter of research for the critics. However, the *Éléments d'idéologie* (1801) by Destutt de Tracy had been edited in Italian by Giuseppe Compagnoni and published by the editor Antonio Fortunato Stella (a good friend of Leopardi) in 1817, who refers to this book in a letter to Leopardi of 3 February 1827. Cabanis's *Rapports du physique et du moral de l'homme* (1802) had been published in Italian in 1820. On Leopardi's eighteenth- and nineteenth-century sources and his philosophy of language see Stefano Gensini, *Linguistica leopardiana* (Bologna: Il Mulino, 1984), and 'Manzoni, Leopardi e lo scacco della lingua', *Bollettino di Italianistica*, 11.2 (2012), 66–81. See also: Cacciapuoti, *Dentro lo 'Zibaldone'*, particularly pp. 8–22; Cecilia Gazzeri, 'Pensiero, parola, corporeità: un nesso ideologico-sensista nella filosofia del linguaggi di Giacomo Leopardi', *Segni e comprensione*, 19.56 (2005), 113–23 (p. 115); Alberto Frattini, 'Leopardi e gli ideologi francesi del Settecento', in *Leopardi e il Settecento*, ed. by Salvatore Battaglia and others (Florence: Olschki, 1964), pp. 253–82.
7. See for instance the reading provided by Camilletti in *Leopardi's Nymphs*.
8. For an example of transference, see *Zib*. 29–30: 'Una giovane nubile educata parte in monastero parte in casa con massime da monastero, esortava la sorella di un giovane parimente libero, a volergli bene, e le ripeteva questo più volte, e con premura, cosa di ch'io informato credetti che questo potesse essere un artifizio dell'amore che non potendo a cagione della di lei educaz. monastica operare direttamente, operava ïdirettamente facendole consigliare altrui un amor lecito, verso quell'oggetto, ch'ella forse si sentiva portata ad amare con amore ch'ella avrà stimato illecito' ('A young woman, unmarried, educated partly in a convent and partly at home with convent precepts, urged the sister of a young man, who was also unmarried, to love him, and repeated this several times, insistently. When I heard about it, I thought that this might be a trick of love, which, being unable, because of her religious upbringing, to operate directly,

operated indirectly, making her recommend rightful love to another, toward that object which she perhaps felt drawn to love with a love that she must have thought was wrong').
9. With regards to the British philosophical tradition, many philosophers and writers were interested in non-aware or latent activities of the mind. A repertoire of quotations can be found in Lancelot Law Whyte, *The Unconscious Before Freud* (London: Tavistock, 1960). However, the empiricist approach of Locke and Hume did not identify the issue of the substantial nature of consciousness as crucial because, as Nicholls and Liebscher observe, 'Since [...] the self or "I" [...] cannot be proven to exist on an empirical basis, the question as to the substantial ground of consciousness is regarded as being unanswerable' (Angus Nicholls and Martin Liebscher, 'Introduction: Thinking the Unconscious', in *Thinking the Unconscious: Nineteenth-century German Thought*, ed. by Angus Nicholls and Martin Liebscher (Cambridge: Cambridge University Press, 2010), pp. 1–25 (p. 5)). In the post-Freudian context, the focus on an unsubstantiated nature also applies to the unconscious, which 'has often been received with skepticism in Anglophone philosophy. This has led to a tendency to refer to a variety of "unconscious mental states" in the sense of an automatic or latent form of cognition, rather than to a single substrate or realm associated with "the unconscious"' (Nicholls and Liebscher, 'Introduction', p. 21).
10. Günter Gödde, 'Freud and Nineteenth-century Philosophical Sources on the Unconscious', in *Thinking the Unconscious*, ed. by Nicholls and Liebscher, pp. 261–86.
11. Nicholls and Liebscher, 'Introduction', p. 23.
12. This is the interpretation drawn by Arnim Regenbogen in Arnim Regenbogen and Holger Brandes, 'Unbewußte, das', in *Europäische Enzyklopädie zu Philosophie und Wissenschaften*, ed. by Hans Jörg Sandkühler, 4 vols (Hamburg: Felix Meiner, 1990), IV, 647–61 (p. 649), referenced in Nicholls and Liebscher, 'Introduction', p. 14.
13. Immanuel Kant, *Critique of Pure Reason*, trans. and ed. by Paul Guyer and Allen W. Wood (Cambridge: Cambridge University Press, 1998), pp. 257, 259.
14. States of non-vigilance (dream, reverie, and shock) inform crucial imagery in Leopardi's creative writing. See for instance Claudio Colaiacomo's reading of Leopardi's poetry in *Camera obscura: studio di due canti leopardiani* (Naples: Liguori, 1992).
15. See Alessandra Aloisi, *Desiderio e assuefazione: studio sul pensiero di Leopardi* (Pisa: ETS, 2014), pp. 150–53. On Leopardi's indirect knowledge of Kant see Antimo Negri, 'Leopardi e la filosofia di Kant', *Trimestre*, 4 (1971), 479–91, and Loretta Marcon, *Kant e Leopardi* (Naples: Guida, 2010), pp. 11–34.
16. Eduard von Hartmann, *Philosophie des Unbewussten: Versuch einer Weltanschauung* (Berlin: Duncker, 1869), the first edition, as used by Nietzsche.
17. Friedrich Nietzsche, *Untimely Meditations*, ed. by Daniel Breazeale, trans. by R. J. Hollingdale (Cambridge: Cambridge University Press, 2007), pp. 66, 249.
18. Analysis of Nietzsche's notes in relation to Leopardi is offered by Marco Brusotti, 'Figure della caducità: Nietzsche e Leopardi', in *Leopardi: poeta e pensatore/ Dichter und denker*, ed. by Sebastian Neumeister and Raffaele Sirri (Naples: Guida, 1997), pp. 319–35 (p. 320). As Brusotti states, the majority of the notes taken in preparation for the second *Untimely Meditation* were made by Nietzsche during the summer and autumn of 1873.
19. On Nietzsche and Leopardi see Nicholas Rennie, *Speculating on the Moment: The Poetics of Time and Recurrence in Goethe, Leopardi and Nietzsche* (Göttingen: Wallstein, 2005), particularly pp. 271–89. See also: Friedrich Nietzsche, *Intorno a Leopardi*, ed. by Cesare Galimberti (Genoa: Il melangolo, 1992); Angelo G. Sabatini, 'Nietzsche e Leopardi', in *Leopardi e il pensiero moderno*, ed. by Carlo Ferrucci (Milan: Feltrinelli, 1989), pp. 173–81; Alessandro Carrera, 'Nietzsche e Leopardi: per una critica della modernità', in *Giacomo Leopardi: estetica e poesia*, ed. by Emilio Speciale (Ravenna: Longo, 1992), pp.11–36.
20. See Fabio A. Camilletti, 'Leopardi *avec* Sade: Impotence and *Jouissance* in "La ginestra"', in *Ten Steps*, ed. by Camilletti and Cori, pp. 205–25. See also Raffaele Pinto, 'L'archeologia delle emozioni: le pulsioni di morte nello *Zibaldone*', in *Lo 'Zibaldone' di Leopardi come ipertesto*, ed. by Muñiz Muñiz, pp. 245–56, and Roberto Mapelli, 'Nichilismo attivo e rigenerazione di civiltà: Leopardi e Freud interpreti della crisi', in *Il Contributo*, 31.2 (2009), 19–30.
21. Roberto Esposito, *Pensiero vivente: origine e attualità della filosofia italiana* (Turin: Einaudi, 2010), p. 12.

22. Roberto Esposito, *Living Thought: The Origins and Actuality of Italian Philosophy*, trans. by Zakiya Hanafi (Stanford, CA: Stanford University Press, 2012), p. 11.
23. Giacomo Leopardi, 'Discorso sopra lo stato presente dei costumi degli italiani' [Discourse on the Present State of the Customs of the Italians] (*TPP*, p. 1015).
24. Philippe Lacoue-Labarthe and Jean-Luc Nancy, *The Literary Absolute: The Theory of Literature in German Romanticism*, trans. by Philip Barnard and Cheryl Lester (Albany: State University of New York Press, 1988), p. 32.
25. See *Zib.* 1657–58.
26. For what concerns the modern entropic character of Leopardi's thought, see my essay '"Time-image" in Poetry and Cinema: Leopardi and Antonioni', in *Ten Steps*, ed. by Camilletti and Cori, pp. 175–203 (pp. 194–203). Claudio Colaiacomo speaks about Leopardi's attitude to ancient and modern times in terms of a 'bipolarità insita nella disposizione leopardiana verso il *moderno*. [...] Il mondo antico è caratterizzato da una superiore varietà e originalità di caratteri usi e costumi [...] mentre la società moderna è caratterizzata da uno spirito di omologazione' [an embedded bipolarity in Leopardi's disposition towards modernity. The ancient world is characterized by a superior variety and originality of characters, habits and customs, while modern society is characterized by a spirit of homologation], with homologation being the social equivalent of a physical condition of entropic uniformity, see 'Post-etica rivoluzionaria: la conquista dell'insensibilità nel discorso leopardiano', in *Il poeta della vita moderna: Leopardi e il romanticismo* (Rome: Sossella, 2013), pp. 83–131 (p. 85).
27. Benjamin, *The Arcades Project*, p. 463 (N3, 1).
28. Ibid., pp. 462 (N2a, 3), 843 (G°, 19).

CHAPTER 2

The Continuum and the Discrete

Leopardi considers the temporal fragment as the essential infinitesimal unit of consciousness: 'Noi speriamo sempre e in ciascun momento della nostra vita. Ogni momento è un pensiero, e così ogni momento è in certo modo un atto di desiderio' ('We always have hope in each moment of our life. Each moment is a thought, and so each moment is in a way an act of desire') (*Zib.* 4146). This statement seems to allude to an uncanny idea of the temporality in our consciousness, because what presents itself apparently as a continuous flux is in fact discontinuous and constituted of infinitely small particles of thought. Leopardi's statement can indeed be interpreted in two complementary ways: one which reads 'ogni momento è un pensiero' in the sense that all our life, all the moments of our life are occupied by thinking, that there is nothing aside from thinking, and therefore thinking appears as a continuous state of the mind; and another which focuses on the equivalence between 'un pensiero' and 'un atto', provided that *atto* means for Leopardi a discrete manifestation.[1] According to this point of view, thinking also appears as an assemblage of tiny, discrete units. At a conceptual level, Leopardi is here concerned with the theory of the continuum and the question of the infinite divisibility of space and time, which had represented a very controversial topic in religion and science over the previous two centuries. Since its origin in Zeno's paradoxes, the basic principles of the theory of the infinitesimal stated that any line was composed of 'indivisibles', that is, points which cannot themselves be divided. But the 'problem that any positive magnitude, even a very small one, can always be divided' was associated with this concept.[2] In the first half of the seventeenth century a group of mathematicians, including Cavalieri and Galileo among the Italians,[3] rediscovered the theory of indivisibles to construct new mathematical systems which would revolutionize the discipline, and, with it, the way the world was conceived. By accepting the concept of a continuum formed by infinitely small particles they allowed for an idea of contradiction and paradox — that extensive lines are composed of non-extensive components — to be at the root of the real, thus destroying trust in the world as 'a perfectly rational place, governed by strict mathematical rules'.[4] This is why the theory of the indivisibles was constantly rejected by the Catholic Church and in particular by the Jesuits. Leopardi is also concerned with this paradox, but, although he shows awareness of the mathematical concept of the 'indivisibles', he prefers to switch his point of view from a purely abstract mathematical concern to its application to the physical world, in which the 'indivisibles' by necessity acquire a certain extension:

> Arrivate anche se potete, agli atomi o particelle indivisibili e senza parti. Saranno sempre materia. Al di là non troverete mica lo spirito ma il nulla. Affinate quanto volete l'idea della materia, non oltrepasserete mai la materia. Componete quanto vi piace l'idea dello spirito, non ne farete mai nè estensione, nè lunghezza ec. non ne farete mai della materia. Come si può compor la materia di ciò che non è materia? Il corpo non si può comporre di non corpi, come ciò che è di ciò che non è: nè da questo si può progredire a quello, o viceversa. Ma finchè la materia è materia, ell'è divisibile e composta [...]. Non v'è scala, gradazione, nè progressione che dal materiale porti all'immateriale (come non v'è dall'esistenza al nulla). Fra questo e quello v'è uno spazio immenso, ed a varcarlo v'abbisogna il salto (che da' Leibniziani giustamente si nega in natura).

> [See if you can get to the atoms and particles that are indivisible and without parts. They will still be matter. Beyond them it is not spirit you will find but nothingness. Refine the idea of matter as much as you like; you will never transcend matter. Compose the idea of spirit as much as you like, you will never create either extension or length, etc., from it; you will never create matter from it. How can one compose matter from what is not matter? The body cannot be composed of nonbodies, any more than what is can be composed of what is not, nor can one proceed from the latter to the former, or vice versa. [...] There is no scale, gradation, or progression that carries one from the material to the immaterial (just as there is none from existence to nothingness). There is a huge space between the former and the latter, and to cross it you'll need a leap (which the Leibnizians rightly deny to nature).] (*Zib.* 1635–36)

Leopardi is here measuring two different perspectives: a purely mathematical one, according to which the idea of the indivisibles is conceivable ('Arrivate anche se potete, agli atomi o particelle indivisibili e senza parti'), and which he implicitly associates with the characteristics of the 'spirit' ('Componete quanto vi piace l'idea dello spirito, non ne farete mai nè estensione, nè lunghezza ec. non ne farete mai della materia'), and a physical one regarding matter as the only substance and for which no purely indivisible extension is given in nature ('finchè la materia è materia, ell'è divisibile e composta'). The way in which Leopardi conceives of time produces the same split perspectives. For instance, Leopardi refers to our necessity to represent the temporal instant 'non esattamente e matematicamente, ma in modo largo' ('broadly, rather than precisely and mathematically') (*Zib.* 3265). In order for our intellect to approach and represent reality through language, we necessarily need to engage in an operation of alteration and approximation of the true essence of time, which makes us see things as either 'indivisibil[i] e non continuat[e]' ('indivisible [...] and not continuous') (when they are in fact divisible and possessing duration), or divisible and continuous, as in the relation between non-continuative and continuative verbs (cf. *Zib.* 1160–63). The previous reflection on the way time appears in our consciousness seems to correspond to these two models: there is the idea of indivisibility of the fragmented temporal unit, the moment, and the idea of a continuum of thought as an all-encompassing state of mind. The latter condition also translates as the temporal form of our lived experience which is subjected to the evaluation of our physical and sensory understanding. The way Leopardi formulates his statement on our perception of time makes us perceive these two dimensions of thought (infinitesimal and continuous, abstract and physical) as coexistent. This also means that a twofold form of representation resides in the very way we articulate our thought. Thinking, Leopardi seems therefore to infer, resides in an intrinsic contradiction or ambiguity. Depending on the perspective adopted to conceptualize thought (or time), we can intend it in the first instance as either continuous or fragmented, but in either case the perspective which has not been primarily selected also appears as the background to the other as a reflex with antithetical connotations. We could indeed figure the condition of constant desiring as a sequence of adjacent singular acts, each directed to its own different targets and emerging from our mind by seconding the impulses of the continuous hidden 'whole' made of the set of both our lucid and unconscious perceptions. Our mind, which cannot figure the infinitely small, is necessarily required to operate a work of adjustment or of enlargement in order to conceive of the divided idea. The reality we perceive as sensory beings and the reality we speculate on as rational creatures do not converge. Furthermore, as both sensory and rational beings, we constantly switch focus from one perspective (natural and led by the senses) to the other (led by reason), which makes our existence intrinsically regulated by a continuous leap between the two. This leap is in itself an inexplicable and almost unnatural happening, because the impulse which activates it, thus causing the switch between the two states, is alien to both: it is an infinitesimal state of being that is not perceived by the senses and is not defined in our reason. Once the leap has taken place, each resetting of consciousness after the move to the new point of view becomes an experience of transmutation and shock.

If Leopardi propends towards a physical rather than abstract approach, and if this general attitude corresponds to a wider set of correspondences between different elements of his speculation, this is not because the mathematical approach in itself is not considered valuable enough.[5] Rather, Leopardi's aversion to abstract thinking aims to avoid precisely the disruptive consequences that it could bring within his own system of thought, namely the insinuation of spiritualism into the conceptual roots of his philosophy. This could have been made possible, had Leopardi embraced the path of mathematical abstraction, thanks to the previously highlighted equivalence between the properties of the 'indivisibles' — which constitute the foundation of mathematics in Leopardi's time — and those of the spirit, on which religion is founded. The infiltration by spiritualism via a philosophical (that is, mathematical) methodology is the danger (and further paradox) that Leopardi tries to prevent. But resisting abstract thinking in general does not mean for Leopardi undermining the new revolutionary mathematical discoveries of the infinitesimal, nor remaining indifferent to its fascination. Quite the opposite, in fact, because the fundamental form of the infinitesimal model, namely the inhomogeneity between whole and parts recurs on many occasions in his writing, hidden behind the surface of a variety of reflections animated by apparently different concerns. Think for instance of Leopardi's reflections on the unhappy states of individuals composing happy masses, or the good nature of individuals who inform evil masses,[6] or the predominance of powerful masses made up of useless individuals.[7] The concept in question recurs also in one of his most crucial analyses of the poetic effect of Anacreon's odes, which is also clearly constructed around the same ambiguous relationship between the parts and the whole: 'Chi le legge posatamente, chi si ferma sulle parti, [...] non vede nessuna bellezza, non sente nessun piacere. La bellezza non istà che nel tutto, sì fattamente che ella non è nelle parti per modo alcuno' ('Anyone who reads them steadily through, stopping at each part, [...] does not see any beauty, or feel any pleasure. The beauty lies in the whole, in such a way that it is not in the parts at all') (*Zib.* 4177). In all these cases the quality of the single element does not correspond to that of the ensemble, in the same way that the lack of extension constituting the nature of the parts conflicts with a certain occupation of space by the line in the theory of the 'indivisibles'. All these examples put into practice a mathematical concept in a wide range of fields, testifying to Leopardi's propensity to generate unexpected contaminations and syncretism between different systems of thought and creative universes. Underpinning these applications is the conviction that the very foundations of our thought, whatever the field or modality of manifestation, is regulated by an uncanny and irreconcilable incongruence. The subject is split between physical appearance and speculative essence, and beneath the surface of the traditional collaboration between senses and intellectual faculties there lies a condition of incommunicability.

Notes to Chapter 2

1. See *Zib.* 1160: 'Atto ed azione propriamente, differiscono tra loro. L'atto, largamente parlando, non ha parti, l'azione sì. L'atto non è continuato, l'azione sì. Questi due verbali actus ed actio [...], a considerarli esattamente, differiscono in questo, che il primo considera l'agente come nel punto, il secondo come nello spazio, o nel tempo' ('Act and action do, strictly speaking, differ. An act, broadly speaking, does not have parts, but an action does. These two verbal nouns, actus and actio, [...] if properly considered, differ in this respect, namely, that the former considers the agent as if at a single point, whereas the latter considers him as if in space, or in time').
2. Amir Alexander, *Infinitesimal: How a Dangerous Mathematical Theory Shaped the Modern World* (New York: Farrar, Straus & Giroux, 2014), p. 9. See also *Seventeenth-century Indivisibles Revisited*, special issue of *Science Networks: Historical Studies*, ed. by Vincent Jullien, 49 (2015).
3. Leopardi mentions Cavalieri in his *Storia dell'astronomia dalla sua origine fino all'anno MDCCCXI*, in Giacomo Leopardi and Margherita Hack, *Storia dell'astronomia dalle origini al 2000 e oltre* (Rome: Edizioni dell'Altana, 2002), p. 231. As for the relationship between Leopardi and Galileo see Gaspare Polizzi, *Galileo in Leopardi* (Florence: Le Lettere, 2007).
4. Alexander, *Infinitesimal*, p. 12.
5. See *Zib.* 231: 'Bisogna distinguere la cognizione materiale dalla filosofica, la cognizione fisica dalla matematica, la cognizione degli effetti dalla cognizione delle cause. Quella è necessaria alla fecondità e varietà dell'immaginativa, alla proprietà verità evidenza ed efficacia dell'imitazione. Questa non può fare che non pregiudichi al poeta' ('It is necessary to distinguish empirical knowledge from philosophy, physical science from mathematics, knowledge of effects from knowledge of their causes. The former are necessary to the variety and fertility of the imagination, to the propriety, truth, realism, and effectiveness of imitation. The latter can only be harmful to a poet').
6. See *Zib.* 112.
7. See Giacomo Leopardi, 'Dialogo di Tristano e di un amico' [The Dialogue of Tristan and a Friend], in *Operette morali* (*TPP*, p. 604); *MT*, p. 222.

CHAPTER 3

The Psychology of Clarity

A crucial statement of extreme divisibility of thinking appears in *Zibaldone* in relation to clarity, where Leopardi refers in particular to the 'infiniti particolari del pensiero' ('infinite subtleties of thought'):

> Il posseder più lingue dona una certa maggior facilità e *chiarezza di pensare seco stesso*, perchè noi pensiamo parlando. Ora nessuna lingua ha forse tante parole e modi da corrispondere ed esprimere tutti *gl'infiniti particolari del pensiero*. Il posseder più lingue e il potere perciò esprimer in una quello che non si può in un'altra, [...] ci dà una maggior facilità di *spiegarci seco noi e d'intenderci noi medesimi* [...]. Cosa ch'io ho provato molte volte, e si vede in questi stessi pensieri scritti a penna corrente, dove ho *fissato* le mie idee con parole greche francesi latine, secondo che mi rispondevano *più precisamente* alla cosa, e mi venivano *più presto* trovate.

> [Knowing several languages affords some greater facility and *clarity in the way we formulate our thoughts*, for it is through language that we think. Now, perhaps no language has enough words and phrases to correspond to and express all *the infinite subtleties of thought*. The knowledge of several languages and the ability, therefore, to express in one language what cannot be said in another, [...] makes it easier for us *to articulate our thoughts and to understand ourselves* [...]. I have experienced this on many occasions, and it can be seen in these same thoughts, written with the flow of the pen, where I have fixed my ideas with Greek, French, Latin words, according to how for me they responded *more precisely* to the thing, and came *most quickly* to mind.] (*Zib.* 94–95; my emphasis, apart from '*fissato*')

The main points of Leopardi's reflection show that he is first of all interested in clarity as a cognitive tool suitable for capturing his own ideas in order to make them available for subsequent retrieval. He is aware of a structural deficiency of language to reflect all the shapes and shades of thought and believes that a broad range of linguistic markers is necessary to correspond to the equally vast nature of fragments of thinking. Foreign words in particular carry nuances of meaning additional to those available in our own tongue and are therefore useful as a precise aid for thought, helping us to avoid hesitations and omissions.[1] From this entry we deduce a certain urgency and anxiety in finding the word that is most capable of corresponding to the idea as quickly as possible, this search for the right word appearing almost like a race and a challenge to error: 'perchè un' idea senza parola o modo di espirimerla, ci sfugge, o ci erra nel pensiero come indefinita e mal nota a noi medesimi che l'abbiamo concepita' ('for an idea without a word or a way to express it is lost to us, or roams about undefined in our thoughts, and is imperfectly understood by we who have conceived it') (*Zib.* 95). But at the same time Leopardi seems also to recognize that there are intrinsic limits in language due to the fact that the perceptions which affect our senses and emotions are so numerous and difficult to grasp, because of their non-conscious nature, that language struggles in the attempt to provide an account of them.

Leibniz also founded his philosophy of clarity on the investigation into the capability of the mind to understand the discrete sensorial elements informing and influencing our perceptions. A parallel for example could be drawn between on the one hand the 'infiniti particolari del pensiero' cited above and the involuntary changes to our soul brought about by a variety of physical circumstances (*Zib.* 3205), and, on the other hand, Leibniz's conception of thinking, in which the faculty to perceive is described as a collection of infinite unregistered impulses within our body, which causes changes destined to remain obscure:

> There are hundreds of indications leading us to conclude that at every moment there is in us an infinity of perceptions, unaccompanied by awareness or reflection; that is, of alterations in the soul itself, of which we are unaware because these impressions are either too minute and too numerous, or else too unvarying, so that they are not sufficiently distinctive on their own.[2]

What is most remarkable is that Leibniz insists on an idea of clarity which is somehow ambiguous, as it is based on the understanding that the visible effects on the whole do not inform one exactly of what happens at the level of the discrete. In the same way, Leopardi's reflection on the nature of time can also be defined as ambiguous, as we have seen, because it allows two types of non-homogenous conceptions to coexist in difference, independently of the chosen point of view on either the continuum or the fragmented moments. In the following passage, Leibniz employs the very effective image of the sound of the sea to explain the relationship between clarity and obscurity:

> To give a clearer idea of these minute perceptions which we are unable to pick out from the crowd, I like to use the example of the roaring noise of the sea which impresses itself on us when we are standing on the shore. To hear this noise as we do, we must hear the parts which make up this whole, that is the noise of each wave, although each of these little noises makes itself known only when combined confusedly with all the others, and would not be noticed if the wave which made it were by itself. We must be affected slightly by the motion of this wave, and have some perception of each of these noises, however faint they may be; otherwise there would be no perception of a hundred thousand waves, since a hundred thousand nothings cannot make something. [...] These minute perceptions, then, are more effective in their results than has been recognized. They constitute *the je ne sais quoi*, those flavours, those images of sensible qualities, vivid in the aggregate but confused as to the parts; those impressions which are made on us by the bodies around us and which involve the infinite; that connection that each being has with all the rest of the universe. It can even be said that by virtue of these minute perceptions the present is big with the future and burdened with the past, that all things

harmonize [...]. These insensible perceptions also indicate and constitute the same individual, who is characterized by the vestiges or expressions which the perceptions preserve from the individual's former states, thereby connecting these with his present state.[3]

In interpreting this passage, which for Henri Ellenberger 'inaugurated the idea' of a 'subliminal world of perceptions' which is 'much wider than the field of consciousness', Gilles Deleuze stresses the ambiguous and somehow uncanny operation performed by Leibniz in maintaining an appearance of continuity with Descartes's thought, while at the same time radically renewing his system of clarity.[4] Indeed, despite the fact that 'no one has better maintained the illusion of a subordination of [...] sufficient reason to the identical', in fact Leibniz creates an alternative to the Cartesian idea of the clear and distinct by suggesting an 'element of difference' in 'the homogeneity of a natural light à la Descartes', and 'provid[ing] it with a differential unconscious'.[5] The Cartesian division between what is clear and what is not loses its meaning in this new 'uncanny' conception of clarity hosting ambiguity and contradiction: 'a clear idea is in itself confused; it is confused *in so far as it is clear*'.[6] Instead, it is the contrast and variation in degree of the various perceptions and, once again, the non-identical correspondence between what emanates from the whole and from its parts, that becomes crucial:

> Either we say that the apperception of the whole noise [of the sea] is clear but confused (not distinct) because the component little perceptions are themselves not clear but obscure; or we say that the little perceptions are themselves distinct and obscure (not clear): distinct because they grasp differential relations and singularities; obscure because they are not yet 'distinguished', not yet differentiated.[7]

Deleuze detects the presence of a boundary line where the interplay between emergence and immersion of thought in the indeterminate of the non-conscious mind is played out:

> These singularities then condense to determine a threshold of consciousness in relation to our bodies, a threshold of differentiation on the basis of which the little perceptions are actualised, but actualised in an apperception which in turn is only clear and confused; clear because it is distinguished or differentiated, and confused because it is clear.[8]

The importance of 'a threshold of differentiation' in Leopardi and the way this image is comparable to certain patterns of the *Zibaldone* writing will be discussed in more detail in the next chapter devoted to Leopardi's use of et cetera. For now it is essential to understand how, on a theoretical level, although Leopardi did not possess the same mathematical background which led Leibniz to build his system of infinitesimals and structure his theory of clarity, nevertheless the sense of a silent and hidden influence of minuscule elements of perception, as well as the crucial character of obscurity participating in the concept of clarity, is also present in his thought. On the one hand, as we have seen, there is his own original interest in the relation between the discrete and the continuum, which derives first of all from his investigation into human beings' perception of time; on the other hand, his focus on the indeterminate and the indefinite as a form of poetic imagination also elicits a certain interest in and sensitivity towards the relationship between 'minute perceptions' and their influence on the general vision:

> È piacevolissima [...] la vista di una moltitudine innumerabile, come delle stelle, o di persone ec. un moto moltiplice, incerto, confuso, irregolare, disordinato, un ondeggiamento vago ec. che l'animo non possa determinare, nè concepire definitamente e distintamente ec. come quello di una folla, o di un gran numero di formiche, o del mare agitato ec. Similmente una moltitudine di suoni irregolarmente mescolati, e non distinguibili l'uno dall'altro.
>
> [The sight of an innumerable multitude is very pleasing indeed, as of stars, or people, etc., a multiple, uncertain, indistinct, irregular, disordered movement, a vague undulation, etc., that the mind cannot define, nor definitely and distinctly, etc., conceive, as with that of a crowd, or a large number of ants, or a rough sea, etc. Likewise a multitude of sounds jumbled up and not distinguishable one from the other.] (*Zib.* 1746–47)

Although Leopardi probably did not have the chance to read directly from Leibniz's 'Premise' to the *New Essays*,[9] from which the quotation on the 'minute perceptions' was taken, Diderot's entry 'Leibnitzianisme', which appeared in both his *Encyclopédie* and the *Encyclopédie methodique*,[10] could offer an effective synthesis (though also mostly based on secondary sources) of Leibniz's idea of an indeterminate and confuse ensemble of perceptual stimuli from which a clear (but not distinct) idea is derived by intuition, as well as the non-absolute reliability of the sign as a means of corresponding to the true essence of reality.[11] Many passages discussing the difference between clear and obscure ideas of the early 'Dissertazione sopra la percezione, il giudizio, e il raziocinio' [Dissertation on Perception, Judgement and Reasoning] (1812),[12] also share many points of interest with a Leibnizian conceptualization of obscurity and distinctness.[13] In the encyclopaedia entry, the focus on compound ideas, also central in the thought of the French Idéologues,[14] lends itself to comparison with Leopardi's reflection on the limited nature of our understanding:

> Nous ne pouvons pas toujours embrasser dans notre entendement la nature entiere d'une chose très-composée: alors nous nous servons de signes qui abrégent [...]. Nous ne pouvons pas saisir à la fois toutes les notions particulières qui forment la connoissance complete d'une chose très-composée.[15]
>
> [We cannot always embrace within our understanding the whole nature of a thing extremely compounded: therefore we need signs which abridge [...]. We cannot know at once all the particular notions which form the complete knowledge of a very compounded thing.]

This both summarizes the concept of 'numberless perceptions' expressed by Leibniz in the 'Premise' and constitutes a solid point of reference for Leopardi's reflection on the 'infiniti particolari del pensiero'. Diderot also alludes to the necessarily symbolic nature of our representations: 'La connoissance d'une chose primitive & distincte est intuitive; celle de la plupart des choses composées est symbolique' [Knowledge of a primitive and distinct thing is intuitive; that of most compounded things is symbolic].[16] With the use of 'symbolic' Diderot/Leibniz conceives of a necessary construct of the mind that is able, by means of the arbitrary sign, to mould a specific set of corpuscular perceptions, in order to inform a shape which can be beheld by our inner eye. But as we have seen, Leopardi had also contemplated the necessity for a 'symbolic' (adjusting) activity of the mind capable of artificially enlarging or approximating infinite discreteness in order to make it conceivable, and expressed the importance of the prompt intervention of the linguistic sign to render a specific concept intelligible.

The arbitrariness of the sign, to which mental clarity is linked, became a central issue of the philosophy of language in the eighteenth century.[17] It interpreted language as the most useful and effective tool to grasp a fugitive reality in order to make it retrievable and repeatable, while at the same time creating an irreducible gap between the 'thing in itself' and the way we encapsulate it through signs, thus rendering it a function of our subjective reality.

The most significant innovative aspects of Leibniz's thought shared by Leopardi with respect to the definition of ideas are that of having presented an idea of clarity which admits shades, approximation, obscurity, and contradiction, and that of having conceptualized language as an essential but at the same time only partial and provisional indicator of the real. Leopardi's reflection on the difference between 'parole' [words] and 'termini' [terms], which has in Beccaria the most direct interlocutor, finds in Leibniz a powerful prototype, albeit limited to the realm of abstract speculation. The encyclopaedia passage indeed introduces the concept of a certain kind of memory intrinsically bound with language, which renders 'une notion telle quelle des mots' [a bare notion of words].[18] This refers to signs which, like Leopardi's 'termini', are directly and scientifically linked with the concepts that they are meant to express, but which have lost or never possessed the deeper and more complex set of senses which evoke the origin of the particular idea, and the subsequent passages of meaning which inform a specific concept, which is instead a propriety of the 'parole'.[19] Leibniz is concerned with analytical thinking and not with poetic imagination, as is the case for Beccaria and Leopardi, but nevertheless there is the sense that a word can be the carrier of different degrees of resonances for the concept it indicates, according to the typology of the sign in question and the presence or absence in the mind of a particular 'history' of the concept itself. Again, there is a tension between the visible and the invisible, as signs which, through writing, present themselves as the 'threshold' of determinacy, can show or hide a variety of complementary thoughts which have participated in the creation of a particular definition.

The encyclopaedia passage also includes a method of analysis analogous to that which Leopardi follows very strictly in the *Zibaldone*:

> Souvent nous n'avons qu'une notion telle quelle des mots, une mémoire foible d'en avoir connu autrefois la valeur; & nous nous en tenons à cette connoissance aveugle, sans nous embarrasser de suivre l'analyse des expressions aussi [l]oin et aussi rigoureusement que nous le pourrions. C'est ainsi que nous échappe la contradiction enveloppée dans la notion d'une chose composée.[20]

> [Often we only have a bare notion of words, a weak memory of having once known their value; and we stick to this blind knowledge without troubling ourselves to follow the analysis of the expressions as far and as rigorously as we could. This is how we miss the contradiction embedded in the notion of a compounded thing.]

Diderot, on Leibniz's behalf, here addresses an issue which had already been crucial in Descartes's thought, namely the power of attention to contrast the vanishing tendency of the mind's constructs. Descartes's focus had been on perception, and more particularly the disappearance of certain ideas from the mind which causes the loss of the sense of clarity and truth for the entire analysis. Descartes believed that a concept, in order to be clear, needs to be fully available in all its parts to our inner sight. It is not enough to remember the conclusions of a certain speculation; instead, all the passages should be equally visible, because as soon as the singular parts of the analysis fade from our memory — and this is inevitable as our mind is not able to remain constantly fixed on a certain idea — doubt arises and new, alternative, and sometimes contrasting possibilities emerge to undermine the previously achieved results.[21] The passage from the encyclopaedia quoted above, which unlike Descartes allows for the imaginative potential of clear ideas composed of obscure details, is concerned with the further cognitive stage regarding ideas encapsulated in the linguistic sign. It speaks about the risk of losing the sense of the multi-layered analytical contexture of the words, which end up referring to ideas whose complexity and origin are no longer perceived. If we now observe Leopardi's definition of what can be conceived as a methodology for writing, one notices the same insistence on the visualization of the progressive stages of thought as a compelling task in the research process, as well as the importance of language in registering all the phases of thinking. The insistence on the need to be able to reiterate this representation through constant training is also evident, as a way to facilitate our minds in the process of visualization in the most accessible and agile way possible:

> È verissimo che la chiarezza dell'espressione principalmente deriva dalla chiarezza con cui lo scrittore o il parlatore concepisce ed ha in mente quella tale idea. Quel metafisico il quale non veda ben chiaro in quel tal punto, quello storico il quale non conosca bene quel fatto ec. ec. *riusciranno oscurissimi al lettore, come a se stessi*. Ma ciò specialmente accade quando lo scrittore non vuole nè *confessare*, nè dare a vedere *che quella cosa non l'intende chiaramente*, perchè anche le cose che noi vediamo oscuramente possiamo, fare che il lettore la veda nello stesso modo, e ci esprimeremo sempre con chiarezza, se faremo vedere al lettore qualunque idea tal quale noi la concepiamo, e *tal quale sta e giace nella nostra mente*. Perchè l'effetto della chiarezza non è propriamente far concepire al lettore un'idea chiara di una cosa in se stessa, ma un'idea chiara dello stato preciso della nostra mente, o ch'ella veda chiaro, o veda scuro, giacchè questo è fuor del caso, e indifferente alla chiarezza della scrittura o dell'espressione propriamente considerata, e in se stessa.

> [It is very true that clarity of expression derives chiefly from the clarity with which the writer or speaker conceives and has in mind a particular idea. The metaphysician who does not grasp a particular point altogether clearly, the

historian who is not well acquainted with a particular fact, etc. etc., *will prove utterly obscure to the reader, as they will to themselves.* But this is particularly liable to happen when the writer does not wish either to *admit* or let it be seen *that he does not clearly understand that thing*, because even in the case of the things that we see obscurely, we can so arrange it that the reader sees them in the same way, and we will always express ourselves with clarity if we show the reader any idea just as we conceive it, and *just as it is and sits in our mind*. Because the effect of clarity is not strictly speaking to cause the reader to conceive a clear idea of a thing in itself, but a clear idea of the precise state of our mind, whether it sees clearly or sees obscurely, since the former is beside the point, and irrelevant to the clarity of the writing or of the expression strictly considered, and in itself.] (*Zib.* 1372–73; my emphasis)

Leopardi here is not stressing the value of absolute clarity ('un'idea chiara di una cosa in se stessa'), but that of the provisionality of thinking, which, while hosting obscurity and uncertainty, can still be valuable as a kind of radiograph of thought. What is most important regarding this passage is not only the humble admission that one's knowledge is limited and subject to improvement, but also the fact that Leopardi understands that there are territories of the psyche which are difficult to reduce to any verbal frames or which simply escape our lucid awareness.

Leopardi believes that the mind can sometimes be oppressed and that it is an intrinsic feature of our memory-structure that sometimes it leaps from one state to another without us being able to explain what happens at the actual point of the transition between one condition and the next. Thus, in order to understand Leopardi's conception of clarity and especially the meaning of the 'obscure clarity' which we will soon encounter also in his writing, one should always remember the two-sided nature of his thinking and the way that the almost obsessive need to reproduce any fragments of thinking through writing is at the same time accompanied by the recognition of the limits intrinsic to our communicative faculties. In Leopardi's view, obscurity does not impede clarity as long as the obscure is registered clearly, namely as it really appears in the mind. This point constitutes an element of originality with respect to the other philosophers of clarity, as it is strongly linked to the daily practice of notebook-writing. If the idea of the arbitrariness of the sign and the impossibility of perfect clarity for compound ideas is contemplated also by Leibniz at a theoretical level, Leopardi pushes his analysis of obscurity further into the realm of praxis, and transforms his approach from descriptive to prescriptive. Obscurity is not only acknowledged but *must* be registered in the practice of writing as the only way to rediscover the writer's own self, by re-encountering a precise state of thought as it presented itself to the mind and was rendered 'untouched' by writing in the course of the chronological succession of the pages of the diary. However, as we shall see, it is not always possible to retrieve thought in its original shape, but it is nevertheless paramount that the effort is monitored, albeit only to acknowledge that thought has undergone changes. Leopardi's use of et cetera, which is analyzed in the next chapter, provides an ideal opportunity to scrutinize how this theoretical awareness is actualized in the daily practice of writing.

Notes to Chapter 3

1. A detailed analysis of Leopardi's use of foreign words in the *Zibaldone* is offered by Roberto Lauro, 'Le idee e le parole: il lessico straniero nello *Zibaldone*', in *Ten Steps*, ed. by Camilletti and Cori, pp. 87–119.
2. Gottfried Wilhelm von Leibniz, 'Preface', in *New Essays of Human Understanding*, ed. by Peter Remnant and Jonathan Bennet (Cambridge: Cambridge University Press, 2000), paragraph 53 (no page number). I am here analyzing points of similarity between Leopardi and Leibniz as far as the idea of 'obscure clarity' is concerned. However, there are also points of divergence between their views, such as for instance Leibniz's idea of the best possible world, which is discussed by Leopardi in *Zib.* 4174, where the statement 'tutto è bene' [everything is good] is inverted to 'tutto è male' [everything is evil], as well as the two philosophers' different conceptions of nothingness. See Moneta, *L'officina delle aporie*, pp. 217–30.
3. Leibniz, 'Preface', paragraphs 54–55.
4. Henri Ellenberger, 'The Unconscious Before Freud', *Bulletin of the Menninger Clinic*, 21.1 (1957), 3–15 (p. 4). See also, by the same author, The *Discovery of the Unconscious: True History and Evolution of Dynamic Psychiatry* (New York: Basic Books, 1970). However, the editors of the recent volume *Archaeology of the Unconscious: Italian Perspectives* (London: Routledge, 2019), Alessandra Aloisi and Fabio A. Camilletti, rightly warn against the temptation (still visible in some aspects of Ellenberger's thought) to consider eighteenth- and nineteenth-century experiences of the unconscious as mere anticipations of the Freudian unconscious.
5. Gilles Deleuze, *Difference and Repetition*, trans. by Paul Patton (New York: Columbia University Press, 1994), p. 213.
6. Ibid.
7. Ibid.
8. Ibid.
9. In general Leopardi's knowledge of German philosophy was second-hand, that is, gathered through the filter of Madame de Staël and articles in the *Biblioteca Italiana* and the *Spettatore*. In *Zib.* 1636, Leopardi discusses Leibniz's ideas on the leap between matter and spirit by referring to the manual by Louis Dutens, *Origine delle scoperte attribuite ai moderni* [Origins of the Discoveries Attributed to the Moderns] (Venice: Bettinelli, 1789), which was present in the Leopardi library. For other sources establishing an indirect contact with Leibniz, such as Valsecchi, Jacquier, Saury, and Brucker see Bortolo Martinelli, *Leopardi tra Leibniz e Locke: alla ricerca di un orientamento e di un fondamento* (Rome: Carocci, 2003), p. 71. See also Moneta, *L'officina delle aporie*, p. 217.
10. Denis Diderot, 'Léibnitzianisme ou philosophie de Léibnitz', in *Encyclopédie méthodique: philosophie ancienne et moderne*, ed. by Jacques-André Naigeon, 3 vols (Paris: Panckoucke, 1791–94), III, 109–27). All quotations from the article are from this edition. Although the family library did not possess a copy of Didérot's great *Encyclopédie*, the *Encyclopédie méthodique* was Leopardi's constant point of reference.
11. On the entry 'Leibnitzianisme' and the presence of Leibniz in the *Encyclopédie* see Khanh Dao Duc, 'Leibniz dans l'*Encyclopédie*', *Recherches sur Diderot et sur l'*'*Encyclopédie*', 48 (2013), 123–42. The author believes that Diderot's own knowledge of Leibniz was also mostly based on secondary sources. Diderot himself lamented the fragmentariness of Leibniz's published work: 'la plus grande partie est dispersée dans les journaux & les recueils d'académies' [the main part is dispersed in journals and academic collections] (*Encyclopédie*, IX, 373a) (p. 125). A certain adaptation of Leibniz's thought to Diderot's own eclecticism also took place in 'Leibnitzianisme', and the same operation was performed by the other authors of the *Encyclopédie* (D'Alembert and Formey) who referred to Leibniz in other entries. Therefore, 'la présence de Leibniz dans l'*Encyclopédie* est principalement une présence du leibnizianisme, à travers différents auteurs' [the presence of Leibniz is mostly a presence of Leibnizianism through different authors] (p. 126). For the purpose of my study, which is to reconstruct generative forms which influenced Leopardi's reflection and notebook-writing, the lack of first-hand references to Leibniz in the *Encyclopédie* entry does not undermine its interest, as it makes it possible to detect the process of formation of a certain sensitivity to issues of clarity which Leopardi also perceived.

12. 'Se le idee si considerino relativamente all'intelletto, chiare saran queste, od oscure; distinte, o confuse; complete, o incomplete; adeguate, o inadeguate: chiare allorchè il loro oggetto può dalla mente esser conosciuto per mezzo di sufficienti indicj dalle idee stesse rappresentati: distinte allorchè la mente comprende le forme, e i contrassegni dell'oggetto rappresentato dalle idee. Se l'intelletto può distinguere, e conoscere tutti cotesti contrassegni la idea appellasi completa, in diverso caso appellasi incompleta. Finalmente può l'intelletto aver di questi contrassegni medesimi una distinta cognizione, e la idea chiamerassi adeguata, o può soltanto confusamente comprenderli, e la idea dirassi inadeguata. Le idee oscura, e confusa sono opposte alle idee chiara, e distinta, mentre la prima rappresenta l'oggetto in modo, che la mente non può di essa formare alcun giudizio, che dagli altri il distingua, e la seconda non addita alcun contrassegno, o forma dell'oggetto' [Ideas considered with respect to the intellect, are either clear or obscure; distinct or confused; complete or incomplete; adequate or inadequate; they are clear when their object can be known by the mind by means of sufficient signs represented by the ideas themselves; distinct when the mind comprehends the forms and the specific signs of the object represented by the ideas. If the intellect can distinguish and know all these specific signs, the idea is called complete; otherwise it is called incomplete. Finally, the intellect can have distinct cognition of these very specific signs, in which case the idea is adequate; or the intellect can only know them in a confused way, in which case the idea is inadequate. Obscure and confused ideas are opposed to clear and distinct ideas; while the first represent the object in a way in which the mind cannot form any judgment of it, the second do not indicate any specific sign or form of the object] (Giacomo Leopardi, 'Dissertazione sopra la percezione, il giudizio, e il raziocinio', in *Dissertazioni filosofiche*, pp. 303–04). Crivelli notes how this *dissertazione* was composed in close adherence to a manual by Odoardo Del Giudice (*Logicae et ontologiae eclecticae elementa ad usum studiosae juventutis* [Elements of Logics and Ontology for Studious Young People]).

13. 'La connoissance est ou claire ou obscure, & la connoissance claire est ou confuse ou distincte, & la connoissance distincte est ou adéquate ou inadéquate, ou intuitive ou symbolique. Si la connoissance est en même temps adéquate & intuitive, elle este très-parfaite; si une notion ne suffit pas à la connoissance de la chose représentée, elle est obscure; si elle suffit, elle est claire. Si je ne puis énoncer séparément les caractères nécessaires de distinction d'une chose à une autre, ma connoissance est confuse, quoique dans la nature la chose ait de ces caractères, dans l'énumération exacte desquels elle se limiteroit & se résoudroit. [...] Dans les notions composées, s'il arrive, ou que la somme des caractères ne se saisisse pas à la fois, ou qu'il y en ait quelques-uns qui échappent ou qui manquent; ou que la perception nette, générale ou particulière des caractères, soit momentanée ou fugitive, la connoissance est distincte, mais inadéquate' [Knowledge is either clear or obscure; clear knowledge is either confused or distinct, and distinct knowledge is either adequate or inadequate, either intuitive or symbolic. If knowledge is at the same time adequate and intuitive, it is really perfect; if a certain notion is not sufficient for the knowledge of the thing represented, it is obscure; if it is sufficient, it is clear. If I cannot state separately the characteristics necessary for the distinction of one thing from another, my knowledge is confused, although in nature the thing has these characteristics, and is limited and resolved within their exact enumeration. [...] Within compound ideas, if it happens either that one does not know at once the sum of the characteristics or that there are some which escape or are missing; or that clear perception, general or particular, of the characteristics be momentary or fugitive, knowledge is distinct but inadequate] (Diderot, 'Léibnitzianisme', p. 117).

14. Compound ideas are central in particular in the philosophy of Destutt de Tracy, to whom Leopardi refers in *Zib.* 1234–36: 'è [...] stabilito dagl'ideologi che il progresso delle cognizioni umane consiste nel conoscere che un'idea ne contiene un'altra (così Locke, Tracy ec.), e questa un'altra ec.; nell'avvicinarsi sempre più agli elementi delle cose, e decomporre sempre più le nostre idee, per iscoprire e determinare le sostanze (dirò così) semplici e universali che le compongono' ('ideologues have already established, in knowing that one idea contains another (thus Locke, Tracy, etc.) and this one yet another, etc., and consists in drawing ever nearer to the elements of things and in breaking our ideas down ever further so as to discover and define the simple and universal substances (if I may put it like this) of which they are made up'). For a study of the philosophy of the Idéologues see Sergio Moravia, *Il pensiero degli idéologues: scienza e filosofia in Francia, 1780–1815* (Florence: La Nuova Italia, 1974).

15. Denis Diderot, *Léibnitzianisme*, p. 117.
16. Ibid.
17. As far as Leopardi's philosophical context is concerned, Roberto Pellerey distinguishes between sign, language, signification, expression, and communication: 'Segni sono singoli elementi che rappresentano ciascuno un'idea astratta o un oggetto concreto. La lingua è invece un sistema di regole e dei [sic] segni che ne organizza l'uso ai fini comunicativi. La significazione è l'atto di attribuzione di un contenuto a un segno mentre l'espressione è l'atto di determinare un segno per un contenuto che si vuole denotare. La comunicazione non è che la trasmissione di un segno da un parlante a un ricevente, il quale potrà comprenderlo se conosce le regole comunicative e attribuisce lo stesso significato, socialmente e generalmente condiviso, per i segni utilizzati' [Signs are individual elements, each representing an abstract idea of a concrete object. Language instead is a system of rules and signs which organize its use for communicative aims. Signification is the act of attribution of content to a sign, while expression is the act of determining a sign for a content that one wants to denote. Communication is nothing other than the transmission of a sign from a speaker to a receiver, who is able to understand it if he knows the communicative rules and attributes the same meaning, socially and generally shared, to the employed signs]; 'Significato e comunicazione: il ruolo della grammatica negli "idéologues"', *Belfagor*, 45 (1990), 369–84 (pp. 369–70).
18. Diderot, 'Léibnitzianisme', p. 117.
19. See *Zib.* 109–11, 1237–38.
20. Diderot, 'Léibnitzianisme', pp. 117–18.
21. In his dedicatory letter to Elizabeth of Bohemia in his *Principia philosophiae*, Descartes writes: 'As long as it [the mind] attends to them [certain common notions], it is completely convinced of their truth. [...] But it cannot attend to them all the time; and subsequently, recalling that it is still ignorant as to whether it may have been created with the kind of nature that makes it go wrong even in matters which appear most evident, the mind sees that it has just cause to doubt such conclusions, and that the possession of certain knowledge will not be possible until it has come to know the author of its being'; *The Philosophical Writings of Descartes*, trans. by John Cottingham, Robert Stoothoff and Dugald Murdoch, 2 vols (Cambridge: Cambridge University Press, 1999), I, 197.

CHAPTER 4

'ec. ec. ec.':
The Determinate and the Indeterminate

The thousands of et ceteras dotted throughout the *Zibaldone* appear with various spellings ('ec.', 'ecc.', 'etc.'), in several different configurations (from the single 'ec.' to 'double' and 'triple' combinations, that is, in sequences of 'ec. ec.' and 'ec. ec. ec.'), in all possible positions (in the body of the text, in the page margins, in between the lines and in relation to intra- and inter-textual cross-references), leading to the most prevalent idea that permeates the pages of the philosophical notebook: excess.[1] The 'ec.' appears both as an indicator of vastness, that is, as the symbol that projects the existing text into potential, but unexplored, territories, expanding from the discourse that produces it, as well as a sign of the division and detail exerted upon a thought that could potentially continue to be subdivided into an infinite number of subclasses, or continue to pass between *almost* identical units separated only by infinitesimal nuances of difference. The 'ec.' is what survives of a totality that cannot be comprehended by our cognitive structure and is destined, exhausted by a period of ordering and classifying of dates into a sequence, to abandon its own elements and allow them to remain confused in something unsaid. After all, if excess really could be manifested in the text, channelling it in all of its cases, aspects, and variations into organized sequences of meaning would involve slowing down the thought until it stopped. The et cetera therefore prove to have a dual value: as well as interrupting, they establish at the same time the trail of cognitive selection and the origin of its movement, the start of the mental 'leap' needed to propel the thought towards new shores, so as to prevent it from stopping. Whereas the form of the abbreviated sign of excess is brief and concise, the exclusion that this alludes to, or from which it emerges as its remainder, is all-encompassing and indeterminate. In its dual function of both leap and bridge in the thought, the et cetera is located in a liminal zone between shape and shapelessness, working in both directions from 'immersion' in the indeterminate, when the discourse fades, and 'emergence' from the indeterminate, when the same presence of the 'ec.' retrospectively captures the attention of Leopardi as a reader and urges him to reconnect it with the interrupted line of thought.

The fact that the et ceteras appear exclusively in note form (with one exception, which will be briefly discussed later), and that the shortest note form 'ec.' is predominant (compared to 'ecc.'), seems to be explained not only by considerations of utility regarding its natural appearance as a flexible note-taking instrument; but also, with respect to the indeterminate thought which it faces, the note form of the et cetera, the final offshoot of the verbal extension of a given discourse, can also be read as meaning that is wounded or eaten by excess, and as a form that experiences the material effect of the shapelessness that it refers to. Unable to channel itself or secure a defined form in the text, the excess reduces the text to fragments, acting on the part of that with which it is in contact, the words 'et cetera', thus revealing the essential limited and punctiform nature of what is thought or spoken, compared to what *could be* thought or said.

By considering what happens to its 'photographic negative', as it were, namely the only case where the et cetera appears in its entirety, it will be possible to provide evidence of the ability of the et cetera to correspond in its form to the semantic meaning in which it is immersed:

> E delle composizioni successive di note, altre riescono melodie a tutti gli orecchi, altre a quelli di chiunque è pure un poco intendente (cioè assuefatto), altre ai mezzi-intendenti più avanzati, altre ai soli veri e perfetti intendenti, ed altre a questi più a quelli meno, o *viceversa, eccetera*. E così il giudizio e il senso della melodia sempre nasce e dipende ed è determinato *dall'assuefazione*, o dalla cognizione di leggi che non hanno la loro ragione nella natura universale, ma *nell'accidentale e particolare uso* presente o passato, e in altre tali cose, le quali leggi ho chiamato di sopra arbitrarie.
>
> [And of all the successive compositions of notes, some appear to all ears to be melodies, others to those of anyone who is even only a little bit knowledgeable (that is, habituated), others to the most advanced of the semiknowledgeable, others only to the real, fully fledged connoisseurs, others more to the former and less to the latter, or *vice versa, et cetera*. Hence the judgment and sense of a melody is born always of, and depends on and is determined by, *what one is habituated to*, or by knowledge of laws, the rationale for which is not to be found in universal nature but *in accidental and particular* present or past usage, and in other such things, which laws I have described above as arbitrary.] (*Zib.* 3232; my emphasis)

The sole occurrence of a full-length et cetera can be explained by a sort of phonic attraction, created by the assonance between the words 'vi-ce-ver-sa' and 'ec-ce-ter-a', and by an extremely close link between signified and signifier where the content of this entry transforms the linguistic form into the meaning that it communicates, and the form of the words corroborates its own content, becoming its actualized manifestation. In fact, the thought discusses a succession of sounds, or notes, and the assonances between 'viceversa' and 'eccetera' indeed produce 'composizioni' of sound. Being the only occurrence of a full-length et cetera in the entire *Zibaldone*, its use is highly 'accidentale', while the assonances produced by the vowel sounds in the two related, mirror-image words, do no more than repeat a sequence, thus generating 'assuefazione' [habituation] to a succession of notes, which the passage is talking about precisely at that moment. The reason why the et cetera appears exceptionally in full-length form is due to the content value and the formal aspect of the vice versa, a whole and unfragmented word, which in order to perform and stage its own intrinsic referral to an opposite, needs to be reflected by another whole word. If in other words saying 'vice versa' means alluding to the inverse of a given class of information, and saying 'et cetera' instead means referring to an excess as the homogeneous continuation of the given class, there is a contrasting semantic relation between the two words, in that they are mirror opposites. To be reflected and realize itself, the vice versa not only needs to come into semantic opposition with another antonym, but that same antonym also needs to reflect the shape of its opposite, and therefore needs to be whole and not abbreviated, as this is where the assonance and the completion of other performative requirements emerge. The reason for this unique unabbreviated occurrence of et cetera is thus explained, and this is invaluable not only in and of itself (because it shows the indissoluble link between thought and word, content and form), but also because it demonstrates the predisposition of the et cetera to performativity, its ability to endure the influence, on the appearance of its own shape, of meanings that involve processes *in limine*, on the threshold of reversals between opposites.[2] If this interpretation carries weight, then even the most abbreviated 'ec.' is part of the same process, it is the 'eaten' et cetera that suffers the action of the indeterminate which lies beyond its determinate form.

Naturally, this philosophical and imaginative dimension works alongside a more concrete level of writing practice. Leopardi avoids the full-length form of the et cetera both because it is not compatible with the haste of thoughts 'a penna corrente' ('written with the flow of the pen') (*Zib.* 95), and because the abbreviated et cetera combinations are easier to distinguish, also making it simpler to identify moments of interruption at a later stage, not only because the *Zibaldone* is designed to be continually reread and rewritten, but above all because it is devoted to clarity, or rather to the reproduction of the precise state of his mind. Leopardi is interested in making moments of indeterminate excess visible and ensuring that these are not confused with more definite moments, in order to be able to retrace the interruption at a later date, not necessarily just to modify or clarify it but indeed to recognize the simple fact that this has occurred and perhaps to try to return to the mental state that had produced it. A very common practice, for example, is inserting combinations of two or three et ceteras before the date, or letting the graphic effect of single or successive et ceteras interact with a wide, blank margin, as if almost wanting to leave open the possibility of returning to add further cross-references that transform the interruption and the indeterminate opening into a new circumscribing framework. It is not by chance that several internal cross-references or notes between the lines are written close to the et ceteras, which therefore offer themselves not only as moments of abandon to excess, but also as possibilities of future consideration and adjustment, as visual reference points for a future rereading. There are also some occurrences of 'etc.' which determine a sudden syntactic rupture in the discourse, but Leopardi does not fail to go back and leave precise coordinates in order to re-establish a connection with the thought. On p. 999 Leopardi talks about language and the link between the ancient state and the modern development of idioms:

> La letteratura latina non potè impedire che la sua lingua non si spegnesse, laddove la greca ancor vive, benchè corrotta, perchè sapendo il greco antico, si arriva anche senza preciso studio a capire il greco moderno. Non così sapendo il latino, a capir l'italiano ec. Onde la presente lingua greca non si può distinguere dall'antica, come l'italiano ec. dal latino, che son lingue precisamente diverse, benchè parenti. E neppure si capisce l'italiano sapendo il francese, nè ec. (29. Aprile. 1821). V. p. 1013. capoverso 1.
>
> [Latin literature could not prevent its language from being extinguished, whereas the Greek language still lives, corrupted though it may be, because if one knows ancient Greek, one manages without a particular course of study to understand modern Greek. It is not the same if you know Latin so far as understanding Italian is concerned, etc. Which is why the present Greek language cannot be distinguished from the ancient, as Italian can, etc., from Latin, which are indeed different, though related languages. And one cannot even understand Italian when one knows French, nor etc. (29 April 1821.) See p. 1013, paragraph 1.] (*Zib.* 999)

The final part of the argument interrupted at 'nè ec.', added to follow a date first written then crossed out, constitutes a further case of an idea being momentarily 'rescued' from its envelopment in the indeterminate, which Leopardi notes down quickly before sharply cutting off the discourse. On p. 1013 Leopardi once again reflects on the link between Latin and Italian, at which point the thought from p. 999 occurs to him again and he completes the unfinished reflection with a further addition on ancient Teutonic and German, the missing piece from the passage cut off at the 'nè':

> Alla p. 999. Così chi sapesse l'antica lingua teutonica, non intenderebbe perciò la tedesca, senza espresso e fondato studio (Andrès, loco cit. di sopra, (p. 1010) p. 253.); non ostante che la tedesca, secondo il Tercier, ec. v. p. 1012. principio. (5. Maggio 1821.).
>
> [For p. 999. Thus, a person knowing the ancient Teutonic language would not on that basis understand German without special and serious study. (Andrés, the passage quoted above (p. 1010), p. 253.) Notwithstanding the fact that German, according to Tercier, etc., see p. 1012, beginning. (5 May 1821.).] (*Zib.* 1013–14)

Complying with the demands of clarity, what initially appeared to be a suspension or interruption marked by the et cetera is therefore transformed into a tool of renewal and explanation. This is due, perhaps, to a certain haste similar to that which led Leonardo da Vinci to abandon his writing with an 'etcetera: because the soup is going cold'.[3] But unlike Leonardo, who, as Carlo Vecce observed, limited his reasoning to the confines of the page, in the *Zibaldone* the continual cross-references within the text and in the margins reveal a thought process that necessitates constantly flicking through the pages.[4] This implies that the connection between the different parts is achieved not so much through moving one's eyes between the top and bottom of the page, but rather through intermittent glances and visual leaps between the inside and the outside of the page, following a model of consultation and rereading that is, so to speak, three-dimensional, absolutely dependent on the depth and thickness of the notebook.

Hidden behind the Leopardian practice of flicking through pages and the physical relationship between the author and his diary are profound cognitive structures at the base of some writing solutions. The desire to make a moment of interruption as easy as possible to decipher at a later date by leaving further instructions illustrates an example of vigilant management of moments of excess in the *Zibaldone*. Only through continued resistance to interruption, and even to the 'temptation' to interrupt — when Leopardi knows, that in that moment the discourse is clear, but it may not appear so to a second reader — can the thoughts be retraced more speedily within such an enormous mass of papers.[5] But in an even greater number of cases, on the microstructural level of the sentence, the et cetera seems to indicate dynamics of inclusion in and exclusion from the linear sequence of thought, and as alluded to earlier, an 'inside' and 'outside', like presence and absence from the lucid supervision of the thought. In these places the et cetera is not accompanied by further indications or renewals in order to make the excess delineated and exact, but, on the contrary, it acts as a mere element to identify the masses of 'dark' and indeterminate thoughts that the writing touches on without being able to stop and illuminate. The 'ec.' constitutes the appearance of the limit between the verbal material of the written discourse and a preverbal matter within the movement of thought that cannot, or is too slow to, emerge clearly outlined in the mind, and is necessarily destined to remain submerged. The four examples that follow are made up of 'ec.'s that appear between coherent elements of the discourse and closely linked syntactic elements, that is, between the noun and its complements, or before subordinate clauses introduced by relative pronouns. We see here a few of the many cases of et cetera used outside lists (that is, et ceteras that do not interrupt a sequence or a list or words, adjectives, or verbs), or et ceteras indicating the attempted emergence of a list aborted by the flow of writing:

> L'odio dell'uomo verso l'uomo [...] è confermato da ciò che accade *nelle persone di una medesima professione ec. fra le quali*, sebben la perfetta amicizia astrattamente considerata è impossibile [...] nondimeno anche la possibile amicizia è difficilissima, rarissima, incostantissima ec.
>
> [Man's hatred toward man is manifested principally and is confirmed by what happens *with people in the same profession, etc., among whom*, though perfect friendship abstractly considered is impossible and in contradiction with human nature, nonetheless even what is possible in the way of friendship is very difficult, rare, inconstant, etc.] (*Zib.* 1724; my emphasis)
>
> Quello che ci desta una folla di rimembranze dove il pensiero si confonda, è sempre piacevole. Ciò fanno le immagini [...] *della vita rustica ec. il cui* grand'effetto deriva in gran parte dalla folla delle rimembranze [...] che producono [...]. Quindi si veda con quanto giudizio i bravi [...] romantici [...] scelgano di preferenza le similitudini [...] per le *immagini ec. della* loro poesia.
>
> [Whatever awakens a host of memories for us, where thought grows uncertain, is always pleasurable. The [...] images *of rural life, etc., whose* powerful effect derives in large part from the host of memories [...] they evoke [...]. Hence it may be seen what judgment the valiant [...] Romantics [...] choose similes [...] as *images, etc., for* their poetry.] (*Zib.* 1777–78; my emphasis)

> La lingua spagnuola [...] dev'esser considerata come speciale e principale conservatrice dell'antichità, della latinità, del volgar latino ec. quanto alla material forma delle parole e alla proprietà *delle loro inflessioni ec. che è quello* che ora c'importa.
>
> [The Spanish language [...] must be considered the special and main preserver of antiquity, of Latinity, of Vulgar Latin, etc., insofar as regards the material form of the words and the property *of their inflections, etc., which is what* we are concerned with here.] (*Zib.* 3573; my emphasis)
>
> Talvolta è propriamente ridicolo a vedere imagini e sentenze e affetti sublimi, e rimoti o dall'opinione o dall'uso volgare, e superiori al comune *modo ec. di pensare*, espressi ne' versi francesi al modo che si esprimerebbe una dimostrazione geometrica, o si direbbe una facezia in conversazione.
>
> [Sometimes it is downright ridiculous to see sublime images and maxims and sentiments, set apart on the one hand from popular opinion or popular use, and superior on the other to the commonplace *way, etc., of thinking*, formulated in French verses in the manner in which one would formulate a geometric proof, or make a witty remark in conversation.] (*Zib.* 1813; my emphasis)

The almost instantaneous response of the writing hand to every impulse of the thought, obtained through the 'ec.', is a sort of cognitive seismograph that reveals the presence of an idea oscillating more or less imperceptibly around the logical sequence of the written line.[6] Some et cetera sequences almost take on the form of a tic, an obsession with capturing the slightest shift in attention. Hardly has a secondary idea exerted the slightest force on the main idea than the hand, almost automatically, logs its presence with an 'ec.', which has the advantage of being a particle of concentrated meaning, easy to write, with minimal impact on the speed of writing, and, even more importantly, an essentially verbal symbol, in line with the strict ban on using non-verbal graphic elements such as 'segnetti e lineette, e punti ammirativi doppi, tripli' ('little signs and dashes, and double or triple exclamation marks') (*Zib.* 225–26), abhorred by Leopardi, who maintained that words, and only words, were authorized to express concepts. Indeed, it is also well-known how in the *Zibaldone*, unlike other authors' diaries or notebooks, there are no graphic signs or non-verbal squiggles (except the minuscule crosses that designate internal cross-references).[7]

It is essential to note how the function of the 'ec.' as a seismographic recording of thoughts occurs not only in the first phase of writing, in the body of the text, but also as an element of rereading and rewriting, namely in the great many insertions of isolated et ceteras (those not forming part of syntactic sentences or passages) between the lines that interrupt the original complete sentence.[8] In some cases Leopardi even seems to add new excess to the already existing excess and, again, it seems important to underline how this operation is not necessarily a quantitative addition but rather an act of clarity and reappropriation in 'difference', as will now be seen. In the following reflection the first and third 'ec.' are added later in order to surround the earlier central 'ec.':[9]

> È da notare che la nostra ben distinta teoria della formazione grammaticale de'
> continuativi e frequentativi [...] serve ancora ad illustrare e mettere in chiaro
> [...] la vera origine di molti participii più moderni, come *actus*, e la loro ragione
> grammaticale; e spiega e scioglie molte anomalie apparenti ec. ec. ec.
>
> [It is worth noting that our quite distinct theory of the grammatical formation
> of continuatives and frequentatives [...] serves to illustrate and bring out
> [...] the true origin of many more modern participles, such as *actus*, and
> their grammatical justification. And it explains and resolves many apparent
> anomalies, etc. etc. etc.] (*Zib.* 2826–27)

Certainly, it cannot be ruled out that the addition could be the result of a comparison between two moments of writing, which would appear to possess semi-determinate and semi-delineated characteristics enabling a comparison between two meanings of excess that both appear in thought (one as a reminder, the other as presence) but are left under the surface in terms of verbal expression.[10] More likely, however, the same, almost mechanical, process of recording a latent idea that only imperceptibly emerges within the flow of thought during the first writing also occurs at the time of rereading. Immortalized in the manuscript, therefore, are the traces of two different 'tremors' in the thought, occurring from the same speculative line.[11] If the precise earlier state of mind cannot be recovered (which occurs both when the original meaning of the initial 'ec.' is forgotten and when the idea is replaced with new additions), the prior symbol of excess, which has by this time become an unrecognizable or in any case 'no longer authentic' foreign body (as it was produced by a different train of thought), must again be personalized through new graphic interventions associated with the new meaning of excess. Even at the peak of indeterminacy, we can see at play an extreme act of clarity, or better 'obscure clarity', exercised in the praxis of writing, which is fundamentally oxymoronic and, in line with the epistemology of excess outlined so far, based on the adjacency of opposite terms in its impulse to register the unregistrable. This is a thought that necessarily lives on a reflexive leap, on a non-coincidence of it with itself in future moments, even though these further thinking moments come from identical premises. This is how temporal irreversibility penetrates forms and means of writing and the 'ec.' becomes at the same time a signal of change as well as of continuation, in that the second moment relates to the first in the same way that the 'one' corresponds with its 'other'. This was also the substantive meaning of the pair vice versa/et cetera, the departure-point of the present argument.

Any element of discourse in the *Zibaldone*, when associated with an et cetera, is capable of assuming the function of a tangential point, potentially projecting the text into infinite lines of meaning. That Leopardi imagined excess in a certain sense as a straight line is suggested by the graphic performance of the et cetera in the thought on p. 1944: 'La vista è il più materiale di tutti i sensi, e il meno atto a tutto ciò che sa di astratto. Perciò la vista e i suoi piaceri sono le predilette sensazioni dell'uomo naturale. ec... ec... ec. V. Costa, dell'Elocuzione' ('Sight is the most material of all the senses, and the least suited to all that has to do with abstraction. Consequently, sight and its pleasures are the favorite sensations of natural man, etc.... etc.... etc. See Costa, Dell'elocuzione'). While referring to Costa's thoughts on materiality and the power of sight, on the manuscript Leopardi transforms the sequence of three 'ec.'s into a visible form, in a linear succession of dots between which the 'ec.'s are carefully arranged, as if each 'ec.' were itself a constitutive part of the line. This abundance of small dots, of which this is the only example in the entire *Zibaldone*, is a precious revelation of how Leopardi envisaged excess. His natural and general resistance to the use of merely graphic symbols has been discussed, and it is important to specify how in this particular case he does not contradict himself; the graphic symbol here does not replace the verbal symbol but is produced by it, providing a representation of how the verbal form appears in the mental dimension and suggesting its evocative power on the sense of sight, both internal and external. The performative power of Leopardian writing, that is the ability of the word to transform itself into what it says, brushes against the upper limit of proximity between verbal form and graphic form.

The logical organization of the thought in excess is widely presented in textual arrangements that could be assimilated with certain geometric conceptualizations. Of course, these are employed here purely as an explanatory tool (that is, without implying that Leopardi used them voluntarily), and discussed by using a process of approximation, given that the present analysis is operating in a broad metaphorical dimension.[12] There are cases of excess that pertain to 'sets' that are related to one another through parentheses, as in the following three examples, where the excess within the parentheses constitutes a 'subset' of the main thought, itself also in excess:

> Anche il delitto bene spesso è un eroismo, cioè p.e. quando il farlo torna in danno o pericolo, e nondimeno si vuol fare per soddisfare quella tal passione ec. tanto più eroismo quanto che bisogna superare tutta la forza della natura reclamante, e dell'abitudine (se si tratta p.e. di un giovane, di un innocente ec.) ec.
>
> [Crime, too, is often a form of heroism, that is, for example, when committing a crime leads to loss or danger, and yet you still want to carry it out in order to satisfy a given passion, etc., and the more heroic, the more need there is to overcome all the power of protesting nature and of habit (if we are talking, e.g., about a young person, an innocent, etc.), etc.] (*Zib.* 72)
>
> Come non è nè letteratura nè lingua nostra quella letteratura e quella lingua che oggidì usano i nostri pedanti affettando e simulando di esser antichi italiani, e dissimulando al possibile di essere italiani moderni, di aver qualche idea che gl'italiani antichi non avessero perchè non poterono, (così forse fece Cic. verso Catone antico ec. o Virgilio verso Ennio ec.?) ec. ec.
>
> [In the same way as that literature and language which our pedants use today is not our literature or language, as they affect and pretend to be ancient Italians, and disguise as much as possible the fact that they are modern Italians, that they have some ideas which the ancient Italians did not have because they could not (as perhaps Cicero did in relation to Cato the Elder, etc., or Virgil with Ennius, etc.?), etc. etc.] (*Zib.* 3465)
>
> Che da' partic. pass. della prima si facciano i continuat. o freqq. in *itare* piuttosto che in *atare*, non dee parer maraviglia quando si consideri l'uso lat. di scambiare

> p. regola l'*a* in *i* breve, in tante altre cose, come ne' compp. (*facio jacio — conficio, conijcio* ec.) ec. Oltre che anche nella prima v'ha molti supini e participii passati in *ĭtus*, de' quali altrove, come *domitus* ec..
>
> [That continuatives and frequentatives in *itare* rather than in *atare* are formed from past participles of the first conjugation is no surprise when you consider Latin regularly changes *a* to short *i*, in so many other cases, such as in the compounds (*facio* [to do] *jacio* [to throw] — *conficio* [to put together], *conijcio* [to throw together], etc.), etc. Moreover in the first conjugation too there are many supines and past participles in *ĭtus*, mentioned elsewhere, like *domitus* [tamed], etc.] (*Zib.* 4086)

The 'boundary' outlined by the parentheses represents the space of action that is graphically closed, or 'finite', of an excess that arises as a sort of lateral germination of the main discourse, subject to a precise channelling procedure. This operation is controlled by a tension between two opposing impulses, one aiming to shrink and constrict, as represented by the parentheses, and the other pushing towards an indeterminate opening or gap, alluded to by the excess inside the parentheses. The result of such a dynamic is a kind of cropping of actual infinity, which cannot in itself be experienced by the human mind, where the 'ec.' remains as its symbol and 'eaten' form: while alluding to infinity, at the same time it represents its 'replacement' in finite written form.

Unlike in the previously cited examples, in the following reflection the division into subclasses is the result of a particular point of view from which the sentence develops, not of a real difference in rank between what is inside the parentheses and what is outside:

> Oggi il mio ingegno sarà svegliatissimo, la mia indole piacevolissima, domani tutto l'opposto, senz'alcuna cagione morale nè apparente, ma certo non senza cagioni fisiche, le quali diversamente affettando l'animo, lo tramutano effettivamente d'ora in ora, di giorno in giorno, di stagione in istagione (fu chi disse ch'ei si trovava più atto a comporre nel sommo caldo o nel sommo freddo che nelle medie temperature dell'anno; la mattina che la sera ec.) ec. ec. e lo ritornano nello stato di prima, ed ora lo rendono atto a una cosa, ora a un'altra, ora a più cose ora a meno, ora più ora meno atto ec. ec.
>
> [Today my mind might be most alert, my character most agreeable, whereas tomorrow it might be quite the opposite, without any moral or apparent reason, but certainly not without physical causes, which, in affecting the mind differently, effectively change it from one hour to the next, from one day to the next, from one season to the next (someone once said that they were better able to write in extreme heat or cold than in the medium temperatures of the year, in the morning rather than the evening, etc.), etc. etc., and return it to its former state, and make it more suitable first to one thing, then the next, then to more things then to fewer, first more suited then less so, etc. etc.] (*Zib.* 3204–05)

If we were to invert the position of the clauses outside and inside the parentheses, and start from the observation 'fu chi disse ch'ei si trovava più atto a comporre nel sommo caldo o nel sommo freddo che nelle medie temperature dell'anno; la mattina che la sera ec.' — now at the beginning of the passage and outside parentheses —

we would see that it would be perfectly logical to consider the reflection that comes from the clause 'Oggi il mio ingegno sarà svegliatissimo' as a subclass of the previous clause (starting from the premise that 'oggi' would sensibly function as a subcategory of *mattine* and *sere*), and it would be just as plausible to include it within the parentheses. It goes without saying that in placing the parentheses Leopardi has of course established which consideration should lead over the other; but it is equally interesting to note how the ranking could be reversed according to a logic of correspondence between the 'exterior' and 'interior' of the parentheses in line with the workings of projective geometry, for which, as observed by Giuliano Toraldo di Francia:

> I punti e le rette all'infinito hanno identica cittadinanza di tutti gli altri punti e rette. E, del resto, quando nasce l'ottica geometrica, si riconosce con lo stesso procedimento che le immagini all'infinito e le immagini al finito hanno identico statuto e sono convertibili le une nelle altre mediante una semplice lente.[13]
>
> [Infinite points and lines have the same citizenship as all the other points and lines. And, moreover, when geometrical optics is born, it is recognized through the same procedure by which infinite and finite images have identical status and can be converted the one into the other using a simple lens.]

The operation of these geometries of excess seems to represent, even with the necessary conceptual approximations, the implementation of the Leopardian conception of knowledge, for which the 'andamento, o il così detto perfezionamento dello spirito umano rassomiglia interamente alla progressione geometrica che dal menomo termine, con proporzione crescente arriva all'infinito' ('advance or so-called perfecting of the human spirit exactly resembles geometric progression, which from the most minimal term through increasing proportions arrives at infinity') (*Zib.* 1924). This works not only in the direction of the infinitely large, of the vastness of knowledge, but also towards an infinitesimal trajectory, as a measure of detail and divisibility, typical of the Leopardian tendency to delve into the microscopic nuances of every part, gradation, or quality of a given concept. Again in the following passage, for example, we observe a certain use of et ceteras that project into excess a list where the components not only have varied and wide-ranging qualities (for example in the sequence 'accrescono, scemano' ('increase, reduce')), but also have minimal semantic differences ('influiscono, cambiano, recano' ('impact on, change, give')):

> Le diverse circostanze fisiche che evidentemente influiscono, cambiano, recano, tolgono, accrescono, scemano, diversificano ec. ec. le passioni o inclinazioni in uno stesso individuo, in diversi individui, in varie nazioni e climi e tempi ec. indipendentemente affatto e dalla volontà e dall'assuefazione; son tante e sì varie che *infinito sarebbe il volerle enumerare e descrivere*, coi loro (evidentissimi e incontrastabili) effetti.
>
> [The different physical circumstances which clearly impact on, change, give, take away, increase, reduce, diversify, etc. etc., passions and inclinations in the same individual, in different individuals, in various nations and climates and times, etc., completely independent of both their will and their habitual

behavior, are so many and so varied that *it would take forever to list and describe them*, with their (most evident and incontrovertible) effects.] (*Zib.* 3205; my emphasis)

Between 'che evidentemente' and 'le passioni' there could potentially be an infinite number of other verbs that can only be differentiated from each other by infinitesimal nuances and that subdivide two poles of discourse that are syntactically very closely related; here again there is a cropping of actual infinity. If the thought really paused to outline all the possibilities the argument would grind to a standstill. In this case too, using a mathematical-geometrical explanatory model seems to be useful in representing this type of excess, which replicates on a conceptual level the problems of limits and squaring the circle, much debated in the post-Newtonian scientific and cultural climate: given a polygon inscribed or circumscribed in the circumference of a circle, even by increasing the number of sides of the polygon there would still remain a minimal margin of non-adherence between the two shapes, and even if the subdivision of the space between them was continued until infinity, they would never overlap. That Leopardi was not well-versed in the subject of differential calculus does not mean that he did not have the opportunity to get a sense of such conceptual developments by means of experience.[14] In fact, it should not be forgotten that the most immediate example of an infinite existing in a finite form was provided to him by a universal and fundamental experience described in his notes, that is, the production of voice and sound using the material and finite sound apparatus of our body, within which infinite combinations can occur: 'sono infiniti i modi di collocare ec. la lingua i denti le labbra ec. quelle parti che formano i detti suoni, e noi vediamo come piccole differenze di collocazione formino suoni diversiss.' ('there is an infinity of ways of positioning, etc., the tongue, the teeth, the lips, etc., those parts that form such sounds. And we see how small differences of position produce very different sounds') (*Zib.* 51–52). In the same way, within the finite writing of the *Zibaldone* one senses the tendency towards an infinite series of possibilities, and between two points of a sentence there could be a virtually unlimited number of sub-concepts that would open up a universe between two apparently connected elements of discourse. Whilst the et cetera allows the argument to continue by jumping from one point in the sentence to another, it reveals, at the same time, the attraction exerted by the details.

It is likely and significant that certain writing dynamics that reflect specific cognitive models (such as the geometric model outlined here) were the result not just of private theoretical readings, but also of Leopardi's experience and frequentation of the *Zibaldone* itself. One need only think about Leopardi's habit of making excess thoughts fill all available space within the pages of the diary, in the margins, or between the lines, to understand how writing allowed him to experiment materially with the problem of limits and shapes inscribed within a frame. This represented a material experience which was in turn transformed into a stimulus for forms internal to writing itself, with a more powerful influence than any other abstract model that Leopardi could or could not have known.

Notes to Chapter 4

1. The 'ec.' spelling is by far the most prevalent form; the 'etc.' spelling only appears in reflections involving classical or foreign languages. The last time a 'triple' et cetera appears is on p. 3994, 20 December 1823. From then on, single et ceteras are only accompanied by 'double' sequences.
2. On the psychological dynamics of reversing opposites that underpin Leopardian poetry (the poems 'L'infinito' [Infinity] and 'La sera del dì di festa' [The Evening of the Holiday]) see Colaiacomo, *Camera obscura*.
3. See Carlo Pedretti, *'Eccetera perché la minestra si fredda' (Codice Arundel, fol. 245 recto)*, XV Lettura Vinciana (Florence: Giunti Barbera, 1975).
4. See Carlo Vecce, 'Leonardo da Vinci', in *Letteratura italiana*, ed. by Alberto Asor Rosa, 16 vols (Turin: Einaudi, 1993), II, 95–124 (p. 110).
5. See, on this subject, *Zib.* 1715, 16 September 1821: 'L'individuo, ordinariamente, è tanto grande o piccolo quanto la società, il corpo ec. la patria, a cui egli specialmente appartiene' ('The individual, ordinarily, is as big or as little as the society, the body, etc., the country to which he particularly belongs'), where 'ec. la patria' is inserted between the lines. It would seem that Leopardi places the reference to the 'patria' immediately after the 'ec.' to ensure that this specific element, already contained in the et cetera, does not risk getting lost in his memory. There is a sort of double game and tension between the temptation to set the writing free and loosen the ties that bind it to his mind, and the duty of clarity that instead tightens this bond and forces him to resist the indulgence of interruption.
6. In his fascinating paper on Leopardian et ceteras, Carlo Vecce mentions the image of the 'internal seismograph' but with a slightly different meaning to the one here, referring to the 'linea terminale di rigo' [bottom line] following Leonardo's et cetera: 'Muta anche la sua forma nel tempo, passando dalla linea che gioca con eleganti arabeschi (i nodi, o i "vinci") alla traccia ticchettante di un sismografo interiore, nel codice Hammer e in testi coevi. [...] Leonardo inventa la "sua" linea terminale per [...] inquadrare esattamente la finestra testuale all'interno del foglio, distinguendola (come in un moderno software di *publishing*) dalla finestra "grafica", dagli schizzi, dai disegni' [Its form also changes with time, passing from the line that plays with elegant arabesques (the knots, or the 'vinci') to the ticking trace of an internal seismograph, in the Hammer Codex and other contemporaneous texts. [...] Leonardo invents 'his' 'linea terminale' [bottom line] in order to [...] put a precise frame around the textual window within the page, distinguishing it (as in modern publishing software) from the 'graphic' window, from the sketches, from the designs] ('Appendice: "Una voce chiamantemi a cena"', in *Tre letture leopardiane* (Recanati: Edizioni CNSL, 2000), pp. 85–106 (p. 96)).
7. Corrado Bologna has commented on the idea of whims and squiggles (in the work of Guicciardini), and highlights some analogies which involve Leopardi: 'Un ghirigoro, un ghiribizzo tutto mentale, è l'*eccetera* di cui Leonardo punteggia i suoi fogli di appunti: così come farà nel suo *Zibaldone*, migliaia di volte, anche Leopardi, non riuscendo la mano a tener dietro alla rapidità del pensiero, e volendo la mente per così dire "far punto", "appuntarsi" un'idea su cui tornare successivamente per imbastire altri più distesi ragionamenti' [A squiggle, a mental whim, is the et cetera with which Leonardo punctuates his pages of notes: later, Leopardi will do the same thing in his *Zibaldone*, thousands of times, his hand not managing to keep up with the speed of his thoughts, and his mind wanting to 'make a note', so to speak, an idea to which he can return later in order to sketch out other, more developed, arguments], 'I ghiribizzi di Guicciardini', in *Francesco Guicciardini tra ragione e inquietudine*, ed. by Paola Moreno and Giovanni Palumbo (Liege: Faculté de Philosophie et Lettres de l'Université de Liege, 2005), pp. 75–107 (p. 102)).
8. In *Zib.* 1249 we find an addition of 'ec.' to a previous insertion in the margin: 'Con questi vantaggi vennero anche dalla stessa fonte molti abusi. Li condanniamo altamente, e conveniamo in questo cogli scrittori che oggidì alzano contro di essi la voce in italia [*sic*], senza convenire in questo che ogni genere di bellezza in una lingua, non debba per necessità riconoscere come sua fonte essenziale e principale l'idioma popolare. Dico della bellezza, ec. la quale conviene alla vera poesia, ed alla bella letteratura, essenzialmente distinta nel suo linguaggio da quello

che conviene alle scienze ec.' ('Together with these advantages, there come many abuses, and from the very same source. We roundly condemn them, and agree in this with the writers who are raising their voices against them in Italy today, though they do not agree that every kind of beauty in a language should of necessity acknowledge popular speech as its principal and crucial source. I refer here to the beauty, etc., that is fitting in true poetry, and in literature, essentially distinct in its language from the kind that is fitting in the sciences, etc.'). For further examples of the insertion of 'ec.' in the body of the text, see *Zib*. 23, 41, 54, 287, 426, 724, 1303, 1325, 1335, 1339, 1361, 1436, 1442, 1523, 1586, 1706, 1712, 1724, 1746, 1779, 1783, 1819, 1822, 1921, 1952, 3381, 3409, 3440, 3518, 3521, 3556, 3623, 3633, 3664, 3667, 3720, 3743, 3820, 3866, 3887, 3895, 3919, 4061, 4069, 4410.

9. See also the insertion of the second 'ec.' in *Zib*. 1881 (9 October 1821): 'Ho detto che l'amor libidinoso considera più le altre forme che quelle del viso. Pur è certo che la più sfrenata, invecchiata, ed abituale libidine, è molto eccitata dalla significaz. vivacità ec. ec. degli occhi e del viso, e respinta da un'assoluta bruttezza, insignificazione ec. di fisonomia' ('I have said that lustful love takes more account of the other forms than of those of the face. Yet it is certainly the case that the most unbridled, ingrained, habitual lust is highly excited by the expression, vivacity, etc. etc., of the eyes and the face, and repulsed by absolute ugliness, lack of expression, etc., in the physiognomy'). Other examples are: *Zib*. 3022–23: 'il passivo ha sovente una significaz. propria attiva o neutra, diversa però da quella dell'attivo, e da quella del medio. ec. ec' ('the passive frequently has its own active or neuter meaning, yet different from that of the active, and from that of the middle, etc. etc.'); and *Zib*. 3401–02: 'Quel carattere di nobiltà, di dignità, di ardire, di semplicità, di naturalezza ec. ec. che distingue gl'idiomi e gli stili greco e latino, non si possono in alcuna lingua del mondo, nè moderna nè antica, esprimer meglio nè più spontaneamente e naturalmente che nella italiana e nella spagnuola' ('That character of nobility, dignity, daring, simplicity, naturalness, etc. etc., which distinguishes Greek and Latin idioms and styles, cannot be expressed better, more spontaneously or more naturally in any other language of the world, ancient or modern, than in Italian and Spanish').

10. A consideration of the psychology of writing linked to the number of 'ec.' forms an appendix to these observations. It is difficult to establish if there is any difference between a single 'ec.' and sequences of two or three 'ec.'s within the dimension of excess. From what has been observed about the seismography in the *Zibaldone* one could hypothesize, however, that rather than a quantitative difference of information in excess corresponding to the different spellings, the number of 'ec.'s reflects the period of time during which the sense of excess is present in Leopardi's mind before he leaps towards new moments of speculation, or before the idea vanishes from his thoughts. If, in other words, the sense of excess lingers a bit longer in the mind (we are, of course, discussing almost instantaneous dynamics), the hand responds with et ceteras in sequences. A particular case is the graphic layout of the 'ec.' on p. 1879: 'Alla p. 1876. Applicate a questo luogo l'inadattabilità riconosciuta della melodia poetica latina o greca alla lingua italiana [...]. E pur la italiana è figlia della lingua latina: così la spagn. la francese ec. ec. ec. ec. (9. Ott. 1821.)' ('Apply to this passage the acknowledged unadaptability of Latin or Greek poetic melody to the Italian language [...]. And yet Italian is a daughter of the Latin language; likewise Spanish, French, etc. etc. etc. etc. (9 Oct. 1821.)'), where the first 'ec.' of the series, on the extreme right margin of the page, is followed by a small segment which separates it from the sequence of the other three 'ec.'s appearing on the line below. Because in all the *Zibaldone* Leopardi never uses more than three 'ec.' in succession, I am inclined to believe that there are two separate groups of excess (the single 'ec.' and the other sequence of three), and that the function of the segment is to separate a partial excess (related to Romance language) from a more general excess which predominantly occupies Leopardi's mind. The first excess represents a stimulus from which Leopardi's thought leaps into a second excess on the theme of 'inadattabilità'. More often, as we shall see, the dynamics of highlighting subordination between different sentences is regulated by the use of parenthesis.

11. This is assuming that both of the added 'ec.'s were inserted at the same time. It is clear that if these were both added separately then we would have to talk about three different 'tremors'.

12. As when referring to linguistic manifestations that could potentially be applied to myriad cases

(and that for this reason are associated here with an idea of 'infinity'), but which strictly speaking are finite, since they are produced by a finite language.

13. Giuliano Toraldo di Francia, 'L'infinito in una scienza finita', in *Le dimensioni dell'infinito/ Les Dimensions de l'infini*, ed. by Umberto Eco, Claudio Chiuderi, and Fernando Caruso, 50 Rue de Varenne: supplemento italiano-francese di Nuovi argomenti, 29 (Paris: Istituto italiano di cultura, 1989), pp. 63–70 (p. 64).

14. See Polizzi, *Galileo in Leopardi*, p. 97, and by the same author *Leopardi e 'le ragioni della verità': scienze e filosofia della natura negli scritti leopardiani* (Rome: Carocci, 2003), pp. 73–78. However, Leopardi's awareness of the development of calculus should not be excluded: the article 'Considerazioni sopra l'uso del calcolo nella fisica', by Geminiano Poletti, for example, appeared in the very same issue of *Antologia* (18 (1825), 44–57) as Pietro Giordani's 'Ode del Monti (Per le nozze dell'egregia donzella Adelaide Calderaia col signor Giacomo Butti)' (pp. 77–78). The 'adjacencies' for Leopardi the reader and Leopardi the writer always provide ample sources of exploration and inspiration. The entry 'Léibnitzianisme' in the *Encyclopédie méthodique* (discussed in Chapter 3) also devotes attention to calculus, and includes an interesting idea of sense-making of infinitesimal derivation, that is, as approximation by way of enumeration: 'qu'est-ce que cette définition, sinon une énumeration suffisante des caractères de la chose?' [what is this definition, if not a sufficient enumeration of the characters of the thing] (p. 117).

CHAPTER 5

Clarity and Confession

The registering of the obscure, which, as we have seen, is central in Leopardi's conceptualization of clarity and deeply informs his praxis of writing, represents the crossroad where Leopardi's philosophical concern meets with broader cultural and autobiographical issues linked to his formation and to profound cognitive structures deriving from his religious upbringing. The concept of obscurity as the complementary component of clarity is addressed by Philippe Goibaut Du Bois in his *Discours sur les Pensées de M. Pascal*, present in the 1701 Amsterdam edition of Pascal's *Pensées*. The author explains how Pascal believed that clarity and obscurity were 'mixed' by God in informing man's potential for divine contemplation, so that those who had not found God yet continued to see obscurely until they put themselves in the right state of mind, instead of indulging in their mistaken search for vain values.[1] While absolute clarity is a prerogative of God only, obscurity is necessary for man's salvation, in order for him to recognize his own limits and finitude. God's presence in the world is therefore 'shaded', neither too bright, nor too obscure, so that man can exercise and perfect his will in his search for God:

> S'il n'y avoit point d'obscurité, l'homme ne sentiroit pas sa corruption. S'il n'y avoit point de lumiere, l'homme n'espereroit point de remede. Ainsi il est non seulement juste, mais utile pour nous, que Dieu soit caché en partie, & découvert en partie, puis-qu'il est également dangereux à l'homme de connoître Dieu sans connoître sa misere & de connoître sa misere sans connoistre Dieu.
>
> [Had there been no obscurity, man would not have been sensible of his corruption. Had there been no light, man would have despaired of a remedy. It is then not only just, but profitable for us, that God should be partly hidden, and partly revealed; since it is equally dangerous for man to know God, without the consciousness of his misery, or to know his misery, without knowing God.][2]

In Pascal, Leopardi found a religious counterpart for the positive value associated with obscurity within the realm of phenomenology. In the same way as in Leibniz's analysis of the intellectual faculties the presence of obscurity does not undermine clarity (which was the case with Descartes), but represents a functional parameter in the relationship between the whole and its parts which still leads to a clear representation, so the concept of clarity as divine contemplation also presupposes the presence of some obscurity 'inserted' by God as a fundamental element for man's salvation. What matters, in other words, is the process of 'clarification' through exercise, and this requires obscurity as the necessary obstacle to be faced and overcome. The exercising of one's free will in contrasting obscurity in the search for good could be compared, in figurative terms, to a dynamic process of fruitful expenditure of energy. It is only in the activity of making use of one's force against a contrary force that advancement on the path towards the light takes place: 'S'il n'y avoit point d'obscurité, l'homme ne sentiroit pas sa corruption'. If the 'dark' obstacles were removed, man would presume to be the same as God, he would terminate any effort to approach God, immobility would replace action and free will would have no objectives towards which to direct itself:

> Fa parte essenziale del mio sistema la proposizione che Adamo ebbe una scienza infusa: ma in questo modo. Ogni essere capace di scelta, anzi tale che non si può determinare all'azione [...] e per conseguenza non può vivere, senza un atto elettivo e definito della sua volontà, ha bisogno di credenze, cioè deve credere che le cose siano buone o cattive, e che quella tal cosa sia buona o cattiva, altrimenti la sua volontà non avrà motivo per determinarsi ad abbracciarla o fuggirla, per decidersi a fare o non fare, all'affermativo o al negativo.
>
> [It forms an essential part of my system — that Adam had infused knowledge, but in the following way. Every being capable of choice, or one, rather, that cannot resolve to act [...], and as a result cannot live, without a chosen and defined act of his will, needs to have beliefs, that is, he needs to believe that things are good or bad, and that this particular thing is good or bad, otherwise his will has no reason for deciding whether to embrace that thing or run away from it, whether to act or not, whether to agree or disagree.] (*Zib.* 437)

Leopardi too, like Pascal, admits the benefit of the coexistence of contrast and antithesis in the explication of the human faculties. This is relevant as it helps to approach a structural polarity of the *Zibaldone*, namely a set of cognitive, religious, and philosophical impulses which seems to contain, at the same time, the poison and its antidote. Franco D'Intino has demonstrated the 'Faustian' inclinations of the *Zibaldone*. The birth of the notebook and most of its writing can be read as the manifestation of Leopardi's drive towards worldliness and experience, with the two allowing for the possibility to sin, which is inevitably linked to the actualization of one's desires. The *Zibaldone* corresponds to Leopardi's attempt to replace the frustrating lack of 'real' life with a 'virtual' world always in expansion, always pushing the boundaries of knowledge and imagination beyond limits. The notebook therefore is a '"slancio", o "salto" [...], e raffigura testualmente lo spazio della tentazione, e della mutazione' [rush, or leap [...], and represents the textual space of temptation and transformation].[3] My hypothesis is that while giving voice to Leopardi's daring attitude to challenging boundaries of content and form in a virtual spatial and temporal journey towards an 'elsewhere' free from the constrictions of tradition (the latter meant as the complex of values, norms, and principles absorbed by Leopardi in his education, as well as the literary and philosophical background of his education), the *Zibaldone* at the same time applies a measure which safeguards its author from the attribution of guilt connected to this very same daring operation he constantly enacts in the text. I believe that it is clarity which absolves this relieving function. While constituting a legitimized commitment to philosophical rigour and intellectual honesty, the search for the clear exposition of ideas is deeply permeated by a religious aura which elicits an ongoing process of 'purgation' of the sinful inclinations highlighted by D'Intino. It is as if any dangerous source of 'evil' intrinsic to writing found its immediate cleansing balsam in the very same act of expressing it, thanks precisely to the *way* (that is, the style and the close links between mind and pen) in which it is expressed.

If we look closely at Leopardi's reflection on clarity, it appears deeply permeated by a religious model in its formulation, and there are specific conceptual roots to his choice of a particular terminology in some passages which we have already encountered. Returning to the *Zibaldone* entry on p. 95, cited at the beginning of Chapter 3, in which we saw how Leopardi insists on the fugacity of thought, on its transient nature which requires constant attention and the prompt intervention of language to fix the concepts in the mind so that an idea does not 'erra nel pensiero come indefinita e mal nota a noi medesimi che l'abbiamo concepita'. As demonstrated by D'Intino, *errare* [to err] or *errore* [error] in Leopardi do not only generally refer to a linguistic discourse but are also the traces of an unconscious dimension which reflects religious structures of sin and guilt which Leopardi absorbed during his upbringing. This system of thought, revolving around an inevitably defeated drive towards perfection (intended both morally and linguistically), never ceases to operate at different depths in Leopardi, even when a direct religious faith has long faded from his heart.[4] The presence of the verb *errare* is therefore the first element which suggests that the concept of clarity, in itself already a crucial component of theological discourses, is intrinsically permeated by a religious aura.[5]

In a note on p. 1372 Leopardi uses a specific vocabulary to warn any researcher who 'non vuole nè confessare, nè dare a vedere' ('does not wish either to admit or let it be seen') that he does not understand something clearly, to transcribe his exact state of mind on paper. The presence of an errant and confused idea is already frustrating enough for an author obsessed with precision and with the objective of rendering the exact and punctual shape of his thoughts, and one who cannot help but feel a sense of sin before the error. Nothing could be worse for the very same author than to risk 'damnation', as it were, for refusing to undertake the painful process of confessing the presence of an 'errant' condition. If orthographic error, as demonstrated by D'Intino, equates to sin in Leopardi's innermost association of ideas, clarity instead is primarily bounded to the practice of confession, the process by which one can be cleansed through 'veridiction'.[6]

The history and the development of the practice of avowal, as studied by Michel Foucault, provide a fascinating reconstruction of the different modalities, psychological implications, and socio-cultural perspectives of confession from ancient times to the nineteenth century. The idea of confession as a form of ethical evaluation of one's daily actions against a background of shared and idealized norms of conduct characterized the ancient period, with particular emphasis in the Stoic and Epicurean tradition. Confession here had nothing to do with the idea of disclosing sins, but was considered as a useful practice of moral self-understanding. It was during early Christianity that confession became a process in which the individual was compelled to search the innermost recesses of his or her soul in order to discover his or her own truest self as the first premise of the path toward salvation. In this period being a penitent was a once in a lifetime condition, it was a prolonged status assumed by an individual at a certain moment of his or her life, which would last for a certain number of years without the possibility of reiteration at the end of the expiation. Being a penitent would imply a specific set of bodily sacrifices within a performative and ritual dimension which also involved the participation of others.[7] The real revolution in the practice of confession, and the setting of the foundations of the confessional practice which would later be institutionalized in the form of a sacrament by the Catholic Church, took place in the fourth and fifth centuries in monastic practices. Here for the first time, confession became strictly bound to verbalization (*confessio oris*), to the act of telling the truth undertaken by the individual to a permanent spiritual guide to whom he would be obliged to show absolute and unconditional obedience. Confession became a permanent constant obligation, as the monk had the duty to inform the guide of any thoughts that crossed his mind, while the spiritual director would address inquisitive questions in order to unveil any possible residues of hidden thoughts. The monk had to renounce his will completely and embrace a state of *humilitas*, *patientia*, and *subditio*.[8] While judicial and medical vocabulary were employed as part of the interrogation, the form of vocal confession was modelled on the dialogical questioning which was adopted in the philosophical schools. Truth-telling about oneself became absolutely pivotal, as did the presence of another person to whom one could confess. Even when the individual was alone he was supposed to behave as if he were with a companion, and in these moments he was supposed to either take notes or virtually pretend that it was the mind itself which performed the function of a book with something to communicate to a readership. What had to be monitored as the most dangerous source of wrongdoing were the movements of one's soul, its errant condition, even though, strictly speaking, at this stage of Christianity it was illusion rather than error which most concerned the Christian. Establishing whether there was illusion, that is, 'whether one's thought was deluding itself', was essential because it was precisely during the moments of confusion or hesitation that the Devil was supposed to present himself in the mind.[9] Early Christianity therefore recommended the constant practice of speaking, even as a mental individual performance: 'may each one write his actions and the movements of his soul, [...] that they be noted in writing, as if they needed to be made known to others', 'Let the written word play the role of our companions'.[10] At the origin of the new 'hermeneutics of the self', all these exhortations were meant to stimulate a constant process of self-explication which was considered good *in itself* because 'the sole fact of speaking out loud and speaking to someone else was in itself an operation of *discretio*', that is, a form of partitive and selective thinking, the opposite of devilish confusion or delusion.[11]

Foucault's insight into the psychological and ideological implications of the origin of avowal in the Christian world helps to shed further light on Leopardi's own confessional conceptual framework as far as clarity is concerned. For instance, one cannot ignore the pressure and anxiety intrinsic to Leopardi's own rule of clarity, when he mentioned the utility of foreign words that 'mi venivano più presto trovate' ('came most quickly to mind') (*Zib.* 95), as if it were a confessional test, in which one promptly needs to fill any gaps in the mind which should not be left on stand-by. This state of readiness does not only characterize the early monastic practice of avowal but is preserved as part of the institutionalized sacrament of confession. For instance the *Catechismo* by Pietro Maria Ferreri, well known to Leopardi and to which we will soon return, exhorts the penitent to commit to a 'confessione [...] sbrigata' [a to-the-point confession], that is, 'breve, e succinta' [brief and succinct].[12] The penitent should not waste time digressing into irrelevant details, but should focus entirely on the crucial and essential sins. One could imply that the whole *Zibaldone* as a writing 'a penna corrente' (*Zib.* 95), while being almost the manifestation of a thought striving to be always 'in focus', is at the same time animated by an urge for verbal action, and for a dynamic correspondence between mind and body, with the pen promptly following any oscillations of thought. After all, is it not the very same intrinsic nature of Leopardi's thought, as precisely a 'thought in motion', that calls for a 'salvific' operation of language in contrasting delusion of thought?[13] Is it not the search for truth — the opposite of delusion — that is a sorrowful but unavoidable mission for the modern (post-Christian) philosopher? Of course, as we have seen, not everything that appears to the mind reflects a clear vision of the self. Sometimes it is the obscure that prevails. But even in this case, what matters in a moving thought, which for its own very same motion is constitutionally 'dangerous', is the dynamic operation of *discretio*, the constant propensity to vigilance and distinction.

From its origins in the monastic practice of 'veridiction', the value *in itself* of the act of speaking (whether the content is clear or not) became central also as an institutionalized and legitimized parameter in the sacrament of confession, and directly linked to the faculty of memory. Some religious sources devoted to avowal represented a solid reference point in Leopardi's formation as a poet. Leopardi's family library hosts numerous ecclesiastical texts, often of Jesuit provenance, dealing with the practice and sacrament of confession, such as manuals for both the confessor and the penitent and guides to the catechism, instructing the reader on all the specific and practical information regarding the procedure, frequency, and conduct of confession. The relationship between the confessor and the penitent, in line with the communicational peer standard, is often described as follows: the confessor behaves like a judge, doctor, and master, while the penitent performs the triple role of prosecutor, offender, and witness, as far as the judicial metaphor is concerned, and as a patient and a pupil in the other two medical and educational scenarios. In the confession as courtroom, the prosecutor appears and lists the crimes of the guilty soul. In the meantime the criminal listens and feels ashamed, and waits for the witness to arrive and confirm the accusations. It is the duty of the pentitent to assume these three roles in front of the priest, who plays the part of the judge and who eventually will assign a punishment to be served. In the same way, the penitent playing the part of the patient has a duty to search for the right doctor to cure his illnesses, and once he has been seen by the doctor he must honestly disclose all the diseases which afflict him before following exactly the prescribed cure. Similarly, the penitent as pupil must be ready to embark on his apprenticeship with humility, by disclosing his doubts and relying on the wisdom of his master: 'nelle cose dubbie non faccia egli da dottore, ma domandi con umiltà, per apprendere quel, che deve sapere' [in dubious things he should not behave as a doctor, but he should ask questions with humility, in order to learn what he needs to know].[14] In all these scenarios, the confession moves from the examination of conscience ('*cordis scientia*') in which the penitent must investigate his own soul in search of all the sins committed since the last confession.[15] A model for this practice is offered by the parable of Santa Margarita da Cortona. As a young girl she had been a sinner, but she then converted to what she considered the true path and devoted her life to God. She noticed, though, that the Lord would only call her by the name of 'poor one' (*poverella*) rather than 'daughter' (*figliuola*). Having asked the Lord why she was being denied the privilege of that title, the Lord replied that she had neglected to acknowledge certain sins which still resided in her heart. She therefore prayed to the Lord that he guide her in completing her examination of conscience, and '[a]ppena fece questa orazione, che si vide innanzi a gli occhi dell'Anima sua tutti quanti i peccati, che avea commessi nella sua vita; e con somma distinzione, e chiarezza [...]. Confessossi così piena di dolore, e con somma contrizione' [as soon as he delivered this prayer she saw, in front of the eyes of her soul, all the sins that she had committed in her life; and with supreme distinction and clarity. Thus so full of sorrow, and with great contrition, she made a confession].[16] From now on, she would be called *figliuola*.

It is already evident from this example that the characteristics which clarity assumes as a form of analytical speculation correspond in no small part to the practice of confession. Our sins, in the same way as the philosopher's thoughts, must be accurately displayed before our inner eye in the most distinct way possible. Although there is not a specific order which the sinner should follow in progressing in his research, nevertheless it is essential to start from the moment of the previous confession and advance according to certain guiding parameters. The Commandments, the institutional precepts and obligations set by the Church allow the sinner to evaluate different kinds of crimes possibly committed. The sinner can then investigate whether a specific crime took place through words, actions, or omissions. As Adrienne von Speyr summarizes:

> L'indole dell'esame di coscienza esige anzitutto che si raccolgano i fatti, che se ne abbia una visione nitida e precisa. [...] I peccati devono essere sentiti non solo come un peso generale di tutti, devono essere ricercati e riconosciuti nel loro numero, nella loro gravità, nelle loro circostanze. [...] La chiarezza, che è richiesta in primo luogo, deriva da quella chiarezza che il Signore ha conservato di fronte al Padre in tutto il suo comportamento e in ogni azione. [...] Tutto il decorso dall'esame al dolore e al proponimento, dalla confessione all'assoluzione è come una successione di atti logica e chiara. Dobbiamo sempre sapere a che punto ci troviamo.[17]

> [The nature of the examination of conscience wants first of all that facts are gathered, and that one acquires of them a clear and precise vision. Sins must

be felt not only as a general common weight, but they must be sought and recognized in their number, gravity, and circumstances. Clarity, which is required in the first place, derives from that clarity which the Lord preserved always in front of the Father, in his behaviour and action. The course between examination and sorrow and resolution, from confession to absolution, is like a logical and clear succession of acts. We must always know where we are.]

Leopardi's reflection on memory and the practice of remembering ordinary situations which memory tends to forget if some special impression does not catch our attention, also presents a certain method for remembering which, as in the practice of confession, not only takes account of the general idea itself, but also of its external peculiar circumstances. By referring to specific factors which might help one to remember, he mentions the practice of 'rianda[re] di mano in mano le altre operazioni di quel tal tempo, le circostanti, le conseguenze, le antecedenze; ovvero proccurando di salire dalle più vicine alle più lontane' ('thinking back, from moment to moment, to the other activities of that time, the circumstances, the consequences, the antecedents, or by trying to go back from the most recent to the farthest') (*Zib.* 2380). If the practice of confession necessarily relies on a certain chronology and succession in time (in the sense that the starting-point for any new examination is the moment of the last confession, which functions as a solid reference in time to begin the search), similarly we could conceive of Leopardi's practice of annotating dates or particular occurrences in his *Zibaldone*, such as religious festivals, as a gesture which provides a rhythm to writing while eliciting, for each temporal reference, a renewed sense of beginning. I am not here implying that the entries of the *Zibaldone* perform the same function that a confession does for the sinner, namely providing a *tabula rasa* of conscience where previous transgressions are absolved, and what counts are only the sins that come afterwards, or in other words the memories which are inscribed from that point onwards. The chronological annotations in the *Zibaldone* never only determine a new beginning of thought for subsequent entries, but they lay down the marker for a certain presence of mind and formalize through a kind of rituality that a certain configuration of thinking has taken place over a certain interval of time. Any *Zibaldone* reader is aware of the fact that chronology and diachrony are constantly challenged by patterns of writing which proceed in recurrent expansion. But it is essential to note also that the very same practice of confession contemplates backward examinations of conscience, as it allows recursive and corrective reflections to be undertaken by the sinner in the assessment of his sins. Furthermore, it is important to remark — and this closely links with the idea of obscure clarity which we have examined in the field of philosophical speculation — that the sacrament of confession also contemplates an idea of radiographic registrations of shades of thought similar to that expressed by Leopardi in his exposition of a philosophy of clarity. The Italian version of the *Catechismo* elaborated by the Council of Trent offers a useful account of these configurations. It exhorts the believers to make sure that the confession be 'nuda, semplice, e aperta, non artificiosamente composta [...]; imperocché la confessione dee essere così fatta, che tali ci mostri al sacerdote, quali noi stessi conosciamo di essere, e manifesta le cose certe per certe, e le dubbie per dubbie' [bare, simple and open, not artificially composed [...]; because confession must be made thus to show ourselves to the priest in exactly the same way we know ourselves to be, and it manifests things which are certain as certain, and things which are dubious as dubious].[18] It is very dangerous, for the salvation of one's soul, willingly to alter a confession by omitting sinful elements from the narrative or modifying the circumstances in which the sin took place. But because confession relies on memory, and memory can fail us, it is perfectly acceptable and without consequence if a penitent forgets or is unable to retrieve all the crimes committed. If this is the case, 'gli basterà confessare i peccati scordati, quando gli ritorneranno a memoria' [it will be enough for him to confess the sins that he had forgotten, when they are recalled].[19] He will be able to return to the priest and report the new findings. The practice of confession is therefore ordered, linear (in the sense that it proceeds in chronological sequence), but at the same time open to recursivity and expansion, provided that the sinner is honest and acts in good faith. The nature of the sin can also be dubious in the eyes of the penitent, or a believer may be unable to assess the gravity of his crimes, or even to determine whether a certain action should be classified as sinful or not. In the case of, as it were, 'obscure sins' — by this I mean sins of which we are not aware and about which we might never become conscious — omitting to declare that they took place does not affect one's salvation (provided that these crimes are of a venial nature), as their remission can still take place as part of a more general process of cleansing and regained clarity:

> Il Concilio di Trento dice, che Gesù Cristo non esige altro da penitenti, se non che dopo un diligente esame, si confessino di que' peccati, de' quali si ricordano: gl'altri poi, che non vengono a memoria, restano compresi generalmente nella medesima confessione; nè si rimettono i soli peccati confessati, ma quelli ancora, che si scordano senza colpa.[20]
>
> [The Council of Trent states that Jesus Christ does not expect from the penitents anything other than that, after diligent examination, they should confess those sins which they remember; then the others, which are not recollected, are comprehended within the same confession; neither are only the confessed sins remitted, but also those which are forgotten without guilt.]

In the same way as for the 'minute perceptions', which in Leibniz's and Leopardi's theories of clarity remain unnoticed by our conscience while still resulting in a general clear outcome for the whole, sins which remained unconsciously unconfessed could still be granted salvation. If instead of a complete unawareness there is a doubtful condition, it is then advisable to express the state of our conscience:

> D. [domanda] *Ma se uno dubitasse di aver fatto un peccato, o di averlo fatto due, o tre volte, e non sapesse dire cosa di certo: In tal caso, come doverebbe confessarsi?* R. [risposta] Lo deve dire come dubbio: *Dubito Padre di aver fatto un tal peccato, Dubito, se l'ho commesso due o tre volte. D. Vediamo, se si confesserebbe bene colui che non potendosi accertare del numero de' suoi peccati, per assicurarsi, si confessasse di un Numero di peccati, maggiore di quello, che si ricorda?* R. Questo è un'errore [sic] gravissimo de' Scrupolosi. Il numero ha da essere quello, di cui ci ricordiamo, nè più, nè meno.[21]

[*Q:* [question] *What if one doubted having committed a sin, or having committed it twice or three times, and were not able to say for sure. In this case, how should one confess?* A: [answer] *One should speak with doubt, and say: I doubt, Father, whether I have committed that sin. I doubt whether I have committed it twice or three times. Q: Let's see whether one would confess in the right way if, not being able to ascertain the number of his sins, to be on the safe side one confessed a number of sins higher than the ones he remembers.* A: This is a very serious error of the scrupulous. The number has to be that which one remembers, no less, no more.]

The process of avowal, like Leopardi's ideal of clarity, requires the sinner to confess the exact state of his mind, regardless of whether he sees clearly or not. The *Zibaldone* meets the essential confessional criteria: the process of 'veridiction' based on the incessant registering of the state of thoughts in written form, a 'thought in motion' which requires a surveillance closely bound to a promptness of language, and, as we shall see later (Chapter 18), the employment of dialogical modalities of expression, in which, as in the traditional confession before a priest, Leopardi assumes the confessional roles of master and student. This general comparison between clarification and confession is not of course intended to promote an idea of the whole notebook as a practice of confession. Confession is a form of thinking (one of many) that appears as a cognitive model emanating from the depths of Leopardi's psyche. It provides structures which act as networks for the communication between and overlapping of different cultural universes (philosophy, religion, and the personal dimension of the art of writing). If Leopardi's errant thought is 'sinful' by nature of this very same erring, clarity of expression represents the immediate and 'continuing' cure, healing the wounds of limitless thought in the very unfolding of thinking and writing.

Notes to Chapter 5

1. Cf. Philippe Goibaut Du Bois, 'Discours sur les 'Pensées' de M. Pascal', in Blaise Pascal, *Pensées sur la religion, et sur quelques autres sujets* (Amsterdam: Henry Wetstein, 1701), pp. 5–65 (pp. 49–50). This text is present in the Leopardi library.
2. Pascal, *Pensées sur la religion*, p. 94 (XVIII, 6); *Thoughts*, trans. by Edward Craig (Andover: Allen, Morrill & Wardwell, 1846), p. 275.
3. Franco D'Intino, 'Il monaco indiavolato: Lo *Zibaldone* e la tentazione faustiana di Leopardi', in *Lo 'Zibaldone' cento anni dopo, composizione, edizioni, temi*, ed. by Garbuglia, pp. 467–512 (p. 511).
4. See Franco D'Intino, 'Errore, ortografia e autobiografia in Leopardi e Stendhal', in *Memoria e infanzia tra Alfieri e Leopardi*, ed. by Marco Dondero and Laura Melosi (Macerata: Quodlibet, 2004), pp. 167–83.
5. See Owen Anderson, *The Clarity of God's Existence: The Ethics of Belief After the Enlightenment* (Eugene, OR: Wipf & Stock, 2009).
6. This word has been adopted by Stephen W. Sawyer as an English neologism translating the French *véridiction*. It stresses the 'root *ver-* for truth, and *diction* for speaking, pronouncing, or telling'; see Michel Foucault, *Wrong-doing, Truth-telling: The Function of Avowal in Justice*, ed. by Fabienne Brion and Bernard E. Harcourt, trans. by Stephen W. Sawyer (Chicago, IL: University of Chicago Press, 2014), p. 19 (translator's note).
7. Ibid., pp. 91–124.
8. See ibid. p. 138.
9. Ibid. p. 148.

10. St Athanasius, *The Life of Antony and the Letter to Marcellinus*, trans. by Robert C. Gregg (New York: Paulist Press, 1980), p. 73 (section 55), quoted in Foucault, *Wrong-doing, Truth-telling*, p. 144. On the importance of this text, which Leopardi read in the version by Domenico Cavalca, see D'Intino, 'Il monaco indiavolato', pp. 488–96.
11. Foucault, *Wrong-doing, Truth-telling*, pp. 148, 150–51.
12. Pietro Maria Ferreri, *Istruzioni in forma di catechismo per la pratica della dottrina cristiana* (Venice: Baglioni, 1790), p. 250. This is the edition present in the Leopardi library.
13. The definition of the *Zibaldone* as a 'pensiero in movimento' belongs to Sergio Solmi, 'Il pensiero in movimento di Leopardi', in Giacomo Leopardi, *Zibaldone di pensieri*, ed. by Anna Maria Moroni, 2 vols (Milan: Mondadori, 1997), I, IX–XXVI.
14. Ferreri, *Istruzioni*, p. 236.
15. Ibid.
16. Ibid. p. 238.
17. Adrienne von Speyr, *La confessione*, ed. by H. U. von Balthasar (Milan: Jaca Book, 2002), p. 138.
18. *Catechismo cioè istruzione secondo il Decreto del Concilio di Trento a' parrochi*, trans. by Alessio Figliucci (Lucca: Giuntini, 1791), p. 312. Leopardi's library hosts a different edition of this text, published in Rome in 1765.
19. Ibid.
20. Giovanni Deliegis, *Dottrina cristiana, ovvero catechismo polemico* (Venice: Occhi, 1764), p. 170. This is the edition present in the Leopardi library.
21. Ferreri, *Istruzioni*, pp. 207–08.

CHAPTER 6

Naturalness and Natural Law

There is another principle in Leopardi's writing which in important reflections in the *Zibaldone* is often coupled with clarity and shares with it a universe of senses that escape the purely literary and stylistic concerns to activate a fundamental religious image: naturalness. In the following passage Leopardi establishes a parallel between clarity and naturalness, on the one hand, and civil and natural laws on the other:

> Una gran differenza tra la legge di natura e le leggi civili, è questa che la legge civile o umana si può dimenticare [...], e infrangerla senza leder la coscienza, (come s'io mangio carne non ricordandomi che sia giorno di magro, o anche ricordandomene, ma per distrazione) laddove la legge naturale non ammette distrazione, e non può accadere che uno la infranga non credendo, perch'ella ci sta sempre nel cuore come un istinto che ci avverte continuamente, e il quale non è soggetto a dimenticanze.
>
> La naturalezza dello scrivere è così comandata che posto il caso che per conservarla bisognasse mancare alla chiarezza, io considero che questa è come di legge civile, e quella come di legge naturale, la qual legge non esclude caso nessuno, e va osservata quando anche ne debba soffrire la società o l'individuo, come non è straordinario che accada.
>
> [A big difference between the laws of nature and the laws of civilization is that civil or human laws may be forgotten through distraction or for some other reason, and broken without troubling the conscience [...], whereas natural laws admit of no such distraction, and it cannot happen that we break them without realizing it, because they are always in our hearts, like an instinct of which we are constantly aware, and which is not subject to forgetfulness.
>
> Naturalness in writing is so imperative that if it were the case that this could be achieved only at the cost of clarity, then I would consider that the latter is like civil law and the former like natural law, which can admit no exceptions and must be observed even when society or the individual will suffer, something not so out of the ordinary.] (*Zib.* 118–19)

Rooted in human behaviour rather than in the manifestations of the physical world, the idea of natural law has constituted the 'measure of right and wrong, [...] the pattern of the good life or "life according to nature"' since the origin of Western culture.[1] Of course, with a historical overview in mind, it would be more appropriate to refer to *ideas* of natural law, as its proprieties have shifted in time according to the diverse values and prerogatives associated in different eras with the concept of 'nature'. Natural law is the principle that presides over the very origins of life, the most essential and deeply ingrained mark of distinction for living beings (human but also animal in certain traditions of thought), which have been granted by nature (or by God), a set of potential basic instincts dependent on each species's or individual's place in the universe. The appearances of natural law in Leopardi's thought testify to an uninterrupted concern with the origin of human behaviour and its relation to natural inclinations which involves a dialogue, at times implicit, at other times explicit, with both ancient and modern theorists of natural law. A brief outline of the origin of this concept in Western culture may help us individuate the crucial elements which can be integrated into Leopardi's thought, as well as the fundamental thinking that was transferred from the sphere of cultural constructs to the style of writing.

The concept of natural law is rooted in Greek philosophy, especially in that of the Stoics, which conceives of an all-encompassing *logos* permeating all things. Here human nature may discover this constant and eternal law presiding over the order of nature by following the impulses of reason whose rules guide man towards the good and whose prohibitions protect him from the dangers of evil. Natural law passes from the Greek to the Roman world to inform, together with the law of the nations (*ius gentium*) and civil law (*ius civile*), the structure of Roman jurisprudence. While Gaius the jurist focuses on the division between *ius gentium* and *ius civile* — the former also coinciding, in his view, with the *ratio naturalis* of natural law — Ulpian introduces a tripartite division between *ius gentium*, *ius civile*, and *ius naturale*, remarking upon a distinction in the function of law between the natural universe and the concerns of the *gentes* [people]. Unlike Gaius, who believed natural law to be the prerogative of the human species only, Ulpian extends *ius naturale* to animals while electing the *ius gentium* as the exclusive prerogative of human beings. In the sixth century Gaius's definition of *ius gentium* (as intrinsically bound to natural law) and the three-fold division of law by Ulpian were both employed as pillars of Emperor Justinian's juridical formalization in the *Institutes* and *Digest*. Through Cicero, who, inspired by the Stoic tradition, associates natural law with a *ratio*, that is, a quintessentially rational order that constitutes the immutable characteristic of human beings, the doctrine of natural law reaches the Christian tradition, which adapts it to the perspective of the Revelation, also elaborating a socio-political programme which was originally absent in the Gospels.[2] Thus St Paul detaches natural law from the purely rational features of positive law and, through a 'voluntaristic' vision, namely the idea that 'human intention [...] comes to existence only in response to the will of the Creator', he makes natural law an emanation of the divine Spirit by means of Grace.[3] Finally, according to the Church Fathers, human beings develop their inclinations by realizing freely (but at the same time teleologically) the course of their own personal history. The actualization varies according to different circumstances and individual potentialities but is part of a universalistic fulfilment of the will of God. This is in particular the view of human law theorized by Thomas Aquinas in his *Summa theologiae*. He associates the aims of natural law with the Aristotelian idea of 'what is right' in terms of justice. Natural law is for Thomas a 'participation' in divine law by any rational being, the objective of any moral law, predisposed by God but actively achieved by human will. The voice of reason is free in Thomas's system, but in realizing itself it reflects the divinely established goals in its inclinations. According to this view, what is right for the individual following his or her own truest rational and metaphysical nature is also right for the species as a whole and in harmony with God's *ratio* of the universe. All the above-mentioned positions were known, directly or indirectly, to Leopardi.[4]

The idea of natural law is present in Leopardi's reflections from the early 'Dissertazione sopra la virtù morale in generale' [Dissertation on General Moral Virtue] (1812) to the 1825 entries of the *Zibaldone*, delineating, from a philosophical point of view, a parable progressing from an initial adherence to the dictates of the Christian paradigms to the rejection of natural law as an absurdity of abstraction. In the 'Dissertazione', Leopardi adopts the tripartite distinction of law as natural, divine, and civil. Underpinning natural law is an inner light of reason (of clear Thomistic derivation) which directs us along a true path of action:

> Le leggi naturali son quelle, che ci impongono, o vietano alcuna cosa per mezzo di un certo interno lume, che chiaramente ci mostra qual cosa debba operarsi, e qual no. Nè questo lume può mai spegnersi nell'uom ragionevole sicchè egli non vegga la deformità, ed empietà di tutte quelle azioni, che alle leggi naturali si oppongono.[5]

> [Natural laws are those which impose on us or prohibit something by means of a certain inner light, which clearly shows us what must be done and what must not. Nor can this light ever be extinguished in the reasonable man so that he does not see the deformity and impiety of all those actions which are contrary to natural laws.]

Divine laws, Leopardi continues in the *Dissertazione*, comprise all the principles of natural law but in their highest essence, as they are meant to make man perfectly virtuous.[6] Civil law, on the other hand, is based on conventions between men established to prevent corruption and oppression and to punish wrongdoing. It is interesting to note that from its first appearance, Leopardi's focus on natural law is linked to a concern with the principle of 'non-contradiction', which is a recurrent theme in the *Zibaldone* as part of his investigation into the aims of nature and the position of human beings in the universal order. In this early work, and just before introducing his previously noted three-fold specification of the types of laws, Leopardi does not question the rule of non-contradiction and makes use of a mathematical example to state its validity.[7] In the *Zibaldone*, and again from a purely speculative viewpoint, the principle of non-contradiction, similarly to that of natural law, is subjected to a progressive confutation. On more than one occasion Leopardi is interested in demonstrating the invalidity of the concept of natural law by insisting on the falsity of its innate character and on the absolute relativity of the concept of 'rightness', which, as history demonstrates, often creates contradiction between what is good (and therefore right) for the individual and what is good for the species.[8] The history of the Fall offers further proof of the incongruity of the innate character of moral law. After (and only after) the sin Adam recognized his own nudity and the moral and spiritual consequences of his new condition, which were previously unknown (cf. *Zib.* 399). If the way Adam acted on his inclinations caused a mutation which was not anticipated by his primordial essence, the idea of an original universal and immutable naturalness begins to crumble.[9] In this respect, Leopardi's position is precisely that of contemplating the role of experience and the praxis of living feared by believers in the revealed character of natural law, of which the following is an example and to whose conclusion Leopardi could easily have subscribed:

> Se per [...] Legge Naturale intendasi non un ordine stabilito dal Creatore, ma unicamente il risultato della educazione, dell'esempio, del costume, e di altre cose simili non sostenute da altra forza che da quella delle conseguenze del vivere presente; [...] egli è cosa chiara che niente si può concepir di più debole e mal sicuro per contenere gli Uomini in dovere. Il Giusto, e l'Ingiusto, il Bene, ed il Male non dipenderanno allora se non se dalla inclinazione, dall'interesse, e dalle congiunture.[10]

> [If by [...] Natural Law one means not an order established by the Creator, but only the outcome of education, example, habit, and other similar factors which are not sustained by any other means than the consequences of present living; [...] it is then clear that nothing weaker and more unreliable can be conceived of in order to contain human beings within a righteous behaviour. Right and Wrong, Good and the Evil will thus depend only on inclination, interest, and circumstances.]

When Leopardi finally turns his attention to natural law in the *Zibaldone* (at the beginning of April 1825), he does so through a dialogue with Constantin François de Chassebœuf de Volney, who had centred his *La Loi naturelle, ou catechisme du citoyen Français* [Natural Law, or the Catechism of the French Citizens] (1793) on the topic of jusnaturalism. Volney was one of the key intellectuals who aimed to provide a new moral, educational, and socio-political programme to post-revolutionary France on the basis of either deist or secular grounds, the latter being the path that Volney and the Idéologues would choose. They were interested, following the teaching of Baron D'Holbach, in building a *science of man* capable of discovering the invariant principles of universal morality hidden behind the peculiarities of single individuals. The core philosophical questions that the thinkers in question were compelled to address were 'whether a metaphysics of divine sanction supported or handicapped moral behaviour' and whether human philanthropy could be elicited by either the abolition of corrupt institutions or 'whether education and the laws faced a more onerous task in enlightening prudential self-interest'.[11] As well as being the dawn of modernity, this was also a new era for the concept of natural law, which, in the aftermath of the American and French Revolutions, became associated with attempts to build a 'theory of natural rights'. The concept of 'right' as a *faculty* to act, which emerges in modern times as the correlative of the concept of 'law' as a *rule* of action, was etymologically intrinsic to the twofold meaning of the Latin word *ius*, and finds now in rationalism, individualism and radicalism its new constituents.[12] The idea of natural law now envisioned, although often still presupposing a divine creation, is 'independent of theological presuppositions', it is a 'purely rational construction, though it does not refuse to pay homage to some remote notion of God'.[13] At the same time, it is individualistic, in the sense that it rises in parallel with the idea of a social contract between individuals, in which the right of the individual is 'exchanged against a counterpart of equal or greater value'.[14] Volney's *Loi naturelle* moves from the idea of natural law to promote an ideal of perfection and happiness for human beings. Its structure is typical of standard Christian catechisms in that it replicates the dialogical form between a questioning position and that of a respondent, and is methodologically deductive in proceeding from the observation of particular cases to the general rule, from the individual to society and the human species. Furthermore, as Ludmilla Jordanova observes, the very same structure of catechisms, 'composed of small units carefully organized into larger structures suggests that they contain classificatory systems, which are always tools for organizing the world'.[15] The authorial voice controls the content transmitted and its reception by the implicit pupil (the respondent), having established from the outset which kind of learning outcome is to be derived from the exchange. Therefore 'the very fact of presenting a universal framework is an authority-claim, and Volney's text does just this for a naturalistic world-view'.[16]

From Volney's *Loi naturelle*, Leopardi transcribes in the *Zibaldone* on 5–6 April 1825 a quotation stressing the positive values of pleasure and pain:

> 'D. Le plaisir est — il l'objet principal et immédiate de notre existence, comme l'ont dit quelques philosophes? R. Non: il ne l'est pas plus que la douleur; le plaisir est un encouragement à vivre, comme la douleur est un repoussement à mourir. D. Comment prouvez-vous cette assertion? R. Par deux faits palpables: l'un, que le plaisir, s'il est pris au-delà du besoin, conduit à la destruction: par exemple, un homme qui abuse du plaisir de manger ou de boire, attaque sa santé, et nuit à sa vie. L'autre, que la douleur conduit quelquefois à la conservation: par exemple un homme qui se fait couper un membre gangrené, souffre de la douleur, et c'est afin de ne pas périr tout entier'.
>
> ['Q. Is pleasure the principal and immediate object of our existence, as some philosophers have told us? A. No: no more than pain is; pleasure encourages us to live, pain pushes death away. Q. How do you prove such an assertion? A. By two palpable facts: first, pleasure, if taken beyond need, brings self-destruction; for example, a man who abuses the pleasures of eating or drinking, damages his health and harms his own life. Second, pain sometimes ensures survival: for example a man who has a gangrenous limb cut off, suffers pain, and that so as not to perish entirely'. Volney, La loi naturelle, ou Catéchisme du citoyen français, chap. 3. à la suite des Ruines (Les Ruines) ou Méditation sur les Révolutions des Empires, par le même auteur, 4.me édition. Paris 1808. p. 359–60.] (*Zib.* 4127–28)

Leopardi extrapolates a section that lends itself to a virtual dialogue with his own 'theory of pleasure', which is centred on the idea of human beings' constant striving towards pleasures that cannot be obtained or that vanish as soon as they are reached. In commenting on Volney's conclusions, Leopardi reverses the French intellectual's optimism regarding the conservational outcomes of pleasure and pain and states the triumph of the principle of contradiction (or of 'cognition'), according to which what seems useful for the individual's existence does not correspond to the benefit of the species:

> Bisogna distinguere tra [...] il fine dell'esistenza universale, e quello della esistenza umana [...]. Il fine naturale dell'uomo e di ogni vivente, in ogni momento della sua esistenza sentita, non è nè può essere altro che la felicità [...]. Ma [...] il fine dell' esistenza generale [...], non è certam. in niun modo la felicità [...] anche perchè [...] la somma e la intensità del dispiacere nella vita intera di ogni animale, passa senza comparazione la somma e intensità del suo piacere [...]; ma ciò non toglie che ogni animale abbia *di sua natura* p. necessario, perpetuo e solo suo fine il suo piacere [...] e così la università dei viventi. Contraddizione [...] spaventevole; ma non perciò men vera: misterio grande, da non potersi mai spiegare, se non negando (giusta il mio sistema) ogni verità o falsità assoluta, e rinunziando in certo modo anche al principio di cognizione, *non potest idem simul esse et non esse*.
>
> [We need to distinguish between [...] the end of universal existence and that of human existence [...]. The natural end of man and every living being, in every moment of being aware of their existence, is not and cannot be other than happiness [...]. But [...] the end of existence in general [...] is certainly not happiness [...] also because [...] the amount and the intensity of pain in each animal's whole life is beyond compare to the amount and intensity of his pleasure [...]; but that does not mean that every animal has not *by its nature* as its necessary, perpetual, and only end, its own pleasure [...] and that goes for [...] the universality of living beings. A [...] terrifying contradiction, but not for that reason any less true: a great mystery, which can never be explained, unless we deny (according to my system) every absolute truth and falsity, and abandon in a certain sense the very principle of our understanding, *non potest idem simul esse et non esse* [the same thing cannot be and not be at the same time.] (*Zib.* 4128–29)

Through a philosophical speculation that arises from his interest in natural law, Leopardi reaches conclusions analogous, with respect to the relations between their constituents, to the ones that we have previously encountered in the system of the unconscious, that is, an incongruity and a lack of correspondence between the essence of the parts (the individuals) and that of the whole (the entire system of nature). A reality of this kind, escaping any logical framework, is regulated by aims which appear delusional and activated by invisible reasons which the human intellect cannot grasp. However, despite the fundamental ontological limitations and falsity of its a priori character thus attributed philosophically to the principle of natural law, Leopardi was fascinated by the metaphorical constellations that it bore, and which could be transposed onto his own vision of poetic creation, once the religious system had been deprived of a rigorous adherence to its dogma and had been adapted as a structure to inform the basis of his natural system.

Notes to Chapter 6

1. Alexander Passerin d'Entrèves, *Natural Law: An Introduction to Legal Philosophy* (New Brunswick, NJ, & London: Transaction, 2009), p. 13.
2. See Marcus Tullius Cicero, *On the Republic and On the Laws*, trans. by David Fott (Ithaca, NY, & London: Cornell University Press, 2014), pp. 98–99: 'True law is correct reason congruent with nature, spread among all persons, constant, everlasting. It calls to duty by ordering; it deters from mischief by forbidding' (*On the Republic*, III, 27).

3. Albrecht Dihle, *The Theory of Will in Classical Antiquity* (Berkeley & Los Angeles: University of California Press, 1982), p. 89.
4. In the Leopardi library, the book by Casto Innocente Ansaldi, *De principiorum legis naturalis traditione* (Milan: Regia Curia, 1742), offered a comprehensive overview on the development of jusnaturalism.
5. Leopardi, *Dissertazioni filosofiche*, p. 251.
6. Cf. Leopardi, *Dissertazioni filosofiche*, p. 252.
7. Cf. Ibid., p. 249.
8. See *Zib.* 209: 'la legge naturale [...] potrà esser considerata come un sogno. Abbiamo si può dire innata l'idea *astratta* della convenienza, ma quali cose si convengano in morale, appartiene alle idee relative. Considerate la morale dei diversi popoli, massimam. barbari. E mettetevi nello stato primitivo dell'uomo. Vedrete che il far male agli altri per vostro bene non vi ripugna. Il vostro simile in natura non è una cosa così inviolabile, come credete' ('natural law can [...] be regarded as an illusion. We have what might be called an innate abstract idea of propriety, but what is deemed to be proper in the realm of morals belongs to relative ideas. Consider the morals of different populations, particularly barbarians. And imagine yourself in the situation of primitive man. You will see that harming others for your own good does not repel you. Your fellows in the natural state are not as inviolable as you might think'); see also *Zib.* 342–43, 452.
9. See also *Zib.* 1640–41, 1710–12.
10. Casto Innocente Ansaldi, *Della necessità e verità della religione naturale rivelata* (Venice: Valvasense, 1755), pp. ccxxi–xxii.
11. Martin S. Staum, *Minerva's Message: Stabilizing the French Revolution* (Montreal & Kingston: McGill-Queen's University Press, 1996), p. 118.
12. Cf. Passerin d'Entrèves, *Natural Law*, pp. 61–62.
13. Ibid., p. 55.
14. Ibid., p. 59.
15. Ludmilla Jordanova, *Nature Displayed. Gender, Science and Medicine 1760–1820* (London & New York: Routledge, 1999), p. 134
16. Ibid.

CHAPTER 7

Naturalization of Religion

When one addresses religious frames of mind in Leopardi, one refers to paradigmatic structures and motifs which persist, more or less consciously, either metaphorically or for their representative potentials. The adoption by Leopardi of elements of Jewish and Christian faith in his own discourse does not presuppose adhesion to those values from the time of the 'mutazione totale' ('total transformation') of 1819 (*Zib.* 144). As Cosetta Veronese and Pamela Williams explain in their study addressing the long-debated issue of Leopardi's atheism:

> He was not a positive atheist, not someone who believes that God does not exist, for on that metaphysical question, when speaking about the invisible world, it would be impossible to say one way or the other. He was an *a*theist in the etymological sense of the word, a negative atheist, someone without a belief in God, without a belief in a supreme personal being who is distinct from the world, and Creator of the world.[1]

The broad and progressive operation which accompanies Leopardi's entire creative activity is the naturalization of the religious system, the resetting of a new philosophical posture which induced his own system of nature and the religious natural system to merge in a formal overlapping. This however emptied religion of its substantial elements of faith and reinforced his own thought with an available set of relationships useful to approach the issues of human ontology and man's position in the natural world. This process can be considered to have been completed already by 1820.

During the early process of detachment from religion, as Claudio Colaiacomo notes, Leopardi's philosophical enterprise was founded on specific requirements which were necessary in order to avoid direct confrontation with theology and to continue drawing from it structures of thought which could aliment his own philosophical ideas. It was essential for Leopardi to avoid having to face directly the crucial ultimate questions on the existence of God and of an afterlife which human reason cannot solve. To achieve this, the natural system had to prove itself to be homogenous but independent from religion.[2] If we look for instance at the *Zibaldone* passage, pp. 2114–16, where Leopardi states that early Christian thinkers had understood the presence of an intrinsic friction between the natural and the rational components of the human condition, we note how each element of the analysis and demonstration is exposed through a parallel between the religious and the natural systems to highlight both their overlapping in terms of form and their divergence in terms of content:

> Tutte queste autorità [Gli antichi pensatori Cristiani, S. Paolo, i padri, e prima anche del Cristianesimo, i filosofi gentili] favoriscono [...] il mio sistema, colla differenza che laddove coloro credevano corrotta e corruttrice la natura, io credo la ragione; laddove essi l'uomo, io gli uomini; laddove essi credevano sostanzialmente imperfetta cioè composta di elementi contraddittorii l'opera di Dio, io credo tale l'opera dell'uomo, e a causa della sola opera dell'uomo, credo non sostanzialmente, ma solo accidentalmente imperfetta l' opera di Dio, e composta non di elementi contraddittorii, ma di qualità acquisite ripugnanti alle naturali, o di qualità naturali corrotte, ripugnanti fra loro, solo in quanto corrotte.
>
> [All these authorities [The ancient Christian thinkers, St. Paul, the Church Fathers, and, even before Christianity, the pagan philosophers] [...] favor my system, with the difference that whereas they believed nature to be corrupt and corrupting, I believe that reason is; where they believed it was man, I men; where they believed that the work of God was imperfect in substance, that is, composed of contradictory elements, I believe the work of man imperfect, and, solely because of the work of man, I believe that the work of God is imperfect not in substance but only accidentally, and is composed not of contradictory elements but of acquired qualities that are repugnant to natural ones, or of corrupt natural qualities, repulsive to one another only because they are corrupt.] (*Zib.* 2115–16)

Leopardi criticizes the negative effects of Christianity on the history of civilization:

> Il Cristianesimo [...] è incompatibile [...] colla sussistenza del mondo e della vita umana. [...] L'uomo non doveva intendere dalla ragione che le cose non valessero a nulla, e fossero infelicissime. [...] L'averlo imparato distruggerebbe la vita, se l'uomo seguisse fedelmente e precisamente i dettami e lo spirito della Religione.
>
> [Christianity [...] is incompatible [...] with the subsisting of the world and human life. [...] Man was not meant to understand from reason that things meant nothing, and were utterly wretched. [...] The fact of having learned it would destroy life, if man faithfully and exactly followed the dictates and spirit of Religion.] (*Zib.* 1426)

But despite this he shapes his irreligious natural worldview through the visual and moral potential of religion, which offers itself as a method and a rule for living through examples and terms of contrast.[3] Leopardi attributes to Christianity the characteristics of a philosophical religion inclining to the 'metafisico, all'astratto, al mistico' ('the metaphysical, the abstract, the mystical') (*Zib.* 336). While he refuses to attribute human imperfection to the corruption of nature, he believes that any forms of decline are derived instead from reason and that a regained natural state is the condition of regeneration to be achieved by an 'oltrafilosofia, che conoscendo l'intiero e l'intimo delle cose, ci ravvicini alla natura' ('an ultraphilosophy, which, through a complete and intimate knowledge of things, brings us close again to nature') (*Zib.* 115). Leopardi is here stating the importance of a hybrid kind of thought which, while acknowledging the irreversible fracture between will to action and self-restraint opened in the human psyche by Christianity and completed by the hyper-rationalism of modernity (of which the French revolution was the ultimate historical manifestation), is capable at the same time of putting aside the modern destruction of all illusion to re-embrace an original inclination towards naturalness and spontaneity.

The expression adopted by Leopardi in referring to a law that resides in our heart ('ci sta sempre nel cuore come un istinto' ('[natural laws] are always in our hearts, like an instinct'), in the quoted *Zib.* 119) evokes the very popular equivalence, in the Christian tradition, between an unwritten imprint, as it were, and the indelible informing power of natural law. This image appears precisely in St Paul's Epistle to the Romans ('When the Gentiles, which have not the law, do by nature the things contained in the law, these, having not the law, are a law unto themselves. Which shew the work of the law written in their hearts' (2:14–15)),[4] and is adopted and commented on widely by all the Patristic authorities.[5] Albrecht Dihle stresses that, in line with the Old Testament component of Paul's thought, the function of the (unwritten) law 'written in our heart' is independent from the gnoseological activity of the intellect, in the sense that no requirement of understanding, let alone interpretation, is needed for man to act according to the law, whereas it is only absolute obedience to the law which constitutes a just manifestation of man's will. Moreover, even a conception of 'inborn or natural knowledge of the law' was not intended in the quoted passage from the Epistle to the Romans.[6] This idea would have fitted well in the Greek moral world, where right action derives directly from right knowledge; however Paul 'only stresses the fact that the gentiles in question did fulfil the Law, but he does not give much consideration to the problem of how they could possibly be aware in some way or another, of its content'. What really mattered for Paul, independently of human knowledge of the divine commandment, was 'the act itself' which 'can be performed [...] with and without the explicit knowledge of the divine commandment [...]. So the [...] work of the Law testifies to the will rather than the intellect of the fulfiller'. Dihle also notes that an analogy could be drawn between Paul's passage of the letter and an extract from the *Testament of the Twelve Patriarchs* (Jud. 20). Here it is stated that 'the deeds man has performed in his lifetime are inscribed on his breastbone to bar witness in the presence of the divine judge'. The difference is that while the author of this text was implicitly addressing Jews who had knowledge of the Torah, St Paul had in mind Greeks or gentiles 'of whom at least some have spontaneously fulfilled the Torah without knowing it and who can, therefore, rely on the testimony of their heart where their life in accordance with the Law is recorded'.[7] In addition to the law written in their heart, those people would have the support of their thoughts and conscience, which for Paul is a direct channel of communication between God and men, to unveil the right or wrong character of their choice, but they were not guided by the rational and geometric orders of the intellect.

The instinctual character of naturalness, as defined by Leopardi, also seems to be in harmony with St Paul's idea of a spontaneous drive independent from rational control. However, this does not mean naturalness as a form of untrained naivety or unbounded expression of feelings; quite the opposite in fact, as Leopardi is convinced that in modern times naturalness is the ultimate outcome of experience and that art is built on that experience: 'il sommo dell'arte è la naturalezza, e il nasconder l'arte' ('the height of art is naturalness and the concealment of art') (*Zib.* 20). It is possible, in other words, to express naturally as if that very form of expression were easy, free, and directly linked to our heart, but regaining the spontaneity which was constitutional of ancient forms of expressions can only be the result of a long apprenticeship. The connections between Leopardi's ideal of writing and the Apostle's image are profound and complex, and the very same idea, promoted by Paul, of an entirely new cultural system having been made use of or having been activated in the form of praxis and without necessary formal compliance to its official regulations intrigued Leopardi, because he himself engaged in an operation of naturalization of the religious system which was thus able to offer structures and forms to his own reflection and writing practice.

Leopardi's above-mentioned reference to the regenerative power of 'ultra-philosophy' is part of a wider speculation which involves crucial comparative elements between the Christian and the pre-Christian world. Just a few pages earlier a sequence of notes begins which is devoted to various topics apparently independent but which are in fact linked by a secret messianic thread. First, Leopardi mentions Clement of Alexandria in relation to the importance of beauty in Greek culture and its recognition as a form of Grace in Christian thought:

> Quanto i greci facessero caso della bellezza, oltre alla parola καλοκἀγαθὸς notata già in questi pensieri, vedi un luogo singolare di un antico in Clem. Aless. cohort. ad gentes c. 4. dopo il mezzo. ediz. di Venez. t. 1. p. 49. lin. ult. p. 17. nel marg. lat. e p. 37. nel marg. gr. Qual è ora quel genitore che domandi a Dio quella grazia come un bene principale e suo proprio e dei figli?

> [Concerning the attention that the Greeks paid to beauty, in addition to the word καλοκἀγαθὸς already mentioned in these thoughts, see the singular passage written by an ancient in Clement of Alexandria, "Cohortatio ad gentes," ch. 4, after the middle, Venice ed., tome 1, p. 49, last line, p. 17 in the Latin margin and p. 37 in the Greek margin. What parents now would ask God for that grace as a principal good for themselves or their children?] (*Zib.* 112)

Then, in the following paragraph, he continues with a reflection on Jesus Christ as the first thinker to equate the concept of society with that of evil, and to posit the idea of worldliness as a nemesis of virtue and action. The next notes are a reflection on patience as 'la più eroica delle virtù giusto perchè non ha nessuna apparenza d'eroico' ('the most heroic of the virtues precisely because it has not the least appearance of heroism'), followed by some linguistic observations on the word *impertinente*, which the *Vocabolario* of the Accademia della Crusca defines as that which does not pertain and is not appropriate ('Che non pertiene, Che non conviene'), a meaning that is part of the semantics of friction and irritation, which in turn, as we shall see, informs Leopardi's conception of grace.[8] There follows a remark on Petrarch's verse as an example of unmediated poetic experience, and

Leopardi observes that he 'versa il suo cuore' ('pours out his heart') and makes it speak: 'lo fa parlare'. A subsequent linguistic remark on the adjective *agevole* ('easily done'), deriving from *agere*, a Latin verb describing action, precedes a reflection on the paradoxical nature of contrast as a propeller of lively feelings. Therefore, before producing the quoted passage on the contrasting relationship between nature and reason and the necessity of an ultra-philosophy to balance the excess of the former through a rediscovery of the latter, Leopardi had engaged in a reflection which seems implicitly to refer to the power of Grace and the messianic Revelation. We find the idea of the stimulating irritation and contrast produced by grace, as well as the image of patience, which is a typical messianic virtue. Moreover, the whole reflection seems to be permeated by an idea of a hybridization of cultural polarities which alludes to the historical and cultural context in which Paul proclaimed his message in his Epistle to the Romans. It is not by chance, in this respect, that the starting-point is the reference to Clement of Alexandria, a passionate reader and interpreter of the Bible, as well as of Greek literature and philosophy, and a crucial figure in Leopardi's education. In his life and work, Clement engaged in the art of the productive re-employment of contrasting cultural impulses. Deeply influenced by St Paul's message, Clement provides a further example of a writer in whom 'man's freedom and responsibility' do not 'result exclusively from his cognitive potential'.[9] A convert to Christianity, Clement lived in Alexandria until, in 202, persecution forced him to move to Palestine, where he died. Eric Osborn defines him as a 'traveller, always moving on', not merely from a biographical point of view, but as an intellectual, his spiritual dimension being deeply informed by the aim to persuade Greeks to embrace the path set out by Christ.[10] In his programme to provide Christianity with a solid philosophical structure, which he grafted from the roots of Greek thought, he lived his spirituality as a continuous dynamic of interaction with philosophical and cultural presuppositions previous to or different from Christianity. The most remarkable enterprise of his versatile explorations was his capacity to combine the mastery of Plato with the message of the Revelation. He chose the path of teaching and writing, believing in the power of writing as the privileged means to transmit (or to conceal to those who are unworthy or not yet ready) the mystery of the Scriptures and the oral teaching of the Apostles. He had absorbed Plato's view on writing as a mere 'image of the voice', which is of crucial importance in Leopardi's own response to the tension between orality and literacy.[11] He considered the Scriptures, the Gospel, and the Epistles as the only truly reliable sources for teaching, and through the authority of the revealed message he franchised the mediated essence of writing from Plato's claim of inferiority. From Plato he also derived the dialogical style of his writing, and in the prologue to his *Stromateis*, Clement discusses the relationship between pupil and teacher in terms of flourishing (the master is the one who plants seeds in the mind of the pupil who eventually develops as a fully grown plant), which shows a kind of sensitivity which could not be ignored by Leopardi when investigating the regenerative power of ultra-philosophy.[12] All these elements touched very sensitive chords in Leopardi's own practice of writing, animated, as we shall see, by profound dialogical and pedagogical aims. More generally, it is the twofold aspect — pagan and Christian — of Clement's thought which Leopardi found fascinating. Clement had performed an operation of absorption of cultural modes into a new system of thought. The porosity to paganism that Clement identified in Christianity reinforced the new religion's own philosophical and representative grounds in a time of intellectual and imaginative *mediocritas*, by which, according to Tertullian, the early establishment of Christianity was affected.[13] Clement represented for Leopardi the role of a precursor by having to face the task of dealing with epochal changes which required a decision on the 'destiny' of all that preceded that change (the pre-Christian world). Still deeply attached to the ancient pre-Christian system of thought which had nourished his formation, Clement was able to create a hybrid construct, as is the model of the Hellenic Christian, from a mutated post-Christian perspective. Clement's management of the two cultural systems turned into a peaceful contamination rather than a collision. This happened because in assigning to Greek culture the formal role of vivifying the language and imagery of Christianity, while leaving to the new religion the command of the substantial existential belief, he could keep the two spheres separate while at the same time favouring a dialogue and enrichment for the new mission.

The case of Leopardi is at the same time similar and antithetical. He also looks at ancient culture as the primary source of imagination and vigour and as a standard of ethical norms of behaviour, but he does so from the perspective of the non-believer who attributes to Christianity precisely the responsibility for having wiped away that primordial world. He speaks from the perspective of a new age of disenchantment, also bearing witness to a paradigm shift, namely the replacement of the eternal with the ephemeral vision of the world (the one which will lead to the new consumerist worldview); but from his own viewpoint it is unhappiness, boredom, and false splendour which accompany and await the isolated individual during and at the end of his biological journey. Leopardi's own mind is also binary in the sense that his inevitable but ambiguous acceptance of modernity reflects the acknowledgment that something has imposed itself as new cultural construct, and has caused changes that are not fully traceable or explainable from the perspective of linear history. However, he is also aware that this process has failed to fully annihilate the powerful re-emergence of the ancient as an antithetical, contrasting source of confrontation. Hence both for Clement and for Leopardi, the Greek world remains a source of beauty and inspiration, but while for the former the core focus is the 'new system' of Christianity and the way it can benefit from the interaction, for the latter the 'old religion' has already manifested all possible damage to the inner and social life of the individual, and the Greek world remains a lost universe which can only be resurrected intermittently by poetic means. Nevertheless, despite the antithetical outcome, Leopardi never ceases to see Clement as a fellow intelligent moderator of the impact of a cultural revolution. And he continues to investigate the modes of contamination of different systems of thought, in search of an explanation of what it means to belong to an era which has attempted to assassinate the past while continuing to appreciate forms of thinking which survive from this destruction. Leopardi's ultra-philosophy is also an operation of repositioning and refocusing. The most radical philosophy, which has experienced a devastating excess of reason, is once again brought back to a middle ground for action, where both horizons of intellectual radicalness and imaginative intuition remain visible and capable of being experienced.

Notes to Chapter 7

1. Cosetta Veronese and Pamela Williams, *The Atheism of Giacomo Leopardi* (Leicester: Troubador, 2013), pp. xxiv–xxv.
2. See Claudio Colaiacomo, 'Al di qua del Paradiso (Su autorità e religione nello sviluppo intellettuale leopardiano)', in *Letteratura e critica: studi in onore di N. Sapegno*, ed. by Walter Binni and others, 5 vols (Rome: Bulzoni, 1975), II, 537–74 (p. 554).
3. See Claudio Colaiacomo, 'Crisi dell' "ancient regime": dall'uomo di lettere al letterato borghese', in *Letteratura italiana*, ed. by Alberto Asor Rosa, 16 vols (Turin: Einaudi, 1982), II, 363–412 (p. 405).
4. St Paul, Epistle to the Romans, in *The King James Version of the Holy Bible*, ed. by Dan Cogliano, 2004, p. 647, <http://www.davince.com/download/kjvbiblea.pdf> [accessed 20 January 2017].
5. A synthesis of the theological debate associated with this passage is also present in a book of the Leopardi library: Scipione Maffei, *Istoria teologica delle dottrine e delle opinioni corse ne' cinque primi secoli della Chiesa in proposito della divina Grazia, del libero arbitrio, e della Predestinazione* (Trent: Parone, 1742), pp. 28–29.
6. Dihle, *The Theory of Will in Classical Antiquity*, p. 80.
7. Ibid.
8. *Vocabolario degli accademici della Crusca* , 4th edn, 6 vols (Florence: Manni, 1729–38), <http://www.lessicografia.it/Controller?E=1078;1756404708;&c1=350;-7;3;-21159276;212722725;&c2=129;-39;3;40;69;1;130;32;5;40;66;1;129;-39;65;-31;69;4;130;1025;5;40;75;13;130;27;3;1646876352;15 45561153;&qi=&q1=impertinente&q2=&q3=&q4=&qr=null&num=20&o=115;-38489505;-1185594668;&idV=1221453;-12;14;6;35;749767733;1982947563;&TDE=impertinente;&TDNE> [accessed 23 January 2017].
9. Dihle, *The Theory of Will in Classical Antiquity*, p. 110.
10. Eric Osborn, *Clement of Alexandria* (Cambridge: Cambridge University Press, 2008), p. 1.
11. See Franco D'Intino, *L'immagine della voce* (Venice: Marsilio, 2009).
12. Franco D'Intino has demonstrated how the permanence of Clement's influence on Leopardi's creative world extends far beyond the initial reference to the Alexandrine theologian's *Protrepticus* in his 'Inno a Nettuno' [Hymn to Neptune] in 1816. In fact it innervates, as if through hidden threads, the imaginative dimension of Leopardi's poetic work including the masterpiece 'A Silvia', which is indeed permeated by the Eleusinian mystics into which Clement had been initiated before converting to Christianity; see Franco D'Intino, 'I misteri di Silvia: motivo persefoneo e mistica eleusina in Leopardi', *Filologia e critica*, 19 (1994), 211–71.
13. Cf. Osborn, *Clement of Alexandria*, p. 24.

CHAPTER 8

Messianic Inclinations

The importance of Jewish messianism in St Paul's thought, as well as the Jewish-Greek linguistic background to his writing in the Epistle to the Romans, has been demonstrated by Giorgio Agamben, as opposed to previous critical approaches to Paul's philosophy, which tended to insist on his role as the founder of a new religion.[1] In addition to Leopardi's interest in the linguistic issues of the Scriptures and in particular the use of the Greek language by Jewish writers, there is a specific component of Paul's relationship with messianic time, highlighted by Agamben, which Leopardi seems to share.[2] It is the idea of a process of renovation primarily as a form of praxis and enactment brought about by the prospect of Grace. This, in Agamben's reading of Paul, is a dynamic undertaking which does not leave the soul invested with messianic hope in a static contemplation, awaiting a remote future fulfilment, but instead requires an active performance, putting into practice the individual's original 'vocation', which the messianic calling does not change or overturn but simply revokes and reactivates: 'To be messianic [...] signifies the expropriation of each and every juridical-factical property [...] under the form of the *as not*. This expropriation does not, however, found a new identity; the "new creature" is none other than the use and messianic vocation of the old'.[3] This process, Agamben observes, was already at play in the Franciscans' way of life, as the friars did not only refuse any form of property, but with the prospect of a new life and a highest, spiritual form of property to be achieved in the afterlife, they invalidated civil law by distinguishing the idea of 'use' (which they practised) from that of 'right of usage', thereby detaching the former from any idea of possession or ownership. Through this operation they created 'a space that escaped the grasp of power and its laws, without entering into conflict with them yet rendering them inoperative'.[4] If we now look back at the *Zibaldone* reflection on clarity and naturalness, we notice how naturalness (which we now suppose coincides with a messianic inclination), has the power to revoke civil law in order to complete its actualization:

> La naturalezza dello scrivere è così comandata che posto il caso che per conservarla bisognasse mancare alla chiarezza, io considero che questa è come di legge civile, e quella come di legge naturale [...] e va osservata quando anche ne debba soffrire la società o l'individuo.
>
> [Naturalness in writing is so imperative that if it were the case that this could be achieved only at the cost of clarity, then I would consider that the latter is

like civil law and the former like natural law, [...] and must be observed even when society or the individual will suffer.] (*Zib.* 119)

Furthermore, when Leopardi speaks about the ultra-philosophy which alone would restore the beatific effects of a life according to nature, he does so by insisting on a particular state of things, as the cognition of truth is ('una [...] oltrafilosofia, che conoscendo l'intiero e l'intimo delle cose, ci ravvicini alla natura'), which the ultra-philosopher is not supposed to cancel but only to deactivate. Elsewhere Leopardi specifies the nature of this deactivation by way of forgetfulness: 'Ai mali della filosofia presente, non c'è altro rimedio che la dimenticanza, e un pascolo materiale alle illusioni' ('There is no other remedy for the ills of modern philosophy than forgetting, and material pasture for the illusions to feed on') (*Zib.* 337). Forgetfulness does not imply the abolition of philosophy but only its revocation.

When Leopardi envisions the specificities of this process and explains the modalities and effects of its taking place, he does so with a language which is deeply permeated by a messianic aura:

> L'uomo disingannato, stanco, esperto, esaurito di tutti i desideri, nella solitudine appoco appoco si rifà, ricupera se stesso, *ripiglia quasi carne e lena*, e più o meno vivamente, a ogni modo *risorge*, ancorchè penetrantissimo d'ingegno, e sventuratissimo. Come questo? forse per la cognizione del vero? Anzi *per la dimenticanza del vero*, pel diverso e più vago aspetto che prendono per lui, *quelle cose già sperimentate e vedute*, ma che ora *essendo lontane dai sensi e dall'intelletto, tornano a passare per la immaginazione sua, e quindi abbellirsi*. Ed egli torna a sperare e desiderare, e vivere, per poi tutto riperdere, e morire di nuovo, ma più presto assai di prima, se rientra nel mondo.
>
> [The man who is disillusioned, worn, and weary, whose desires are all exhausted, in solitude gradually recovers, recuperates, *gains what is almost a new lease on life*, and, more or less vigorously, does in any case *revive*, even if he is a man of the most discriminating intelligence and assailed by the most terrible misfortune. How can this be? perhaps through the knowledge of what is true? On the contrary, *it is through the forgetting of what is true*, through the different and vaguer aspect that *things already seen and experienced* and now *distant from the senses and the intellect assume when they return and pass through his imagination and are thereby made beautiful*. And he once again comes to hope and to desire, and to live, only to lose everything all over again, and to die again, but somewhat more quickly than before, if he goes back into the world.] (*Zib.* 681–82; my emphasis)

Through the deactivation of existential law (the 'vero'), things which persist in their old identity ('cose già sperimentate e vedute') are subject to a revocation ('ora [...] lontane dai sensi e dall'intelletto') and a subsequent regeneration ('tornano [...] ad abbellirsi'). Agamben prefers to speak of messianic time not in terms of the 'end of time', but as the 'time of the end', the time that time, in the same way as a poem which is being read, takes to come to an end.[5] The image of the poem employed by Agamben seems all the more appropriate when read in light of Leopardi's work. Colaiacomo has demonstrated how Leopardi's poetry and his reflection on the effect of poetic creation, where he compares the effect of Anacreon's odes to a refreshing breeze (*Zib.* 30–31), is deeply permeated precisely by a focus on reading and the ephemeral time of any reading experience. More generally in Leopardi's verse, the reader's point of view is often projected in the poem as a central presence, as if there were a merging of the printed life of the text with the organic life of the reader. Much like the process theorized by Schlegel, the subjective experience of the reader is not only a necessary material starting-point of the reading experience, but an organic articulation of the work of art; vice versa, the work of art can also be considered as a kind of prosthesis of the reader.[6] The reader acts in the mechanism of the text as a propellant force for the unfolding of the text's meaning. His presence presupposed in the fabric of the text is necessary in order for poetry to be communicated and received, but because the life of the poem depends on the time of the reading experience, the poetry expressing itself through the viewpoint of the reader also reverberates, through his own eyes and voice, the progressive image of its end. The poetic experience can be received and felt as a living organism only by way of usage and consumption: 'L'opera si è avvivata, rubando la vita al lettore. Quando la simbiosi si interrompe, il lettore si trova di fronte un'immagine di morte, che è in fondo un'immagine di se stesso' [The work has become alive by robbing the reader of his or her life. When this symbiosis is interrupted, the reader faces an image of death, which is, in fact, an image of himself or herself].[7] Colaiacomo observes how by connecting the life of the work of art to the life of the reader, Leopardi revolutionizes the idea of the literary canon, in the sense that canonicity derives now not from an external objectifying operation which crystalizes the work of art in an abstract fixity, but rather, the canon becomes a function of the living experience of the reader.

In analogous terms, according to Agamben's reading, St Paul's voluntarism is a much more active and 'present' condition than the one which might derive from the idea of the soul's simple obedience to a commandment whose realization depends on faith in a distant, abstract object. At the same time, Leopardi's ultra-philosophy can be viewed as a form of messianic salvation in the sense that the perspective of regeneration intrinsic to ultra-philosophy moves away from the deactivation of the principles of modernity that made its intervention necessary. But in the same way that in the 'Dialogo di Federico Ruysch e delle sue mummie' [Dialogue of Frederick Ruysch and his Mummies] Ruysch's 'resurrected' mummies have only a limited amount of time to communicate with the scientist, so Leopardi's modern messianic praxis is time-limited, ephemeral, and reversible. The ideas of salvation, hope, and regeneration, while borrowing forms of thinking from eternal perspectives, remain functions of human beings' creaturely condition and of the temporally limited effect that a text is able to exercise on the reader.[8]

Notes to Chapter 8

1. See Giorgio Agamben, *The Time That Remains: A Commentary on the Letter to the Romans*, trans. by Patricia Dailey (Stanford, CA: Stanford University Press, 2005).
2. See *Zib.* 999–1000.
3. Agamben, *The Time That Remains*, p. 26.

4. Ibid., p. 27.
5. Cf. Ibid., p. 83.
6. Cf. Colaiacomo, *Il poeta della vita moderna*, p. 72.
7. Ibid., p. 75.
8. In the 'Dialogo di Timandro e di Eleandro' [Dialogue of Timander and Eleander] Leopardi ironically lets Eleander state that a text cannot have an effect on the reader lasting more than one hour, and even less for those readers who live in big cities, for whom the duration of the temporal rapture never surpasses the half hour, see Michael Caesar, ' "Mezz'ora di nobiltà": Leopardi e i suoi lettori', in *Leopardi a Firenze*, ed. by Laura Melosi (Florence: Olschki, 2002), pp. 461–71.

CHAPTER 9

Naturalness as the Style of Grace

From the realm of philosophical speculation Leopardi's messianic inclination translates into the practice of writing by applying to prerogatives of style the forms and aims of theological Grace. Indeed, if the idea of clarity of language is intrinsically permeated by meanings and allusions which confer on it powers analogous to those of confession, naturalness is invested with a similar power. This results from the equivalence established by Leopardi between naturalness and natural law, and the bond between grace and naturalness that he identifies in the aesthetic realm: 'Pare che la grazia consista in certo modo nella naturalezza, e non possa star senza questa' ('It seems that in some way grace consists in naturalness and cannot exist without it') (*Zib.* 199). Natural law, as envisioned from a theological perspective, is based on the relationship between nature and Grace and on the fact that human nature carries within it the image of God:

> Tale immagine può attuarsi solo per opera della grazia di Dio che suscita nell'uomo la sua risposta personale. Nella sua risposta, sotto l'impulso della grazia, l'uomo instaura un rapporto esplicito di comunione con Dio e con i suoi simili, attua le potenzialità proprie della sua natura e quindi nelle sue stesse scelte storiche si realizza come persona.[1]

> [This image can be actualized only by means of divine Grace, which stimulates in man his own personal response. In his response under the impulse of Grace, man establishes an explicit relationship of communion with God and with his fellow human beings; he actualizes the potentialities of his own nature and therefore he realizes himself as a person in his historical choices.]

Thomas Aquinas insists on participation as the constituent of Grace, when he defines it as 'a kind of sharing in divinity given to thinking creatures' (3a. 7–15).[2] The individual exposed to the influence of divine Grace is naturally inclined to multiply its effects by effusing about his beatific experience to others. Leopardi reflects on aesthetic grace in terms which escape clear-cut definition. In dialogue with Montesquieu, grace is a *je ne sais quoi*, a 'non so che' ('that certain something') (*Zib.* 198) that strikes the eye of the beholder.[3] It is an effect of surprise, achieved by 'dar più di quello che si prometta' ('giving something more than is expected') (*Zib.* 198). From a 'fanciullo che parla o vero opera' ('young boy speaking or doing something') to 'alcuni difettuzzi in un viso' ('certain minor flaws in a face'), such as a 'naso rincagnato' ('a snub nose') or an 'occhio un po' falso' ('a slight squint'), to 'parlar bleso' ('talking with a lisp') (*Zib.* 199–200), what is common to all manifestations of grace is their propriety of visual and intellectual provocation. It represents a stimulus to curiosity by attracting and pushing the soul deeper into the search for the intriguing essence of the object of interest, which resists our grasp. Unlike beauty, which strikes and reveals its power in one single outburst, grace spreads its effects over time, and requires the active attention of the viewer who is unable to prevent his intellectual faculties from seeking further the source of this pleasing aesthetic tickling: 'la grazia ha successione di parti, anzi non si dà grazia senza successione. Quindi veduta una parte, resta desiderio e speranza delle altre. [...] Perciò la grazia ordinariamente consiste nel movimento' ('grace reveals itself bit by bit, in fact you cannot have grace without this succession. So that, having seen part of it, you desire and hope to see more. [...] Hence grace usually consists in movement') (*Zib.* 198). In the manifestations of what Schiller defined as the accidental quality of grace, the subject perceives the actions he performs as his own (as he is confident that he is mastering his own self) and, at the same time, as belonging to someone or something else (as they seem to happen by themselves).[4] In this conceptualization of grace, which is similar to Leopardi's, the subject is transported towards the object and aims to 'participate' in its nature, which echoes the properties of divine Grace, by virtue of which man tends to penetrate the divine essence, to receive bliss, and to conform himself to God. Contrary to the modern (Romantic) trend adopted by those whom Leopardi defines as 'poeti descrittivi' ('descriptive poets') (*Zib.* 21), who indulge in minutial enumerations of details of a certain figure or scene, and in so doing annihilate the function of imagination, Leopardi believes in an ideal of writing in which the poet and the listener or reader become one thing, where the poetic effect is the outcome of a shared activity of creation and a common lived experience of the poetic utterance. Only the reader who 'sa mettere la sua mente nello stato in cui era quella dell'autore' ('know[s] how to put himself in the same state of mind as that in which the author was') and is capable of 'pensare colla stessa profondità dell'autore' ('thinking as deeply as the author') (*Zib.* 348) can fully grasp the poetic essence. Vice versa, with respect to the creator, only the one who possesses a good 'comunicativa' ('skill of communication') (*Zib.* 1376) can initiate this process and let the reader 'intend[ere] la verità, l'evidenza di quei sentimenti' ('understand the truth, the force of those feelings') (*Zib.* 347). In this transaction and communion of senses, the inanimate (the poetic word) comes to life, and between the poet and the listener a sensible effect of the poetic word can be perceived activating a 'vita del discorso' ('life of discourse') (*Zib.* 952). Therefore, the reader participates in the poet's dynamic of creation by assimilating, through channels which are corporeal before being intellectual, the poetic matter itself. The word is somehow resurrected, so to speak, from its inert state through a process of embodiment, which produces beneficial effects. The transforming power of poetry had already been explored by Vico, who had also established a polarity between truths reached through cognition and unmediated experiences of naturalness. In his *Institutio oratoriae*, and under the influence of Cicero's *De oratore*, he refers to 'things' which 'seem to be speaking forth by themselves',[5] without the mediation of the orator ('quando a parlare non sembra che sia l'oratore, quanto le cose stesse').[6] For Vico the function of naturalness is to elicit a process of becoming, as when in the *New Science* he refers to the producer who 'col *non intendere*, egli *di sè fa esse cose*, e col *trasformandovisi lo diventa*' ('when he does not understand he makes the things out of himself and becomes them by transforming himself into them').[7] As in the trope present throughout the humanistic tradition, in Vico poetic creation is reminiscent of divine creation.[8]

Clayton Koelb has studied the cultural significance of the attention devoted by Romantic philosophy and literature to the practice of writing and reading. He has found the presence of a powerful religious model, that of the resurrection of the flesh, active in shaping the conceptualization of reading as a dynamic of the revivification of dead matter:

> The process of writing and reading exemplifies every aspect and subtlety of the interaction between matter and spirit. Indeed, it is hardly possible to overstate the theoretical complexity of a process that involves taking thought embodied in a living creature, reembodying such thought in language, and embodying that language yet again in material objects; then, conversely, extracting language from material objects and thought from linguistic structures to reembody them once again in a living organism. Far from evading or suppressing the material, the Romantic century lavished upon matter its most consistent and careful intellectual scrutiny.[9]

Koelb believes that the root of this conception of a living word, and the source for the Romantic concern with processes of verbal resurrection, reside in St Paul's Second Epistle to the Corinthians. Here the apostle was interested in asserting the power of the revealed word, but in having to confront the new faith with the long-established written tradition of the Old Testament, he could not rely on any existing written sources. For this reason, in referring to 'our epistle written in our hearts', and to the acknowledgement that God made him and his followers 'ministers of the new testament', he intended to undermine the power of the bare word and insisted on the fact that this ministry was founded not on 'the letter' but on the spirit, 'for the letter killeth, but the spirit giveth life'.[10] Paul is alluding to the salvific essence of holy Grace, which constitutes the only condition for the revivification of the written text. In doing so he is inaugurating a new way of conceiving of the power of transformation and transportation of the word, now applied to written rather than oral culture, which for centuries had been bound to the aims of transforming people through rhetoric and persuasion. According to Koelb, Paul's epistle had a specific reference in mind, that is Plato's *Phaedrus*, and in particular the end of the dialogue, where Socrates maintains the importance of words 'written in the soul' rather than on paper, at which point Phaedrus comments by referring to the 'living, breathing discourse of the man who knows, of which the written one can be fairly called an image'.[11] Whereas in Plato the contraposition between the dead and the living involves the written and the spoken utterance respectively, in Paul — who unlike Plato lived in an era of a growing writerly mentality — a shift takes place, and the separation between the two conditions is now solely intrinsic to the written world. What now constitutes the divide between the life and death of the word is the presence or absence in the written text of the divine Spirit.

Paul stressed the revivifying power of the Revelation transforming the death brought about by the consequences of Adam's sins into a new life of redemption. For some thinkers, such as Fichte in *Über Geist und Buchstab in der Philosophie* [On the Spirit and the Letter in Philosophy] (1795), the importance attributed to the 'spirit' — meant not necessarily in its direct reference to the Scripture but as a figure for the creative force that the poet transmits to the text in order to bring it to life — produced a shift in the way the poetic creation was conceived in relation to the divine, and the Son, rather than the Father, bringing new life to the flesh became the model for comparisons. Poetic creation for Fichte does not bring life *ex nihilo*, as in the Father's model, but out of death. Similarly to the salvific intervention of Christ, the poet infuses life into the dead matter of language, which acts as a necessary medium between writer and reader.[12] For Leopardi the concept of naturalness is also permeated by a Christological aura, especially for its redemptive function counterbalancing the presence of Adam, who recurs in the *Zibaldone* as a powerful symbol of error, mutation, and irreversibility.[13] While the Christian proto-modernity started to affirm the inner viewpoint of the self, at the same time society started to change from a place of shared values and harmony of intents, to represent the breeding-ground for selfishness and self-interest. Society started to mutate and become 'the world':

> Gesù Cristo fu il primo che personificasse e col nome di *mondo* circoscrivesse e definisse e stabilisse l'idea del perpetuo nemico della virtù dell'innocenza dell'eroismo della sensibilità vera, d'ogni singolarità dell'animo della vita e delle azioni, della natura in somma, che è quanto dire la società, e così mettesse la moltitudine degli uomini fra i principali nemici dell'uomo.
>
> [Jesus Christ was the first to establish, define, delineate, and personify with the name *world* the idea of a perpetual enemy of virtue, innocence, heroism, and real feeling, of all singularity of mind, life, and actions, of human nature, in short, which is to say society, and thus placed the multitude of men among the major enemies of mankind.] (*Zib.* 112)[14]

Christ is for Leopardi the first visionary of modernity, the one who, from the very same new modern perspective that would also be his own, sacrifices himself to promote an alternative of clarity and naturalness of vision to the dominating destructive values of his era. His path, despite the responsibilities of Christianity for having originated the very extinction of the ancient world, somehow also displays the characteristics of an ultra-philosophy. Contrary to the ancient world where naturalness was the spontaneous way of being and living, in Christian thought the Fall impedes access to man's original nature, and a state of naturalness can only be conceived of as man's return to nature by miraculous means: 'da questo stato di corruzione, l'esperienza prova che l'uomo non può tornare indietro senza un miracolo' ('experience shows that from this state of corruption man cannot turn back without a miracle') (*Zib.* 403). The fact that Leopardi already by 1819 has freed himself from a true adherence to Christian dogma does not stop his aesthetic ideals from continuing to benefit from a religious conceptual framework. This is made possible by the fact that Leopardi's focus on graceful regeneration seems to be mostly internal to his reflection on language rather than on more speculative aspects of ethical and ontological philosophy. Already Pascal had identified the strengths of Christ's revolution in a combination of clarity and 'sincerity' in his language, which means adherence to things as they really are in nature, that is, naturalness: 'JESUS-CHRIST parle des plus grandes choses si simplement, qu'il semble qu'il n'y a pas pensé, & si nettement neanmois, qu'on voit bien ce qu'il en pensoit. Cette clarté jointe à cette naïveté est admirable' ('Jesus Christ speaks of the most sublime subjects with such simplicity, that he seems not to have thought on them; and yet with such accuracy, that what he thought is distinctly brought out. This union of artlessness with perspicuity, is admirable').[15] Pascal's Christ is the antithesis of affectation, as he is so close and so in harmony with the nature he describes that simple words inform an image that immediately strikes the listener. The result of Jesus's naturalness of language is marvel, similar to the desirable effect theorized since the Renaissance with respect to aesthetic grace. Associating a resurrecting power with Christ's words is the means by which the essence of holy Grace can be borrowed almost imperceptibly by Leopardi as a form of thinking for aesthetic ideals, without necessarily having to face in his borrowing and overlapping of forms the theological assumptions regarding Christ's divine nature as the Son of God. The naturalness of Christ's language actually allows Leopardi to bypass the problem of (dis-)belief. This is also the operation envisioned by Leopardi in his references to the revivifying power of poetry. We can identify in Leopardi a net polarity between cognition and overly descriptive attitude on the one hand, and the natural, simple, and naive style of 'una bella negligenza' ('a beautiful negligence') (*Zib.* 21) on the other, mirroring the attitude of the ultra-philosophical poet who lets the word manifest itself without declarative interferences which reveal the poetic objectives.

We are moving here at a level of formalization and metaphorization where the Christian model and its key concepts (transformation, resurrection, and Grace) are emptied of their direct meaning and religious authority to inform a point of view on nature and literature. These two, on the other hand, offer themselves as signifiers and condensers of a cultural surplus (religion), which continues to reform itself in mutated shapes. The following reflection on French language, for example, reveals how, hidden beneath what would at first sight appear a purely linguistic concern, there lie crucial concepts evoking sin and salvation:

> La lingua francese non fa una difficoltà al mondo di *spogliare* la lingua greca secondo i suoi bisogni e in questi ultimi tempi se n'è *empiuta e satollata* straboccchevolmente, onde già fanno dizionari delle parole francesi derivate dal gr. cosa per altro scellerata che *guasta* quella lingua orrendamente [...], riducendola in certo modo ad angoli e perchè non c'è cosa più nemica della natura che l'arida geometria, *le toglie tutta la naturalezza e la naïveté*, e la popolarità (onde nasce la bellezza) e la *grazia* e la venustà, e proprietà.
>
> [The French language does not have the slightest difficulty about *robbing* the Greek language according to its needs, and in recent times *has stuffed and sated itself* to excess. There already exist dictionaries of French words taken from Greek, a criminal act, moreover, that *damages* that language horrendously [...],

and reduces it in a certain sense to angles. And, because there is nothing more unfriendly to nature than dry geometry, *it takes away all the naturalness and naïveté of language*, its popularity (from which its beauty comes) and its *grace* and comeliness, and propriety.] (*Zib.* 48; my emphasis, apart from *naïveté*)

This reflection once again proposes motifs of the narrative of original sin. Through an act of 'nourishment' and 'denudation', French (the modern language par excellence) causes the loss of the primordial state of the Greek language, and leads it to a corrupted condition. Indeed, it '[si è] empiuta and satollata' of Greek scientific words, thus making it 'guasta' and depriving it of naturalness, naivety, and grace. At the other end of the spectrum is Leopardi's appreciation of Dante, for whose 'resurrecting' style he would use a similarly praising tone to that employed by Pascal in relation to Jesus: 'con due parole desta un'immagine [...] lascia molto a fare alla fantasia, ma dico a fare non già a faticare' ('conjures up an image with two words [...] leaves plenty for the imagination to do, and I say do rather than struggle') (*Zib.* 57). The natural Christological ease of Dante's style has nothing to do with affectation and effort, with toil being the identifying connotation of the sinful Adamic state.

Movement, marvel, and participation are therefore the stylistic graceful treats which Leopardi appreciates the most, and which his *Zibaldone* writing constantly produces as outbursts of poetic salvation. If we consider for instance the sequence of prose and poetry in the following passage we are faced with a sudden emergence of the poetic image evoked by the reflection in prose:

> L'utile non è il fine della poesia benchè questa possa giovare. E può anche il poeta mirare espressamente all'utile o ottenerlo (come forse avrà fatto Omero) senza che però l'utile sia il fine della poesia, come può l'agricoltore servirsi della scure a segar biade o altro senza che il segare sia il fine della scure. La poesia può esser utile indirettamente, come la scure può segare, ma l'utile non è il suo fine naturale, senza il quale essa non possa stare, come non può senza il dilettevole, imperocchè il dilettare è l'ufficio naturale della poesia.
> Sentia del canto risuonar le valli
> D'agricoltori ec.
>
> [Usefulness is not the purpose of poetry although poetry can be useful. And the poet can be or deliberately intend to be useful (as Homer may perhaps have done) without usefulness being the purpose of his poetry, in the same way as a farmer can use an axe to scythe crops or for some other purpose without scything being the purpose of an axe. Poetry can be indirectly useful, in the same way as an axe can scythe, but usefulness is not the natural purpose without which it could not exist, in the way that it could not exist without delight, for to give delight is the natural office of poetry.
> I heard the valleys ring
> With farmers' song, etc.] (*Zib.* 3)

The two lines of poetry are of course evoked by the theme discussed in the prose passage, but between the two parts there is a creative leap which is impossible to express and reduce to discourse. The leap takes place between the vigilant consciousness of the prose and the dream-like nature of the verse, which enacts the pastoral theme of the prose clearly evoked by the word 'scure'.

There is a limit beyond which even the most controlling and self-reflexive attitude cannot penetrate to explain how the creative mind works in the moment in which one discursive state of mind transforms into a poetic image, and Leopardi's consistent interest in the *punto* [point] in his work — 'punto di morte' ('the point of death') (*Zib.* 2183), or the point of falling asleep (*Zib.* 290) — shows his interest in leaps of consciousness.[16]

Thus the confession of obscurity reveals itself as an important means of 'redemption' from the fear of error and sin, precisely as it legitimizes the kind of poetic praxis exemplified in the passage cited above (p. 3), in which the word is almost left to roam freely to create meaning and images. At the same time, the eruption of the image functions as a path of creative liberation and salvation of the idea. Confirmation of this interpretation can be found in the following reflections:

> Il secol d'oro di una lingua o di qualunque altra disciplina, non è quello che la prepara, ma quello che *l'adopra*, [...] e *la forma*; [...] il cinquecento formò e determinò la lingua italiana in maniera ch'ella *guadagnando nella coltura e nell'ordine, non perdè nulla affatto nella naturalezza* [...], (quanta è compatibile colla chiarezza [...]).

> [The golden age of a language or of any other discipline is not, in fact, the age that prepares it but the one that *uses it*, [...] and *shapes it*; [...] the sixteenth century shaped and fixed the Italian language in such a way that, *as it gained refinement and order, it lost nothing at all in naturalness* [...], (or as much as is compatible with clarity [...]).] (*Zib.* 707–08; my emphasis)

> E si vede in fatti, chi conosce un tantino la storia de' regni, come *i massimi avvenimenti sieno spesso derivati da piccolissimi affettucci* di quel re, di quel ministro ec. *da menome circostanze, da una passioncella, da una parola, da una ricordanza, da un'assuefazione individuale*, da un carattere particolare, da inclinazioni; da qualità, accidenti della vita, amicizie o nimicizie ec. contratte dal principe o dal ministro ec. *nello stato privato*.

> [And anyone who knows the slightest thing about the history of kingdoms will in fact observe that *the most major events often stem from the most fleeting and unconsidered impulses* of some king or minister, etc., *from trifling circumstances, from a whim, a stray word, a recollection, an individual habit*, from a particular personality, from inclinations, from attributes, accidents in the course of a life, friendships forged or animosities incurred, etc., by a prince or minister, etc., *in his private capacity*.] (*Zib.* 709–10; my emphasis)

If we look closely at these reflections we realize that Leopardi is here in fact subtly thinking of the two possible aspects of clarity and naturalness: the first is the kind of exposition which presents itself as aimed towards an ordinated, controlled, and perhaps linear discourse, which is structured in order to be understood in the easiest possible way. But the second part of the text shows a different kind of creative potential where it is the minor, unordinary, accidental natural event or isolated sign ('affettucci', 'una parola'), that *happen* 'nello stato privato', much like in the *Zibaldone*, and cause the most impressive revolution and ingenious invention. Indeed, it is also important to stress Leopardi's fully modern envisioning of the potential of chance when he writes: 'quante scoperte delle più sostanziali, e *dell'uso il più quotidiano* [...] non le debba l'uomo se non al puro e semplice caso' ('how many of the most important discoveries of this kind, and most often *in everyday use* [...], man owes to pure and simple chance') (*Zib.* 835; my emphasis).

The reflexive confession, which allows one to admit that an idea is not clear or perfectly defined in the mind, serves somehow to legitimize the advent of the unexpected and preludes the liberation of poetic grace. Furthermore, as human history has shown, details and apparently isolated events can reveal the most powerful significance at a later stage, when the circumstances of further reading and writing activate a constellation of meaning which was not fully visible at first. As Esposito observes, the idea of grace in the Roman and Christian juridical system is the salvific overturning of a practice of excess which in its theological and political foundations has since the beginning been based on a disproportion between sin, or crime, and punishment. The latter, he states, is closely linked to a:

> Figura dell'eccesso che, nel rituale della messa a morte pubblica, conduce la pena ben al di là del suo necessario ruolo emendativo rispetto al condannato e dissuasivo nei confronti di chiunque volesse seguirne l'esempio. [...] È solo questa — l'eccedenza di senso che si scarica pubblicamente sul corpo del colpevole — a restaurare, con una misura infinitamente maggiore dell'offesa ricevuta, la sovranità ferita nella sua sacertà dal delitto.

> [Figure of excess that, in the public ritual of execution, leads the punishment well beyond its necessary role of correcting the offender and acting as a deterrent to anyone wanting to follow his example. [...] Only this — the surplus of meaning that is publicly discharged on the body of the offender — can restore, to an infinitely greater degree than the offense received, the sovereignty whose sanctity has been wounded by the crime.][17]

In Dante there is a powerful, archetypal literary paradigm of this unbalanced retribution in the *contrapasso*, a system in which the punishment only apparently fits the crime. In fact, argues Esposito, Dante seems more than once to depict an ordeal of prolonged life in death, so that the sinner can be exposed to an overdose, so to speak, of perennial sorrow, 'come se la rappresentazione della pena inseguisse un punto di fuga invisibile' ('as if the representation of the punishment chased after a vanishing point that remains invisible').[18] However, in Dante and in his juridical system of reference, there is an even more potent demonstration of divine supremacy in the concession of grace, which acts on the very same law imposed by the sovereign (be it the king or God) as a decision to reverse judgement and contravene his own very verdict. Grace brings about a state of exception:

> Tale potere, ridando la vita a chi l'aveva persa, in un certo senso è, per il sovrano, una prerogativa ancora più divina del diritto di uccidere, perché esprime la potenza decisionale di disattivare la propria decisione, instaurando uno stato di eccezione rispetto allo stesso sistema di norme da lui imposto.

> [This power of restoring life to those who had lost it is in a certain sense an even more divine prerogative for the sovereign than the right to kill: because it expresses a ruler's power of decision to block his or her own decision, establishing a state of exception to the same system of rules he or she had imposed.][19]

This exercise of power, which is at the root of Western political and religious systems, is also at the root of Leopardi's conception of ultra-philosophy. This is a supreme state of intellectual power which constantly contravenes and annuls its own philosophical presuppositions based on truth, thus to revert to a state of illusion. In the same way, Leopardi's textual practice, which is inescapably exposed to an excess of sense (as Leopardi's use of et cetera makes manifest), employs naturalness as a means to escape the rules and laws of speculative writing and gain salvation from poetic singularities.

 The profound religious and aesthetic dimension, in which clarity is both a rigorous philosophical approach and at the same time the channel through which Leopardi's inner impulses towards confession can be vented, and where naturality paves the way towards a stylistic strategy that appeals to the reader while at the same time recreating and revivifying the naturalized spirituality of the writer, sheds light on the value of the *Zibaldone* as a daily practice. These senses provide the vital link — in the form of imaginative pleasure, surprise at unexpected creation, and satisfaction in renewal and rediscovery of past thinking — for the extended continuation of the notebook. If the messianic presents itself theologically as the 'time of the end', as the time that time takes to approach the end, the *Zibaldone*, in its daily progressive advancement, its continuously changing shape and unfinished state, is also a measure of the time that passes, and of the time 'that remains' to a notebook which is not a proper work of art, which would not be able to become so, and which could be terminated at any time. This passing of time does not project expectations into the realm of the eternal, but rather into the ephemeral praxis of everyday life. Writing is the spark that keeps Leopardi's imagination alive as, in his 'Dialogo di Torquato Tasso e del suo genio familiare' [Dialogue of Torquato Tasso and His Guardian Spirit], Tasso's recollection of Leonora conveys a 'brivido di gioia' ('shudder of joy'), full of graceful irritation, which 'dalla cima del capo mi si stende fino all'ultima punta de' piedi; e non resta in me nervo né vena che non sia scossa' (*TPP*, p. 529) ('from the crown of my head to the very tips of my toes; and there is not a nerve or a vein in my body that is not shaken by it', *MT*, p. 92). The same character is astonished that:

> Il pensiero di una donna abbia tanta forza, da rinnovarmi, per così dire, l'anima, e farmi dimenticare tante calamità. E se non fosse che io non ho più speranza di rivederla, crederei non avere ancora perduta la facoltà di essere felice. (*TPP*, p. 529)
>
> [The thought of a woman has such power as to restore my soul, as it were, and make me forget so many calamities. And if it were not for the fact that I have no more hope of seeing her again, I would think I had not yet lost the ability to be happy.] (*MT*, p. 92)

The hope of a final re-encounter with supreme beatitude has gone, but the beneficent recreation of the soul through constant revocation or forgetting of truth is still achievable. The precious source which makes this experience renewable for Leopardi is the writing of the *Zibaldone*.

Notes to Chapter 9

1. Gianfranco Ghirlanda, *Il diritto nella chiesa, mistero di comunione: compendio di diritto ecclesiale* (Rome: G & B Press, 2014), p. 27.
2. Thomas Aquinas, *Summa theologiae*, ed. by Liam G. Walsh, 61 vols (Cambridge: Cambridge University Press, 2006), XLIX, 5 (3a 7–15).
3. Cf. *Zib.* 198–203. For a reflection on grace as the *je ne sais quoi* see Camilletti, *Leopardi's Nymphs*, pp. 19–31.
4. Cf. Martino Rossi Monti, *Il cielo in terra: la grazia fra teologia ed estetica* (Turin: UTET, 2008), p. xiii.
5. Giambattista Vico, *The Art of Rhetoric (Institutiones oratoriae 1711–1741)*, ed. by Giorgio A. Pinton and Arthur W. Shippee (Amsterdam: Rodopi, 1996), p. 3.
6. Giambattista Vico, *Institutiones oratoriae*, ed. by Giuliano Crifò (Naples: Istituto Suor Orsola Benincasa, 1989), p. 5.
7. Giambattista Vico, *La scienza nuova 1744*, Laboratorio dell'ISPF, XII, 2015, digital ed. by Centro di Umanistica Digitale dell'ISPF-CNR and based on the critical ed. by Paolo Cristofolini and Manuela Sanna (Rome: Edizioni di Storia e Letteratura, 2013), p. 115; *The New Science*, trans. by Thomas Goddard Bergin and Max Harold Fisch (Ithaca, NY, & London: Cornell University Press, 1970), p. 88.
8. Cf. Francesco Botturi, 'Ingegno verità storia: filosofia dell'immaginaio vichiano', in *Simbolo e conoscenza*, ed. by Virgilio Melchiorre (Milan: Vita e pensiero, 1988), pp. 127–68 (p. 130).
9. Clayton Koelb, *The Revivifying Word: Literature, Philosophy, and the Theory of Life in Europe's Romantic Age* (Rochester, NY: Camden House, 2008), p. xi.
10. Ibid. p. 6.
11. Ibid.
12. Ibid., pp. 16–20.
13. See for instance *Zib.* 394–439, 446–51, 1773.
14. See also *Zib.* 611.
15. Pascal, *Pensées*, p. 75; *Thoughts*, p. 258.
16. See Antonella Del Gatto, *'Quel punto acerbo': temporalità e conoscenza metaforica in Leopardi* (Florence: Olschki, 2012).
17. Esposito, *Pensiero vivente*, p. 140; *Living Thought*, p. 147.
18. Ibid., p. 142; p. 149.
19. Ibid., p. 143; p. 150.

PART II

Physical Sciences

CHAPTER 10

Towards a Philosophy of Life and Technique

Leopardi operated in a time of multi-disciplinarity which valued dialogue between different areas of scientific inquiry as well as humanistic and scientific interchange. The absence of clearly structured specializations made it perfectly natural to seek relationships and assess the recurrence of common conceptual patterns between different fields, and the lack of a fully formed scientific language still entitled thinkers to pronounce judgements on natural science or physics through a more general philosophical lexicon. Certainly Leopardi was not a scientist in the most rigorous meaning of the word, in the sense that he did not make use or produce systematic theorization of scientific instrumentation, nor worked towards a formal language capable of the transmission and logical applicability of general scientific laws.[1] Nevertheless he received a broad scientific education especially (but not exclusively) through Jesuit formation, and his interest in science emerged in his early years, with the *Dissertazioni fisiche* [Dissertations on the Physical Sciences] (1811) and the *Storia dell'astronomia* [History of Astronomy] (1815) being clear examples of his early erudite scientific culture and passionate engagement with Enlightenment sources.[2] Scientific sensibility continued to accompany his philosophical reflection and poetic activity throughout his work. Speculations on Copernican and Newtonian physics not only serve as themes for many of his *Zibaldone* entries and creative work — in particular, the moral tale 'Il Copernico' [Copernicus] — but they also act as terms of comparison and representation for non-scientific concepts that Leopardi depicts through recourse to mechanical, astronomical, or biological images. The ideas of void, gravitation, and the lifespan of animals, for instance, are constant sources of poetic inspiration in the *Zibaldone*. However, what is most important to note is the role that certain scientific impulses play in shaping notebook-writing. Similarly to what has been already noted for certain religious and mathematical categories, science too becomes a generative matrix for forms of thinking, in that it provides models for functions and relations between different parts of the discourse, thus structuring the very appearance of writing. Furthermore, certain concepts are polyvalent and while being operative as religious and stylistic forms — grace is an example par excellence — they also assume scientific forms (for example tension is analogous to grace in its prolonged effect on the transmission of power, as we shall see in Chapter 13). This activates resonances of meaning which break through different conceptual boundaries, resulting in ideas which are creatively unstable, fleeting, and evocative, even when reflections with no immediate poetic aims are concerned.

Leopardi's view of the physical world is typically Galilean, in that he conceives of motion and often illusory knowledge deriving from immediate sensation as the common principles of both the microscopic and macroscopic universes. Newton had demonstrated that even objects which look immobile on the surface of the earth are in fact part of a more general and invisible motion, which results from the influence of the planets on each other. Gravitational force simplified the idea of an ineluctable power precipitating objects not because their self-produced actions are directly responsible for their motion, but because of conditions intrinsic to the perennial, invisible, and universal system in which they are situated and which influences them from a distance. It is not by chance that a very suggestive image of gravitational fall is explicitly linked to Adam in Leopardi's notes drafted in preparation for his poem 'Inno ai patriarchi' [Hymn to the Patriarchs] (1821):

> Ad Adamo. Tu primo contempli la purpurea luce del sole, e la volta dei cieli, e le bellezze di questa terra. Descrizione dello stato di solitudine in cui si trovava allora il mondo non abitato [...] dagli uomini [...]. [L]e frutta pendevano senza che la loro vista allettasse alcuno a cibarsene, e immagine della futura nostra caducità, si rotolavano già mature appiè dell'albero che le aveva prodotte. (*TPP*, p. 470)
>
> [To Adam. You are the first to contemplate the purple light of the sun, and the vault of the heavens, and the beauties of this earth. Description of the state of solitude in which the world found itself, not populated [...] by human beings [...]. Fruits were hanging without the sight of them appealing to anyone to eat them, and — image of our future caducity — ripening, dropping, and rolling at the bottom of the tree that had produced them.]

The laws of physics reiterate the same pattern that religion prescribes to human kind, reproducing the sense of an unavoidable exposure to invisible forces outside our control. In the same way as, according to the Scriptures, any human being coming to life carries an unavoidable bond with the first sinner, so any component of the physical world is subject to the same laws of attraction as those of the primordial powers which generated and maintain the life of stars and planets. The causes and reasons of gravitational force operating in the material world alluded to in the passage quoted above, however, seem even more remote and inexplicable than Adam's impulse to sin, given that the latter was at least tempted through his own gaze and by the intervention of the serpent to eat the apple, while in the vast physical world in which Adam roamed as the only creature, and which extended beyond the reach of his sight, fruit fell from the tree 'senza che la loro vista allettasse alcuno'. It is important to underline that in the way that the two different ideas of 'falling' are described, the law of gravitation is integrally applied, subtly linking the symbolic with the real, the religious with the physical. Adam will 'fall' symbolically in a near future subsequent to his Edenic condition narrated in this passage, but if, through this very image, a gravitational force is evoked and activated, then the rest of the existing objects in that system of reference must also respond to the same influence. Hence the fruit from the tree will also fall, albeit physically — an allusion to a general sense of exposure to a principle of 'precipitation' abridging subliminally the two universes of senses, the world of the spirit and the world of matter, under one comprehensive universe of signification.

This powerful force, whose origins are inexplicable, has a notable impact on Leopardi's imagery, leading him to embrace an idea of science which is primarily descriptive, led by the aim of comprehending the relationships between elements of the physical world but renouncing any hope of grasping the ultimate causes. As we shall see, at the same time as re-evaluating the importance of knowledge as an extension of the sensible, Leopardi also seems to be inclined towards a philosophical posture which would be fully embraced only later in Western philosophy. He discovers the uncanny vicinity between subject and object of observation, the merging of the two statuses which Cartesian and Lockean philosophy had once kept apart. On a theoretical level, principles of perspective and Newtonian optics continue to be operative in his thought, and we have already analyzed the productive implications of forms deriving from projective geometry. At the same time, however, these more consolidated philosophical conceptions co-exist alongside still untheorized (or, to Leopardi, theoretically unknown) but effectively operative models of visuality, anticipating a drive towards externality which manifests itself first in electric and magnetic imagery, and which later was to be fully explored by retinal optics, stereoscopic imagery, and telegraphic technology.

The laws of thermodynamics revealed in the course of the nineteenth century how the physical world is regulated by processes of energy conservation and conversion into different forms, but also the tendency of dynamics of effort expenditure to conserve energy in dissipated forms. Although Leopardi could not have known the idea of entropy, an awareness of dissipation can be detected both in certain speculations and in his praxis of writing, or more precisely in the frequent re-employment of certain images. If we consider the following reflection on the history of language there is a clear preservative pattern shaping the idea of the divergence of idioms. Leopardi believes that as long as a language is actively immersed in the dynamics of production and change, its truest essence is preserved:

> Tutto può degenerare e degenera, fuorchè le parole e le lingue astrattamente considerate. [...] E ciò che s'intende per corruzione di esse non è altro che *allontanamento dal loro stato e forma primitiva*, o da quello che presero quando furono stabilite e formate. *Altrimenti le lingue e le voci non si corromperebbero mai.*

> [Everything can and does degenerate, aside from words and languages abstractly considered. [...]. And what we mean by corruption in languages is simply *a divergence from their primordial state and form*, or from the one they assumed when they were established and formed. *There is no other sense in which languages and words can ever be said to be corrupted.*] (*Zib.* 1936–37; my emphasis)

This reflection could be represented with reference to conservative systems of forces in classical physics, such as for instance the gravitational force in an ideal isolated environment, which transforms the potential energy of a certain falling body into kinetic energy, and even though the two forms of energy are different, the total amount of energy is preserved. But there is also the sense that certain mutations are irreversible and while they are essential determinants of the time arrow of a certain linguistic evolution, there is a progressive disappearance of pathos associated with words. Language is destined to be altered in such a way which makes it difficult to retrieve its original features; the power of words continues to persist, but only abstractly speaking — that is, in an intangible and unused way, as in the status of entropy. In Leopardi's philosophy of language this means that eventually words exhaust, so to speak, their emotional font, and the cultural history to which they allude progressively fades and becomes flattened in the uniformity of present usages.

As far as Leopardi's praxis of writing is concerned, we will look at the way in which Leopardi's mnemotechnic of images generates equivalences — and therefore uniformity — between concepts apparently unrelated while true cyclical recurrence is in fact precluded from human thought, condemned to irreversibility. Leopardi's daily annotations not only produce singularities of expression, unique images, and isolated outcomes strictly linked to the specificities of the textual environment, but they also reveal a certain power of self-generation by the image. A diffusion of images in the notebook results from a kind of automatism in writing, which assimilates Leopardi's creative praxis to the reproductive power of technique and modern simulacra. Clarity assumes here a further significance, being not only the controlled examination exercised by the self-aware subject, but also the incendiary vividness obtained through excessive proximity to the real. Images and 'originals' from the world of matter seem at time to overlap, and while the process of vivification of the image allows Leopardi to realize fully his poetic aims, at the same time there are dangers of chaos and loss of identity to be guarded against.

In the rest of this second part, I aim to explore how the *Zibaldone* becomes the materialization of Leopardi's approach to the physical world, by investigating the way in which concepts of motion, cohesion, and exposure are transferred from the realm of external observation to the complicated fabric of the text, either expressed through demonstrative writing or in the form of images. The first step will be to analyze the way writing in motion takes possession of an augmented and extended horizon of knowledge.

Notes to Chapter 10

1. Cf. Flavio Vetrano, 'Giacomo e la scienza: suggestioni dell'infinito, riflessioni sull'eternità', in *Giacomo Leopardi e il pensiero scientifico*, ed. by Giorgio Stabile (Rome: Fahrenheit 451, 2001), pp. 169–75 (pp. 169–70).
2. Leopardi's early scientific instruction in Recanati was mainly based on the manuals by Jean-Antoine Nollet and Jacques Mathurin Brisson, as well as on later collections of scientific materials by various authors of ecclesiastic provenance, such as Lorenzo Altieri and Francisque Jacquier, the Jesuits Aimé-Henri Paulian and Stefano Pace, and the laymen Saverio Poli and Francesco Dandolo. See Paolo Casini, 'L'iniziazione di Leopardi: filosofia dei lumi e scienza newtoniana', in *Giacomo Leopardi e il pensiero scientifico*, ed. by Stabile, pp. 59–77.

CHAPTER 11

The Heading 'Vitalità, Sensibilità' (I): Leopardi's Elastic Writing

The 'Index' heading 'Vitalità, Sensibilità: il grado dell'amor proprio e dell'infelicità del vivente, è in proporzione di esse' [Vitality, Sensibility: The Living Being's Degree of Self-love and Unhappiness is in Proportion to These], comprising a list of nineteen entries between pp. 1382,2 (24 July 1821) and 4133,2 (9 April 1825), appears to be a useful lens through which to explore the nature and directions of the movements of Leopardi's thought. This heading represents a prime example of demonstrative prose and offers complex philosophical reasoning using a range of syntactical structures. Because my interest concerns specifically the relationship between content and forms of expression, 'Vitalità, Sensibilità' allows me to explore in detail how certain ideas are produced and retrieved often in a tight sequence of connected sentences. In some cases, in order to highlight specific developments in the discourse, I will also consider reflections which are generated in the page- and paragraph-entries listed by Leopardi, but which extend further in subsequent paragraphs not mentioned in this specific 'Index' heading. I will also make reference to the intra-textual cross-references linked to the notes of the entry in question, in order to underline the expanding structure of Leopardi's thought. The chart shown below attempts to provide only a basic and partial illustration of the articulation and complexity of the motion of Leopardi's thought. My aim here is to show how the linearity of the notes included in the 'Index' entry only represents the tip of the iceberg of a complex set of relations hidden beneath the surface of the selected 'Index' reflections.

In attempting to model the development of Leopardi's thought through the lens of this specific theme, I aim to demonstrate the influence of a certain scientific interest transferring itself from the physical world to Leopardi's revising strategies. The first reflection of the heading 'Vitalità, Sensibilità' (24 July 1821) presents itself as an addition to what was already exposed by Leopardi in his 'theory of pleasure', and indeed this entry is also part of the 'Index' heading 'Piacere (Teoria del)' ('Pleasure (Theory of)'). Here Leopardi stresses the links between sensitivity and desire for pleasure, the unobtainability of the latter and the consequent necessary unhappiness of living creatures: 'quanto più gli organi del vivente sono [...] sensibili, [ovvero] quanto è maggiore la vita naturale del vivente, tanto più sensibile e vivo è l'amor proprio [...] e quindi il desiderio della felicità ch'è impossibile, e quindi

The Heading 'Vitalità, Sensibilità' (I)

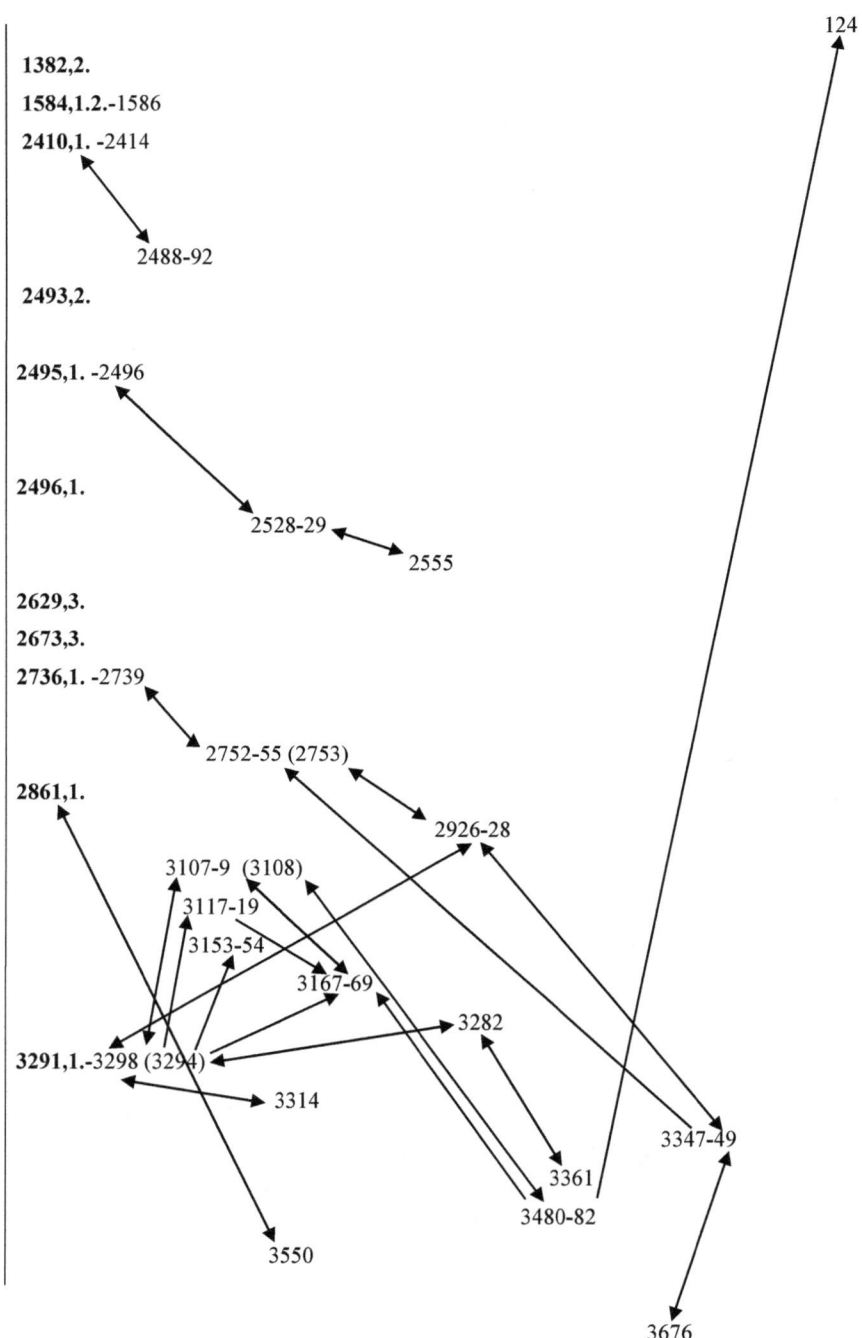

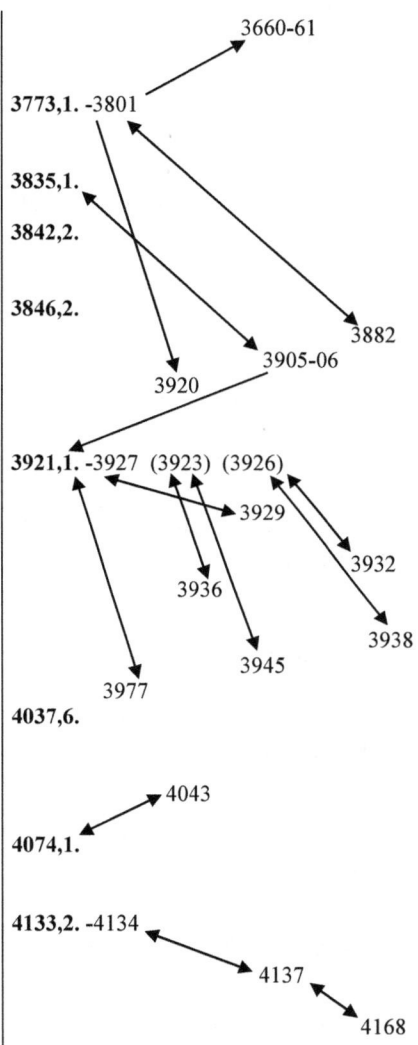

Above and left: Chart of the 1827 'Index' heading 'Vitalità, Sensibilità: il grado dell'amor proprio e dell'infelicità del vivente, è in proporzione di esse' and of the internal cross-references.[1]

l'infelicità' ('the more the organs of a creature are [...] sensitive [...] in short, the greater the natural life of a living being is, the more sensitive and keen is its self-love [...] and hence its desire for a happiness that is impossible, and hence its unhappiness') (*Zib.* 1382). This opening reflection functions as the basic structure of the heading 'Vitalità, Sensibilità' by introducing its key foundational concepts and their relationship. The second thought included in the heading (*Zib.* 1584, 29 August 1821), addresses the idea of the return of sensitivity as a form of melancholy. It examines the condition which Leopardi considers the most suitable to human happiness, that is, 'uno stato o di piena vita, o di piena morte' ('a state either of complete life or one of complete death'), either absolute exaltation and energy or full 'torpore' or 'noncuranza attuale o abituale' ('torpor or uncaringness, current or habitual'). From this consideration it derives that 'il giovane senz'attività [...] è nello stato precisamente il più infelice possibile' ('a young person without activity [...], is indeed in the unhappiest state possible') (*Zib.* 1586). Because self-love cannot be deactivated and it necessarily brings about desire, both in the young and the old, Leopardi concludes that the only state prescribed by nature which allows the highest degree of happiness is distraction.

In the following reflections listed in the initial section of the heading 'Vitalità, Sensibilità' (*Zib.* 2410,1, 2493,2, 2495,1, 2496,1, and 2629,3) the opening proposition is restated and reinvestigated through progressive inclusion of further details examining causes and effects as well as the range of application of the principles analyzed. It is interesting to note the modality through which Leopardi progresses in his speculation, that is, through preliminary repetition of the premises previously discussed, which are then subject to further expansion. Theoretical passages and links between the parts are reiterated in forms analogous to those already present in previous entries, until a new element of the speculation is introduced and is absorbed into the analysis to become itself part of what would constitute a premise to be retrieved and expanded. I believe it is useful to examine in detail the way his argument proceeds by comparing two reflections (*Zib.* 1382, the heading opener, and 2410–14) which, despite their length and complexity, I shall quote in full to detect correspondences. As for the second passage, I also include portions of the text subsequent to the paragraph listed in the 'Index' (*Zib.* 2410,1):

> Alla mia teoria del piacere aggiungi che quanto più gli organi del vivente sono suscettibili, sensibili, mobili, vivi, insomma quanto è maggiore la vita naturale del vivente, tanto più sensibile e vivo è l'amor proprio (ch'è quasi tutt'uno colla vita) [b1] e quindi il desiderio della felicità ch'è impossibile, e quindi l'infelicità [a1]. Così accade dunque agli uomini rispetto alle bestie, così a queste pure gradatamente, così agl'individui umani ec. più sensibili, imaginosi ec. rispetto agli altri individui della stessa specie. [c1] E l'uomo anche in natura, è quindi ben conseguentemente, il più infelice degli animali (come vediamo), perciò stesso che ha più vita, più forza e sentimento vitale che gli altri viventi. [d1]

> [To my theory of pleasure add that the more the organs of a creature are receptive, sensitive, mobile, keen, in short, the greater the natural life of a living being is, the more sensitive and keen is its self-love (which is almost identical

to life) [b1] and hence its desire for a happiness that is impossible, and hence its unhappiness [a1]. As it is with beasts so too it is with men, so too it is with the former to varying degrees, so too with the more sensitive, imaginative, etc., human individuals, etc., as compared to other individuals of the same species. [c1] And man also in nature is therefore very logically the unhappiest of the animals (as we see), through the very fact of his having more life, more strength and feeling of life than other living beings. [d1]] (*Zib.* 1382)

Dalla mia teoria del piacere segue che per essenza naturale e immutabile delle cose, quanto è maggiore e più viva la forza, il sentimento, e l'azione e attività interna dell'amor proprio, tanto è necessariamente maggiore l'infelicità del vivente, o tanto più difficile il conseguimento d'una tal quale felicità. [a2] Ora la forza e il sentimento dell'amor proprio è tanto maggiore quanto è maggiore la vita, o il sentimento vitale in ciascun essere; e specialmente quanto è maggiore la vita interna, ossia l'attività dell'anima, cioè della sostanza sensitiva, e concettiva. Giacchè amor proprio e vita son quasi una cosa, non potendosi nè scompagnare il sentimento dell'esistenza propria (ch'è ciò che s'intende per vita) dall'amore dell'esistente, nè questo esser minore di quello, ma l'uno si può sempre esattamente misurare coll'altro. E tanto uno vive, quanto si ama, e tutti i sentimenti di chi vive sono compresi o riferiti o prodotti ec. dall'amor proprio: il quale è il sentimento universale che abbraccia tutta l'esistenza; e gli altri sentimenti del vivente (se pur ve n'ha che sieno veramente altri) non sono che modificazioni, o divisioni, o produzioni di questo, ch'è tutt'uno col sentimento dell'essere, o una parte essenziale del medesimo. [b2]

Dal che segue che l'uomo avendo per la sua natura ed organizzazione esteriore ed interiore maggior vita, maggior capacità di più vasta e più numerosa concezione, maggior sentimento insomma, o maggior sensibilità di tutti gli altri viventi, dee necessariamente avere maggiore intensità, attività, ed estensione o quantità o sentimento d'amor proprio, che non ne ha verun altro genere di viventi. Quindi l'uomo per essenza propria e inseparabile, è, e nasce più infelice, o meno capace di felicità che verun altro genere di viventi, o di esseri. [c2]

Questo si deve intendere dell'uomo naturale. Ma siccome questa capacità ed intensità e forza ed attività di sentimento della quale egli è naturalmente provveduto sopra ogni altro animale, rende il suo spirito più conformabile, più suscettibile di sempre maggior sentimento, più raffinabile, vale a dire più capace di sempre più vivamente e più variamente sentire; anzi siccome essa capacità non è altro che conformabilità, e suscettività di nuovo sentimento, e di nuove modificazioni dell'animo; così l'uomo, perfezionandosi, come dicono, cioè crescendo la forza e la varietà e l'intimità del suo sentimento, e perciò prevalendo in lui sempre più lo spirito, cioè la parte sensitiva, al corpo, cioè alla parte torpida e grave; acquista egli e viene di secolo in secolo necessariamente accrescendo la forza e il sentimento dell'amor proprio, e quindi di secolo in secolo divien più, e più inevitabilmente infelice. [d2] Dal che segue che...

[From my theory of pleasure it follows that, as a result of the natural and unchangeable essence of things, the greater and more lively the power, feeling, and action and internal activity of self-love, the greater necessarily is the unhappiness of the living creature, or the more difficult it is to achieve any sort of happiness. [a2] Now, the stronger life is, or the life feeling in each being, and especially the stronger the inner life is, or the activity of the mind, that is, the sensory and conceptualizing substance, the stronger the force and feeling of self-love. For self-love and life are almost one thing, the feeling of one's own existence (which is what is meant by life) being inseparable from love of the one who exists, nor can the latter be less than the former, but each can always be exactly measured by the other. And as one lives, so one loves oneself, and all the feelings of one who lives are included in or ascribed to or produced, etc., by self-love, the universal feeling that embraces all existence. And the other feelings of the living being (if there are any that are truly other) are only modifications, or divisions, or products of this, which is the same as the feeling of being, or an essential part of the self. [b2]

From this it follows that man, having by his nature, and by his outer and inner organization, greater life, greater capacity for vaster and more numerous concepts, in short, greater feeling or greater sensibility than all other living beings, must necessarily have a greater intensity, activity, and extent or quantity or feeling of self-love than any other type of living being. Hence man by his own inseparable essence is, and is born, more unhappy, or less capable of happiness, than any other type of living creature or being. [c2]

This must be understood as referring to natural man. But since the capacity and intensity and force and activity of feeling with which he, more than any other animal, is naturally provided makes his spirit more adaptable, more susceptible to increasingly deeper and more refined feelings, that is to say more capable of feeling with increasing intensity and variety, and, indeed, since that capacity is nothing but conformability and susceptibility to new feelings and to further modifications in the mind: so man, perfecting himself, so to speak, that is, increasing the strength and variety and depth of his feelings — and with, therefore, the spirit increasingly prevailing in him, that is, the sensitive part, over the body, that is, the sluggish and heavy part — acquires self-love and as from century to century its force and feeling necessarily increase, hence from century to century he becomes more, and more inevitably, unhappy. [d2] From which it follows that...] (*Zib.* 2410–14)

The first reflection develops four specific ideas which are retrieved and explored further in the second extract. The correspondences are as follows: first there is the theme of the direct proportion between unhappiness and inner sensitivity, strength, and activity, which the two speculations develop respectively from 'Alla mia teoria del piacere' to 'quindi l'infelicità' (a1), and 'Dalla mia teoria del piacere' to 'tal quale felicità' (a2). The second idea occupies only a short sentence in brackets in the first entry '(ch'è quasi tutt'uno colla vita)' (b1), while it is developed in depth in the second passage from 'Ora la forza e il sentimento dell'amor proprio è tanto maggiore quanto è maggiore la vita, o il sentimento vitale in ciascun essere' to 'parte essenziale del medesimo' (b2). The third focus is the comparison between human beings and other living creatures. In the first passage it occupies the space of one sentence from 'Così accade dunque' to 'stessa specie' (c1), while in the second quotation the same idea is expanded largely through use of asindetic coordinations, from 'Dal che segue' to 'o di esseri' (c2). The fourth point is on the natural state of man, which occupies the first extract from 'E l'uomo anche in natura' to 'gli altri viventi' (d1), and the second from 'Questo si deve intendere dell'uomo naturale' to 'inevitabilmente infelice' (d2). It is essential to note how, in this corresponding portion of the second text, Leopardi is not satisfied with stating the initial assumption about the innate unhappiness of human beings, but introduces the subcategory of conformability and perfectibility through which man progressively assumes more refined spiritual qualities, a higher level of sensitivity and therefore unhappiness. This newly emerged focus becomes predominant and absorbs all Leopardi's attention to project the speculation onto horizons which had been unseen in the first entry. The analytical scheme of the opening entry has served Leopardi as an orientating tool, as a line of inquiry which has been retrieved in order to find a sense of direction. But once the order of ideas has been recollected, the speculation independently expands. This practice of reannotating core points of a particular reflection has the aim of revising and memorizing thought. Leopardi uses writing as a tool to fix ideas in the mind through reiteration. This was a constituent practice of Jesuit instruction and the *Ratio studiorum* makes constant reference to revision (see Chapter 18). It is however also important to note how the traces of the traditional Jesuit methodology inherited from Leopardi's upbringing work in conjunction with other equally effective models deriving from his scientific interest and background of reference.

If we leave the heading 'Vitalità, Sensibilità' for a moment to consider the reflection on pp. 3197–3206, (where 3197,1 is part of the heading 'Assuefazione. Assuefattibilità e conformabilità dell'uomo. Attenzione. Imparare. Ingegno. Disposizioni naturali. Facoltà umane' ('Habit. Habit-forming Ability and Adaptability of Man. Attention, Attentiveness. Learning. Intelligence. Natural Dispositions. Human Faculties')), we notice the heavy use of Leopardi's previously noted method of retrieving and expanding his thought further, which extends to the entirety of his demonstrative writing. Here one encounters a similar practice of arranging all the theoretical achievements of the preceding entries of the heading 'Assuefazione' in a synthetic and clearly ordered way, with comparative references linking all possible parts of the already explained discourse:

> *Ho dimostrato* come l'uomo debba quasi tutto alle circostanze, all'assuefazione, all'esercizio; *quanta parte* di ciò che si chiama talento naturale, *e diversità o superiorità o inferiorità di talenti*, non sia per verità altro che assuefazione [...]. *Io però non intendo con ciò di negare che non v'abbiano diversità naturali fra i vari talenti* [...]; *ma solamente affermo e dimostro* che tali diversità [...] sono molto minori di quello che altri ordinariamente pensa. Del resto che gl'intelletti [...] differiscano naturalmente [...] è cosa, come da tutti e sempre creduta, così vera e reale, *e dimostrata da molte osservazioni, le quali, o alcune di esse, verrò qui sotto segnando per capi, sommariamente però, ed in modo che sopra ciascun capo potrà e dovrà molto più estendersi il discorso di quello che io sia per estenderlo.*
>
> [*I have sought to show* how man owes virtually everything to circumstance, habituation, and practice; *how much* of that which is referred to as natural talent, and *diversity* and superiority or inferiority of talent, is in fact no more than habituation [...]. By this, however, *I do not mean to deny that there is a natural difference between the various talents* [...]. *I merely affirm and demonstrate* that such [...] diversities are much more limited than other people ordinarily suppose. Mind you, no one has ever doubted [...] that the intellects [...] differ naturally [...], and [it] is *demonstrated by many observations which, or at least some of which, I shall identify hereunder by means of headings, in summary fashion, so that the subject may,*

indeed should, be developed more extensively under each heading than I do here.] (*Zib.* 3197–98; my emphasis)

Having revised points already explicit in the previous pages of the *Zibaldone*, in the second part of this extract Leopardi declares that he wants to list 'sommariamente' observations which have already been demonstrated by himself and by others, which will serve him as hints to expand his discourse further at a subsequent moment. We could represent this methodology of going back to previous findings in order to gather new intellectual energy through the metaphor of the release of a spring which has previously been compressed. The compression has allowed the device to collect its potential energy. Similarly, knowledge already acquired is used by Leopardi as potential for boosting his thought. Leopardi had shown particular attention to elastic force already since his early 'Dissertazione sopra i fluidi elastici' [Dissertation on the Elastic Fluids] in which he had investigated, through the help of seventeenth- and eighteenth-century sources from Descartes to Malebranche and Newton, the properties of elastic fluids, that is, those substances which 'si sforzano di ricuperare lo stato, in cui erano prima, che da una forza estranea venisser costretti ad abbandonarlo' [strive to regain the state in which they were before being forced to abandon it by an external influence].[2] In the *Zibaldone* Leopardi makes use of elastic imagery to depict moral and creative attitudes, such as for instance when he discusses human indifference as a spring which has lost its potential for expansion (cf. *Zib.* 959).

In post-Newtonian times, the spring was very often employed as an image for human feelings and behaviour and to represent the human capacity for moral and physical adaptability and flexibility. The lexicon of elasticity was borrowed by different disciplines. As Andrea Campana notes, in politics, especially under the influence of Montesquieu's *Esprit des lois*, expressions such as 'ressort du governement' [spring of government] spread to inform a material and physical view of political management.[3] At the same time, in the medical and physiological fields, scientists started to focus more and more on the 'elasticity' of fibres and organs, as for instance in the work of Friedrich Hoffmann and Georges Louis Leclerc de Buffon. The latter, in particular, represented a fundamental point of reference for Leopardi's own interest in natural history as well as the idea of flexibility and sensitivity of the fibres as a vehicle for knowledge. Furthermore, in his 'Discorso sull'indole del piacere e del dolore' [Discourse on the Nature of Pleasure and Pain], Pietro Verri draws a parallel between the initial compression, release, and extension of a spring and the effect of sorrow on our soul:

> Una molla di fino acciajo stassene immobile sin tanto che non venga compressa: il mistero della sensibilità vi ha molta rassomiglianza; l'uomo privo di sensazioni rimane parimenti immobile: comprimilo, addoloralo, ei si rannicchia in sè stesso, e si move. Se la compressione è passaggera e tenue, la molla ribalzando se ne libera, e nel primo slancio si dilata anche oltre il limite in cui prima trovavasi; così la sensibilità, se il dolore sia moderato e passaggero, al cessare di esso la gioja sembra che la dilati e la estenda anche quasi fuor di sè.[4]

> [A spring of thin steel remains immobile inasmuch as it is not compressed: the mystery of sensitivity much resembles this; man deprived of sensations remains

equally immobile: compress him, cause him suffering, and he withdraws into himself, he moves. If compression is short-lasting and slight, by rebounding the spring will release it, and in the first extension it expands even beyond the limits within which it previously was; thus is sensitivity: if pain is moderate and transient, when it ends joy seems to expand and extend it almost beyond itself.]

Similarly, in expressing the idea that pleasure can only result from the overcoming of sorrow, Kant refers to our vital force as a reaction to an antithetical impediment exercised within certain productive limits. He believes that our actions are driven by an inner impulse, spontaneous and not dependent on reflection, which constantly pushes us into activity after our inner spring has been compressed.[5] If not completely identical, Leopardi's view on the absence of pleasure in our existence and the idea that our condition can only oscillate between sorrow and boredom certainly shares much potential for dialogue with that of Kant.[6] What I am interested in underlining, aside from their specific philosophical views, is the presence of a scientific model able to provide metaphorical constellations for the physical and moral world, and, more specifically, an image of elasticity in which advancement results from a force that produces an initial receding motion. At a formal level, Leopardi's methods of expanding his argument seems to function in a similar way, by retrieving notions which project his writing backwards, onto the already expressed, while at the same time boosting his speculative potential through the addition of more details which elicit the release of energy towards the new. It is important to stress how memory itself generates a semantic field invested with elastic imagery. For instance, Leopardi compares the emergence of involuntary recollection to the motion of the 'spring of our memory' (cf. *Zib.* 184, 24 July 1820). It is also essential to remark how Verri's awareness of the importance of maintaining the compression of a spring within a certain limit, and more generally the principle of balance in the exercise of action, was also present in Leopardi's own theorization of the intellectual faculties intervening in the production of thought. When referring to the physiology of attention, for instance, Leopardi remarks how it is productive only when not pushed to an extreme. Attending to a certain object excessively, indeed, transforms attention into its opposite, that is, distraction.[7] At the opposite end of the spectrum, when an operation is performed repeatedly in a mechanical way, its effect on the mind becomes negligible and we lose sense of its constituent parts.[8] Leopardi describes processes of habit-memory with focuses analogous to those which will later inform Bergson's formulation in *Matter and Memory*, in which 'the memory of the lesson [...] like a habit, [...] is acquired by the repetition of the same effort', and this requires 'first a de-composition and then a re-composition of the whole action'.[9] But as far as the writing in motion of the *Zibaldone* is concerned, there is also in Leopardi the sense of a contribution offered by language to the production of thinking, 'perchè noi pensiamo parlando' ('for it is through language that we think') (*Zib.* 94–95). From this perspective, the practice of 'elastic writing' at the core of the theoretical speculations of the *Zibaldone* functions as a balanced tool for combining revision with production of thought. Each new entry which reiterates previous focuses is always led by concerns and interests which renew existing materials from the present perspective. In this way writing serves as the measured framework for exercising thinking. While favouring speediness in retrieval of thought and establishing new connections, the writing process does not affect attention and keeps alive the intellectual exposure to all the senses implied by a specific topic.

We shall now return to the heading 'Vitalità, Sensibilità' to note how, after the series of 'elastic' reflections expanding the content of the opening entry (2410,1, 2493,2, 2495,1 2496,1, and 2629,3), the following reflection included in the heading is the shortest of the whole heading list, condensing, through an aphorism from an 'ancient poet' quoted by Plutarch, the essential meaning of 'Vitalità, Sensibilità': '*Dei beni umani il più supremo colmo È sentir meno il duolo*. Sentenza che racchiude la somma di tutta la filosofia morale e antropologica' ('"The supreme human good is to feel sorrow less". A judgment that contains the height of all moral and anthropological philosophy') (*Zib.* 2673,3, 19 February 1823). The proverbial and sententious character of this maxim gives the sense of a universal truth, thus concluding and sealing with a final impulse the speculation undertaken up to that moment on the theme in question. From this moment onwards, Leopardi considers the analyses expanded in previous entries to be assimilated. Interestingly, the style of the following reflection changes to an assertive tone, showing confidence and mastery of a subject which has been deeply scrutinized and which can now be elucidated with some intellectual authority:

> *È cosa indubitata* che i giovani, [...] non solamente soffrono più che i vecchi [...], ma eziandio [...] sentono molto più di questi il peso della vita [...]. E questa si è una conseguenza dei principii posti nella mia teoria del piacere. Perciocchè ne' giovani è più vita o più vitalità che nei vecchi [...]; e dove è più vita, *quivi* è maggior grado di amor proprio [...]; *e dove* è maggior grado o efficacia di amor proprio, *quivi* è maggior desiderio e bisogno di felicità; *e dove* è maggior desiderio di felicità, *quivi* è maggiore appetito e smania ed avidità e fame e bisogno di piacere: *e* non trovandosi il piacere nelle cose umane è necessario che dove n'è maggior desiderio *quivi* sia maggiore infelicità, ossia maggior sentimento dell'infelicità; *quivi* maggior senso di privazione e di mancanza e di vuoto; *quivi* maggior noia, maggior fastidio della vita, maggior difficoltà e pena di sopportarla, maggior disprezzo e noncuranza della medesima. *Quindi tutte queste cose debbono essere* in maggior grado ne' giovani che ne' vecchi; *siccome sono*; massime in questa presente mortificazione e monotonia della vita umana, che contrastano colla vitalità ed energia della giovanezza; in questa mancanza di distrazioni violente [...]; *in somma* in questo *ristagno* della vita al cuore e alla mente e alle facoltà interne dell'uomo, e del giovane massimamente. Il qual ristagno è micidiale alla felicità per le ragioni sopraddette.
>
> [*It is something beyond doubt* that the young, [...] not only suffer more than the old [...] but even [...] are much more aware than they are of the weight of life [...]. And this is indeed a consequence of the principles laid down in my theory of pleasure. Because in the young there is more life or more vitality than in the old [...]. And *where* there is more life, *there* is a higher level of self-love [...], *and where* there is a higher level or efficacy of self-love, *there* is a greater desire and need of happiness, *and where* there is greater desire of happiness, there is a greater appetite and craving and avidity and hunger and need of pleasure. *And*

when this pleasure is not found in human things it is inevitable that where there is a greater desire for it, *there* is greater unhappiness, or greater consciousness of unhappiness, *therefore* a greater sense of privation and lack and emptiness, *therefore* greater boredom, greater vexation in life, greater difficulty and torment in bearing it, greater scorn and indifference toward the same. *Therefore all these things must be* at a higher level in the young than in the old. *As they are*, especially in this present mortification and monotony of human life, which are at odds with the vitality and energy of youth, in this lack of violent distractions [...], *in short*, in this stagnation of life in the heart and in the mind and in the internal faculties of man, and especially of the young. *And this stagnation* is lethal to happiness for the reasons stated above.] (*Zib.* 2736–38; my emphasis)

Note the confident affirmation of the validity of Leopardi's propositions, '*è cosa indubitata*', 'tutte *queste cose debbono essere* [...]; *siccome sono*', and the use and repetition of the conjunctions and connectors '*e*', '*quivi*', '*dove*' that confer a rapid rhythm to his summarizing prose. It is as if writing here performs the function of rehearsing memorized contents which require a final test to allow him to proceed with confidence. However, when Leopardi gets to the concept of 'ristagno', the tone of his prose (not quoted here) changes, he has reached a new point of reflective 'compression' and his analysis once again adopts the slow attentive focus typical of research in progress.

The section of the heading so far analyzed provides the textual application of Leopardi's theory of clarity. Leopardi has weighed every single aspect of a specific focus, explored its links and expanded its range of application through his 'elastic writing' until he is satisfied with his findings. Having reiterated his analyses he has become used to their different parts, he 'è pienamente entrato nel campo delle speculazioni, [...] ed essendo sicuro delle sue idee, *non ha più bisogno di fissarle* e dichiararle' ('has entered fully into the field of speculations, and being sure of his own ideas, *he no longer needs to define* and explain them in some manner or other even to himself") (*Zib.* 1374, 23 July 1821; my emphasis). The degree of clarity gained by Leopardi about the structuring constituents of 'Vitalità, Sensibilità' allows him to detach himself from the core principles of the heading to explore peripheral themes — and I am using the term 'peripheral' only relatively speaking, as these entries become central to other thematic headings of the 'Index'. It is not by chance that in the chart of 'Vitalità, Sensibilità' the first swarm, so to speak, of entries involving intra-textual cross-references is generated from *Zib.* 2736,1–2739, that is, from the previously analyzed passage where Leopardi rehearses his speculative arguments. As the chart shows, the swarm originates from *Zib.* 2739 to involve, among other entries, *Zib.* 2752–55, 2926–28, 3347–49, 3291–98, 3107–09, 3117–19, 3167–69, 3153–54, 3480–82, with some of these connected by mutual references and generating further intra-textual links. In this post-'rehearsal' swarm of references, *Zib.* 2752–55 is connected to *Zib.* 2736–39 because of its theme on the feeling of life, which it develops from the point of view of the influence of the seasons: 'In primavera [...] è maggiore il sentimento della vita, a causa della diminuzione e torpore di esso sentimento cagionato dal freddo' ('In spring [...] the feeling of life is greater, because of the diminution and lethargy of feeling brought on by the cold') (*Zib.* 2752). This aspect is explored further: 'in parità di circostanze, l'uomo [...] è meno scontento [...] durante l'inverno che durante la state' ('in the same circumstances a man [...] is less discontented [...] during the winter than during the summer') (*Zib.* 2926–28). At this point a switch of focus to the perspective of the nations is expanded further:

> Queste considerazioni vanno applicate al carattere delle nazioni che vivono in diversi climi, di quelle che sogliono passare la più parte dell'anno al coperto e nell'uso della vita domestica e casalinga a causa del rigore del clima, e viceversa ec.
>
> [These considerations should be applied to the character of nations that live in different climates, of those that are used to passing most of the year under shelter and leading a domestic and homely existence because of the rigors of the climate, and vice versa.] (*Zib.* 2928)

The reflection on p. 3347 is connected to this passage through its comparison of northern and southern populations, drawn on the basis of the influence of the climate on their character. Therefore, through progressive expansions from the initial theme we have reached analyses which, if extrapolated from the web of connections, would appear autonomous and independent of the starting-point (*Zib.* 2736–39, for instance, is mostly focused on the comparison between young and old people with respect to their vitality and desires). *Zib.* 3347 is autonomous enough to be indexed also under a separate heading ('Inverno, estate. Questa più malcontenta ec. ec. quello più rassegnato ec. ec.' ('Winter, summer. The latter more dissatisfied, the former more resigned, etc. etc.')). From this viewpoint, Cacciapuoti's definition of 'genetic derivation' of one entry from another is effective, not only to highlight explicit and subterranean bonds between thoughts, but also their capacity to assume a certain self-sufficiency which constitutes their clear and distinct individuality.[10]

The *Zibaldone* could be opened randomly and small portions of the text (even extracted from long speculations) would be able to communicate essential specific contents as well as the relationships between their internal parts clearly and exhaustively (although there are of course exceptions). Because they host constant retrieval of previous materials that helps to visualize the entirety of the speculation all at once in the mind's eye, some entries have condensed within themselves all the logical components of a certain discourse without the need for further inquiry. As reader of his own notes, Leopardi seems at times to regard his research as complete. Yet repetition never means absolute sameness. Leopardi's own satisfaction with his accomplished research is rarely a definitive end and has limited duration. In general, once a cross-reference reactivates the circulation of interest, or as soon as diachronic connections are re-established, the Leopardian universe exceeds its limits and new galaxies of thought are discovered. Compactness and expansion are the essential complementary but contrasting components of the *Zibaldone's* development, which is thus constantly exposed to reshaping forces with both short- and long-term impacts requiring careful work of adjustment.

Notes to Chapter 11

1. The numbers in bold, on the vertical line on the left, represent the entries of the 'Index' heading in question. The other numbers are the internal references in the *Zibaldone* with which the entries of the 'Index' are connected. In general, numbers signal the page (i.e. 1584), paragraph (i.e. 1584,1 — with comma), and, when applicable, sentence in the paragraph (i.e. 1584,1.2 — with full stop). This follows Leopardi's 'Index' manuscript. At the end of each page number in the heading, Leopardi used a full stop (i.e. 1584,1.2.), which I omit when I refer to these entries in my discussion. The dash and number which follow some of the numbers are my addition and signal the page until which that particular reflection continues. When the intra-textual references signalled by the arrows fall within those pages (i.e. neither the first nor the last page of the reflection), the exact page which contains the intra-textual connection is given in brackets (i.e. (2753)). For more details regarding Leopardi's explanation of this 'Index' convention, see Chapter 19, n. 5. As for the arrows, I have followed the model by Marco Riccini, in which the double-headed arrows link pairs of thoughts connected by mutual references. Arrows with one head only represent references which are univocal, or in other words which are only present in one of the two connected entries and the entry towards which the arrow is directed does not reciprocate a reference (See Riccini, 'Lo *Zibaldone di pensieri*', p. 86).
2. Giacomo Leopardi, 'Dissertazione sopra i fluidi elastici', in *Dissertazioni filosofiche*, p. 187.
3. See Andrea Campana, *Leopardi e le metafore scientifiche* (Bologna: Bononia University Press, 2008), pp. 69–78.
4. Pietro Verri, 'Discorso sull'indole del piacere e del dolore', in *Discorsi* (Milan: Marelli, 1781), pp. 1–100 (p. 96).
5. Cf. Amedeo Vigorelli, *Il disgusto del tempo: la noia come tonalità affettiva* (Milan & Udine: Mimesis, 2009), pp. 27–28.
6. See *Zib.* 3622, and 'Dialogo di Torquato Tasso e del suo genio familiare' (*TPP*, p. 531).
7. Cf. *Zib.* 3950–51, 4016.
8. See *Zib.* 2378.
9. Bergson, *Matter and Memory*, trans. by Nancy Margaret Paul and W. Scott Palmer (London: Allen & Unwin, 1919), pp. 89–90.
10. Cf. Cacciapuoti, *Dentro lo 'Zibaldone'*, pp. 79–89.

CHAPTER 12

❖

Swarms of Birds: The Heading 'Vitalità, Sensibilità' (II) and Leopardi's Self-adjusting Thought

As part of a recent project on collective animal behaviour, a team of international researchers led by Andrea Cavagna has investigated the motion of flocks of starlings to assess the modalities of their frequent changes in group direction. Because each change represents a risk of exposure to predators that can take advantage of isolated birds, it is essential for the birds' preservation that the flock maintains cohesion. This study has demonstrated that the birds which turn first are physically close to each other. From a certain localized place in the group the decision to turn is transmitted from bird to bird, so that each bird is able to adjust its own trajectory on the model of its closest neighbour's flight; as Cavagna notes: 'the alternative view, namely that the turn is caused by an external stimulus hitting all birds at the same time, would imply an independent response of each bird and thus a spatially unstructured distribution of the delay times, whereas we always find a clear spatial modulation of the delays'.[1] The flock's system is non-hierarchical, in the sense that the role and position of each bird constantly change. The individuals who are ahead make more effort, because, as in any other aerodynamic system, those who come afterwards can exploit for their own motion the vortexes created by the preceding ones. Changes in position are naturally frequent in such aerial performances so as to maximize physical fitness, and peripheral birds can suddenly assume leading positions. In this self-adjusting and non-centralized system, each bird interacts with a certain number of other individuals (normally six or seven at its sides) regardless of their distance. As Cavagna explains, 'by interacting within a fixed number of individuals, rather than meters, the aggregation can be either dense or sparse, change shape, fluctuate and even split, yet maintaining the same degree of cohesion'.[2] For this reason 'the topological interaction is indispensable to maintain a flock's cohesion against the large density changes caused by external perturbations, typically predation'.[3]

Although the mathematical equations explaining the transmission of the information of direction change between birds has only recently been discovered, the incredible harmony of the flocks and the compactness of myriad birds moving as if they were one continuous flow has always inspired admiration and curiosity among poets, scientists, and common spectators. In the nineteenth century, the naturalist Paolo Lioy (1834–1911), who refers to Buffon's *Histoire naturelle des oiseaux* [The Natural History of Birds] as one of his points of reference, shows to have clearly observed the anti-hierarchical shifts between birds:

> Taluni Uccelli che viaggiano a stormi si dispongono in modo nel volare da rendersi più facile il fendere l'aria; così le Gru sfilano a schiere [...] rassomiglianti ad un Y rovescio; [...] l'uccello che sta alla punta come condottiere viene successivamente sostituito da quello che il segue [...].
>
> La organizzazione degli Uccelli è la più favorevole per abitatori dell'aria. Ad essi interessava una grande leggerezza per sostenersi sulle ale senza molta fatica, ed è per tale ragione che le loro ossa sono sparse di cavità aeree comunicanti coi polmoni; il calore stesso del loro corpo dilata l'aria che contengono.[4]
>
> [Some birds that travel in flocks, assume a flying formation which makes it easier for them to rend the air; in the same way, cranes are seen to fly in swarms similar to an inverted 'Y' shape. The bird that is ahead as a leader is subsequently replaced by the one that follows.
>
> This organization of birds is the most favourable for these inhabitants of the air. They need great lightness to sustain themselves on their wings with no effort, and it is for this reason that their bones are filled with air cavities and connected to their lungs. The very heat of their body dilates the air that they contain.]

Leopardi too was impressed by their collective motion and in the *Zibaldone* he refers to 'la moltitudine degli uccelli i cui stormi sono innumerabili' ('the multitude of birds, whose flocks are innumerable') (*Zib.* 71), while in the 'Elogio degli uccelli' [In Praise of Birds], also inspired by Buffon, he depicts the birds' sudden change of trajectory:

> Cangiano luogo a ogni tratto; passano da paese a paese quanto tu vuoi lontano, e dall'infima alla somma parte dell'aria, in poco spazio di tempo, e con facilità mirabile; veggono e provano nella vita loro cose infinite e diversissime; esercitano continuamente il loro corpo. (*TPP*, p. 573)
>
> [They change place every moment; they pass from one region to another as distant as you please, and from the lowest to the loftiest regions of the air, in a short space of time and with marvellous ease; in their lives they witness and experience an infinite number and variety of things; they continuously exercise their bodies.] (*MT*, p. 167)

However, there are further hidden references in his work which allow one to interpret Leopardi's ornithological interest as a sign of his dialogue with a long-standing history of ideas.

It is the aim of this chapter to show how the flight of birds constitutes not only a trope for imagination but also a form for organization of thought. By unveiling the roots of the transposition of the flock's motion from the realm of animal observation to that of creative writing, it will then be possible to employ the dynamism of the birds' flight as a model to interpret the self-adjusting modalities of the text. This means that there are deviations and self-confutations in Leopardi's analytical trajectories which the discourse registers in their ongoing development. Changes of viewpoint that contradict previous statements are investigated by Leopardi with the same rigour and clarity as any proof of confirmation. What matters for Leopardi is that when a change of direction takes place all the elements of the discourse continue to maintain cohesion, that is, a functional relationship with the other parts. Like for birds in a flock, no component should be left in isolation.

In favouring interaction between zoology, myth, and the creative imagination surrounding the birds' flight, Leopardi shares a tradition of thought which dates back to the origin of Western civilization, and in particular to Greek and Latin culture. Olga Monno has reconstructed the literary 'migrations' of the crane imagery in classical and Christian texts from Homer to medieval times, and has highlighted how, in addition to their natural behaviour and physiological characteristics, it was mainly the cranes' flight and migratory dispositions that lend themselves to processes of metaphorization.[5] In the *Iliad*, Homer employs the simile of a flock of shouting and disorderly assembled cranes attacking the Pygmies to describe the conflict between the silent and well-organized Greeks and the loud and disordered Trojans.[6] To this legend Leopardi refers extensively in the chapter 'Dei pigmei e dei giganti' [On Pygmies and Giants] of his 'Saggio sopra gli errori popolari degli antichi' [Essay on the Popular Errors of the Ancients], where he mentions the legacy of Homer's tale in authors such as Ovid and Boios, while he refers to Aristotle as an example of independent employment of the image of the flock (*TPP*, pp. 921–23). Plutarch (in *De sollertia animalium* [On the intelligence of Animals]) and Aelian (in *De natura animalium* [On the Nature of Animals]) refer to the triangular shape of a flock of cranes as a strategy which cuts through the air without unsettling the cohesion of their formation. Cicero, in *De natura deorum* [On the Nature of Gods], refers to Aristotle's observation regarding the compactness of birds, which allows the flocks to move through the air as one only body, with full solidarity between the single parts.[7]

In the Latin literary tradition, while the formation of birds continues to be associated with that of soldiers in an army, in some cases the flock of cranes moves from symbolizing destructive chaos to representing the positive qualities of hopefulness and encouragement emanating from their sound. Both Virgil and Juvenal focus on the sound effect of the flock, and explain the compactness of the assemblage as deriving from the spread of sound between birds, with the latter author referring in particular to a 'nubes sonora' [clamorous cloud], in a passage quoted by Leopardi in his 'Saggio sopra gli errori': 'Ad subitas Thracum volucres nubemque sonoram | Pygmaeus parvis currit bellator in armis' ('When the clamorous clouds of Thracian cranes swoop down | They're charged by the Pygmy warrior in his miniature armour').[8] Writers also offered visual aids for definitions of the flock's forms. In particular, Lucan refers to the aerodynamic V-shaped disposition of the flock and the unsettling effect of the Noto wind, which causes the rupture of the V: 'Et turbata perit dispersis littera pinnis' ('until the letter is broken and disappears as the birds are scattered').[9] This reference belongs to a broader set of attributions of 'semiological' value to the flock,[10] or in other words to literary references insisting on the comparison between the birds' configuration and the letters of the alphabet, which had a certain popularity through the centuries in European literature and finds in Dante one of the most authoritative examples:

> E come augelli surti di rivera,
> > quasi congratulando a lor pasture,
> > fanno di sé or tonda or altra schiera,
>
> sì dentro ai lumi sante creature
> > volitando cantavano, e faciensi
> > or *D*, or *I*, or *L* in sue figure.
>
> Prima, cantando, a sua nota moviensi;
> > poi, diventando l'un di questi segni,
> > un poco s'arrestavano e taciensi.
>
> (Dante, *Paradiso*, XVIII, ll. 73–81)

Like birds that rise above a river bank | and, chorusing in joy at food they find, | form flying discs and various other shapes, | so, deep in light, these holy creatures sang | and, as they winged around, they now assumed | the figure of a D, then I, then L. | Singing, at first, the notes of their own tune, | They then (becoming one of these three signs) | paused for a moment and let silence fall.[11]

Here, in the contrast between the singing voice of the pre-literal bird-like shape ('prima, cantando') and the silent fixity of the literal configuration an entire universe of signification is condensed, alluding to the passage between the world of orality — lively and outgoing ('moviensi') — to that of the literary — static, introverted, and reflexive ('s'arrestavano e taciensi'). In the course of the centuries, scientific and encyclopaedic treatises also continued to reproduce the alphabetic model and the previously quoted passage by Lioy is an example of this representation. Therefore, although the question of the transmission of messages relating to route changes between birds had to wait millennia before being answered, it is essential to note that the roots of flock-imagery in Western culture were since the beginning associated with a certain attention to collective communication and performance resulting from the cohesion of the single parts, as well as the visual association of the birds' flight with human language.

The relevance of the flock-imagery in Leopardi's thought appears stronger when considering its further cultural transmigration into Christian culture. In Jerome and Rabanus Maurus, among others, flocks of cranes are the symbol of monastic life. Cranes collaborate as part of an organized ensemble in which leadership alternates with labour and obeying the guidance of others.[12] The birds' speed of response to sudden impulses and variations becomes a figure of promptness in engaging with monastic activities. Order and discipline are represented in the flock's structured motion, while the other relevant connotation of vigilance associated with the 'sentinel' crane — an image resulting from their standing on one leg only, which suggests they never allow themselves to be too comfortable in sleep — functions as a symbol of the monk's moral vigilance against the assaults of evil. This further sense cannot have escaped Leopardi's attention when he refers to the 'ordinanza delle grù nei viaggi che fanno, della sentinella o svegliatrice che tengono' ('the organization of cranes [and the fact that] they use some birds as sentinels or lookouts in their migratory flights') (*Zib.* 288). However, one finds in Leopardi a further metaphorical charge for the flock imagery, in which the collective flight is associated with the ephemeral connotations of modern life, namely the abundance of printed material and broad circulation of goods, as well as the abrupt changes in and brevity of fashions and trends.[13]

Leopardi discusses his views on the advent of consumerist society in many pages of the *Zibaldone*, as well as in his moral tales, but it is precisely through reference to a flock of cranes that in the 'Palinodia al marchese Gino Capponi' [Recantation for Marchese Gino Capponi] (1835) he ironically depicts business transactions and the productions of the printing press:

> Fortunati color che mentre io scrivo
> Miagolanti in su le braccia accoglie
> La levatrice! a cui veder s'aspetta
> Quei sospirati dì, quando per lunghi
> Studi fia noto, e imprenderà col latte
> Dalla cara nutrice ogni fanciullo,
> Quanto peso di sal, quanto di carni,
> E quante moggia di farina inghiotta
> Il patrio borgo in ciascun mese; e quanti
> In ciascun anno partoriti e morti
> Scriva il vecchio prior: quando, per opra
> Di possente vapore, a milioni
> Impresse in un secondo, il piano e il poggio,
> E credo anco del mar gl'immensi tratti,
> Come d'aeree gru stuol che repente
> Alle late campagne il giorno involi,
> Copriran le gazzette, anima e vita
> Dell'universo, e di savere a questa
> Ed alle età venture unica fonte!

Lucky are they whom, as I write, | the midwife welcomes mewling in her arms! | It's envisioned that they'll see | those sighed-for days when, thanks to long research, | we'll know, and every infant will imbibe | with the milk of its beloved nurse, | how much weight of salt and how much meat, | how many bushels of wheat his native city | devours each month, and as well how many | births and deaths the old prior marks down: | when, by the agency of mighty steam, | newspapers, printed by the thousands | in a second, the universe's soul and life | and the one font of wisdom | for this time and times to come! | will cover plain and hill | and even the vast tracts of the sea, I think, | as often an array of cranes flight | will hide the light from the broad countryside.[14]

Figures of modern city life make their appearance in this stanza: the busy shopkeeper who registers (perhaps in a double entry notebook) the consumption of goods, while the registrar's office calculates the changes in population resulting from polar shifts of birth- and death-rates. After providing a glimpse of a dynamic city life, the view of the poem moves to an aerial perspective of a flock of cranes overseeing a variety of landscapes which they traverse in a speedy and compact motion, with the connotations of speed and resistance representing the birds' special instincts for survival. The first of these allows them to escape the grasp of predators through a sudden change of direction, while the latter allows them to venture far and wide to explore more suitable territories and climes before returning to their place of origin. These senses lend themselves to describing the motion of the *Zibaldone* writing, which alternates between long expansive and recursive excursions with sudden changes of perspective and style. However, further meanings which re-enforce this interpretation are hidden in Leopardi's ornithological image.

In the 'Palinodia', the image of the cranes and their intrinsic natural qualities are used to represent the fast-paced rhythm of the creation of printed material, as well as the seriality deriving from mechanical reproduction. The employment of this figure in Leopardi's poem seems therefore to represent a reverse ironic reference to the previously mentioned symbolism assumed by these birds in the Western tradition, which was well known to Leopardi: the disciplined and time-consuming effort of the crane-scribe is now replaced by the hastily-produced uniformity of the crane-machine. The co-existence of these two cultural models cannot be detached from the significance that the *Zibaldone* itself had started to assume in the later years of annotation as a mirror of antithetical tensions. It is first of all essential to note how the reference to the 'lunghi studi' makes the *Zibaldone* — the most material concretization of Leopardi's constant study — an actual, albeit hidden, presence in this stanza. The private notebook, so meticulously kept and preserved and hidden from sight, which was the result of restless yet disciplined activity, had started, at least after 1831, to take on a less hermetic perspective. Already since the spring of that year, Leopardi had started to contemplate the possibility of revealing his very private craft to others. Elisabetta Brozzi has indeed identified in a letter of May 1831 (undated) to Louis de Sinner, in which Leopardi transcribes some philological notes on Theon taken from the *Zibaldone*, the first sign of Leopardi's new openness: 'Ho trovato fra le mie carte questa osservazione sopra Teone, che [...] vi trascrivo. Notandus usus modi infinitivi in Theone sophista, progymnasm. 2, ed. Basil., p. 36' [I have found among my papers this observation regarding Theon, which [...] I shall transcribe for you: 'the use of the infinitive mode in Theon the sophist is to be noted', *Progymnasmata* 2, Basel edition, p. 36] (*E*, II, 1791).[15] This unprecedented sharing of content of the *Zibaldone* is then repeated in a subsequent letter to Sinner of 1 June 1831, where Leopardi sends his friend part of his philological 'Note varie a poesia e prosa greca' [Various Annotations to Greek Prose and Poetry], comprising observations recorded in the *Zibaldone* between January 1821 and March 1829, and which are also listed under the 'Index' heading 'Filologia. Passi d'autori, spiegati, corretti, ec. ec.' ('Philology. Passages from authors explained, corrected, etc. etc.'). However, this revolutionary gesture does not come without a filter, as the notes sent in the May 1831 letter are written in Latin rather than Italian: 'Theo sophis. progxymnasm. 2. hoc est de narrat. ed. Basileae 1541. p. 36. L'infinito usato in modo affatto italiano. (Bologna 24. Gen. 1826.)'] ('Theon the sophist, "Progymnasmata" 2, that is "De narratione," Basel 1541, p. 36. The infinitive used in a way which is quite Italian. (Bologna, 24 Jan. 1826.)') (*Zib.* 4163). This choice of language, which suggests a final subconscious attempt to prevent the direct exposure of the *Zibaldone*, can be explained by the fact that Leopardi's act of opening up the diary carries a significance which extends far beyond the content of his private epistolary exchange.[16] In disclosing the *Zibaldone*, albeit as partially and cautiously as possible,

Leopardi is implicitly allowing his writing to face the potential anonymity of a public readership. Although the immediate recipient is in this case a single individual, Leopardi acknowledges the more general principle that in his time circulation of knowledge or ideas, even if through the most confined channels, equals dispersion. As far as the reception of his work is concerned, Leopardi's aims were now more sceptical than those had motivated him to submit his early work to the attention of authoritative personalities such as Pietro Giordani, Vincenzo Monti or Angelo Mai. Then, the young Leopardi was searching for confirmation and affirmation of his qualities, although he had already reached the conclusion that it was 'by no means easy to create a "poetic space" in which the audience, the speaker, and the event could be accommodated in an effective relationship', especially given all the material and psychological variables connected with the internalization of poetry.[17] Here, having long been well aware of his own genius but without hope of finding a real communion of literary intent, Leopardi is consigning his ideas to his faithful friend while his general drive towards project-planning has already started to decline and reverse into a form of 'resigned patience', which the entire enterprise of the indexing clearly subsumes.[18] Rather than searching for hints which could help him produce new publishable material, Leopardi is in fact experimenting with chance. The problem, before being one of reception and management of information, is philosophical. The moral tale 'Parini, ovvero della gloria' [Parini, or Concerning Fame] clearly expresses Leopardi's view that perfect coincidence between the sender and the receiver of a message is impossible, and any communication is in fact miscommunication. In modern times, displaying one's thinking necessarily means altering it and being altered by the contact with others. Even the apparently least subjective type of reflection, philology, has for Leopardi an immense emotional, autobiographical, and literary value. Philology is the means through which, from the beginning of his education, Leopardi tried to construct not only his reputation with his readership but also a more intimate dialogue with and understanding of his authors. Philology is also the dynamic balance that regulates Leopardi's contrasting impulses, namely the attempt to pursue glory as a drive to escape his restricted family world and, conversely, once he is away from Recanati, the need to return to a familiar and methodical comfort-zone of habit.[19] In creating a bridge between the *Zibaldone* and the outside world, Leopardi's attitude is also twofold. On the one hand, through Latin, there is the last attempt to 'protect' the *Zibaldone* notes from a stranger's intrusion; this is the 'old' Leopardi persevering in his monkish and disciplined attitude. On the other, as in the garden of Eden, Leopardi (in a serpent-like mode) is offering the fruit of his study to his friend while at the same time concealing its nature and appearance. It is indeed necessary to stress how the philological note transcribed in Latin at the bottom of the letter contains a specific reference to crucial meanings expressed previously to Sinner. Already in a letter of 17 February 1831 to his friend, Leopardi had referred to his *Zibaldone* ('mes observations') as a work with a form for which only the definition of 'mélanges' could adequately render its fragmented and multifarious nature: 'Mais je persiste à croire que la forme de *mélanges* est la seule sous laquelle mes observations puissent être rédigées' [However I continue to believe that the form of a heterogenous miscellany of thoughts is the only one in which my observations could be edited] (*E*, II, 1774). In stating the difficulty of finding available terminology, Leopardi is implicitly recognizing the unprecedented, modern character of his thoughts. This observation is part of a wider reflection included in the letter on the current status of modern readership and the ephemeral and variable nature of fashions:

> J'avoue que je suis ordinairement peu touché de ces propos: *tel ou tel genre n'est plus à la mode*. On le remet à la mode, si l'ouvrage est bon: et si l'ouvrage est mauvais, la mode ne saurait pas le soutenir. Aussi me semble-t-il que ce ne serait pas *entrer dans le monde philologique*, que de paraître comme philologue dans un Journal. (*E*, II, 1774)
>
> [I must admit that I am generally little impressed by the following remark: *this or that genre is no longer in fashion*. It can be made fashionable again if the work is good; and if the work is poor fashion alone could not sustain it. Therefore it seems to me that appearing as a philologist in a journal would not mean *entering into the philological world*.]

Following this consideration, Leopardi adds the news that he has collected some 'strictly philological' notes which could be of interest to his interlocutor, and promises Sinner that he will soon share them with him:

> Je fais extraire de mes pensées les morceaux *strictement* philologiques, en espérant de vous les faire parvenir par occasion sûre. Je vois que c'est peu de chose: il y a quelque note léxicographique, et deux observations sur Théon, qui pourront vous intéresser. (*E*, II, 1774)
>
> [I have the *strictly* philological parts extracted from my thoughts, hoping to send them to you when a safe opportunity arises. I can see that it is a small thing: there are some lexicographical notes and two observations on Theon, which might interest you.]

As we have seen, in the later letter of May 1831 to Sinner Leopardi keeps his word by transcribing the note on Theon. But if we take a closer look at Leopardi's philological note we can detect how it goes far beyond a mere 'strictly philological' interest. Already in the letter of 17 February, Leopardi had mentioned to his friend a certain plan regarding his 'Saggio sopra gli errori popolari degli antichi'. He had disclosed that he had contemplated the idea of selling this early work under a different name:

> Pour ce qui est de l'*Essai* sur les erreurs populaires, je consentirais à le vendre même pour le nom, c'est-à-dire à ce qu'il fût publié sous le nom d'un autre; car, croyez-moi, sans le refondre entièrement, il est impossible de le rendre un ouvrage capable de nous faire honneur. (*E*, II, 1774)
>
> [When it comes to the *Essay* on popular errors, I would consent to sell it, even when it comes to the name, or in other words, that it be published under another name; because, believe me, without reshaping it completely it is impossible to make it a work capable of doing us honour.]

This intention is restated in the May letter:

> Non ostante l'indulgenza colla quale voi giudicate del *Saggio su gli errori popolari*, io sinceramente persisto a credere che il venderlo tal qual è in anima e corpo, cioè anche per il nome, sia il migliore, e forse il solo uso che possa farsene. E se ciò si potesse presentemente far con profitto, io ve ne pregherei. V'assicuro ch'io sono intimamente convinto che da quel libro non possa venirmi onore alcuno, e però la questione è di trarne la maggior somma possibile di denaro. (*E*, II, 1789)
>
> [Despite your indulgence in judging my *Essay on the Popular Errors*, I honestly continue to believe that selling it as it is, body and soul, meaning also when it comes to the name, would be the best use one could make of it, and perhaps the only use to be made of it. And if this could be done now and with profit, I would kindly ask you to do so. I can assure you that in my innermost self, I am convinced that I could obtain no honour from that book, and therefore the only point is to be able to get from it the greatest sum of money possible.]

In this letter where, as we have seen, extracts from the *Zibaldone* make their way out of the notebook for the first time, a Faustian Leopardi has clearly adopted the perspective of the modern pragmatic and utilitarian businessman who would be willing to 'sell body and soul' in exchange for money. If we now observe the final allegedly 'strictly philological' observation which Leopardi borrows from his diary (from *Zib.* 4190, 16 August 1826) and with which he closes the letter, we find a brief reference to Fazio degli Uberti: 'Noster *Fazio degli Uberti* in poemate *Dittamondo*, l. I. c. 29, v. 18, *Che mi vendrei se fosse chi comprare*, i.e. *chi mi comperasse*' [Our *Fazio degli Uberti* in the poem *Dittamondo*, b. I. c. 29, l. 18, *as I would sell myself if there were anyone willing to buy*, i.e. *anyone willing to buy me*] (*E*, II, 1791). Far from restricting his focus solely to philology, Leopardi is subtly adapting the content of his philological homage to his own condition, that of a modern author whose unfavourable economic circumstances force him to bargain honour for profit. In that this quotation is inspired as much by personal as by philological aims, it functions almost as a signature legitimizing the first 'transaction' of the *Zibaldone* with materials leaving the diary and being released into the world. Leopardi has sneaked into his apparent purely philological concern a self-referential message which almost serves the purpose of a modern receipt, a kind of preliminary contract stating a precise intention. I am inclined to believe that in sending his philological notes to his friend, it is the effect that this operation has on his own self, rather than some kind of urge for homage, that he desires the most. As a modern and self-aware Adam, he is living through (and recording on paper) a transition while monitoring self-reflexively the way in which he is being transformed by this event, namely in the passage from the condition of the crane-scribe to that of the crane-machine evoked in the 'Palinodia'. In transcribing the *Zibaldone* notes — and it should be noted that the meaning of the title of Theon's work to which Leopardi is referring, the *Progymnasmata*, is 'preparatory exercises' — he induces this mutation, inspired to do so by self-interest and self-scrutiny. His attempt to divulge his philological notes through the eyes of his friend can be read as the first self-imposed test to verify the emotional and intellectual impact of the 'opening process' — of giving oneself up to the unexpected.

In the same way that the 'eaten' et cetera represents the threshold between the determinate and the indeterminate, and in so doing carries within itself the wound of the insinuation of the indeterminate in the text, so the philological fissure opened by Leopardi towards a less private and less self-constructed world, testifies to the advancement of the 'outside world' — the crane's predator — towards the enclosed space of the diary. The increasingly rare and fragmented notes of the later years of the notebook are a clear manifestation of Leopardi's inclination to material rather than imagined or reflected experience. Life had eventually presented itself in the form of a need for unfiltered exposure to the sensible and the real. Therefore, as with the et cetera and the crane symbolism, when the writing of the *Zibaldone* comes to an end in 1832, it is as if real life and real experience have finally taken possession of Leopardi's vital impulses which were previously fully directed towards notebook-writing. It is as if pure life, the predator, has devoured the notebook, the crane-letter, crane-scribe, and crane-disciple. The ironic employment of the flock of cranes as an image for modernity in the 'Palinodia', while showing the grip that the 'outside' world is exercising on Leopardi in the 1830s, at the same time alludes to and legitimizes the *Zibaldone* as the textual testimony of this mutation from crane-scribe to crane-machine. However, Leopardi's welcoming of the imagery of the crane into his poetic work does not imply that this metaphor remains 'still', so to speak, at the level of the declarative, that it functions as a mere conceptual framework representing the author's attitudes and efforts related to the diary as opposed to new editorial trends. Instead, it is 'alive' within the *Zibaldone* universe, as its pregnancy at a conceptual level translates into structuring forms of motion for Leopardi's reflections. As for previously-analyzed forms of writing, I am here addressing the conceptual liminal zone in which a metaphorical constellation becomes actualized in Leopardi's organization of thought. The informing idea, even when not consciously or directly addressed, provides a set of relationships between parts of the discourse which recur in a variety of speculative domains. I am not looking at the way in which Leopardi explicitly associates flocks of birds with writing, but at the way in which a certain assemblage of ideas contains intrinsic relationships which correspond in form to the flock's behaviour. In the same way that leading birds change direction and are then followed by the whole flock, similarly in the *Zibaldone* the emergence of leading ideas can cause a change of speculative route to which the entirety of both immediately and distantly-related concepts conform.

In order to investigate this further form of thinking, it is now essential to conclude the analysis of 'Vitalità, Sensibilità' that has served as a sample case of analytical writing. The later entries under this heading provide a significant example of the revision in progress which Leopardi applies to his own ideas, requiring a certain readjustment of his general discourse under the influence of the modifications that occurred. This later part of the heading will also allow us to investigate the philosophical implications of Leopardi's practice of expansive writing.

On pp. 3291–96 Leopardi discusses the difference between egoism and self-love. The first is a kind of 'specie' [species] of the second and manifests itself 'quando l'uomo ripone il suo amor proprio in non pensare che a se stesso [...], rigettando l'operare per altrui con intenzione [...], d'indirizzare quelle medesime operazioni a se stesso come ad ultimo ed unico vero fine' ('when man employs his self-love solely in thinking of himself [...], in rejecting the possibility of acting in favour of others with the intention [...] of directing those same actions toward himself as if toward their ultimate and sole true end') (*Zib.* 3291). While self-love is directly proportionate to life, egoism is 'in proporzione inversa' ('inversely proportionate') (*Zib.* 3294–95). The sacrifice of the self and of one's self-love, on which acts of compassion are based, is in fact the self-sacrifice operated by self-love, and can only take place in those souls in which self-love is abundant. For this reason, it can be found in young people, in the ancients, and in all sensitive human beings, while the 'torpidi e insensibili e duri e d'animo tardo e morto, e [...le] donne [...] in genere hanno maggior quantità e forza d'egoismo, e minore d'amor proprio' ('the dull, insensitive [...], and [...] women [...] generally speaking have more, stronger egoism, and less self-love') (*Zib.* 3294). However, as far as women are concerned, Leopardi believes that 'potrà farsi un'eccezione in favor [loro] quanto alla compassione' ('an exception may be made for women insofar as compassion') (*Zib.* 3296), because not only does compassion require a great deal of self-love and vital force, but also that these qualities be present in a refined and delicate way. Similarly to the moderns when compared to the ancients, women are believed to possess a higher degree of delicacy and refinement of the soul than men, which makes them more compassionate. In contrast, from the point of view of force and vitality, their weakness renders them less keen to help others and 'meno misericordiose e benefiche degli uomini' ('less merciful and charitable than men') (*Zib.* 3297). At this point Leopardi adds a further consideration which reverses his previous points. 'Tutto insieme compensato' ('Hence overall'), that is, from the general analysis of quantitative and qualitative prerogatives, women are:

> In verità, generalm. e per natura, più egoiste [...] degli uomini. Perocchè molto maggior parte ha nella beneficenza [...] l'intensità, la forza, l'abbondanza della vita, e quindi dell'amor proprio, che la delicatezza e raffinatezza dell'animo disgiunte dalla forza [...] del medesimo. E ciò non pur negli uomini rispetto alle donne, ma generalm. in chi che sia, rispetto a chi che sia.
>
> [Women really are generally and by nature more egoistic [...] than men. For intensity, strength, abundance of life and therefore of self-love have a much greater part in charity [...] than do delicacy, and sophistication of mind separated from the strength [...] of self-love. And this not just in men compared with women, but generally in whoever, compared to whomever.] (*Zib.* 3297–98)

In the course of the reflection Leopardi moves from highlighting the state of exception represented by women (which can be summarized as: although women are weaker and less vital than men, nevertheless they are more compassionate thanks to the delicacy of their organs) to reinforcing and confirming the general rule: as far as compassion is concerned, the influence of women's delicacy is less effective than the consequences of their weakness and therefore they are more egoistic than men. This is an example of Leopardi's deviation of viewpoint, a kind of philosophical veering which is transmitted from the specific consideration on women to a generalized perspective: 'E ciò non pur negli uomini rispetto alle donne, ma generalm. in chi che sia, rispetto a chi che sia'. If we now consider the notes on pp. 3921–27, which focus again on the same theme of vitality and self-love, it is possible to observe how the change of direction that occurred in the evaluation of women's behaviour, which led to their relocation from a state of exception to one of confirmation of the rule, ends up influencing the entirety of the following reflection on self-love. The newly-discovered truth about the prevalent effects of weakness finds now application to all the other aspects of his analysis. This begins with a recapitulation of the links between self-love and unhappiness, and the dependence of self-love not so much on the strength of the body but more on the strength of the spirit. These two strengths, adds Leopardi, are generally inversely proportioned: the greater the bodily strength, that is, the external activity of the individual, the lesser the strength of the soul, that is, the internal activity, and vice versa. At this point Leopardi includes an important proviso: 'Ma questo si deve intendere, posta una parità di circostanze nel rimanente' ('But this has to be understood, assuming an equality of circumstances in the remainder') (*Zib.* 3925); and clarifies his statement with two examples, one drawn from the animal world and the other from his speculation on women:

> Se il leone ha più forza di corpo che il polipo, non p. questo egli è men vivo del polipo. [...]
>
> Se la donna è di corpo più debole dell'uomo e la femina del maschio, non ne segue che generalmente e naturalmente la donna e la femmina abbia più vita, e sia più infelice del maschio. *Converrebbe prima affermare* che di spirito la femmina sia o più o altrettanto forte, cioè viva ec., che il maschio; *ed accertarsi o mostrare* in qualunque modo, che al minor grado della sua forza corporale rispetto al maschio non risponda generalmente nel suo spirito una certa qualità di organizzazione [...] da cui risulti che generalmente e naturalmente [...] la femmina abbia men vita interna [...] del maschio, con un certo e proporzionato ragguaglio al minor grado di forza corporale che ha la femmina rispetto al maschio. Io credo onninamente che sia così.
>
> [I mean, that if the lion has more strength of body than the polyp, it is not therefore less alive than the polyp. [...] If woman is in body weaker than man, and the female than the male, it does not follow that generally and naturally the woman and the female have more life and are more unhappy than the male. *It would be necessary first to establish* whether in spirit the female is more or equally strong, that is alive, etc., than the male, and *to ascertain or show* in some way whether or not to the lesser degree of her corporeal strength with respect to the male there corresponds generally in her spirit a certain quality of organization [...], from which it turns out [...] that the female has less internal life [...] than the male, with a certain and proportionate equality to the lesser degree of corporeal strength which the female has with respect to the male. I entirely believe that this is the case.] (*Zib.* 3925–26; my emphasis)

It is evident how Leopardi rehabilitates the motifs of weakness and delicacy which he had considered when, in the reflection on pp. 3291–97, he had attempted to remark on what at first sight presented itself as a state of exception for women with respect to compassion. But the change of direction which made him correct his assumptions leads him now to rethink the complete philosophical asset of the theme in question and to elaborate a new plan of speculative action. Indeed, reincorporating an exception back into the rule imposes the need to verify all the different components which constitute a certain truth, and he concludes that:

> Bisogna aver molta pratica [...] di applicare i principii generali agli effetti anche più particolari e lontani, e di scoprire [...] i rapporti anche più astrusi [...]. Questa protesta intendo di fare generalmente per tutti gli altri principii e parti del mio sistema sulla natura.
>
> [One must have much practice [...] in applying general principles to effects which are more particular and distant, and in discovering [...] even the most abstruse [...] ones. I intend this protestation to be taken generally for all the other principles and parts of my system on nature.] (*Zib.* 3927)

There is nothing further from the system than an exception to the system, and therefore there could be no more evident confirmation of the laws of the system than an exception relocated within its remit. This analytical practice, Leopardi adds, can be achieved only through habit and skill, namely the two characteristics that underpin both the art of clarity and the art of flying for a flock of cranes. One leading idea which creates a shift in viewpoint transmits its senses to both adjacent and distant concepts, and thus the speculation is capable of self-adjusting, to maintain cohesion and fuel productive advancement.[20]

With his 'protest' Leopardi reaches the climax of his demonstrative tension in 'Vitalità, Sensibilità'. However, if we investigate the last heading entry (*Zib.* 4133), written on 9 April 1825, it is possible to detect a more irreversible inversion in Leopardi's philosophical premises, which is in line with the general weakening of Leopardi's analytical impulses in the post-1824 *Zibaldone*, and is the basis of the attraction which the outside 'lived' life is starting to exercise. The entry on p. 4133 opens with the statement that all creatures are unhappy, more or less according to their degree of sensitivity and self-love: 'Gli enti sensibili sono p. natura enti *souffrants*, una parte essenzialmente *souffrante* dello universo' ('Sensitive beings are naturally *souffrants* [suffering], a part of the universe that is essentially *souffrante*'). At this point Leopardi introduces a realization which dissolves any trust in the gnoseological potentialities of any philosophical system. Nature, he writes, is founded on a 'imperfezione essenziale' ('essential [...] imperfection'), that is on the fact that all its creatures endure the existence of the natural order in spite of the damage that is done to them and at the expense of their own happiness and wellbeing. Their existence is necessary for the preservation of the species but is harmful to individuals. However, Leopardi continues, even this most evident truth is based on a structural misunderstanding on the part of the human intellect, as is the assumption that the animal kingdom is the main constituent of nature. In fact, this is false and animals occupy only a very small place in the natural order. As humans who are bound to our creaturely life and viewpoint, our own way of evaluating and orienting ourselves within the natural system is founded on an essential and unredeemable mistake, as well as on the application of a completely arbitrary point of view:

> Questo nostro giudizio viene dal nostro modo di considerar le cose [...] comparativam. [...]; *modo e giudizio naturale* a noi che facciamo parte noi stessi del genere animale e sensibile, *ma non vero*, [...] nè conforme al giudizio e modo [...] di pensare della natura universale.
>
> [This judgment of ours comes from the way we consider things [...] comparatively [...]; *a natural way of judging* for us who are ourselves part of the animal and sensitive genus, *but not a true one*, [...] nor one which [...] conforms to the judgment and to the way of thinking [...] of universal nature.] (*Zib.* 4134; my emphasis)

Reason is an insufficient tool, in that it is not homologous with the system in which it would like to operate, which is destined to remain contradictory, as a 'misterio grande da non potersi mai spiegare' ('a great mystery, which can never be explained') (*Zib.* 4129). Human beings are therefore forced to renounce the 'principio di cognizione' ('principle of our understanding'), while it is certain that nature's ends do not coincide with man's, whose only endeavour is to achieve happiness. Leopardi has reached here a complete reversal of the illuminist trust in the faculty of reason and in its speculative tools, such as the practice of comparison and the power of analogies to which he devotes much attention in previous reflections of the *Zibaldone*.[21] Drawing on Bayle, Leopardi considers reason 'piuttosto uno strumento di distruzione che di costruzione' ('an instrument of destruction rather than construction') (*Zib.* 4192). It can be employed to reveal our errors and highlight our ignorance, but it cannot be used to produce the truth. This new philosophical posture is founded at the same time on the full reception of visual evidence (or better, of what presents itself to our eyes as evidence) and abstention from judgement. When speaking about the capability of matter to feel and think, and human beings' difficulty in accepting this truth rationally, Leopardi stresses the importance of intellectual insight: 'E se non l'intendiamo [...], neghiamo noi per questo che la materia non sia capace di queste cose, *quando noi vediamo* che lo è?' ('And if we do not understand it, [...] do we therefore deny that matter is capable of doing these things, *when we see* that it is?') (*Zib.* 4252; my emphasis). Leopardi is in other words stating that our faculty of comprehension is limited to our capacity to be exposed to as much evidence as possible that comes from experience. But it is pointless to attempt to interpret the ultimate substance of reality because it is destined to remain unknown: '*Astenghiamoci* [...] dal giudicare, e *diciamo che questo è uno universo*, che questo è un ordine: ma se buono o cattivo, non lo diciamo' ('*Let us abstain* [...] from judging, and *let us say that this is a universe*, that this is an order. But let us not say whether it is good or bad') (*Zib.* 4258; my emphasis). Our intellect can only describe what presents itself to the mind's eye in the immediacy of perception and across the broadest possible spectrum, aiming for an 'accrescimento del sensibile' [an increase of the sensible].[22] Understanding coincides now not with depth of knowledge but with clarity and expansion of evidence. Leopardi is proposing an aerial and horizontal way of conceiving of knowledge, a dominance of space rather than profundity. This corresponds, on a philosophical level, to the admiration expressed in the moral tale 'Elogio degli uccelli' (1827) for those creatures who 'abbondano soprammodo della vita estrinseca' (*TPP*, p. 573) ('abound exceedingly in the external life', *MT*, p. 167). However, unlike these creatures, which are instinctually able to merge completely with 'the open', the ultra-philosopher Leopardi conceives of modern extrinsic life not as a natural phenomenon originating from the senses, but as the extreme consequence of a philosophy which, having penetrated the ultimate limits of intellectual speculation, traces backwards its own steps.[23] The philosophical realization attained by Leopardi in these pages of the *Zibaldone*, written in 1827 like the 'Elogio', effectively legitimizes clarity, 'whether [the mind] sees clearly or sees obscurely' (*Zib.* 1372), as the privileged objective of inquiry. In doing this, the religious forms of 'veridiction' prescribing clarity as a *starting* premise for experience converge and overlap with an *atheist* philosophical conclusion reaching clarity as the *final* shore of speculation. As in the 'vice versa, et cetera' (*Zib.* 3232) meaning, diametrically polar conceptions end up meeting and merging as oxymorons.

The next step for Leopardi is to leap into a further unmediated experience which fully puts into practice his new gnoseological awareness. From 1832 onwards, he decides to embrace a full visual, horizontal spectrum of experience without the filter of the deep analytical reflection of notebook-writing. When the *Zibaldone* terminates Leopardi has not stopped his philosophical path, he has only changed its form of expression by actualizing or embodying the final remaining message in his diary. While life had up to that point converged in the *Zibaldone* as a reflected form, it is now the *Zibaldone*'s final message which is lived and performed in the practice of everyday life. Leopardi embraces an integral exposure to life while at the same time accepting its modern status as an ephemeral simulacrum, as a reality devoid of meaning and more suitably approachable by technical skills rather than philosophical scrutiny.

Notes to Chapter 12

1. Andrea Cavagna, 'Information Transfer and Behavioural Inertia in Starling Flocks', *Nature Physics*, 10 (2014), 691–96.
2. Andrea Cavagna, 'Interaction Ruling Animal Collective Behavior Depends on Topological Rather than Metric Distance: Evidence from a Field Study', *Proceedings of the National Academy of Sciences of the United States of America*, 105 (2008), 1232–37 (p. 1235).
3. Ibid., p. 1232.
4. Paolo Lioy, *Lo studio della storia naturale* (Florence: Le Monnier, 1857), pp. 301–02.
5. Olga Monno, '"Migrazioni" della gru: da Omero ai simboli medievali', *Vetera Christianorum*, 45 (2008), 91–111.
6. Homer, *Iliad*, III, ll. 1–9: 'And when each of them was marshalled with their leaders, | the Trojans went with a shriek and a war cry, | like birds, just as the shriek of cranes arises in the sky, | the ones who, fleeing storm and endless downpour, | fly with a shriek over the streams of Okeanos | bringing slaughter and death to Pygmy men; | high in the air, they provoke dread strife; | but the Achaeans went in silence, infused with might, | eager in their hearts to protect one another'; cited by Leonard Muellner, 'The Simile of the Cranes and Pygmies: A Study of Homeric Metaphor', *Harvard Studies in Classical Philology*, 93 (1990), 59–101 (p. 59).
7. Cf. Oddone Longo, 'La migrazione delle gru', in *Volatilia: animali dell'aria nella storia della scienza da Aristotele ai giorni nostri*, ed. by Oddone Longo (Naples: Procaccini, 1999), pp. 153–72 (pp. 163–64).

8. Juvenal, *Satyra*, XIII, ll. 167–68 (*TPP*, p. 921); *The Sixteen Satires*, trans. by Peter Green (London: Penguin, 1998), p. 101.
9. Lucan, Pharsalia, v, l. 716, *The Civil War (Pharsalia)*, with an English trans. by J. D. Duff (Cambridge, MA: Harvard University Press, 1977), p. 292–93.
10. Cf. Monno, '"Migrazioni" della gru', p. 93.
11. Dante Alighieri, *The Divine Comedy: Paradiso*, trans. by Robin Kirkpatrick (New York: Penguin, 2012), p. 406.
12. Cf. Monno, '"Migrazioni" della gru', p. 106.
13. I discuss the theme of ephemerality in Leopardi in my article 'Ephemera: The Feeling of Time in Leopardi's *Canto notturno*', *Italian Studies*, 67.1 (2012), 70–91.
14. Leopardi, *Canti*, ll. 135–53 (C, pp. 267–70).
15. See Elisabetta Brozzi, 'Le note filologiche dello *Zibaldone*', in *Lo 'Zibaldone' di Leopardi come ipertesto*, ed. by Muñiz Muñiz, pp. 183–89.
16. On the theme of 'hiding' from exposure to the dangers of the world see Franco D'Intino's analysis of the five linguistic filters that Leopardi employs in the 'Martirio de' Santi Padri' [Martyrdom of the Holy Fathers] in Giacomo Leopardi, *Volgarizzamenti in prosa (1822–1827)*, ed. by Franco D'Intino (Venice: Marsilio, 2012), pp. 52–53.
17. Michael Caesar, 'Poet and Audience in the Young Leopardi', *The Modern Language Review*, 77.2 (1982), 310–24 (p. 310).
18. For this reading of the meaning of Leopardi's 'Index', see D'Intino, 'Il monaco indiavolato', pp. 511–12.
19. See Brozzi, 'Le note filologiche dello *Zibaldone*', pp. 184–86.
20. This finds correspondence in the micro-structure of the *Zibaldone* syntax. Alessio Ricci highlights Leopardi's modes of balancing sentences through the correlations between subordinates and the detachment of conjunctive locutions; see 'Sintassi e testualità dello *Zibaldone di pensieri* di Giacomo Leopardi, parte II', p. 36.
21. See *Zib.* 348, 947, 1090, 1650, 1702, 1836, 1853, 2020.
22. Colaiacomo, *Il poeta della vita moderna*, p. 24.
23. For a reading of 'Elogio degli uccelli' with respect to the 'open', see Alessandra Aloisi, 'Elogio dell'inoperosità: Agamben e Leopardi', *Italian Studies*, 72.3 (2017), 282–91.

CHAPTER 13

Electric Thought

By way of creative illumination Leopardi often forms images and suggests poetic landscapes which his writing only imperceptibly announces before their apparition suddenly attracts the reader's attention. There is a kind of kinetic and electric energy running through his figurative thought, regulating the emergence of images and their influence on the surrounding text. The *Zibaldone* reader perceives an image in formation progressively permeating Leopardi's thought, but it is often challenging to reconstruct its links with the linear discourse. Its irradiation, rather than being dependent on the core themes or focuses leading Leopardi's rational argument, is often generated by specific words or combinations of words which trigger subliminally the emergence of an image. It is not a matter of obvious relationships between cause and effect, nor of the development of existing philosophical points, but of sparks of interaction between concepts within a certain lexical field. Often the image starts to take effect on Leopardi's writing well before its shape is fully formed in the text. Vice versa, a permeating image continues to exercise its influence on the subsequent discourse even when Leopardi's attention has apparently moved on. Words here function as luminous appearances of subterranean currents of thought. For this reason it seems appropriate to compare Leopardi's figurative thought to a magnetic field exercising its potential on the surrounding text: the closer the text is to the source, the stronger the influence over it, with the dynamics in question operating under the effect of invisible forces. I am referring to specific moments of the text in which an image simply occurs, germinated by a discursive argument, and concentrates all the senses that the speculation includes. Once created, it releases its semantic power to generate other images or new phases of argument, a form of electric writing.

The imagery of electricity and magnetism, which between the seventeenth and the nineteenth centuries offered a range of metaphors that were adopted to explain the functioning of broader physical and cultural activities, from medicine to politics and communication, were a strong influence on Leopardi's formation and continued to constitute in the *Zibaldone* a close tie between the realm of science and other structuring forces, above all religion and aesthetics, especially as far as the crucial concepts of grace and beauty are concerned. Before addressing the text to interpret the *Zibaldone* as a field of tensions, circulation, and release of imaginative potential, it is important to provide some preliminary clarification of the terminology and theory of the time. I am here using the concept of 'electric tension' as an explicatory model for the textual interactions between image and discourse. In physics, 'tension' describes the potential difference in a conductor which is responsible for the electric current, or in other words the flow of electric charges between two points of the electric circuit. In Leopardi's time, the science of electricity availed itself of the concepts of balance and charge difference, but because electricity was considered a branch of the more general 'science of fluids', the manifestations of electric current were attributed to the behaviour of electric fluid rather than to the motion of corpuscular charges. Also, the idea of positive and negative charges had nothing to do with the later concepts of proton and electron, but was usually associated with a quantitative measurement: it was meant as greater or lesser presence of electric fluid in the material in question. However, the idea of difference of energy as a stimulus for a certain motion aimed at restoring balance was at the basis of the known physical system, and in particular it was considered as the element in common between related phenomena such as gravity, electricity, and magnetism. Reality presented itself to observation and to rational understanding as an unstable set of dynamics and forces in constant interaction. As far as the concept of 'electric tension' is concerned, prior to Georg Simon Ohm's 1826 formulation of the laws that for the first time explained the relationships between tension, intensity of charge, and resistance of the conductor, the most popular conceptualization was that also shared by Alessandro Volta, who stressed the balancing and communicational principles of electricity. Tension is defined by the Italian scientist as:

> Lo sforzo che fa ciascun punto del corpo elettrizzato per disfarsi della sua elettricità, e communicarla ad altri corpi: al quale sforzo corrispondono generalmente in energia i segni di attrazione, ripulsione, &c. e particolarmente il grado a cui vien teso l'elettrometro.
>
> [The endeavour by which the electricity of an electrified body tends to escape from all the parts of it, to which tendency or endeavour the electrical phenomena of attraction, repulsion, and especially the degree of elevation of an electrometer, correspond.][1]

Elsewhere Volta insisted on the equivalence between tension and energy and on its expanding impulses: '[L'] energia [...] che chiamo *tensione di elettricità*, [...] è [...] lo stesso che lo sforzo di spignersi fuori' [The energy that I call *tension of electricity* [...] is [...] the same as the effort of something launching itself outwardly].[2] As J. L. Heilbron observes, in Volta the conceptualization of tension had been anticipated by the idea of 'saturation', which described certain processes of attraction between bodies and the electric fluid that were driven by a specific 'striving for fulfilment', that is, by the need to reach a certain state of charge. Saturation is thus a:

> State [...] in which the integrated attractions of its particles for electric fluid are precisely *satisfied*. This integrated attraction may be altered by any process, mechanical or chemical, that displaces the particles relative to one another; friction, pressure, and perhaps evaporation, electrify bodies by *destroying existing patterns of saturated forces* and redistributing electrical fluid.[3]

Even when the correct level of charge is reached, saturation is a provisional and precarious state, for sudden changes of physical and chemical parameters have the power to unsettle the charge and to activate new dynamics of satisfaction. It is interesting to note how, in structural terms, Volta's idea of saturation shares much with Leopardi's conceptualization of 'tendenza' [tendency], which is an essential component of his theory of pleasure. While the human soul tends towards the satisfaction of infinite pleasure, unlimited in both extent and duration, this striving is destined to remain frustrated, prevented as it is by nature in principle (cf. *Zib.* 165). Therefore, 'l'infelicità dei viventi, universale e necessaria, non [...] deriva da altro, che da questa tendenza, e dal non potere essa raggiungere il suo scopo' ('the universal and necessary unhappiness of living beings, consists in and derives from nothing other than this tendency, and from it not being able to reach its goal') (*Zib.* 4186). Even those pleasures which are exceptionally satisfied immediately lose their appeal and become dull experience, thus requiring a new drive for pleasure. This renders the dynamics of desire a continuing sensory instability in search of satisfaction, and our imagination the tool to extend our understanding of reality, in a ceaseless and unbalanced interplay between deficiency and attainment of pleasure. 'Tendency' to pleasure can therefore be conceived of as a potential difference between a charged pool of pleasure, which is constitutionally located beyond the reach of human beings, and the latter's intrinsic deficit of pleasure, which constantly forces man to project his expectations further. It is essential to stress the influence exercised by science on Leopardi's theory of pleasure, which traditionally is interpreted only from literary and aesthetic viewpoints. If the gaze is an essential component of the poetics of the sublime, similarly, fixed observation and distant projections of sight were also the constituents of the modern scientific approach, which perceived a strict bond between thinking and the capacity to see beyond immediate appearance. Already in Locke and Condillac, and in the French Idéologues, the eyes were considered the first agents of empirical knowledge, for building an understanding of a reality which rarely manifests itself in its totality, and which often instead merely appears partially through signs and symbols. Visual interpretation was considered the most immediate tool that allowed one to grasp these manifestations and see beyond the first layer of matter. However, the discovery of gravity, electricity, and magnetism challenged the idea of science as a discipline based on observation. These new phenomena revealed the presence of invisible forces active between objects, impulses which manifested themselves through 'final' outcomes but of which it seemed impossible to determine the origin and internal mechanisms. The electric spark or the alignment of the poles in a calamite were typical examples of visible effects deriving from hidden causes.

During the first half of the eighteenth century, and in the first decades of the nineteenth century, Europe became fascinated by theories, or pseudo-sciences, which claimed to possess the key to understanding all those invisible and mysterious forces regulating natural laws. Many microscopic behaviours of matter which could not be explained through rigorous physical approaches were attributed to the dynamics of the fluid, which functioned as a conveniently malleable theoretical tool in which a mixture of objective observations and subjective convictions converged.

The fluid could be adapted to explain a variety of natural systems, those of gravity and electricity as well as those of air and fire. It was, in Bachelard's words, 'une monstruosité epistémologique' [an epistemological monstrosity], which paradoxically in its pretentious scientific claim easily lent itself to metaphysical manipulations.[4] In the new scientific fervour it was through claims of scientific rigour that the leap between polar ontological systems such as science and superstition, and matter and spirit, took place. For instance, the alleged existence of bodies and microscopical creatures hidden in matter was often explained through a kind of observation permeated by superstition from which hyper-rationalist conclusions were drawn, so detaching science from the experimental method. As Robert Darnton observes:

> The progressive divorce of science from theology in the eighteenth century did not free science from fiction, because scientists had to call upon the imagination to make sense of, and often to *see*, the data revealed by their microscopes, telescopes, Leyden jars, fossil hunts, and dissections. That their eye alone could not decode nature seemed clear from scientific observations of mermaids and little men talking in rocks; and that machines need not improve perception followed from reports of fully developed donkeys seen through microscopes in donkey semen.[5]

These scientific approaches were based on the visual power of imagination, and as Francesca Montesperelli enphasizes, a connection was perceived between the temporal extension of thought and the spatial horizon of the optical field.[6] A common impulse to challenge the unknown was shared by both the 'science of rapports' and the 'coup d'œil' [rapid glance] of eighteenth century philosophy on the one hand, and the penetrating vision of the mesmeric imagery of nineteenth-century literature on the other, with its developments in the field of spiritism and esoterism. However, in the course of the cultural events that occurred in the period between these two philosophical visual approaches, the horizon of investigation had changed. The epistemological hole opened up by phenomena of attraction had progressively required science to make a preliminary choice between either abandoning or remaining faithful to matter as the sole object of speculation.

The way Leopardi makes use of the electric model shows his understanding of the scientific crisis of his time. His reflections on the abuses of reason exercised by Christianity and spiritualism show an understanding of the thin line separating approaches to the physical and the metaphysical worlds. His interest in a conception of science as the search for the solution of a mystery is manifest already in his early *Dissertazioni fisiche*, in which he repeatedly stresses the idea of a reality which hides itself from sight and which should be investigated solely through the scientific tools at one's disposal. As already discussed, in the science of his day electricity was thought of as a continuous force. Without a corpuscular model, which was to appear only at the end of the nineteenth century, in those conceptualizations which contemplated the possibility of fluids being composed of particles, these particles were considered as 'evanescent', with an almost imperceptible and negligible effect on the behaviour of the body as a whole. This modelling of the whole and its parts was necessary to describe a kind of matter which was suspected of infinite divisibility, but of which no account could be given of the constituent parts through a coherent theoretical model. Leopardi, who as we have seen reflects in many ways on the problem of divisibility, from the issue of the void in the *Dissertazioni fisiche* to the previously encountered question of time as an infinite succession of instants, is a clear example of the intellectual impasse of his time in conceptualizing a reality which apparently shows itself as continuous, but which is suspected of being composed of discrete elements. The model of the fluid offered the possibility to switch attention from the problem of the parts and concentrate on the unitary behaviour of the body, conceived as the totality of its parts. For instance, the electric spark or the electric shock implied an instantaneous event as the electric current traversed the whole body and was then discharged. It is a manifestation which finds in Leopardi a corresponding image in literature in the definition of 'impressione improvvisa dell'intero' ('the sudden [...] impression of the whole') (*Zib.* 4177) that he employs to express the effect of Anacreon's odes, which is also compared, as we have seen, to a 'fresh breeze' (*Zib.* 31). The act of reading educes the rapid flow of electric current, subliminally participating, through the reference to the shock — a sudden undefinable feeling — in the broader semantic field of the 'current' evoked by the breeze. The final pleasure resulting from the beauty of Anacreon's poetry parallels the impression of the electric shock passing from the electric circuit to the body of the receiver. This means for Leopardi that literature produces primarily a sensory and physical impression which, like electricity, acts through embodiment. To stress how the effect of beauty manifests itself not by way of attention to the parts but as an exposure to the whole, Leopardi compares beauty to an electric shock and grace to a state of prolonged irritation:

> L'effetto della grazia non è di sublimar l'anima, [...] o di renderla attonita come fa la bellezza, ma di scuoterla, come il solletico scuote il corpo, e non già fortemente come la scintilla elettrica. Bensì appoco appoco può produrre nell'anima una commozione e un incendio vastissimo, ma non tutto a un colpo. Questo è piuttosto effetto della bellezza che si mostra tutta a un tratto, e non ha successione di parti.
>
> [The effect of grace is not to exalt the soul [...] or to leave it amazed, as beauty does, but to shake it, the way tickling shakes the body, not powerfully, like an electric shock. It is true that little by little it can produce excitement and a raging fire in the soul, but not all at once. That is more the effect of beauty, which manifests itself in an instant rather than gradually.] (*Zib.* 198)

A current of air, with its 'sudden impression of the whole', and electric current, with its final spark, come together in Leopardi's representation of beauty. In contrast, grace involves constant stimulation, a persistent active impulse or tendency to reach out to the object of interest. Here the physical properties of grace reproduce the paradigm of participation at the heart of theological Grace. The overall electric imagery as a set of surfacing impressions produced by agents of a fugitive and subliminal nature is clearly a structuring feature of these two crucial poles of Leopardi's aesthetic thought, with the scientific and the religious galaxies functioning as communicating providers of imagery. Of these two poles, Leopardi suggests, the pair 'grace-tension' is the most durable form of intellectual stimulation, because, as Galvani had already demonstrated, 'when equilibrium is established, there is no motion'.[7] This effect of stasis is precisely what remains when the other pair, beauty and electric shock, has released its power, turning potential energy into a sudden explosion exhausting all force. This corresponds more generally to an important motif recurring in different ways in Leopardi's thought, namely the philosophical danger hidden in any static conditions of uniformity. Leopardi's thought insists on action, motion, and performance as the only means to avoid direct exposure to truth, and thus to aliment forms of imagination and desire. Paradoxically, the attraction of beauty is that it can be a vehicle for the loss or the paralysis of poetic potential. As in the case of any other all-embracing phenomena, in one glance beauty exposes the object as a scrutinized form, revealing the void that this gnoseological experience leaves behind. It leaves the observer motionless, contemplating a still horizon. Life is also paralleled to poetry in Leopardi's representation of beauty through the electric metaphor, and while this image of beauty conveys the sense of the brief duration of life, implicit in the instantaneous discharge of the electric burst, there is reference to aesthetic fleetingness, as the darkness which follows the flash evokes inspirational death.

The official acceptance of the equation between life and the electric spark dates back to 1788, when Charles Kite in his *Essay on the Recovery of the Apparently Dead* presented to the Royal Human Society of London, provided the definition of a dead body as that of a corpse which does not react to electric stimuli and suggested that the distinction between apparent and absolute death could be drawn on how the body responded to the principle of irritability.[8] From this formulation the idea of the electric spark as the essence of life was deduced. The metaphorical constellation of electricity had also often been linked to life in the eighteenth-century iconographic representations of the release of energy, which often portrayed an outstretched index finger much like the emblematic picture of God transmitting the vital spark to Adam in Michelangelo's *Creation of Adam* in the Sistine Chapel.[9] However, there was also an equally powerful reverse universe of senses associated with its uncontrollable power. In explaining the process through which animal electricity leaves the body to be released outwardly, Galvani stresses its stupefying and annihilating effect:

> This one thing seems particularly proper and peculiar of the torpedo and cognate animals that at their will and pleasure they can direct electricity outside the skin, and expel it so that it completes its circulation outside the body, and with such quantity and force that it exhibits a spark, [...] so that it produces a [...] violent sensation and sometimes makes such an impact on the animalcules that fall into the path of its circulation, that it either kills or stupefies and terrifies them.[10]

Furthermore, in the eighteenth century electricity in the atmosphere provided a clear manifestation of the dangerous force and lethal potential of lightning and thunderstorms. Therefore, the medical uses to which electricity could be put had to be carefully monitored. Safe parameters in the 'quantity of electricity' ensured a beneficial intensity which brought about healing rather than destruction.[11] The study of death by fulguration became a topic of research in the field of animal electricity. Felice Fontana, for instance, in his 1775 *Ricerche filosofiche sopra la fisica animale* [Philosophical Research on Animal Physics] remarks on how the lethal effect of electricity works by eliminating from the muscles the power of response: 'Ogni cosa era morta in essi, il principio del moto era distrutto' [Everything was dead in them, the principle of motion had been destroyed].[12] Excess of electricity dissolves the body's natural and constituent dynamic properties, and 'un corpo colpito dal fulmine restava ancora organizzato, ma perdeva l'organizzazione necessaria alla vita, perché senza movimento non c'era vita' [a body hit by lightning still remained organized, but lost the organization which is necessary to life, because without motion there was no life].[13] One finds this also in Leopardi's application of electricity to aesthetics. Subsequent to the sudden and integral fulfilment brought about by beauty, any possibility of intellectual interaction with the details is precluded. Beauty extinguishes any hopeful expectation of modelling and reshaping partial understanding with a view to further improvement and refinement of the aesthetic experience, which is the driving force for any artisan attending to his daily craft, as it is for Leopardi in the writing of his *Zibaldone*. In contrast, grace and tension are forces that produce enduring desire and intellectual activity. The creative experience parallels the vital physiological desire for pleasure in essential operations of sense perception. It is not by chance that the most tensive image of the entire *Zibaldone*, the one of the effect of Anacreon's odes, is also a model of recursive thought. Leopardi here does not only *talk about* electric current, but there is actual tension also in his own efforts to express the effect of Anacreon's odes through words capable of depicting their ephemeral nature. On three occasions marking different steps in the chronological evolution of the *Zibaldone* (pp. 30–31, 3441–42, 4177), Leopardi addresses the peculiarity of Anacreon, finally to declare (*Zib.* 4177), the defeat of the power of argument to the imagination: the pleasure conveyed by Anacreon's odes is so fugitive, he says, and so 'ribelle ad ogni analisi' ('resistant to all analysis'), that it can only be depicted through images, with the employment of the adjective 'ribelle', a hapax in the *Zibaldone*, stressing the exceptionality of the stylistic challenge. This is a non-comprehensive, fugitive intellectual experience which, while apparently presenting itself as impossible for Leopardi's to understand, is the fuel that feeds curiosity and keeps writing going by activating a formal and semantic cross-cultural polyphony.

The themes of beauty and grace, which are philosophically and aesthetically linked to the dialectics between the parts and the whole, also carry, as we have seen in the first part of this volume, religious references in Leopardi, thus creating an already multifaceted system of signification connecting aesthetics, poetry, and (pseudo-)science. To these cultural universes one should add epistemology, as the electric model also seems to be borrowed by Leopardi to provide an interpretation of the way the human intellect approaches the real. In the 'Dissertazione sopra l'elettricismo' [Dissertation on Electricity] Leopardi employs the concepts of affinity and aversion to describe the conductors:

> Le proprietà principali del fluido elettrico possono [...] ridursi a tre vale a dire alla sua meravigliosa tendenza *all'equilibrio* alla sua particolare *affinità* con i corpi conduttori ed in ispecie con il calorico, e alla sua quasi [...] *avversione* con i corpi non conduttori.[14]

[The main properties of electric fluid can be reduced to three, that is, its marvellous tendency *to balance*, its particular *affinity* with conductors and especially the caloric, and its near-*aversion* to non-conductors.]

Similarly, the idea of the leap from the material to the spiritual realm, which is unattainable in nature, is expressed in terms of ontological non-conductibility: between the two realms 'v'è uno spazio immenso, ed a varcarlo v'abbisogna il salto' ('There is a huge space [...], and to cross it you'll need a leap') (*Zib.* 1636). Human thinking, when it tries to conceive of the immaterial, is analogous to an electric fluid which launches itself from the material pole to the opposite spiritual pole without being able to cross the 'huge space', which is a non-conductor.[15] The conceptual affinity is supported by the fact that on more than one occasion Leopardi conceives of thought as a 'circuit': 'Non si pensa se non parlando. Quindi [...] quanto la lingua di cui ci serviamo pensando, è più lenta, più bisognosa di parole e di circuito per esprimersi, [...] tanto [...] è più lenta la nostra concezione' ('We think only by speaking. Hence [...] the slower the language we use in thinking, the more in need of words and circumlocutions to express something [...], the slower [...] is [...] our mode of conceiving') (*Zib.* 2212).[16] The word *circuito* was traditionally used to convey a more general spatial idea of 'Rotondità, Cerchio' [Roundness. Circle], as well as a long-winded kind of discourse, or circumlocution.[17] However, its employment to describe the route run by the electric current spread in scientific publications of the nineteenth century and was definitely in common use in the Italian language by the second half of the nineteenth century.[18] The phenomenon of the fluid which throws itself out of the circuit and in so doing produces light was described as 'salto della scintilla' [leap of the spark] — and even today we commonly refer to the 'salto di corrente' [leap of current] to describe a power cut. It was not uncommon to find this expression in the scientific treatises of the time, and one relevant occurrence is for instance in an 1831 issue of *Antologia* (a journal regularly read by Leopardi), in the article 'Sopra la forza elettromotrice del magnetismo' [On the Electromotive Force of Magnetism] by Leopoldo Nobili and Vincenzo Antinori. The article describes, for example, how, by interrupting an electric circuit, 'la corrente, ch'era già in giro, s'accumula [...] sul luogo dell'interruzione, che acquista quivi la tensione necessaria per lanciare la scintilla. Una tale tensione manca nell'altro caso di chiudere il circuito, e con ciò manca pure il salto della scintilla' [the current, which is already circulating, accumulates at the place of the interruption. This thus acquires the necessary tension to launch the spark. Such tension is not present in the other case when the circuit is closed, and together with it also the launch of the spark does not happen].[19]

Electric tension thus offered Leopardi an epistemological model to define the possibility of knowledge. In his search for understanding, man often only possesses the evidence of a final event rather than the awareness of the intermediate relationships between its constituents. Reason is challenged by the ambushes of invisible forces, but it nevertheless must continue to wander in the circuit of matter without abandoning the physical path.

Now that the theoretical relevance in Leopardi's thought of conductors, charges, poles of attraction and effects manifesting at a distance has been clarified, it is important to interpret how the electric and magnetic model actively shapes his writing. The notes in question develop independently and are therefore located at a certain temporal distance (the temporal gap often being signalled by Leopardi through the date), which is a necessary requirement to examine the patterns of emanations and leaps of electric discourse. However, the distance between notes is at the same time limited (in terms of notes present on the same page or on subsequent pages), which allows me to monitor, as it were, the warming influence of Leopardi's writing on the surrounding text. The following passage, followed by three accompanying notes (*Zib.* 255–57; my emphasis), provide a first example of thought in tension:

> L'uomo superiore, [...] si può dire [...] che si avvezzi a pregiare piuttosto che a dispregiare. [...] Siccome *prima egli non istimava se non le cose lontane, le quali, in quel modo in cui egli le concepiva, non erano reali*, si può dire che il numero delle cose reali ch'egli stima vada sempre crescendo, se bene diminuisca [...] il numero assoluto delle cose ch'egli stimava, perchè sono molte più quelle cose ch'egli pregiava lontane, e disprezza vicine, di quelle che da principio non curava, ed ora è necessitato a pregiare.
>
> [The superior man, [...] one could say [...] is these days more likely to praise than to disparage. [...] While *before he valued only distant things, which, in the way he conceived them, were not real*, you could say that the number of real things that he values goes on increasing, even if the standard of absolute value diminishes [...] of things that he used to value. Because there are many more things that he used to appreciate from a distance and thinks little of close up than those that at first he did not care about but now is obliged to appreciate.]
>
> Si mise un paio di *occhiali fatti della metà del meridiano co' due cerchi polari*.
>
> [He put on a pair of *glasses made from half the meridian with the two polar circles*]
>
> Una casa pensile in aria *sospesa con funi* a una stella. (1 Ottobre 1820.)
>
> [A house hanging in the air *suspended by ropes* from a star. (1 October 1820)]

It is part of a broad set of reflections disseminated in the *Zibaldone* about the different way of approaching reality in the passage between antiquity and modernity. In ancient times, states Leopardi, human beings had a low opinion of concrete reality because they tended to project themselves into illusionary dimensions of thought. They were persuaded of the existence and obtainability of illusions. As a result of modern disillusion and hopelessness, man has been forced to reapproach the real as the only realm of experience that is left following the 'strage delle illusioni' [slaughter of illusions].[20] On 1 October Leopardi rereads the passage written the day before and creates an image which is the materialization of the world of illusions evoked in the previous entry. Both images, 'Si mise un paio di *occhiali fatti della metà del meridiano co' due cerchi polari*' and 'Una casa pensile in aria *sospesa con funi* a una stella', represent an unreal, ancient way of perceiving remoteness through the lens of imagination, to which he refers in the previous reflection. The argument has actualized itself in the form of an image. Discursive thinking has leapt up and sparked a poetic creation. While this textual transformation provides evidence of the strong bond between philosophical and poetic thinking, the subsequent note shows how the interplay between the two takes place in both directions, from discourse to image and from image to discourse. The observation which follows on vivacity as the mother of grace is also intrinsically linked to the idea of tension evoked by the two images, with tension here constituting both the general conceptual framework of reference discussed in this chapter and a specific thematic motif of these representations. One can see how the text creates a chain of prolonged irritation, as the reflection on vivacity and 'languor' as sources of grace condenses in itself a sense of tension, electric tension, activated by a different kind of tension — the mechanical tension of 'ropes' and 'meridian' of the preceding images. Each link in this electric chain adds to the semantic aura of the surrounding thoughts, thus actualizing in the text the essential form of irradiation which is of scientific but also religious origin.

Another example of magnetic interaction between subsequent passages which are only apparently independent and which focus on different thematic concerns (*Zib.* 62–63; my emphasis), describes the disposition of soldiers at the Battle of Issus and then makes literary reflections on comedy and the effect of new similes:

> Nella gran battaglia dell'Isso, *Dario collocò i soldati greci mercenari nella fronte della battaglia*, [...] *Alessandro i suoi mercenari greci proprio nella coda* [...]. [E]ra chiaro che tutta la confidenza dei Persiani stava in quei 30^m· greci, e pure eran greci anche i mercenari d'Alessandro [...] ed egli li poneva alla coda. Quindi è chiaro ch'egli confidava più nel resto che in questi, e *quello che era il più forte dell'esercito Persiano era il più debole del Macedone.*
>
> [In the great battle of Issus, *Darius placed the Greek mercenary soldiers in the front line*, [...] *Alexander placed his Greek mercenaries at the very back* [...]. [I]t was clear that the Persians placed all their hopes in those 30,000 Greeks, and yet Alexander's mercenaries were also Greek [...] and he put them at the rear. It is therefore clear that he placed more trust in the others than he did in these, and *what was strongest in the Persian army was weakest in the Macedonian army.*]
>
> Della distinzione del ridicolo in quello che consiste in cose e quello che in parole, data da me in altro pensiero vedi il Costa della elocuzione p. 70. e segg.
>
> [As to the distinction between comedy of things and comedy of words, which I described in another thought, see Costa, Della elocuzione, pp. 70ff.]
>
> Una similitudine nuova può esser quella dell'agricoltore che nel mentre che miete ed ha i fasci sparsi pel campo, vede oscurarsi il tempo ed una grandine terribile rapirgli irreparabilmente il grano di sotto la falce: ed egli quivi tutto accinto a raccoglierlo, se lo vede come strappar di mano senza poter contrastare.
>
> [A new simile could be that of a farmer who is reaping, his sheaves scattered about the field, and sees the weather darken and a terrible hailstorm snatch the grain away irreparably from beneath his scythe; and he there, ready to harvest it, sees it being ripped from his hands without being able to do anything about it.]

As in the previous example, there is an effect of tension originating in the initial entry which is passed on to subsequent entries. There is a polarity in the collocation of mercenary soldiers in the two armies: at the front of the battle for Darius, at the rear for Alexander. These diametrical dispositions are also 'charged' antithetically. On the Persian side the non-mercenaries are the weak soldiers and the mercenaries the strong. On the Macedonian side, the non-mercenaries are the strong soldiers and the mercenaries the weak. This formation recalls the figure of an electric circuit with two poles of opposite charge. In terms of form this entry therefore seems to generate subliminally the idea of electrical current. According to the electric and magnetic model here employed, this reflection should be capable of producing an emanation of senses traversing and permeating the surrounding text. In the following note, at a first sight Leopardi's concerns might seem to belong to a completely different conceptual field, as he briefly refers to Paolo Costa's treatise *Della elocuzione* [On Elocution], which thematically does not have anything in common with ancient battle formations. However, the passage in question from Costa reads as follows:

> Si può [...] cavare ridicolo dalle parole composte di nuovo, che esprimono alcuna deformità del corpo o dell'animo [...]. Siffatte maniere che direi quasi deformità della lingua, poichè dall'uso si allontanano, essendo convenienti alle cose significate stanno bene, e perciò inducono a ridere e han lode di graziose; ma se poi in forza dell'uso divengono proprie, perdono, a somiglianza delle vecchie metafore, alquanto della grazia primiera.[21]

> [It is possible to obtain a comic effect from newly compound words which express some deformity in the body or soul. These manners, which I would almost define as deformities of language because they distance themselves from ordinary usage, conform to the things signified and are appropriate, and therefore they induce one to laugh and are praised as gracious, but, if as a result of use they become proper, they, like old metaphors, lose their pristine grace.]

The reference to grace alerts us to a possible live wire. Contemporary theories on metaphor, such as for instance Paul Ricœur's study on living metaphors, define the process of metaphorical consumption described by Costa and known already to Aristotle as one of the possible outcomes of *metaphorical tension*. In order for the metaphorical effect to be alive, or polysemantic, it is necessary to perceive a leap arising from the unexpected and unusual relationship between the metaphorical terms ('tenor' and 'vehicle').[22] Conversely, when a certain relationship between images has become conventional and almost automatic, the metaphorical tension decreases and the evocation weakens to the point of becoming synonymous with the original meaning.[23] Leopardi's brief reference to Costa is therefore also invested with a concern with tension, which we have reached from an initial theme of ancient battle evoking, through its lexical disposition, a subtle conceptual reference to electric conductors. But there is more. This apparently simple bibliographical reference does not stop the textual energy and continues to act as a creative conductor. It is not by chance that, immediately afterwards, Leopardi adds his note on the topic of a new simile and employs precisely an image that is somehow electrified through its reference to the hail storm, that is, an atmosphere electrically charged by nature. Once again, Leopardi's magnetic field of thought expands through charges and discharges in a fruitful interplay between discursive and poetic tensions.

The science of electricity is therefore another constituent form of the *Zibaldone* writing, and the ideas of conductor and conductibility of thought serve as suitable theoretical models to describe Leopardi's tendency to create circuits in which ideas attract each other as if they were differently charged polarities. Electric currents figure the movement of a writing 'a penna corrente' (*Zib.* 95), that is, a textual form assuming shape in the very same praxis and immediacy of its actualization.[24] The text becomes a living organism, self-nourishing through motion and variation, and by expansion and thematic leaps in a constant process of energetic production. Thus Nietzsche conceived of the 'living thing', which is such because it 'wants to *discharge* its strength — life itself is will to power — : self-preservation is only one of the indirect and most frequent *consequences* of this'.[25] Already Schlegel had conceptualized an equivalence between style, that is the effect of language on the receiver, and the electric spark, especially as far as polemic dialogical interaction is concerned — a form of expression also largely employed in the *Zibaldone*, as we shall see in Chapter 19. Schlegel referred to a 'fiery kind' of reason 'that actually makes wit witty, and gives an elasticity and electricity to a solid style'.[26] While opposing the 'soporific monologues of revered philosophers, he was hoping to reignite the "fire" of controversy', stimulating a dialogue with oneself and offering 'combinatorial incentives', to be completed by the reader in an infinite range and variety of possibilities corresponding to the real and changing status of their living conditions.[27]

Leopardi seems to take part in this electric line of thought which conceives of language as a living medium of emanation, 'creating involvement in depth', as electric light and power do, in the words of Marshall McLuhan.[28] Despite the sequentiality and chronological distance between fragments, the creative tension in Leopardi's circuits fills gaps and reactivates motion-pictures as in a process of film editing. Leopardi's fragments on polar circles and stellar ropes, for instance, with on the one hand the sense of discontinuity that they transmit because of their individual stances, and on the other the sense of communication, obtained through subtle semantic affinities, assume in the reader's imagination the speed and amalgam of senses characteristic of film, which carries us 'from the world of sequence and connections into the world of configuration and structure'.[29] Before and even without making sense of Leopardi's intended meaning in these images, the reader perceives his passage of thought from one figure to the other as a form of movement, independently from the specific contents or 'real' associations between the metaphors and images employed. In transmitting a sense of tension independent of the actual content, writing itself, *the medium*, like light, *is the message*. Leopardi's understanding of the effect of the electric spark as an image of beauty parallels McLuhan's conceptualization of cubism as 'an instant sensory awareness of the whole' where 'segments of attention have shifted to total field'.[30]

The *Zibaldone* accompanied Leopardi for fifteen years due to its inner renewable power, which almost certainly took strength from external stimuli such as Leopardi's reading, his dialogue with the ancient and modern literary world, as well as his own creative work and recurrent motifs in his philosophy; yet it also survived and persisted thanks to self-induced reasons which are intrinsic to the same process of note-taking, and at one with the non-programmatic contingency of the 'moment' of the practice of writing. In the second half of the nineteenth century, together with the development of thermodynamics and its interest in the conservation of energy, as well as with the rise of the discipline of psychology, which started to look at mental processes independently from direct sensorial responses, a new interest in habit and automatic physiology started to focus attention on the body as creator of its own inner functioning. Although Leopardi on a theoretical level was still very much bound to eighteenth-century physics and to associationism, there are already traces of this new sensibility in the *Zibaldone*, where thought emanates as a renewable form, independently from direct and explicit thematic associations between the entries involved in Leopardi's intellectual magnetism. As we shall see in the next chapters, it is not only the vivifying character of self-production which Leopardi faces in his daily relations with the text, for the vitalism that he shares with early-Modernist thinkers also brings with it the dangers and consequences of excess that can be generated by a thought with ample margin for expansion and freedom of action.

Notes to Chapter 13

1. Alessandro Volta, *On the Method of Rendering Very Sensible the Weakest Natural or Artificial Electricity (Del modo di rendere sensibile la più debole elettricità sia naturale, sia artificiale)* (London: Nichols, 1782), pp. 23, 58.
2. Alessandro Volta, 'Continuazione delle osservazioni sulla capacità de' conduttori elettrici e sulla commozione che anche un semplice conduttore è atto a dare eguale a quella di una boccia di Leyden. Del signor Alessandro Volta in una lettera al signor De Saussure', in *Opuscoli scelti sulle scienze e sulle arti*, 22 vols (Milan: Marelli, 1778), I, 289–312 (p. 293).
3. J. L. Heilbron, *Electricity in the 17th and 18th Centuries: A Study of Early Modern Physics* (Berkeley: University of California Press, 1979), p. 414.
4. Gaston Bachelard, *L'Activité rationaliste de la physique contemporaine* (Paris: PuF, 1951), p. 93.
5. Robert Darnton, *Mesmerism and the End of the Enlightenment in France* (Cambridge, MA, & London: Harvard University Press, 1968), p. 12.
6. See Francesca Montesperelli, *Flussi e scintille: l'immaginario elettromagnetico nella letteratura dell'Ottocento* (Naples: Liguori, 2002), p. 101.
7. Luigi Galvani, 'From *De Viribus Electricitatis* (1791)', in *Literature and Science in the Nineteenth Century: An Anthology*, ed. by Laura Otis (Oxford: Oxford University Press, 2002), pp. 135–39 (p. 136).
8. Cf. Luke Antony Francis Davidson, 'Raising Up Humanity. A Cultural History of Resuscitation and the Royal Humane Society of London, 1774–1808' (unpublished doctoral thesis, University of York, 2001), p. 164.
9. Nina Zimmer and Bodil Holst, 'Representations of Electricity: The Development of a Visual Language for Electrical Phenomena', *Interdisciplinary Science Review*, 27.4 (2002), 257–70 (p. 262).
10. Galvani, 'From *De Viribus Electricitatis* (1791)', p. 139.
11. Cf. Paola Bertucci and Giuliano Pancaldi, 'Introduction', in *Electric Bodies: Episodes in the History of Medical Electricity*, ed. by Paola Bertucci and Giuliano Pancaldi (Bologna: University of Bologna Press, 2001), pp. 5–15 (p. 13).
12. Felice Fontana, *Ricerche filosofiche sopra la fisica animale*, 5 vols (Florence: Cambiagi, 1775), I, 188.
13. Lucia De Frenza, 'La morte e l'elettricità: esperienze di elettrofisiologia tra XVIII e XIX secolo', in *Storia della definizione di morte*, ed. by Francesco Paolo De Ceglia (Milan: Franco Angeli, 2014), pp. 251–74 (p. 252).
14. Giacomo Leopardi, 'Dissertazione sopra l'elettricismo', in *Dissertazioni filosofiche*, pp. 222–32 (pp. 226–27; my emphasis).
15. See *Zib.* 1635–36.

16. In *Zib.* 2042 the electric imagery appears in the adoption of the word 'circuito' in connection with 'condotto': 'queste immagini risultano in lui da una copia di parole e di versi, che non destano l'immagine senza lungo circuito, e così poco o nulla v'ha di simultaneo, Giacchè [*sic*] anzi lo spirito è condotto a veder gli oggetti appoco appoco per le loro parti' ('his images come from an abundance of words and lines, which give rise to the image only after a long circuitous path; and so there is little or nothing simultaneous about him, for the spirit is led, instead, to see objects little by little, through their parts'). See also *Zib.* 4223.
17. See *Vocabolario degli Accademici della Crusca quarta impressione*, <http://www.lessicografia.it/Controller?c1=350;-7;3;-21159276;212722725;&c2=129;-39;3;40;69;1;130;32;5;40;66;1;129;-39;65;40;69;4;130;1025;5;40;75;13;130;27;3;652660136;1238720506;&qi=&qr=null&num=20&o=105;-44382125;-308820822;&q1=circuito&EdCrusca4=1> [accessed 14 February 2017].
18. The Tommaseo-Bellini Dictionary lists seven different entries for meanings of *circuito* linked to the science of electricity: 'circuito elettrico' [electric circuit], 'circuito elettrico ordinario' [ordinary electric circuit], 'circuito elettrico della boccia di Leida' [electric circuit of the Leyden jar], 'circuito galvanico' [Galvanic circuit], 'circuito magneto-elettrico' [electro-magnetic circuit], 'circuito termo-eletrico' [thermo-electric circuit], 'circuito voltiano o voltaico [Voltian or voltaic circuit] (Niccolò Tommaseo and Bernardo Bellini, *Dizionario della lingua italiana*, 8 vols (Turin: Unione tipografico-editrice, 1861–79), <http://www.tommaseobellini.it/#/items> [accessed 14 February 2017]).
19. Leopoldo Nobili and Vincenzo Antinori, 'Sopra la forza elettromotrice del magnetismo', *Antologia*, 131.11 (1831), 149–61 (p. 154).
20. Giacomo Leopardi, 'Discorso sopra lo stato presente dei costumi degli italiani' (*TPP*, p. 1013).
21. Paolo Costa, *Della elocuzione* (Bologna: Riccardo Masi, 1827), p. 73. The Leopardi library contains an 1805 edition printed in Venice.
22. The definitions of 'tenor' and 'vehicle' are those of I. A. Richards, *The Philosophy of Rhetoric* [1936] (Oxford: Oxford University Press, 1965).
23. Cf. Paul Ricœur, *The Rule of Metaphor: The Creation of Meaning in Language*, trans. by Robert Czerny, Kathleen McLaughlin, and John Costello (London & New York: Routledge, 2003).
24. On the meaning of 'a penna corrente' (*Zib.* 95) see Luigi Blasucci, 'I registri della prosa: Zibaldone, Operette, Pensieri', in *Lo 'Zibaldone' cento anni dopo, composizione, edizioni, temi*, ed. by Garbuglia, pp. 17–35 (pp. 20–21). See also Emilio Peruzzi, 'Stesura e stile', in Giacomo Leopardi, *Zibaldone di pensieri*, , ed. by Peruzzi, I, XLIX–LXI, and Ricci, 'Sintassi e testualità dello *Zibaldone di pensieri* di Giacomo Leopardi', parte I', p. 184, where the author insists on the *Zibaldone* writing as a 'scrittura dal coefficiente di progettazione ridotto' [writing with a limited degree of project-planning].
25. Friedrich Nietzsche, *Beyond Good and Evil*, ed. by Rolf-Peter Horstmann and Judith Norman, trans. by Judith Norman (Cambridge: Cambridge University Press, 2002), p. 15.
26. Friederich Schlegel, 'Critical Fragments', in *German Aesthetic and Literary Criticism: The Romantic Ironists and Goethe*, ed. by Kathleen Wheeler (Cambridge: Cambridge University Press, 1984), p. 43.
27. Guillaume Lejeune, 'Early Romantic Hopes of Dialogue: Friedrich Schlegel's Fragments', in *Literature as Dialogue: Invitations Offered and Negotiated*, ed. by Roger D. Sell, special issue of *Dialogue Studies*, 22 (2014), 251–70 (p. 258).
28. Marshall McLuhan, *Understanding Media: The Extensions of Man* [1964], (Cambridge, MA, & London: MIT, 2002), p. 9.
29. Ibid., p. 12.
30. Ibid., p. 13.

CHAPTER 14

Disenchanted Mnemotechnics

Leopardi's search for perfect natural images reflects a practice of representation which can be defined as organic. While maintaining the mnemonic function that the art of memory since antiquity associated with visuality, Leopardi's images — their creation and their effect on the crafting of thought — extend far beyond the spatial constructions of traditional mnemotechnics and the imprinting processes of Lockian sensationalism, where the mind produces images by receiving and storing sensory stimuli. In Leopardi, as in late nineteenth-century art and philosophy, visuality is deeply embedded in the physiology of the body, in its variable conditions and its sometimes automatic responses. Leopardi's *imagines agentes* bind to the concepts that they are chosen to express so that the recurrence of a certain reflection triggers its specific image, and vice versa the image favours the retrieval of a certain line of thought; this is visible for instance in the image of gravitation and acceleration used to depict the idea of progress, of which Leopardi writes, 'in matematica o fisica *non si può trovare più giusta immagine* di detti progressi, che il moto accelerato' ('*there is no more apt image* of this progress in mathematics or physics than that of accelerated motion') (*Zib.* 1767; my emphasis). Indeed, on p. 1732 Leopardi had already used gravitational motion to express the idea of the improvement of human faculties: 'la celerità de' progressi dello spirito umano si accresce in proporzione degli stessi progressi, come il moto de' gravi, il quale benchè sempre gradato, sempre proporzionatamente si accelera' ('the swiftness of the progress of the human spirit increases in proportion to that progress itself, like the motion of bodies which, though always gradual, always accelerates proportionately'). The elected image seems therefore inseparable from its generating idea, and this pairing also recurs at *Zib.* 2002. However, the value of the image does not always remain fixed and immutable, but is subject to variation and change. There is an ephemeral constituent that projects Leopardi's retrieval strategies far from the enduring and accumulative character of ancient mnemotechnics and close to the modern consumption of the image as a commodity. The passage between the two conceptions was set in motion in the eighteenth century, when the nature of man started to be investigated in order to find sources of happiness which could be recognizable and quantifiable, and reality started increasingly to be seen as a provider of 'objects' and signs assessed according to measurable and visible proofs.[1] Once the correspondence between signifier and signified lost hold and unicity, signs and objects became consumable and replaceable. Equivalences and displacements took place between elements of reality and signification which were previously assigned relations of exclusivity in the realm of knowledge. Leopardi was fully aware of this change, as is demonstrated for instance by his interest in the way fashion and ephemeral values create homogeneity and subjugation to trends whereas before there was originality of expression and spontaneous imagination. Equally telling is his envisioning of a general tendency towards uniformity affecting modern man in all possible spheres, from emotions to social practices, to language. As for the latter in particular, Leopardi's reflection on the disappearance of multiple synonyms and on the monopoly of signification assumed by certain few words clearly testifies to his concern with the progressive depletion of the richness of language. Certain words, Leopardi believes, gained an expressive territory that used to belong to a variety of words, thus diminishing the propriety of language.[2] Also, along a line of thought which might resonate with thinkers from Maine de Biran to Bergson, Leopardi was keen to investigate the flattening effect of habituation and repetition on the faculties of thought and on the way we represent reality and are shaped by it. As we have seen, this sensitivity regulates his own approach to study, as is evident in the continuous interplay between reiteration and vivifying expansion in the prose of his diary.

However, philosophical speculation is not the only type of writing that is modelled by habituation, and the persistence of images in the *Zibaldone* can also be explained in the context of Leopardi's revisiting of the pages of his notebook. It is through constant re-reading and re-employment that an image originally intended as the most suitable (that is, 'perfect', absolutely 'apt', or the most natural, in Leopardi's words) can be moulded and applied to a broad range of topics, thereby losing its exclusivity and favouring equivalence between different discourses.[3] In the same way, as for the general tensions at play in the *Zibaldone* as a whole, the formation of images is also where aspiration to the ultimate and unique configuration of thought comes to terms with the reshaping and sometimes levelling power of praxis and experience.

This is evident by following the movements of one of the most recurrent and allusive images of the *Zibaldone*, namely that of soft dough, which serves as an image of conformability:[4] '*Ciascun uomo è come una pasta molle, suscettiva d'ogni possibile figura, impronta ec. S'indurisce col tempo, e da prima è difficile, finalmente impossibile il darle nuova figura ec. Tale è ciascun uomo, e tale diviene col progresso dell'età*' ('*Each man is like a soft dough, susceptible to every possible shape, impression*, etc. It hardens over time, and at first it is difficult, and finally it is impossible to give it a new shape, etc. Such is each man, and such he becomes as he grows older') (*Zib.* 1452; my emphasis). Later the image of soft dough is retrieved and reapplied in an analogous way to express conformability, this time with the general category of 'man' giving way to the more specific 'fanciullo':

> *Il carattere de' fanciulli essendo ancora formabile, la significazione della loro fisonomia, è anch'essa da formarsi, e la corrispondenza fra l'interno e l'esterno è minore, o meno determinata, in quanto l'uno e l'altro aspettano la forma che riceveranno dalle circostanze, e sono ancora quasi pasta molle e da lavoro.*

[*Since children's characters are still in the process of being formed, the meaning of their physiognomies is itself yet to be formed*, and the correspondence between the inside and the outside is less, or less defined, inasmuch as both await the form they will receive from circumstances, and are still *as it were a soft paste to be worked*.] (*Zib.* 1905; my emphasis)

This proves itself as one of the most effective and long-lasting similes in the *Zibaldone*. Conformability indeed is also the topic at the origin of Leopardi's reflection on the structuring components of signification. From its first appearance the relation between the signifier and the signified is denoted by qualities of transience and lightness. Leopardi explains how children's physiognomy conveys little signification to the spectator, given that signification is a product of habit and assuefaction. To the eyes of the observer who associates the external facial expression to the inner character of the child, 'ciò che ora ne apparisce è passeggero, oltre che alla fine è di poco conto, e nel genere delle bagattelle' ('what now appears of them is fleeting, aside from the fact that in the end it is of little account, and a mere trifle') (*Zib.* 1906). The changing body of the child is itself emblematic of the more general mobility and instability of signification. Leopardi is here stating the arbitrariness of the sign, its variability as a function of the transient intrinsic features of the content it is meant to express. Universal and absolute truths have disappeared from Leopardi's horizon and nothing impeded that which presents itself as the most secure and reliable evidence from acquiring unexpected contrary connotations sooner or later. But he is also asserting a further level of variability, namely the fact that the relation between signifier and signified depends on the conditions of the receiver, as his or her degree of exposure and habituation to the relation changes the value associated with it:

> L'effetto della significazione della fisonomia umana, riconosce anch'esso per sua prima cagione ed origine l'esperienza e l'assuefaz. [...] La significazione [...] non esisterebbe, se ciascun uomo non osservasse l'effetto generale, e gli effetti particolari, momentanei ec. che per natura produce l'interno sul viso.
>
> [The first cause and origin of the effect of meaning in the human physiognomy is also acknowledged to lie in experience and habituation. [...] The actual meaning [...] would not exist if each man did not observe the general effect, and the particular, momentary, etc., effects that what is inside naturally produces on the face.] (*Zib.* 1930–32)[5]

It is the process of recurrent observation which shapes signification. Meanings are not fixed forever and signs become marks of changing values in time. Any mnemotechnic relying on the image as a reminder of past thought has now to presuppose an idea of memory as a mobile recurrence of forms which might vary in their nature, rather than as a provider of static loci for fixed contents.

In a later passage Leopardi focuses on certain linguistic considerations, especially concerning the German language. Its most distinguishing characteristic, he states, is that it is able to acquire all properties belonging to other modern idioms. This is possible because German is not yet fully formed, and its lack of rigidity allows for it to be easily moulded, thus absorbing all the peculiarities of other languages.

After mentioning the main quality of the German language, that is, its adaptability, Leopardi employs once again the simile of the soft dough, which he had previously defined as the image par excellence of human conformability. It is essential to note how, having introduced the image of the dough, the privileged term for analogy — the conformability of the child — also reappears. As soon as the image is named its related concept also immediately resurfaces:

> La lingua tedesca *non è ancora abbastanza formata*; e perciò solo le sue ricchezze e facoltà non hanno limiti: [...] *ell'è come una pasta molle* suscettibile d'ogni figura, d'ogni impronta, e di cangiarla a piacere di chi la maneggia; *simile appunto al fanciullo prima dell'educazione*, il quale è suscettibile d'ogni sorta di caratteri e di facoltà.
>
> [*The German language is not yet sufficiently formed*, and so its resources and capabilities are limitless. [...] *It is like a soft dough*, receptive to every shape, every imprint, which can change at the pleasure of whoever is handling it, or *like an unschooled boy* who is receptive to every sort of attribute and faculty.] (*Zib.* 2080; my emphasis)

The image of the soft dough acts as a kind of gateway to a different imaginative field, that of childhood and its learning potentialities, thus also expanding the original simile from a two-way- to a three-way-analogy. Like Leopardi's arguments, so his thinking through images proceeds through expansion. And in the same way that philosophical expansion reveals the need for seen and experienced evidence, thus the frequentation of an image exposes the image itself to the variables of usage. A few pages after the above-mentioned passage, in a discussion on the ancient roots of German and Italian, Leopardi compares Teutonic with Latin. While Latin was able to anchor its roots in time, live out its life, and eventually die out, Teutonic was never fixed and still lives on in modern languages which 'derivano dall'antico senza interruzione' ('derive from the ancient without interruption') (*Zib.* 2082). The following simile, which Leopardi employs to explain the differences between the two languages, is revealing of the influence of previous writing on the persistence of the image:

> L'antico teutonico dunque non si può diversificare dal moderno tedesco, né considerar questo e quello *come due individui, ma come un solo, anticamente fanciullo, oggi adulto*. Dove che l'italiano p.e. e il latino sono due individui parimente maturi, e diversi l'uno dall'altro. Tutto ciò non prova l'adattabilità e *conformabilità* particolare della lingua tedesca, ma la *conformabilità* comune a tutte le lingue non mai state formate.
>
> [Ancient Teutonic cannot, therefore, be differentiated from modern German, nor can the former and the latter be considered *two individuals, but are one, a child in the past, today an adult*. Whereas Italian, e.g., and Latin are two equally mature individuals, and different from one another. All of that proves not the adaptability and particular flexibility of the German language but the *flexibility* common to all languages that have never been fully formed.] (*Zib.* 2083–84; my emphasis)

The image of the child here emerges under the influence of the three-way-simile previously quoted. In the course of the *Zibaldone* a kind of transitive relation —

namely the mathematical property stating that if 'a' is related to 'b', and 'b' is related to 'c', then 'a' is also related to 'c' — is formed between the poles of the analogy: first there is the relationship between human conformability and soft dough (in *Zib.* 1452, 1905); then the analogy between the German language and the dough (in *Zib.* 2080, in the first part of the simile) and the three-way relationship between German, dough, and the child (again in *Zib.* 2080); and finally the parallel between German and the individual's conformability. The element 'child' in the course of its movements between one relation and the other has changed its function: in the first relation it is the first term of analogy, that is, the concept to which the image of the soft dough provides visual expression. In the three-way simile and in the last quoted relation between the German language and human conformability the 'child' modifies its status and becomes the second term of the simile, or in other words the image of language which is now its concept. All these developments are possible thanks to the mnemonic value of the image, in which a certain representation adheres to the concept it depicts and follows its movements through the pages. However, as in any experience of endurance over time, modification occurs and the image can change its initial value, as is evident in the last entry where the 'soft dough' appears, once again in conjunction with a reflection on the German language:

> *Altro è che una lingua sia pieghevole, adattabile, duttile; altro ch'ella sia molle come una pasta.* Quello è un pregio, questo non può essere senza informità, voglio dire, senza che la lingua manchi di una forma e di un carattere determinato, di compimento, di perfezione. Questa informe mollezza pare che si debba necessariamente attribuire alla presente lingua tedesca [...]. Ciò vuol dire ch'ella è una *pasta informe e senza consistenza alcuna.*
>
> [*It is one thing for a language to be pliable, adaptable, versatile, quite another for it to be as soft as dough.* The former is a good quality, the latter implies formlessness, or rather, implies the language lacks form or a determined character, in terms of achievement and perfection. It seems that such flabby formlessness should be necessarily attributed to the present German language [...]. That means that *it is a formless dough and without consistency.*] (*Zib.* 4191; my emphasis)

Compared to the previous reflections on German language, the image of the dough here provides a strikingly negative connotation: whereas in the previous entries the dough represented the vivifying adaptive potential of language, here it is employed to express a lack of form and character. However, even from a reversed critical perspective the original image does not abandon the primary idea (language) and the representation itself, once again in a performative outcome, is subject to the remoulding and reshaping it is intrinsically elected to signify. The soft dough occupies a stable and secure place in Leopardi's imagination also thanks to the fact that it possesses the visible and tangible character of a concrete example, which gives it striking metaphorical power. For this reason, the image of the soft dough can start to circulate freely in the *Zibaldone*, expanding its range of influence and generating a kind of seriality in its web of multiple references. But it is as if the value of the elected sign, similarly to any commodities subjected to trends of fashion, had some kind of lifespan, its popularity and decline responding to changing waves of interest. The core visual metaphorical field (revolving around the poles of conformability, adaptability, and malleable bodies) is associated with a system of figurative internal cross-references (centring on the 'dough' and the 'child') which are related and independent from any possible alternative semantic meanings. The soft dough is so effective an image that it monopolizes the imaginative territory for conformability. The recurrence of the image becomes somehow self-sufficient. In the core metaphorical field there is, in the words of Baudrillard, a kind of 'autonomization', emancipation and liberty of the signs, which start to 'exchange among themselves exclusively', while at the same time stretching the metaphorical flexibility of the image to encompass wider aspects of the real (from human growth to language).[6] But this also means that as use of the sign grows, its value mutates. While new objects inserted into the play of images expand the reality of reference, the sign (the soft dough) broadens its range of action to become allusive of antithetical values, namely positive conformability and negative lack of form, the latter resulting from its very extreme malleability. By exploiting the whole spectrum of values of the image and including senses which contrast with previous senses in the history of his image, Leopardi allows his own writing to become abstracted from the individual meanings progressively employed. The last negative connotation assumed by the dough in referring to the German language does not annul the praiseworthy moulding qualities of the dough expressing the child's conformability. Both senses continue to co-exist, but this co-existence of opposites, seen from the perspective of the *Zibaldone* as a whole, seems to allude to a higher level of form assumed by notebook-writing than that of a work with chronological development and sequentiality of thought. In the course of the reflection additional senses have been discovered and added to the matrix of signification. Significance extends beyond the individual expressions associated with the image and coincides with the very *movement* of thought in time. From this perspective, the writing of the *Zibaldone* could be read, again borrowing from Baudrillard, in terms of 'simulacra surpass[ing] history', that is, as a rapport between production and reproduction: 'the real message, *the real ultimatum,* lay in reproduction itself' and 'production, as such, has no meaning'.[7] Applied to notebook-writing, this means that attention on particular occurrences only (production) obscures the forms that the image assumes in its circulation and reusages, and neglects its performative outcomes. Instead, it is only the full lifespan and reproduction of the image that can reveal its full range of action, including the self-referential effect that the image of the dough ends up exercising on itself as it becomes the site for the *expansion* of senses, *remoulding* of contents, and *adaptability* of linguistic components, which become visible only when writing is studied not just for its contents but as a *medium of transformation* of contents. As we have seen, the image of the soft dough creates an enclosed and almost autarchic regimen of textuality, which in general in Leopardi becomes more exclusive when the image is more perfect, and the more it is automatically generated in the moment of creation the more its appearances multiply.[8]

Leopardi's sensitivity to disenchantment does not go as far as to assert his full anticipatory vision of the postmodern world of simulation theorized by Baudrillard; nevertheless, his language of images proves that the roots of a mechanism of simulacra are already present in his diminishing confidence in the gnoseological possibilities of the subject with respect to a reality which has withdrawn stable references of signification and ontological answers to the nature of human existence. Images are long-lasting in Leopardi's *Zibaldone*, but as they emerge from a non-programmatic praxis of writing, they are equally unstable in their reference value. Leopardi's employment of the image of the soft dough seems to exemplify this process. The image most suitable and faithful to the concept continues to activate memory and promote further research, but the relation between signifier and signified, that is between image and idea, changes its value as the *Zibaldone* progresses and becomes a variable function of time and assuefaction rather than a fixed signpost. Also, not only is the meaning associated with the dough subject to variation, but, as we have seen, it is the very same statuses of concept and image that in the expansion of similes exchange roles. In the course of the pages the signifier becomes the signified and vice versa. This reflects a more general shift in the observing subject's position which originated in the early decades of the nineteenth century and was fully achieved by Modernism, as the visual subject, more and more coincident with its own corporeality, begins to be involved in a process of equivalence and exchange with the reality observed.

As Crary remarks, modernity can be defined by two parallel processes, that is, the 'remaking of the observer' and the 'proliferation of circulating signs and objects whose effects coincide with their visuality'.[9] In the course of the nineteenth century, the role of the observer in acquiring evidence becomes one of participation in generating the meaning attributed to the reality observed, rather than mere recognition from a position of detached scrutiny. A further level of equivalence to that involving objects is reached between subject and objects of observation, that is between the two poles of the process of understanding which used to be distinct. When the physiology of the observing subject becomes paramount in determining cognition, the observer begins to occupy the same plane of consistency with the reality which it would like to investigate. Observer and the observed become two categories continually exposed to mutual influence and variation, with this surface of interaction replacing the distance that traditionally separated the point of view of the analytical subject from the reality investigated. As we shall see in the next two chapters, Leopardi's use of images is telling of a more general cultural and conceptual shift which occurs in the nineteenth century and which he is one of the earliest thinkers to perceive.

Notes to Chapter 14

1. Cf. Jean Baudrillard, *The Consumer Society*, trans. by Chris Turner (Los Angeles, CA, London, New Delhi & Singapore: Sage, 2008), pp. 49–55.
2. See *Zib*. 1500–01: 'il tempo [...] sopprime quindi naturalmente una buona parte de' sinonimi, conservandone solo uno o due per significato, che prevalendo appoco appoco nell'uso, fanno dimenticar gli altri ec. Così le lingue perdono appoco appoco necessariamente di ricchezza e di proprietà, a causa della sinonimia' ('time [...] naturally suppresses a fair proportion of the synonyms, retaining only one or two per meaning, which, as they gradually prevail in ordinary use, cause the others to be forgotten, etc. Thus necessarily the languages gradually lose wealth and propriety because of synonymy').

3. See *Zib.* 1432, 1767, 3534.
4. On the concept of conformability in Leopardi see Aloisi, *Desiderio e assuefazione*, pp. 97–108.
5. On the role of assuefaction in the process of signification alluded to in the image of the soft dough see Antonella Del Gatto, *Aspetti della mimesi nella modernità letteraria: premesse petrarchesche e realizzazione romantica* (Sesto Fiorentino: Apice, 2015), pp. 97–106.
6. Jean Baudrillard, 'Symbolic Exchange and Death', in *Selected Writings*, ed. by Mark Poster (Stanford, CA: Stanford University Press, 1988), pp. 119–48 (p. 125).
7. Ibid., p. 138.
8. The recurrence of the images of the refreshing breeze to express the effect of Anacreon's odes and of gravity exemplifying the progress of human spirit fit this emancipatory prerogative of the image generating an exclusive circuit of signification.
9. Crary, *Techniques of the Observer*, p. 11.

CHAPTER 15

❖

The Hypnotic Image: A Preliminary Contextualization

Between 1810 and 1840 a new regimen of visuality was affirmed in aesthetics in conjunction with new optical technical and anatomical advancements.[1] The eighteenth-century model of the camera obscura started to be challenged by new focuses on physiological optics. In the camera obscura, the framing of a visual experience where an extrapolated image of the mobile reality outside is projected inside a dark room can be used as an exemplary model for the conception of an interiorized mechanism of interpretation for the analyzing subject. This device reproduces, in its structure, the basic idea of the eye as a lens through which the penetrating light impresses an image according to geometrical and linear correspondences and proportions. The light penetrates the aperture of the camera projecting mimetic figures of the outside world, in the same way as in the equivalent classical physiological model the reality to be experienced is located outside the subject, while the apparatus for experience is located inside, in the mind, which receives objects of the real to be analyzed in the form of impressions conveyed by the senses. This reflects a more general understanding of perception as a process involving positions and roles for both subject and object of observation which are stable, constant, and operating through association. Instead, the retinal model, which in the course of the nineteenth century replaced the camera obscura model, relied on a more complex knowledge of the structure of the eye. In this new conceptualization, our optical apparatus is understood to function in response to a system of diffractions and opaque reverberations in the retina, in which 'the passage of light into the eye is anything but unmediated' and light itself, no longer thought of as travelling in linear segmentation, is conceived of as 'a form of luminous energy that strikes a dense mosaic of receptors'.[2] Unlike the previous geometrical conception, the parameter of duration is here fundamental, as the impulses received by the retina originate the optical perception via mutual and progressive activation of a complex system of nerves.

This new visual regimen, which is indebted to the electric and magnetic imagery of the eighteenth and nineteenth centuries, sees the body in its most extrinsic interaction with the outside world and in its variable responses, and as determiner not only receiver of perception. Perception itself is not something to be enclosed within the mind that treats it as a separated object of study, but a maker of the very same subjectivity that is constantly reshaped and renewed in the encounter with the real. It is on the basis of this plane of action, where subject and object are mutually influenced and redefined, that Crary chooses the definition 'observer' as opposed to that of 'spectator' to express the prerogatives of the new modern visual subject. While the term 'spectator' remains confined to a passive idea of 'looking at' something, 'observer' carries a performative aspect in its etymology from the Latin *observare*, which alludes to conforming one's action to specific conventions or practices. It refers to a system of discourses, cultural constructs, and social norms with which the acting visual subject interacts: 'there is no observing subject prior to this continually shifting field'.[3] The subject cannot help but respond to these impulses in making his choices while at the same time modifying the value of the impulses received according to its movements. In relating the process of signification to an organic transformation, that of the child's growth, Leopardi seems to have made his own the new sense of immanence and permeation between subject and object of observation. He also seems to attribute to perception and, more generally, to understanding, the prerogatives of a process unfolding in time, rather than an immediate univocal response to a sensorial stimulus. The Newtonian model, which in his early 'Dissertazione sopra la luce' [Dissertation on Light] Leopardi had considered for instance in his reflections on the transmission of light as a mere process of reception — that is, light as either reflected or absorbed by the eye — appears as too unproblematic an explanation of the continuing changing variables of perception, discussed later on in the *Zibaldone*.[4] Here in describing the importance of assuefaction in determining judgment and decoding sense perception, like Goethe and Schopenhauer Leopardi affirms an important property of the mind: its capacity to produce understanding as a progressive action, and its power to adjust. In his *Theory of Colours*, Goethe described the changing qualities of the afterimages produced in and by the eyes under certain light conditions, and insisted on them being a visual product independent of the outside reality where the visual process initially begins. Schopenhauer, instead, stressed how retinal conditions determine phenomenological perception of a reality which assumes gnoseological status dependent on the physiological prerogatives of the subject, in a strong interlacing of aesthetics and biology. In his system of thought, perception is not passive reception but an activity of the nerves.[5] Similarly, when Leopardi describes the adjusting power of the mind in approaching new data which are interpreted through recourse to existing experience, he is also projecting his phenomenology away from the Cartesian model of a dualistic reality into a more complex, subjectivized realm of knowledge formation, in which the mind is the site and the producer of understanding. In the following entry, for instance, Leopardi clearly affirms that judgement is reached through an adjusting movement of consciousness, which allows exposure to a new melody to change initial aural discomfort into enjoyable recognition:

> Le armonie o melodie affatto nuove ordinariamente non piacciono che agl'intendenti, i quali sentono la difficoltà, e le raffrontano colle regole ch'essi conoscono ec. E questi medesimi provano a primiss. giunta un senso di discordanza, che però presto svanisce, e ch'essi immediatamente ravvisano per

illusorio: ma si può dir che ogni assoluta novità in fatto di musica contiene e quasi consiste in un'apparenza di stuonazione.

[Wholly new harmonies or melodies normally only please the knowledgeable, who appreciate the difficulty, and compare them with the rules that they know, etc. And even they experience at the very beginning a sense of discordance, but this soon vanishes, and they immediately perceive it to be illusory. Yet one could say that every absolute novelty in music contains and as it were consists of an appearance of disharmony.] (*Zib.* 1873–74)

Here the mind is not merely the apparatus elaborating ideas transferred by the senses. In addition to the movement proceeding from the senses to the intellectual analysis, there is a further level of perception moving in reverse from the intellect to the senses, which takes place after, not prior to, the formulation of judgement. The intellect, Leopardi believes, possesses a kind of 'sensorium' acquired at a mature stage of the thinking process, when the intellect has already been involved in cognitive operations which have produced familiarity. This participates in further sensorial evaluation, in that it determines the way subsequent impulses are perceived by the senses, as Leopardi states in a discussion of our appreciation of melodies: 'le assuefazioni cagionano, siccome fra noi, il senso e il piacere d'esse melodie' ('habituation that occasions as it does with us, the meaning and pleasure of those melodies') (*Zib.* 3213). The role of the mind is not only to assess materials provided by the senses, but to influence the very experience of perception. Therefore when Leopardi writes that 'gl'intendenti giudicano, e giudicando sentono (cioè col fattizio, ma reale sensorio dell'intelletto e della memoria) secondo i principii e le norme della loro scienza' ('the knowledgeable make judgments, and as they judge they listen (that is, with the artificial but real perception of intellect and memory) according to the principles and norms of their science') (*Zib.* 3218), he means that the intellect personalizes the nature of perception by actively participating in the interaction with external reality. The very same distinction between what is outside and inside the mind blurs in this system of diffractions, given that the idea of an external objective reality awaiting assessment is overtaken by this more dynamic conception of the intellect as intervening in the most variable and exposed plane of immanence.[6] The fact that the separation between outside and inside is not in place anymore also means that, while the mind is much more involved in the process of perception, it is also more exposed to unpredictable effects and capturing experiences. The reality from which the intellect was protected by the sensorial filter is now the surface on which the intellect leans and from which its sensorium emanates. It is on the basis of this *physiology of exposure* that for Leopardi the principle of measure and moderation is of great importance.

This physiological perspective also reflects broader cultural concerns with ideas of infiltration, influence, and control, which in the course of the eighteenth and the nineteenth centuries had become crucial in the new phenomenon of mesmerism, or 'animal magnetism' (the first system of psychological healing introduced in France by Viennese doctor Franz Anton Mesmer), and its development into the science of artificial somnambulism and hypnotism. Mesmerism was located at a crossroads between contrasting and at times antithetical conceptualizations and practices. It was the direct product of modern science while at the same time taking inspiration from pre-modern thought, combining new technological tools such as the galvanic battery with spiritual experimentations with clairvoyance and thought transfer.[7] Although polemic reactions and objections were not lacking, odd and unconventional practices and wonderful experiments had a massive power of suggestion if not of persuasion. These new practices linked to the discovery of the unconscious flourished around the belief in the healing or corrective power transmitted by extremely gifted practitioners to individual or collective pathologies. They acted by exploiting what were believed to be hidden components of the body and manipulatable operations of the mind. From Mesmer's alleged cosmic fluid, the unobstructed circulation of which had to be restored in the human body, often through touch, in order to re-establish harmonic balance between the organs, to Puységur's belief in the 'action of thought upon the vital principle of the body', because 'thought moves the matter', to the enchanting sight of hypnotists manipulating the unconscious will of their subjects; in all these manifestations of the magnetic age, suggestion, imagination, and empirical treatment had expanded the boundaries of matter to include invisible forces and processes which were previously relegated to the field of the supernatural.[8] Contaminations were felt to be taking place between the sphere of the human and that of the machine. Through the voice of the hypnotist, the subject, who 'lit sans les yeux' [reads without eyes], was thought to increase his or her intellectual faculties and strengthen his or her power of perception.[9] Some artificial somnambulists were believed to acquire extreme clarity of inner vision and clairvoyance to the point of becoming capable of reading other people's mind as well as scrutinizing the interior of their own body to detect the nature and location of their illnesses, and to establish an appropriate cure for the disease. In Italy, one of the first and most sensitive scientists interested in mesmerism and practices of the occult — the latter always analyzed through experimental and rational means — was Francesco Orioli, a good friend of Leopardi during the time that the poet spent in Bologna (on three different occasions from 18 to 27 July 1825, 29 September 1825 to 12 November 1826, and from 26 April to 21 June 1827). As demonstrated by Gaspare Polizzi, Orioli was both a direct and indirect source for Leopardi.[10] Direct because, while part of the same circle of Bolognese friends, in late 1825 Orioli had the opportunity to discuss in person with Leopardi his own multi-faceted erudition on matters of electricity and animal magnetism, and it was probably Orioli who suggested to Leopardi Ludovico Antonio Muratori's *Della forza della fantasia umana* [On the Power of Human Imagination], the seventh chapter of which is devoted to 'Sonnamboli, detti anche nottambuli' [Somnambulists, Also Called Noctambulists].[11] But Orioli also inspired Leopardi indirectly through his own work. While it was thanks to Orioli's research on 'paragrandini' [hail rods] (probably known to Leopardi before Orioli's 1826 article on 'De' paragrandini metallici' [On Metallic Hail Rods]) that Leopardi developed the idea of imaginary tools such as 'parainvidia [...], paracalunnie o paraperfidia o parafrodi' (*TPP*, p. 506) ('a parajealousy, a paracalumny, paraperfidy or parafraud', *MT*, p. 55), which appear in the 'Proposta di premi fatta dall'accademia dei sillografi' [Announcement of

Prizes Offered by the Academy of Sillographers], the Leopardi library also hosts the four volumes of the journal *Opuscoli scientifici* [Scientific Papers]. Here, in Orioli's 1817 article on mesmerism, it was probably his depiction of the figure of Tasso and his spirit which inspired the representation which Leopardi would employ in his *Operette*. It is worth noting how Tasso is considered by Orioli as a subject extremely prone to transforming into real and concrete presences figures that in a balanced state of mind would only remain as inconsistent representations. Tasso appears as a typical example of one in which desire:

> Ariva [*sic*] [...] a dipinger sugli occhi il fantasma d'un oggetto che non è presente, e a farne udire ciocchè in realtà non ascoltiamo, e a farne gustare il sapor di cibi immaginarj, e l'odore di aromi che non sono, e a farne infine palpare e trovar solidi gl'idoli che mentre sono interiori vengono da noi trasportati all'esterno.[12]

> [Gets to depict in his eyes the ghost of an object which is not present, to make one hear that which in fact one does not hear, and to make one taste the flavour of imaginary food and the scent of aromas that do not exist, as well as to make one touch and feel solidity in idols which, although internally produced, are transported outside.]

This is a typical description of 'somnambulistic lucidity', that is, a high stage of somnambulism characterized by faculties of extreme intellectual vividness and penetration, which is discussed thoroughly by Orioli also in the chapters devoted to 'chiarovisione' [clairvoyance] and 'sonno magnetico lucido' [lucid magnetic sleep] in his treatise on animal magnetism, which he authored in 1842.[13] An unprecedented degree of self-awareness was reached by the somnambulist subject compared to other medical or psychological conditions, which also helped transform the idea of the patient from a passive to an active subject. Capable of training his or her own faculty of vision and clairvoyance through appropriate somnambulistic education, the somnambulist patient progressively learned to vivify his capacity of introspection through verbal elaboration.[14] He could see the past and the future as if they were the present, in a flattening of temporal perspectives in which objects normally distanced through the deep and smoothing filter of remembrance or imagination appeared to the mind's eye with unnatural but hyper-realistic closeness. While in this state of lucid sleep, the patient was not only capable of activities normally performed in an awakened state, but he was also able to imitate perfectly the features and movements of people who had been connected in the 'magnetic chain'. The somnambulist became almost a sleeping replica of the authentic subject, which led to many associations between this phenomenon and metaphors of reflections in mirrors and automatons.[15] At the same time, by fixing himself in absolute concentrated attention, the patient under hypnosis paradoxically abandoned extrinsic vitality to enter a state of isolation from the external world, with the latent journey of the mind often eventually terminating with silence and deep sleep. While the person was constantly exposed to the risk of degenerating into mechanistic automatism, the machine was sometimes believed to possess marvellous intuitive characteristics.[16] Conversely, ways in which to potentiate the sensory and rational operations of the machine were also studied in order to investigate the possibility of it assuming operational faculties which could be easily confused with those of a person. Frankenstein provides perhaps one of the most exemplary tragic models of this embodiment.

Mesmerism developed into different branches which transformed the original idea of magnetic fluid into different conceptualizations, such as the divine afflatus for the mystics, the spectres for the spiritualists and the will for the metaphysicians. In all these cases, it was the idea of an expanded cognitive potential, often manifesting hidden dynamics of the mind, to represent the common ground of interest, which also allowed Freud to consider earlier psycho-pathological practitioners and researchers of the invisible transmittable powers of the mind as the fathers of modern psychoanalysis.[17]

The mesmeric and hypnotic age — with a proper science of hypnotism having been developed after James Braid's theorization in the early years of the 1840s — is thus permeated by two complementary but inverse tendencies, namely to explore the acquisitions of an augmented extension of intellectual power, and at the same time to invigilate and warn against the destructive and irreversible consequences of its excess. In late eighteenth-century philosophical treatises exploring the prerogatives of the mind one can already find the roots of this twofold tension between curiosity towards and prudent refrain from the challenges of thought extension and advancement of the image. This is evident for instance in Christoph Wilhelm Hufeland's *Die Kunst, das menschliche Leben zu verlängern* [The Art of Prolonging Life] (1796), a book well known to Leopardi, who read it in the Italian translation by Luigi Careno.[18] In the chapter devoted to 'Agreeable Stimulants of the Senses and of Sensation Moderately Used', Hufeland considers intellectual stimula as essential for prolonging human life, especially when 'by their immediate influence on the vital power, they enliven, strengthen, and exalt it'. However, he adds, it is essential not to exceed with 'a certain cultivation and refinement of our sensibility', and 'in stimulating the senses also great care must be taken not to exceed the proper measure; for the same enjoyment which, when used in a moderate degree, is capable of restoring, may, if used too much, consume and exhaust'.[19] We have already seen how the same ambivalence inhabited the electric imagery of the spark, which was associated with an idea of beneficial energy but one that could also provide a deadly shock when excessively charged and unsupervised (Chapter 13). And it is precisely the comparison with electricity and magnetism which Hufeland uses to describe the 'vital power', the living principle which can persist in a *state of liberty* even when it is enclosed in the body, which it inhabits in a latent way, appearing only when activity is required for preservation, in the same way as only a certain irritation reveals the presence of electricity in a body.[20]

In the nineteenth century, mesmeric and hypnotic imagery continue to propose an idea of 'freedom' connected to exercises of control and penetration of the body and mind performed by the practitioner. Freedom to traverse the boundary of the other's self-domain to master the attention and operations of the patient is normally conceded by the patient to the healer in mesmeric sittings, but it is also often abused by mesmerists and hypnotists such as the likes of Svengali (in George Du Maurier's novel *Trilby*) for devious ends. Animal magnetism acts as a point of convergence between the religious, the scientific, and the linguistic, and ideas of daring and breaching the limit are their common denominators.

Certain essential expressive and philosophical achievements in Leopardi's work are deeply affected by a subterranean influence of animal magnetism, despite Leopardi's lack of explicit references. It is not by chance, for example, that in the *Disegni letterari* [Literary Projects] ideas related to electricity, motion, magnetism, as well as 'occult and active forces' (such as those employed by mesmerism) are placed in a central position in a list of themes which are of structural importance:

> Inni agli Dei filosofici; Natura, Necessità, Materia, Uomo o genere umano, Arte o industria umana, Passioni, Speranza, Forze occulte ed attive della materia, Elettricità, Moto, Magnetismo, Calor centrale, Sole, Caso o Fortuna nelle cose umane, Universo o Tutto, Ragione, Immaginaz.[21]
>
> [Hymns to the philosophical gods. Nature, Necessity, Matter, Man or humankind, Art or human industry, Passions, Hope, Occult and active forces of matter, Electricity, Motion, Magnetism, Core heat, Sun, Chance or Fortune in human matters, Universe or Whole, Reason, Imagination.]

The presence of mesmeric concepts within core words of Leopardi's philosophical system is telling of their importance and wide range of application. The variety of analogies that animal magnetism naturally favoured in the course of the nineteenth century is helpful to explain how it permeated the mind of a thinker that shows a propensity for metamorphoses and metaphorization between different cultural discourses. From a thematic point of view, as will be shown in the next chapter, in the *Zibaldone* Leopardi's concerns with ideas of moral and aesthetic possession and domination are formulated with references to the classical social and moral system of values. But at the same time a more complex interchange between the ancient and the modern is at play in his entries, reflecting the way animal magnetism broadly rehabilitated and re-proposed classical inter-personal norms and constructs under a modern psychological guise, often also absorbing Christian moral and spiritual preoccupations.

Providing the background to the contaminations between different cultural manifestations of the mesmeric spirit will allow us to interpret certain uses of the images in the *Zibaldone* beyond their most immediate meaning and classical world of reference, and to uncover the presence of a certain kind of modern visuality and interest in the 'real', which was to find full expression only later in the nineteenth century.

Documents reporting 'case studies' of episodes of magnetization (with the term here being intended, broadly, as the equivalent of mesmerism as well as of hypnotic or artificial somnambulistic induction) often moved from personal experiences of patients and magnetizers, to include references to the venue of the somnambulistic process, the hygienic and moral state of the subjects, and to explain the stages of magnetic sleep with nuances of language which absorbed a variety of expressive codes, from those proper to both rural societies and aristocratic medicine. Within these frameworks, references to both medical and Catholic ethics were constant. Master and subject were often presented as tied by one exclusive magnetic bond, while preserving their autonomy at the end of the magnetic process. Giordana Charuty, writing with regard to French sources, notices how mesmeric procedures focused on 'tying the souls', 'crossing fluids', and 'receiving ecstasies': 'La "foi ardente" emprunte, ainsi, un langage religieux pour assimiler la relation maître/sujet à celle de Dieu et du Christ, et pour qualifier le lien d' "âme" à "âme" qui doit unir les deux opérateurs' [The 'burning faith' borrows, thus, a religious language in order to assimilate the relation between master and subject to that between God and Christ, and to qualify the connection from 'soul' to 'soul', which is meant to conjoin the two magnetic ministers].[22] The dialogical modalities between master and subject employed in reporting the magnetic experience contain the seeds of the first expressions of the modern autobiographic posture. A new sense of conceiving of the subject in terms other than those of sensationalism was propelled by animal magnetism, as 'tout comme la pensée onirique, la parole somnambulique relève d'une autre forme de succession des idée, qui échappe au controle de la conscience et de la volonté' [exactly as in the case of oneiric thought, the somnambulist's talk highlights another type of succession of ideas which escapes the control of consciousness and will].[23] The concept of personal identity started to change together with the idea that the mind might not be a single self-present entity. It switched its place from self-assessment to the testimony of others. Because the subject's memory followed independent and separate patterns in the two states of vigilance and sleep — the subject in one state did not recollect the portion of life he had experienced in the other state — only other people, acting as observers and witnesses, could provide proof of his personal identity.[24] But this also meant the birth of a new model of the self which was disenfranchised from theological logic. While the behaviour of latent consciousness and will made it difficult to attribute moral responsibilities as a matter of lucid deliberation, a process of substitution of magnetic marvel with religious transcendence intervened. This was necessary to fill the philosophical and conceptual gap opened up by the lack of rigorous conceptualization and terminology available to describe new unconscious dynamics of the mind and different modalities of assessing its operations physiologically and morally. However, on the one hand a new sense of an out-of-vigilance error, which escaped the traditional possibilities of remission of Christian morality, presented itself to the sensibility of the believer; on the other, the whole system of Christianity seemed to provide available answers, the process of allegorization often allowing religion to be metabolized together with magnetic imagery in order to elicit structures and correspondences from which to borrow a language and build the basis of a yet unformed 'intellectual belief' in magnetism.[25] But at the same time, during the magnetic and hypnotic age there were significant cases which moved the status of religion to that of an 'emotional belief', that is, a set of conventions which are not (or no longer) logically justified but that instead meet our needs as a form of '*prudence* (in view of *all* the needs of our being) of the kind of emotional activities the belief subserves'.[26] This is for instance the reading provided by Robert Milder with respect to the 'unpardonable sin' sought by Ethan Brand, the fiendish protagonist of Nathaniel Hawthorne's eponymous short story, who devoted the last years of his life to the domination and possession through magnetic means of the soul and mind of the young female character, to finally annihilate himself in completion of his enterprise. Despite and beyond the fact that, in line with Hawthorne's puritan moral vision, magnetic abuse is explicitly associated with Christian sin, there is an ambiguous duality of perspectives at play. Milder argues that the heavy burden of morality and Christian allegorization associated with the core themes of the tale acts as a kind of overarching creative structure which belongs more to the narrative dimension than to the author's real perception of the natural dimension of the story. In his Berkshire notebook which depicts the same provincial world which would also appear in *Ethan Brand*, Hawthorne's notes seem much more rational and far less transcendental compared to the narrative. A detailed reading of the text allows the critic to reach the conclusion that the narrative seems to undermine the meaning of religion through the very same obsessive employment of its forms, so that by insisting on the theme of a sin that is *beyond* God's forgiveness, Hawthorne in fact projects the idea of an unprecedented sin outside God's sphere of influence, thus effectively depriving punishment of a concrete place in the reader's imagination and undermining the validity of supreme religious means. This transforms God into a disempowered presence and confers deeper significance on a human being who is truly disenchanted:

> The dreadful task of extending man's possible guilt beyond the scope of Heaven's else infinite mercy' is concomitantly a work of situating man in a religious world and extending his power and majesty, even to the point of abridging divine sovereignty and outdoing God, much as Ethan Brand feels that in boldness of thought and deed he has outdone the Devil.[27]

It seems appropriate here to apply Milder's reading of Ethan Brand as 'an allegorist who reacts against the prospect of empty naturalism by recreating an imagined word fraught with spiritual meaning' to a broader tendency of the magnetic imagery as a whole.[28] The parallel psychological universe disclosed by magnetic science and the lack of scientific models capable of fully describing mental processes operating unconsciously, made the recourse to pre-existing moral and religious structures even more necessary, as a mask to cover the theoretical fragility in approaching the new modern unconscious on behalf of an age which was still unprepared to rebuild conceptual paradigms on the ruins of rationalism and associationism.

The sense that the various magnetic practices were overcoming a threshold of some sort, be it physical or mental, and the fact that this operation was perceived as exceeding the normal freedom and possibility of human operativity are at the roots of the various associations of magnetic performance to divine creation and the primordial Adamic state of being, which populate magnetic treatises or reports in the nineteenth century. The association between magnetic and primordial intellectual power is highlighted for instance by Francesco Guidi, author of an 1854 treatise on animal magnetism, in a reflection on the Fall which finds many echoes in Leopardi's own philosophical treatment of the theme:

> Chi ha dato ad esseri, spesso ignoranti nello stato di veglia una perspicacia tanto penetrante e una scienza tanto profonda? Chi oserebbe negare che non sia una scintilla del genio che l'uom ebbe nella creazione dalle mani dell'Onnipossente prima della sua caduta?[29]
>
> [Who gave to creatures so ignorant in the state of vigil such penetrating perspicacity and deep knowledge? Who would dare to deny that this is a spark of the genial spirit that man received in the creation from the hands of the Almighty before his fall?]

Leopardi's position regarding the intellectual condition of Adam subsequent to the Fall diverges in that he believes that as a consequence of sin Adam's clairvoyance actually increased rather than decreased. However, he also associates with sinful Adam an image of illumination and lucidity which carries immense significance, both theoretically and, more personally, creatively:

> Questo squilibrio, questo contrasto di due qualità divenute allora incompatibili [la carne e lo spirito], provenne e consistè nell'incremento e preponderanza acquistata dalla ragione; e la degradazione dell'uomo non fu quella della ragione. nè della cognizione, nè l'offuscaz. dell'intelletto. Anzi dopo il peccato, e mediante il peccato l'uomo ebbe l'intelletto rischiaratissimo, acquistò la scienza del bene e del male, e divenne effettivamente per questa, quasi unus ex nobis, disse Iddio.
>
> [This imbalance, this clash of two qualities that had become incompatible, originated and consisted in the increase and predominance of reason; and the degradation of man was not that of reason or of knowledge, or the obfuscation of the intellect. Indeed, the intellect of man was greatly illuminated after his sin, and by way of his sin. He acquired the knowledge of good and evil, and became effectively in this way 'quasi unus ex nobis' ['as one of us'], in the words of God.] (*Zib.* 434)

Leopardi's entire conceptualization of the roots and course of modernity revolves around the idea of the abuse of reason exemplified by the first man, and as we shall see in the next part of this book, his own *Zibaldone* also has to come to grips, on a performative level, with the same realization that took hold of Adam (see Chapter 20). It is therefore useful to explore further the background of these contaminations between the magnetic and Adamic imagery, as well as the way in which language was also affected by similar psychological and moral concerns.

Numerous texts proposing comparisons between the religious and the magnetic fields are listed for instance in the first chapter of Lisimaco Verati's treatise on animal magnetism devoted to the various opinions concerning its origins. Verati is not himself a supporter of these readings, but the number of sources provided testifies to an increasing inclination of early nineteenth-century theorists to favour an overlap between religion and pseudo-science which is significant from the point of view of recurrent forms of thinking that this operation implies. From Verati one learns for instance that: 'Avvi talun magnetista che fa risalire l'esistenza del magnetismo animale [...] alle costole del padre Adamo; imperciocché tiene per fermo, che il sonno nel quale appunto rimase privo della costa, destinata a formare la sua bella compagna, fosse magnetico' [There are some magnetizers who date the existence of animal magnetism back to Adam's ribs; and therefore they are convinced that the sleep in which Adam was deprived of his rib, which would form his beautiful companion, was a magnetic one].[30] I have already stressed how the iconographic imagery of electricity interacted very closely with artistic representations of the myth of the origin, such as for instance Michelangelo's *Creation of Adam* (see Chapter 13). In Verati's treatise we find an analogous operation with respect to the Scriptures, as the story of the Fall is revisited and subjected to a transposition which deconstructs its various moments and symbols so that each component finds its new place in the ambiance of mesmerism.[31] For example, in order to show how animal magnetism 'manomette e contamina' [manipulates and contaminates] the Holy Scriptures,[32] the author mentions interpretations which highlight the persistence of atavistic ritual and gestures in the practice of magnetism:

> Quando il gran sacerdote nel benedire il popolo invocava il nome del Signore, alzava le tre prime dita della mano, tenendo le altre due inclinate (posizione magnetica), e nel momento dell'ispirazione, secondo la testimonianza dei sacri libri 'la mano di Dio discendeva sopra di lui (cioè Dio lo magnetizzava), e così gli comunicava lo spirito profetico'; [...] quando Mosè volveva riempir Giosuè dello spirito profetico, gl'imponeva la mano sul capo.[33]

> [When the great Priest invoked the name of God in his blessing of the people, he would raise three fingers of his hand and keep the other two inclined (as in a magnetic posture), and in the moment of inspiration, according to the testimony of the sacred books, 'the hand of God descended above him (that is, magnetized him), and in this way it communicated to him the prophetic spirit'; [...] when Moses wanted to fill Joshua with the prophetic spirit he would impose his hand on his head.]

Animal magnetism, with its codes of practice based on touch and the visual capture conducted by the hands and eyes of the magnetizer, could easily superimpose its modern imagery on ancient symbolic cultural systems deriving from Roman law. However, visual and physical performances were not the only territories that lent themselves to processes of absorption and contamination. The voice of the magnetizer was also a powerful tool for the penetration of the patient's mind, and thus also the verbal sign became subject to manipulation of the religious into the pseudo-scientific. The analogical potential of magnetism, which was centred on its naturalness, was recognized by Verati, this time discussing its linguistic implications:

> Per assicurarci del carattere naturale dell'azione di Gesù in certi atti miracolosi, [...] noi dobbiamo cercare dei corrispondenti fenomeni nel dominio di quelle contingenze che son riguardate come naturali; ora qui il magnetismo animale forma, com'è noto, il punto centrale di tutte le analogie che possono rintracciarsi. Noi vi riscontriamo [...] un'azione curativa, non già della mano che offre un rimedio, [...] ma della mano che semplicemente tocca, della sola imposizione di essa, in virtù della quale Gesù così spesso guariva. [...] Pure noi troviamo, senza immediato contatto, l'efficacia della semplice parola, ed eziandio della volontà del magnetizzatore [...]. In questo dominio [...], veggiamo similmente estendersi i limiti delle facoltà di percepire, ed apparire una lucidità ed una veduta a distanza che ci ricorda molte particolarità della vita di Gesù, secondo la evangelica narrazione.[34]

> [In order to be persuaded of the natural character of Jesus's actions in certain miraculous events, [...] one must seek for correspondent phenomena in the realm of those situations which are regarded as natural; now, animal magnetism constitutes, as is well known, the centre of all analogies that can be found. One could individuate a healing function in the hand offering a remedy, or even in the hand which is simply touching, by virtue of which Jesus so often healed; at the same time one can find the effectiveness of the bare word operating without direct touch, and of the will of the magnetizer. [...] In this respect one can see that both cases extend the limits of the faculty of perception; a certain lucidity and distant sight appears that reminds one of many episodes of Jesus's life, according to the Gospel.]

Words can trigger powerful beneficial effects, extending the horizon of clarity, augmenting perception, and overcoming the ordinary limitations of human faculties. However, words can also be as dangerous as any other physical procedures when used carelessly. A sense of the limit had to be ensured to safeguard the patient's body from harmful manipulations, especially when implements such as needles were applied to the body of the sleeping patient for punctures, incisions, or burnings. Similarly, words could harm the spiritual wellbeing of the soul when administered without control. As Paolo Costa explains in his *Del modo di comporre le idee* [On the Ways to Compose our Ideas], words can travel from mouth to mouth and, by crossing the boundaries of different ideas, can *awaken* and convey meanings which they did not carry at the beginning of their journey:

> Molte sono le parole che andando di bocca in bocca risvegliano nelle diverse menti diversissimi concetti; molte quelle, che trapassando da un'idea a significarne un'altra, recano alla seconda gli elementi proprii della prima. Per queste cagioni il linguaggio diventa un istrumento di falsità, che le strane opinioni tramanda di gente in gente, di generazione in generazione.³⁵

> [There are many words which, passing from mouth to mouth, awaken in different minds many different concepts; many words which cross from one idea to signify another idea, and carry into the second certain meanings which are proper to the first. For this reason language becomes an instrument for falsity, as it multiplies strange opinions from people to people and from generation to generation.]

The transmission of words refers to a latent process of insinuation and circulation of ideas from mind to mind, which lends itself to comparison with practices of magnetization, the idea itself behaving in the mind as if it were a person 'awoken' from sleep under the effect of, so to speak, 'the fluidic chain' of other ideas. Verati extends the analysis of the effect of the images even further, by discussing a degree of vividness in which the image almost changes its ontological status to move into the dimension of the real. According to the degree of energy and clarity that they carry, certain creations of the mind switch from the status of idea to that of image, and from this to sensation, which is the effect normally produced by the outside reality on the body. Similarly to Orioli's conclusions regarding Tasso's psychological state, for Verati in madness and other pathological conditions an excess of vividness characterizes the representational progress and, in the same way as in dreams, certain images 'riescono anche forse più vivaci delle sensazioni impresse in tempo di vigilia, e [...] alcuni pazzi [....] scambiano le loro imagini colle vere sensazioni attuali' [appear even more vivid than sensations imprinted in time of vigil, and [...] some crazy individuals [...] mistake their images for actual and true sensations].[36]

The traditional question on the nature of the relationship between the 'original', and its representation through the image, known since Aristotle, is posed here with a focus on the body as producer and at the same time receiver of its own manifestations. Between the 'thing' and its 'image', a relation of homogeneity of effect can arise which overcomes the normal dialectics of mutual dependence, whenceforth the image gives life to the thing by allowing it to take a form in the mind, while vice versa the image needs an original source in the real from which to flourish. In the case of extreme sensitivity induced by dream, illness, or madness, an abstract thought can reach the same level of concreteness as the actual life that produced it. The body can be hit by the image with the same intensity and modalities as it is by the object in its immediate physical manifestations, producing analogous sensations to those aroused by 'le sensazioni degli oggetti attualmente sottoposti agli organi sensiferi' [the sensations of objects when they are presented to the organs of sense].[37]

In this sensibility towards ideas of crossing, overcoming boundaries, and dominating the mental sphere of others, one finds the roots of those particular fears of and attractions to the vivification of the image, which emerged more evidently towards the end of the nineteenth century, especially in the study of hysteria and other nervous pathologies. The new sense of reduced distance between the original and the copy as well as the hyper-clarity induced by the extreme vicinity of the object of the gaze become more and more compelling with the growth of the consumer society, and also determine new interests in the creative arts. In painting, for instance, this new visuality can be found in the diversified artistic line which includes Wilhelm von Köbell (who in his paintings depicted backgrounds which are often in abrupt communication with the foregrounds), Turner, Manet, and Seurat, who conceive of the observing eye of the viewer as participating in the logic of the work of art.[38] Here the viewer's gaze is often pulled towards the scene represented while the subjects of the painting seem to enter into communication with life outside the canvas. In some of Turner's work produced in the 1840s (*Light and Colour (Goethe's Theory) — The Morning After the Deluge* (1843) and *The Angel Standing in the Sun* (1846), in particular), the looking eye of the viewer emerges from the circular brushstrokes of the painting as intrinsically merged with the scene represented, and the sun depicted also alludes to the 'the pupil of the eye and the retinal field on which the temporal experience of an afterimage unfolds'.[39] Somehow, the form of the painting continues outside itself in the artistically formless body of the viewer while the work of art is permeated by the viewer's presence, creating 'a zone where forms become indiscernible'.[40]

The parable of magnetic culture from the eighteenth to the early twentieth century is therefore one in which progressive substantiation of the invisible also brings about a more physical experience of vicinity. The image switches ground, and from being a mere object of contemplation it starts to inhabit the body in a more concrete, fulfilling, but also uncanny way. In the next chapter we will look at the way in which Leopardi's relationship with his own images shows crucial signs of his preoccupations with concepts of aesthetic abuse, intellectual domain, and loss of creative identity. His use of forms of attenuation protecting the creator (and reader) from the direct impact of an image is clearly an expression of this multi-layered sensitivity, where the sense of error and fear of excess are conjoined with a tendency to explore and expand the metaphoric might of language.

Notes to Chapter 15

1. See Crary, *Suspension of Perception*.
2. Ibid., p. 153.
3. Crary, *Techniques of the Observer*, p. 6.
4. Cf. Giacomo Leopardi, 'Dissertazione sopra la luce', in *Dissertazioni filosofiche*, pp. 197–207 (p. 205).
5. Cf. P. F. H. Lauxtermann, 'Five Decisive Years: Schopenhauer's Epistemology as Reflected in His Theory of Colour', *Studies in History and Philosophy of Science*, 18.3 (1987), 271–91.
6. Cf. my 'Intelletto', in *Lessico leopardiano 2016*, ed. by Novella Bellucci, Franco D'Intino and Stefano Gensini (Rome: Sapienza Università Editrice, 2016), pp. 57–63.
7. Cf. Betsy van Schlun, *Science and the Imagination: Mesmerism, Media and the Mind in Nineteenth-century English and American Literature* (Berlin: Galda & Wilch, 2007), pp. 10–12.
8. Armand-Marie-Jacques de Chastenet, marquis de Puységur, *An Essay of Instruction: Teaching the Method of Magnetizing*, trans. by John King (New York: J. C. Kelley, 1837), p. 61.
9. Brigitte Baptandier, 'Le Texte en filigrane', in *Du corps au texte: approches comparatives*, ed. by Brigitte Baptandier and Giordana Charuty (Nanterre: Société d'ethnologie, 2008), pp. 7–24 (p. 19).
10. See Gaspare Polizzi, 'Alla ricerca dello "specioso" e dell' "insolito": Francesco Orioli e Giacomo Leopardi', *Lettere italiane*, 60.3 (2008), 394–419.
11. Ludovico Antonio Muratori, *Della forza della fantasia umana* (Venice, Pasquali: 1745), pp. 64–88. Leopardi's library holds the 1830 edition, published by Masi in Bologna.
12. Francesco Orioli, 'Lettera II. Mesmerismo nella sua maggior semplicità. Definizione del medesimo. Forza del desiderio, della volontà, della speranza, della fiducia, del timore, dell'attenzione nel produrre o nel togliere i morbi e generalmente nel perturbare il corpo: riflessioni generali e particolari', *Opuscoli scientifici*, 1.2 (1817), 117–40 (p. 124). On this text and the relationship between Orioli and Leopardi see Polizzi, 'Alla ricerca dello "specioso" e dell' "insolito"', pp. 411–13.
13. Francesco Orioli, *Fatti relativi a mesmerismo e cure mesmeriche* (Corfù: Tipografia del governo, 1842), pp. 282–307.
14. See Adelina Talamonti, 'Prefazione', in Clara Gallini, *La sonnambula meravigliosa: magnetismo e ipnotismo nell'Ottocento italiano* (Rome: L'Asino d'oro, 2012), Kindle edition, location 85.
15. Cf. Gallini, *Magnetismo e ipnotismo nell'Ottocento italiano*, location 844.
16. Cf. Montesperelli, *Flussi e scintilli*, pp. 161–62.
17. See Maria M. Tatar, *Spellbound: Studies on Mesmerism and Literature* (Princeton, NJ: Princeton University Press, 1978), pp. 3–44.
18. See my 'Ephemera', pp. 81–88. Leopardi mentions Hufeland in *Zib.* 352, and in his *Operette*, more precisely in a note to the 'Dialogo di un fisico e di un metafisico' (*TPP*, p. 525) ('Dialogue of a Physicist and a Metaphysician', *MT*, p. 254).
19. Christoph Wilhelm Hufeland, *The Art of Prolonging Life*, 2 vols (London: Bell, 1797), II, 266–67. On the relations between Leopardi and Hufeland see Loretta Marcon, 'La ragione, il corpo, la vita. Kant, Hufeland, Leopardi', *Rivista di letteratura italiana*, 25, 2 (2007), 49–70 (p. 61).
20. Cf. Hufeland, *The Art of Prolonging Life*, I, 43–44.

21. Giacomo Leopardi, *Disegni letterari* (*TPP*, p. 112).
22. Giordana Charuty, 'Somnambules à la lettre', in *Du corps au texte*, ed. by Baptandier and Charuty, pp. 151–84 (p. 172).
23. Baptandier, 'Le Texte en filigrane', p. 20.
24. See Daniel Pick, *Svengali's Web: The Alien Enchanter in Modern Culture* (New Haven, CT, & London: Yale University Press: 2000), p. 77.
25. For the difference between intellectual and emotional belief see I. A. Richards, *Practical Criticism: A Study of Literary Judgement* (London: Kegan Paul, 1930), pp. 271–91.
26. Ibid. p. 277.
27. Robert Milder, *Hawthorne's Habitations: A Literary Life* (Oxford: Oxford University Press, 2013), p. 10.
28. Ibid., p. 11.
29. Francesco Guidi, *Trattato teorico-pratico di magnetismo animale considerato sotto il punto di vista fisiologico e psicologico* (Milan: Turati, 1854), p. 101.
30. Lisimaco Verati, *Sulla storia teoria e pratica del magnetismo animale*, 4 vols (Florence: Bellagambi, 1845), I, 10–11. Lisimaco Verati was the pseudonym of Giuseppe Pellegrini.
31. Ibid., p. 12.
32. Ibid., p. 13.
33. Ibid.
34. Ibid., p. 15. I discuss further the analogies between religion and animal magnetism in my forthcoming article, 'Italian Mesmerism, Religion and the Unconscious: Irresistible Analogies from Muratori to Morselli', in *Archaeology of the Unconscious*, ed. by Aloisi and Camilletti, pp. 113–40.
35. Paolo Costa, *Del modo di comporre le idee e di contrassegnarle con vocaboli precisi*, 3rd edn (Parma: Fiaccadori, 1838), p. 13.
36. Verati, *Sulla storia teoria e pratica del magnetismo animale*, III, 87. I analyze this passage further, as well as the importance of the vivification of the image in Leopardi, in my forthcoming article 'Ipnotismo e iperrealtà: spunti per un dialogo tra Leopardi e il postmoderno', *Italian Studies*, 74. 3 (2019).
37. Verati, *Sulla storia teoria e pratica del magnetismo animale*, III, 87.
38. Cf. Crary, *Techniques of the Observer*, pp. 126, 139–43.
39. Ibid., pp. 139–40.
40. Gilles Deleuze, *Francis Bacon: The Logic of Sensation*, trans. by Daniel W. Smith (London & New York: Continuum, 2002), p. 46.

CHAPTER 16

❖

Leopardi's Philosophy of Exposure and Attenuation

Leopardi's conception of writing is expressed in his criticism of the declarative style of certain authors who elicit pleasure 'mediatamente, cioè mostrando come ce lo possiamo proccurare' ('indirectly, showing how we can obtain it'), while poetry brings pleasure 'immediatamente, cioè somministrandocelo' ('immediately, provides it for us') (*Zib.* 21). This reflects a more general reassessment of issues of personal identity which originated in Europe during the 1820s and which projected into the realm of self-hood the new questions on integrity and contamination also raised by the magnetic imagery discussed earlier. This reconceptualization of personal identity was founded, as demonstrated by Angela Esterhammer with respect to the English context, on a tension between theories and creative practices insisting on an ideal of an interiorized and autonomous self, on the one hand, and, conceptions of an interpersonal, interactive and performative self on the other.[1] The latter views, such as for instance in the case of William Hazlitt, valorize the self's character by means of personification and agency, even implying the possibility that an identity might be replicated by an imagination capable of projecting itself into fictional selves and assuming their characteristics. This performative imagination transports the features of an imagined and future self into the real and organic life of the present self. It is precisely through their interest in the ways in which identity can be multiplied and replicated that early nineteenth-century thinkers develop the idea of a discontinuous and vulnerable self which had already interested eighteenth-century intellectuals such as David Hume and Adam Smith. In this idea of a multiplication of selves the nineteenth-century philosophical conceptualization of personal identity takes ownership of the perception of social changes brought about by the growing seriality and replicability intrinsic to contemporary advances in technology, the advent of modern city life, as well as the consumeristic and commodified economy.[2]

Although Leopardi does not produce a fully articulated theory of the self, the focus on processes of sympathy activated by writing is crucial in his thought because in his view this represents the means through which poetry triggers beneficial illusions. It is precisely on the basis of this performative ideal that the *Zibaldone* becomes the centre of absorption and irradiation of cultural impulses which act directly on its structure and mould Leopardi's language, thus often *transforming* the text into what it is talking about. As already shown, the case of electricity is an example par excellence, as whenever Leopardi considers more or less explicitly themes recalling ideas of tension, the text itself assumes the shape of a circuit or an electric spark (see Chapter 13). However, the destructive potential of electricity and the uncanny manifestations of magnetism are also the models which allow Leopardi to conceptualize an ideal of moderation in processes of textual performance. Excessively exposing an uncontrolled imagination to the influence and effects of the other self (be they real or fictional) can represent a threat to personal identity. The following analysis of forms of mitigation in the *Zibaldone* aims to reconstruct the way Leopardi's writing mirrors dynamics of attraction to and distancing from the enchantment of the text.

Attenuation, or mitigation, a linguistic phenomenon studied mainly within pragmatics, is a collection of strategies for the protection of 'l'agire linguistico da vari rischi interazionali' [linguistic agency from various interactional risks], and functions as a mode of adaptation and control in interactive communication.[3] Morphemes of approximation or uncertainty (for example 'almost', 'that is to say', 'I would say') can be found associated with any part of the sentence attenuating the degree of responsibility of the speaker, and at the same time softening the responsibility requested on the part of the interlocutor. The classification devised by Claudia Caffi distinguishes three general types of mitigation: 'cespugli' [bushes] where, to mitigate the content of a proposition, the speaker keeps a certain distance, conferring approximation or vagueness ('a bit', 'a certain', 'a kind of', etc.); 'siepi' [hedges], used to attenuate the illocutionary impact ('unless I'm wrong', 'I would say', 'as it were', etc.); and 'schermi' [shields] where the origin of the proposition alleviates or deviates responsibility away from the speaker by different attribution of the content source (as in 'quote unquote' or indirect speech).[4] As well as applying to the speaker's point of view (speaker-oriented), where it reduces the degree of adhesion to the proposition, mitigation can project itself onto that of the receiver, to silence or sweeten the impact of a valuation, whatever advice or criticism it might involve. If, from time to time, mitigation assumes characteristics of subjectivity, possibility, uncertainty, and approximation, the general reason it is required is a condition of danger or excessive exposition intrinsic to the expression, and the need to soften its effect or range of application.

As mentioned before, attenuation is a very flexible strategy, applicable to various elements of the sentence as required; for as a figure of the contingency of communication, it can be accommodated in styles more or less charged with literary intention, lending itself in the written text to privileged analyses of the degree of dialogicity, explicit or implicit, in a text. It is no coincidence that the *Zibaldone*, where the dialogical vein has recently been emphasized, frequently uses mitigating measures, the adoption of which corresponds each time to different aspects of Leopardi's reflection and poetry.[5] Attenuation can work as a harmonious component compared to the poetics of vagueness and the indefinite, or as a sign of the adoption of a scientific method. Given the absolute relativity of any judgement within a reality that is fleeting and unstable, every declaration of truth has to come to terms with a level of possibilities mitigating its impact or incisiveness.

I intend to analyze here a specific category of mitigation, that is, the attenuated metaphors or images where the interaction between concepts is tempered by the presence of indicators of approximation which slow down or render opaque the process of transference between tenor and vehicle. This is sometimes a sign of hesitation, or at other times gives an aura of further vagueness to the metaphorical process, already by nature virtually indefinite and open to a multiplicity of possible outcomes. In metaphors, the attenuation can assume very different evocative functions, from complete participation and pertinence on the one hand, to purely graphic mitigation on the other. For the former, the following passage from the 'Cantico del gallo silvestre' [The Canticle of the Wild Cock] is representative of the type of mitigation integrated with the image: 'E tu medesimo [sole], tu che *quasi un gigante* instancabile, velocemente, dì e notte, senza sonno né requie, corri lo smisurato cammino che ti è prescritto; sei tu beato o infelice?' (*TPP*, 576) ('And you yourself [sun], you who *like a tireless giant*, swiftly both day and night, with neither sleep nor rest, run the unending course that is prescribed you; are you full of bliss or of misery?', *MT*, p. 172). Here we have attenuation with extreme poetic effect: the 'quasi', while first seeming to emphasize the absence of metaphorical identity, is instead at one with the image itself. It enlivens the senses of immeasurability, conferring vagueness and approximation on the metaphorical application of the word expressing excess (the 'giant'), which already escapes any definite representation. The double strength of the 'quasi', in its approximate and comparative meaning (in the sense of 'as if' and 'little less than') softens the semantic weight of the word beside it and confers a further sense of vastness and indefiniteness to the metaphorical idea. In this case, therefore, the attenuation only *appears* to hinder the integral metaphorical transfer, while in reality reinforces its senses (the excess, accessible only approximately).

A second case of mitigation which is, as it were, an intermediary between assimilation and distance from the image, is the reflection on the expectations of the old man in *Zib.* 3268–69. Leopardi finds himself discussing the process of deferment characterizing the way the elderly man relates to hopes. Because the old fellow knows from experience that the possibility of pleasure is denied to man, and therefore being unable even weakly to experience desire, he attempts to project his hopes as far away as possible, so that the object of desire can never be near enough to fully demonstrate its unreachability and vanity: 'le sue speranze [del vecchio] ne divengono tarde e pigre e lente e quasi trascurate (benché sempre però bastantemente vive per mantenerlo e *quasi allattarlo*, come alla vita umana indispensabilm. ricercasi.)' ('his hopes become tardy, lazy, and slow, and almost neglected (although still sufficiently alive to maintain and *almost suckle him*, as is indispensably necessary for human life)') (*Zib.* 3268–69; my emphasis). The 'almost' is introduced to attenuate the oxymoron generated by the courageous juxtaposition of old age and breast feeding, the two periods in human life that are furthest apart; but on closer view, its decelerating effect is only illusory, and instead seems to open the way to a reflective space that does not negate but reaffirms the truth of the image and of the existential paradox described. The continuation of the reflection, 'come alla vita umana indispensabilm. ricercasi', leaves a trace of a further meditative movement and reaffirms the validity of the seemingly incongruent image.

Instead, in the following cases, hedges, bushes, and shields of mitigation, such as 'per così dire' [so to speak], 'si può dire' [one might say], 'vogliamo dire' [by which I mean], 'pare' [it seems as though], plentiful in the *Zibaldone*, give attenuation the function of a brake not directly integrated in the image: 'le sue canzoni sono coperte *si può dire* ugualmente di uno strato di perfetta e formale mediocrità' ('every single poem is, *one might say*, equally covered with a layer of perfect formal mediocrity and frigidity') (*Zib.* 27; my emphasis, as is the case for all following examples in this sentence); '[la letteratura latina] venuta, *per così dire,* a lotta colla greca, [...] dovè cedere' ('[Latin] literature, when it came into conflict, *so to speak*, with Greek literature [...] had to yield') (*Zib.* 996); 'le opere [dei settentrionali] nascono tra le pareti di una camera scaldata da stufe; le opere [dei meridionali] nascono, *p. così dire*, sotto un cielo azzurro e dorato, in campagne verdi e ridenti, in un'aria riscaldata e vivificata dal sole' ('the products of northern imagination are born within the walls of a room heated by stoves, while those of the southern are born, *so to speak*, beneath a blue and golden sky, in green and smiling fields, in air warmed and vitalized by the sun') (*Zib.* 3681–82); 'il desiderio del piacere diviene una pena, e *una specie di travaglio abituale dell'anima*' ('the desire for pleasure becomes a torment, *a kind of habitual anguish of the soul*') (*Zib.* 172); '[la nostra lingua] non saprà [...] scrivere in nessun modo ai contemporanei; o lo farà [...] *quasi* trasformandosi in un'altra [lingua], o *vogliamo dire*, facendosi provincia e suddita di un regno straniero' ('our language [...] will not be able to [...] write in any way to contemporaries, or it will do so [...] *practically* turning itself into another language, *by which I mean* becoming a province and subject of a foreign kingdom') (*Zib.* 778–79); 'la traduzione inaffettata [...] *si può chiamare* un dimezzamento del testo' ('an unaffected translation [...] *can be called* a slicing in half of the text') (*Zib.* 320); 'Le passioni e i sentimenti dell'uomo *si può dire* che da principio stessero nella superficie, poi si rannicchiassero nel fondo più cupo dell'anima, e finalmente siano venuti e rimasti nel mezzo' ('*It could be said* that human passions and feelings were at first on the surface, then they huddled deep in the darkest depths of the soul, and finally they arrived at the halfway point and stayed there') (*Zib.* 266); 'La ricchezza [...] suol dare allo stile un certo splendore, abbondanza, e *forse* scialacquo' ('wealth [...] tends to produce a certain splendor, abundance, and *perhaps* excessive lavishness in style') (*Zib.* 4241); '*Pare* che l'anima nell'addormentarsi deponga i suoi pensieri e immagini d'allora, come deponiamo i vestimenti, in un luogo alla mano e vicinissimo, affine di ripigliarli, subito svegliata' ('*It seems as though* when the soul goes to sleep it puts aside that set of thoughts and images, just as we leave our clothes in a convenient place near at hand so that we can put them on again as soon as we wake up') (*Zib.* 184). In addition to the examples already given, the following might be considered the most representative: 'Io sono, *si perdoni la metafora*, un sepolcro ambulante, che porto dentro di me un uomo morto, un cuore già sensibiliss. che più non sente' ('I am, *pardon the metaphor*, a walking sepulchre, and inside me I carry a dead man, a once very sensitive heart that feels no more') (*Zib.* 4149; my emphasis). Mitigation, an observing presence watching over the act of written communication, signals an operation of control aiming to prepare for the impact of the image. It activates a process of defence from the image through graphic intrusion within tightly cohesive syntactical forms, such as subject and verb, verb and complement, or between co-ordinated complements of the same verb. These are attenuations with an almost neutral power, intervening with minimal modification of the meaning. A case in point is that of *Zib.* 27, where the attenuation 'si può dire' is inserted later and between the lines. It seems like the trace of a desire to assert control over the image and almost to register an evaluation of its appropriateness from the outside, as if Leopardi wanted to forewarn any reader or interlocutor (primarily himself). This would allow time to realize that a metaphorical form is about to appear while reading and this would both increase the attention on the appropriateness of the image, as well as mitigate its illocutionary force.

In his practice of cautious writing and control over his own images, Leopardi maintains an attitude of refrain from excess which, during the magnetic age was felt as necessary and praiseworthy in the face of practices which could lead to the loss of personal identity. Although, on a theoretical level, Leopardi does not link his own relationship with writing to an explicit magnetic sensitivity, he does however refer to the power of language in terms of possession and dominance. His framework of reference are relations of power in the classical world, which were in turn appropriated by many theorists of magnetism as fertile ground for imagery and for describing doctor-patient relationships in magnetic sessions.

It is useful to digress from attenuating metaphors for a moment in order to consider certain essential reflections on creative methods and the relationship between language and idea, thus to explore the way in which essential historico-social paradigms appear outside their own specific area, disguised in the form of a philosophy of language. The objective is to highlight not only the positive and imaginative poetic strength of the metaphor, but also the destabilizing elements and the risks attenuation is meant to prevent, either consciously or otherwise. This links with both Leopardi's discourse on the real (namely its ontological essence and its representability) and his reflection on the dominion of thought.

Leopardi discusses the relationship between word and mind: 'ciascun vocabolo anche semplicemente considerato nella sua profferenza, [...] ha tanto corpo, e per così dire persona, e tanta consistenza, che basta a ferire i sensi' ('any word even when simply considered in its pronunciation, [...] has sufficient body, and so to speak individuality, and sufficient consistency, to strike the senses') (*Zib.* 2953), while elsewhere he reflects on the fact that 'la lingua riguardo alla mente di chi l'adopra, contenga non solo i segni delle cose, ma quasi le cose stesse' ('language in relation to the mind of the person who uses it contains not only the signs of things, but almost the things themselves') (*Zib.* 1701). Concentrated in these two passages we find the three fundamental concepts — person, body, and thing — upon which since its origin Western culture has established a relationship between man and reality.[6] While considering the concepts of person and thing, it can be seen how in Leopardi the two founding cultural paradigms outlining their form and substance, that is, the areas of Roman law and of theology (specifically regarding the nature of the Trinity and Christ) are absorbed, profoundly affecting his thought on language so much as to shape, within his reflection, a conceptual entity definable as the 'linguistic person'. This is hardly a captivating definition but works perhaps at least as a theoretical reminder of the complexity of the very nature, physiognomy, characteristics, and operations of language. The 'linguistic person' acts on and influences the body and the mind, according to those same dynamics adopted by human beings in their relationship between the body and the outside world. To glimpse the risks intrinsic to the workings of this 'linguistic person' inside the mind is also to identify the essential reasons for a defence from them, which is one of the functions of the object of this analysis, attenuation.

Roberto Esposito emphasizes how the Western world has long produced various traditions of thought employing a binary logic in which person and thing interact in terms of possession. While the person is that entity recognized on the basis of the act of appropriation and consequent property of the thing (a person is originally defined in terms of what one *has* as against what one *is*), the thing does not possess an autonomous identity but is passive compared to the subject to which it belongs, or rather defined as something possessed.[7] Property, once linked to war, always starts from an initial appropriation, and this was so before the transference of property became legally binding. For a thing to become unquestioned property, it had to have been snatched from nature or from other men.[8] This principle of property has resulted in a lack of prominence of the living body in constituting the concept of a person and its social recognition. The person is a double entity whose biological constituent has been relegated to a subordinate position or a purely functional one for the purpose of obtaining property and enhancing intellectual or spiritual power. In the same way, Esposito highlights how the process of disembodying the subject corresponds to a parallel dereification of the object. This is not only because the object is a function of the subject that owns it but above all because, within the expressive and epistemological relationship between man and thing, we have turned to the world of ideas, to language, and to the word, to channel the object and make it representable. The thing has become a mere referent of the idea or of language, an allusion on behalf of a sign that makes it emerge from the undifferentiated, while irreversibly distancing it as an immediate body. Furthermore, not only does the philosophical tradition of Descartes, Locke, and Kant decree that the separation between person and thing should also be reiterated within the same subjectivity, with the idea of self-awareness of one's own behaviour reducing the part of the self acting as object of examination of the observing self, but an irreparable fracture between person and thing also supports the entire theological scaffolding. The category of person in the dogma of the incarnation of Christ separates the identity of the individual into two halves, splitting spiritual nature from bodily nature. Thus begins the fundamental tension between the necessary subjugation of the body by the spirit (for which being a person is consolidated in proportion to both the distance one maintains from the object, as well as the control exercised on the body), and the rebellion and resistance of the body against such spiritual domination.

The following extract from the *Zibaldone* reveals how Leopardi's linguistic reflection is infused with a sense of the theological person and the incarnation and deposition of the body:

> [Nella lingua francese e nell'ebraica] lo stile si riduce ai nudi concetti [...] in quella perché *i concetti non hanno ancora onde farsi un corpo, in questa perché l'hanno deposto*; in quella perché *la materia è ancora scarsa a vestir lo spirito, in questa perché lo spirito ha consumato la materia, è ricomparso nudo del corpo di cui s'era vestito*, ha prevaluto alla materia, e tutta l'esistenza è spiritualizzata, né si vede o si tocca oramai [...] quasi altro che spirito.
>
> [In French and Hebrew] style is reduced to bare concepts [...]; in the former because the *concepts do not yet have the wherewithal to make themselves a body*, in the latter because *they have laid it aside*; in the former because *there is as yet scant matter with which to clothe the spirit*, in the latter because *spirit has consumed matter, it has reappeared divested of the body in which it had clothed itself*, it has prevailed over matter, and all of existence is spiritualized, nor henceforth does one see or touch, [...] anything almost other than spirit. (*Zib.* 2912; my emphasis)

The concept of the theological person, having transferred itself to within a different system of conceptual linguistic correspondences, leaves traces of its original provenance through lexical signals. The same can be said of the sphere of law, for the evolution of language seems to reproduce the appropriating structure between person and thing described, and many reflections on language treat the relationship between words or between idioms as dynamics of expropriation, appropriation, and usurpation of property. The following passage refers to 'parole [...] domiciliate' ('words which have settled here and become citizens'), to the 'porte della scrittura' ('the gates of writing'), to 'cittadinanza' ('citizenship'), and to 'diritto naturale' ('natural law'):

> Infinite sono le antiche *parole straniere domiciliate, e fatte cittadine della nostra lingua* [...]; che come quest'uso è sempre fecondo, *così le porte della scrittura e della cittadinanza, sono sempre aperte, per diritto naturale* [...]. E questa è una delle massime, e più naturali e legittime e ragionevoli fonti, della novità, e degl'incrementi necessari della favella.
>
> [There are any number of old *foreign words that have settled here and become citizens of our language* [...]; and, as such a usage is always fruitful, *so the gates of writing and citizenship* are *always open, by natural law* [...]. This, then, is the greatest, and most natural and legitimate and reasonable source of innovation, and of necessary additions to a language.] (*Zib.* 786–87; my emphasis)

Instead, in the following quotations there are references to 'nomi restati in proprietà' ('names which have continued to be the property of'), to usurped senses,[9] and to an echo of *mancipium*, the practice of transferring property symbolized by the placing of the hand, a clear testimony to a contamination of linguistics and of the semantic sphere of the law: 'Tutte simili cose [...] non hanno ricevuto il nome se non mediante metafore, similitudini [...], i cui nomi hanno servito [...] ad esprimere le cose non sensibili; e spesso sono *restati in proprietà* a queste ultime, *perdendo il valor primitivo*' ('All such things, aside from the fact that they [...] only received their names through metaphors, similes [...] whose names have served [...] to express things that are not perceptible. And often they have *continued to be the property of the latter, while losing their original value*') (*Zib.* 1388; my emphasis); '*la prepotente forza dell'uso fe' sì che il senso traslato si mise in luogo del proprio e ne usurpò le funzioni*' (' "[...] the overwhelming power of usage caused the transferred meaning to stand in for the proper meaning and to usurp its functions [...]" ') (*Zib.* 1110; Leopardi is here quoting from Vincenzo Monti); 'Non avendole dunque i latini né create né formate [le discipline], ma ricevute quasi *per manus* belle e fatte, neanche ne crearono né formarono, ma riceverono parimente il linguaggio' ('the Latins had neither created nor shaped those disciplines, but had received them virtually *per manus* [handed down] and ready-made, they did not create or shape the language, but received it in the same way') (*Zib.* 747–48).[10] The appropriative dynamics and relationships between person and thing to which Leopardi alludes in these passages are all within the linguistic system, as if they reproduced the structure of the real, the relationship between persons, and between these and things. The rebuilding of the scaffolding of the outside world within the linguistic and cognitive world is revealed further in the following reflection, where Leopardi includes an explicit parallel between person (human) and 'linguistic person':

> Nelle parole si chiudono e quasi si legano le idee, come negli anelli le gemme, anzi s'incarnano come l'anima nel corpo, facendo seco loro come una persona, in modo che le idee sono inseparabili dalle parole, e divise non sono più quelle, sfuggono all'intelletto e alla concezione, e non si ravvisano, come accaderebbe all'animo nostro disgiunto dal corpo.
>
> [Ideas are enclosed and as if bound up in words, like gems in rings, in fact they are incarnated like the soul in the body, making with them a kind of person, so that the ideas are inseparable from the words, and when they are separated they are no longer ideas, they escape the intellect and conception, and are not recognized, as would happen to our soul if it were separated from the body.] (*Zib.* 2584)

Hence the traditional dichotomy between body and spirit, thing and person, seems to be at play in Leopardi's employment of the religious and legal cultural pillars. However, the process by which language encapsulates thought involves a further level of exposure of the mind, resuscitation of the real, and reification of thought, which inverts the direction of appropriation. The reality transported in the mind in the form of an image can come back to life and subjugate the mind. In the reflection just quoted (as in the already cited *Zib.* 2912), the fundamental relevance of the body in determining the person stands out. It almost turns on its head the traditional paradigm that the body is subject to the spirit; there would be no person, says Leopardi, if the soul were taken out of the body. We are witness then to a kind of multiplication or interior replication of the person in the 'linguistic person'. It is not only an innocuous similitude but a conceptual node of enormous philosophical significance. It should be noted how the following reflection reiterates the image of replication in the process of incarnation between word and idea:

> Il posseder più lingue [...] ci dà una maggior facilità [...] d'intenderci noi medesimi, applicando la parola all'~~cosa~~ idea che senza questa applicazione

rimarrebbe molto confusa nella nostra mente. Trovata la parola in qualunque lingua, [...] la nostra idea [...] ci rimane ben definita e fissa nella mente, e ben determinata e circoscritta. Cosa ch'io ho provato molte volte, e si vede in questi stessi pensieri scritti a penna corrente, dove ho *fissato* le mie idee con parole greche francesi latine, secondo che mi rispondevano più precisamente alla cosa, e mi venivano più presto trovate. Perché un' ~~cosa~~ idea senza parola o modo di espirimerla, ci sfugge, o ci erra nel pensiero come indefinita e mal nota a noi medesimi che l'abbiamo concepita. Colla parola prende corpo, e quasi forma visibile, e sensibile, e circoscritta

[The knowledge of several languages [...], makes it easier for us [...] to understand ourselves, and to apply the word to the ~~thing~~ idea, which, without that application, would remain confused in our mind. Having found the word in whatever language, [...] our idea becomes clear and settled and consistent and remains fixed and well-defined in our mind, and firmly determined and circumscribed. I have experienced this on many occasions, and it can be seen in these same thoughts, written with the flow of the pen, where I have *fixed* my ideas with Greek, French, Latin words, according to how for me they responded more precisely to the thing, and came most quickly to mind. For an ~~thing~~ idea without a word or a way to express it is lost to us, or roams about undefined in our thoughts, and is imperfectly understood by we who have conceived it. With the word, it takes on body and almost visible, tangible, and distinct form.] (*Zib.* 95)

This passage is also valuable in clarifying the way in which Leopardi balances the use of 'thing' and 'idea' when he refers to thought, and the conceptual undertones that the two words assume. Two corrections involving these two words have taken place in this passage. In the opening sentence, Leopardi in fact first uses 'cosa' and later substitutes it with 'idea'. Even if the undertone of the meaning is almost imperceptible, it would seem that Leopardi prefers to adopt 'idea' for the conception that already finds itself in correspondence with the word, when the 'linguistic person' is formed or being formed. Subsequently, a further correction again replaces 'cosa' with 'idea'. This substitution might at first seem to be in contrast with the logic of clarity that is supposedly in harmony with 'idea'. On closer inspection, it occurs in reality not in the function of the senses of the first period of belonging ('un'idea senza parola [...] ci sfugge'), but in the function of (and probably in conjunction with) the later interlinear addition 'Colla parola prende corpo, e quasi forma visibile, e sensibile, e circoscritta'. It is the emphasis of the distinct and intelligible concept, added in the revision phase, which probably determines the insertion of 'idea' in substitution of 'thing'. The latter is more apt, as will be seen, to describe less clear mental states of uncertain property. 'Thing' underlines an as yet unrelated mass of thought ('senza parola'), and is unable to form part of the dispositive of the person, going round and round in the mind as an excluded presence and 'mal nota'.

The advent of the word is not limited to giving a shape to the thing, which would otherwise remain in indeterminate flux, through the process of distinction which starts when it is named; it also sets off a further passage. The word retransforms the idea into an integrated object ('visibile', 'sensibile', e 'circoscritt[o]'), intending by 'object' a relational entity, that which interposes itself as an obstacle so as to demand recognition, allowing experience of the object within the mind.[11] Note how the issue underlying the relationship between person and thing is not the ultimate essence of the real, as it is for example with the unknowable 'thing in itself' of Kant, of which the mind can only possess an equivalent (but not coinciding) thought. Nor, with reference to Leopardi's reflection, can one speak of a commonality of outcomes with the Aristotelian philosophical tradition of *auto to pragma* that leads to Hegelian phenomenology by holding the essence of the thing as a pure function of the subject; the word here lends its own voice to the truth of substance unfolded through its automatic development within thought. Even if there are some points of contact, especially where the possibility of a self-produced idea in the mind is concerned, Leopardi holds dearest to his heart the relational status between person and thing, the process of approach that induces the *experience* of the thing and its renewability by means of words. The power of the word, making the physicality of the thing visible, sensorial, and formal, actively establishes an *almost* equivalence with the way of experiencing the thing in offering ourselves to the outside world. It is clear though that the ontological problem, even if it is not addressed directly, returns at the point of outcome. The two experiences, the sensorial action with which we relate to the outside world and the reactivation of its memory and emotional bearing in reproducing the experience of the object through the word, cannot fail to raise a number of questions regarding the nature of the real. If the experience of the real is renewed by the word, what is the relationship between external and internal reality? What is transferred from the thing in the process of reproduction of the real: how does the thing come to inhabit the person to the point that they encounter it in the mental space as if the thing had given itself to the immediacy of being present and alive? Leopardi does not enter into a systematic debate on the nature of the real and the way it appears, but provides a partial reply. Rather than looking at the essence, he considers the means, maintaining that in the human mind the 'idee sono [...] legate alla parola' ('ideas are [...] linked to the word'), which in turn is 'inseparabil[e] dalla cosa, è la sua immagine, il suo corpo' ('is inseparable from the thing, it is its image, its body') (*Zib.* 1701). He seems to imply that the part of the real that can be known is its image and that the image *is* in fact the real in the *form* in which it presents itself to the mind. Disconnected from its relationship to the mind, it is not possible to comment on its external substance, yet *the effect* of the thing on the person remains intact due to the word which evokes it. For this reason, the word is not a distant and empty symbol but a real body captured in its interactivity. However, similarly to what happens in the magnetic imagery between subject and object of observation, the two states of the thing (external and internal, that is in the form of the word) seem to have reached extreme proximity. For this reason, through attenuation, Leopardi interposes a thin film of ontological division between them, separating the inert from that which, through and in the body, has life. The 'quasi' present both in the quotation *Zib.* 95 quoted above, as well as in the entry which constitutes my starting-point ('la lingua riguardo alla mente di chi l'adopra, [contiene] non solo i segni delle cose, ma quasi le cose stesse', *Zib.* 1701), must be interpreted in this sense. This separation of entities through a very light marker of mitigation ('quasi') can be read as an automatic gesture aimed at avoiding total assimilation between the two worlds, the human and the real, of which Leopardi had conceptualized the maximum limit of adjacency. On this subject, in the following passage, Leopardi discusses the effect of the loss of a loved one on our cognitive capacity. It constitutes an example of the alarming penetration into our mind of an *other* reality, not assimilable in the sphere of thought. This *other* reality shares with the material external reality a connotation of irreducible foreignness, independently of the determination of its substance. A further case of correction is to be noted between 'cosa' (literally 'thing', translated in the English *Zibaldone* as 'situation') and 'idea', this time to the advantage of the former, increasing the already numerous occurrences of 'cosa' in the passage:

> L'idea di una grave sventura (come anche di qualunque grande e strana mutazione di *cose* [...]) che ci sopraggiunga, massimamente improvvisa, non si può concepire intera, se non altro ne' primi momenti; anzi è sempre confusissima, debolissima, oscurissima, e diffettosa. [...] [P]onete che vi si annunzi la morte di uno de' vostri cari [...]. Il dispiacere, [...] il dover considerare quella persona in *un modo tutto diverso dal passato*, cioè come morta, [...] tutte queste *cose* che si presentano in folla alla vostra mente, vi cagionano una confusione un imbarazzo uno stupore tale, che voi in luogo di considerare ciascuna parte della ~~idea~~ cosa, non ne considerate nessuna, non siete capace di valutare né l'estensione né la profondità né la natura della *cosa*, né di formarvene un concetto preciso, e *restandovi* solamente l'idea in genere e confusamente, non siete capace di pensarvi, né vi pensate formalmente, non dirò perché non vogliate pensarvi, ma perché non sapete pensarvi. E quindi accade quella *cosa* osservatissima che *le grandi mutazioni*, sieno disgrazie, sieno fortune, al primo momento istupidiscono, e non è se non col tempo, che voi considerandone ciascuna parte, ne cominciate a piangere o rallegrarvene separatamente. Giacché questo pure è notabile, che l'atto del piangere o rallegrarsi [...] cade sempre sopra una parte della *cosa*, non già sul tutto, perché l'anima non è capace di abbracciar questo tutto, in uno stesso tempo.
>
> [The idea of a great misfortune (and also of any major, unexpected change [...]) that overwhelms us, especially if it happens suddenly, cannot be grasped in its entirety, at least not at first; instead, it is always very confused, very weak, very obscure and deficient. [...] But supposing you are told of the death of a close member of your family [...]. The dismay, [...] the need to think of that person *in a completely different way from the past*, that is, as dead, [...] all these *things* crowd into your mind, creating such confusion, awkwardness, and stupor that instead of considering each aspect of the situation you cannot think about any, are not capable of evaluating the extent, the depth, or the nature of it, or of forming any precise conception of it, but *are left with* just a confused, general idea; you are unable to think about it, and do not think about it properly, I do not say because you do not want to, but because you do not know how. What happens, then, is something often noticed with all great changes, whether misfortune or good fortune, that at first you are stunned, and it is only with time that, as you reflect on each part of it, you begin to weep or rejoice part by part. For this too is noteworthy, that the act of weeping or rejoicing [...], happens only in relation to a part of the thing, not the whole, because the soul is not capable of embracing the whole, all at once.] (*Zib.* 366–67; my emphasis)

It is also no coincidence that the profusion of the word 'cosa' characterizes a passage dominated by the concept of a distinction shockingly trespassed by death, as is the mutation between a former condition homogenous to our nature as a living person, and another state, that of the dead reduced to the condition of a thing. A closer look at the connotation of the word 'cosa', as used here by Leopardi, reveals moments of conceptual deadlock, of crises of recognition due to direct confrontation and exposure to the presence of the 'other'. 'Cosa' is more a shade of a cognitive block compared to 'idea', which signals instead a prospect of intelligibility from the visual perspective of one who has taken *a step back* from direct and close vision of the 'cosa' (*'restandovi* solamente l'idea in genere e confusamente'). While normal language contexts circumscribe as much of the thing as is visible and sensitive, distancing and reducing it to the status of possession, in the condition of loss the mind finds itself coping with a changed idea that in a Lacanian way inhabits it as a Thing: a Thing once familiar and now unrecognizable and unrecognizably 'divers[a] dal passato' ('in a completely different way from the past'). Unlike normal situations of thought production, the 'linguistic person' is defenceless, the relationships of power are inverted and the thing has usurped the mental space with no possibility (at least at first) of reappropriation by thought.

In normal contexts uninvolved with mutations causing dangerous contact between ontological statuses, the poet, 'quasi per magico incanto, a che che sia che *gli venga alle mani*' ('of whatever *comes into his hands*, as though by placing it under a spell'), through the word, changes the aspect of things while still maintaining their status of reality, and knows how to 'vestirle, adornarle, abbellirle' ('dress, adorn, and embellish them') (*Zib.* 3222; my emphasis) through images. Normally it is the same metaphorical nature of language that allows this recreational reverberation of senses, keeping alive the influence of etymological origins and of a series of expansions undergone by the word while, over time, crossing different semantic territories.[12]

It is also no coincidence that Leopardi assimilates the poetic transformation to magic. Until late antiquity, legal ceremonies involved certain rituals that contained elements of magic. Institutions such as the *mancipatio*, the *stipulatio*, and the *vindicatio* contained features of supernatural and religious origin which were preserved in their ceremonial. The performative power of the word, like that of prayer, gave access to a new reality not immediately visible, conserving principles of duty and authority within; it fused together a play between novelty and tradition, between unique event in the present and reabsorption of relational modes into the frames of the known and of the culturally stratified:

> The methods followed in legal acts were the same as those followed by men attempting to shape other worlds they could not fully see or perfectly control, whether the imagined world of political community or the perceptible world of the divine. They were, for centuries, the methods that best achieved the ends that citizens and jurists most wanted. By being both familiar and traditionally efficacious, such methods made law an 'embedded' rather than a separate sphere of action, and engaged the immense power of a world of belief on the side of order in human affairs.[13]

The magical power of the word, to which Leopardi alludes, subterraneously connects the creative dimension with the deep conceptual magma of the original paradigm of the person and property, as it manifested itself in the practice of law. At the same time, it registers the insinuation of a dimension of risk or danger that also surrounds the magical.

The theoretical model of property lends itself as a representative structure for metaphor primarily because of the latter's constituent tension or conflict between tenor and vehicle, which operates a transfer of fluctuating and unstable semantic properties, thus characterizing the vivifying power of the metaphorical image. Recent studies show that the foundational principle of metaphor is its stepping beyond the 'threshold of conflict', and the continuous semantic adjustments required for comprehension that lead to *finding* the analogy — the latter not therefore broached but acquired, conquered — in the interaction between terms.[14] If the condition of loss exposes the mind to an extreme vulnerability in the face of the Thing, the confrontation of the entity not immediately reabsorbable by the thought is an essential feature of the metaphor. That which Leopardi defines as 'property of language', or 'una lingua ardita [...] capace di scostarsi nelle forme, nei modi ec. dall'ordine e dalla ragion dialettica del discorso' ('a bold language, that is, capable of moving away in its forms and expressions, etc., from the order and dialectic reasoning of discourse'), is a magical richness, as fruitful as it is dangerous, demanding continual control:

> Quanto più qualsivoglia imitazione trapassa i limiti dello strumento che l'è destinato [...], tanto più esce della sua natura e proprietà, e tanto più si scema la maraviglia, come se nella scultura che imita col marmo s'introducessero gli occhi di vetro, o le parrucche invece delle chiome sculpite. E così appunto si deve dire in ordine alla scrittura, la quale imita colle parole e non deve uscire del suo strumento.
>
> [The more any sort of imitation oversteps the limits of the instrument intended for it [...], the more it abandons its nature and properties, the more does wonder diminish, for example, if glass eyes or wigs for sculpted tresses were introduced in sculpture, which imitates with marble. And precisely the same goes for writing, which imitates with words, and must not abandon its instrument.]
> (*Zib.* 977)

Property of language protects dynamic semantic relationships built in time and condensed in words and images held together in a precious but fragile balance. However, language can exercise its own property excessively and thus denaturing itself: for in the very nature and essence of the metaphor lies the risk of it expanding until it is consumed by the same vital lymph of the word onto which it is grafted. This takes place precisely through dynamics of appropriation and *taking possession*: 'l'idea primitiva significata propriamente da [...] vocaboli traslati è mangiata a lungo andare dal significato metaforico il quale solo rimane' ('for the original idea properly signified by those metaphoric words was consumed over time by the metaphoric meaning, which alone remains') (*Zib.* 2469). As long as the etymologies of the words used can still be perceived, 'l'idea ch'elle destano, è quasi doppia' ('the idea that they awaken is, so to speak, double') (*Zib.* 1703), but at the peak of the process of metaphorical consumption, the metaphorical action turns on the word and, as if by magic, annihilates its own meaning, depriving it of its soul, and leaving only a dry and naked body.[15] Thus the 'linguistic person' is reduced to the state of a 'linguistic thing', inert and no longer able to constitute a person.

The function of attenuations integral to the image, such as those analyzed at the beginning of this chapter, contributes to enhancing the metaphorical nature of the language, emphasizing the image's reverberations and distancing the sight of the thing in its alien, static, frontal nudity. While they appear to mitigate and confound the image, protecting the mind from an excessive exposure to the bare thing, they keep the internal metaphorical conflicts active and fruitful. The philosophical valency of invigilating attenuations is different. Beneath their use lies Leopardi's attempt to guard over the characteristics of the metaphor that can compromise the balance of the relationships of property of the 'linguistic person'. It is essential to keep in mind how the legal system that I have adopted as a frame for the current discourse, based on the idea of expropriation and appropriation of the thing by the person in Roman civilization, is used to bear witness to continuous imbalance and movement between the two poles of person and thing. Esposito reminds us how in cases of compensation for credit, for example, the creditor could do whatever he wanted with the body of the insolvent debtor. He could mete out every kind of violence and even go as far as to deny the return of the body of the deceased debtor to his family. In the blink of an eye the person could fall into the depths of the thing. The slide between the statuses of person and thing was so frequent in ancient Rome that 'nessuno resta[va] tutta la vita, dalla nascita alla morte, persona' [nobody remained a person from birth to death] and everyone used to transit 'almeno per un certo periodo, per una condizione non lontana da quella della cosa posseduta' [at least for a certain period through a condition not far from that of the possessed thing].[16] Transposing these observations into the Leopardian philosophy of language, and keeping in mind the live effect of the language on the same physical experience of the reader, temporal and emotive, a quite radical extension of the philosophical consequences of such dangerous richness of language is seen, while certain preoccupations that today animate the biopolitical discipline can be glimpsed. As will be seen, in defining the relationship between word and person in Leopardi it no longer seems sufficient to refer to language as a mere thought form, possessed by the human mind which uses it as instrument or as thing. In fact, language can loosen itself from possession by the mind and the relationship of power between person and thing, between thinker and the thought, can be reversed, causing momentary loss of those faculties that constitute the person.

In an important entry (*Zib.* 25–26), Leopardi alludes to a word that can reach the point where it reduces the same mind which produces it to an object:

> Alle volte, la collocazione, diremo, fortuita delle parole, quantunque il senso dell'autore sia chiaro tuttavia a prima vista produc[e] ne' lettori un'altra idea, il che, quando massime quest'idea non sia conveniente bisogna schivarlo, massime in poesia dove il lettore è più sull'immaginare e più facile a creder di vedere e che il poeta voglia fargli vedere quello ancora che il poeta non pensa o anche non vorrebbe. Ecco un es. Chiabrera [...]: Ora il bel crin si frange, E sul tuo

sasso piange. *Si frange* qui vuol dire si percuote, e intende il poeta, colle mani ec. Il senso è chiaro [...]. Ma la collocaz. casuale delle parole è tale, ch'io metto pegno che quanti leggono la Canz. del Chiabrera colla mente così sull'aspettare immagini, a prima giunta si figurano Firenze personificata [...] che percuota la testa e si franga il crine sul sasso del Zanchini [...]. Ora, lasciando star se l'immagine ch'io dico sia conveniente o no, certo è che non è voluta dal poeta, e ch'egli perciò deve schivare questa illusione quantunq. momentanea [...] eccetto s'ella non gli piacesse come forse si potrebbe dare il caso, ma questo non dev'essere se non quando l'immagine illusoria non nocia alla vera e non ci sia bisogna di ravvedimento per veder questa seconda, giacché due immagini in una volta non si possono vedere, ma bensì una dopo l'altra il che quando fosse, potrebbe anche il poeta lasciare e anche proccurare questa illusione, dove pure non noccia al restante del contesto, perch'ella non fa danno [...] destando immagini delle quali non sia evidente la ragione, ma quasi nascosta, e tale che'elle paiano accidentali, e non proccurate dal poeta in nessun modo, ma quasi ispirate da cosa invisibile e incomprensibile.

[Sometimes the, let us say, fortuitous arrangement of words, however clear the author's meaning might be, produces a different idea in the minds of readers upon first reading. This must be avoided, especially when it is inappropriate, and especially in poetry, where the reader uses more imagination and more easily believes that he is seeing something and that the poet wants him to see something which the poet has not thought of or would not even wish to. This is an example from Chiabrera [...]: 'Ora il bel crin si frange, / E sul tuo sasso piange' ["Now her lovely hair is broken, and on your stone she cries"]. *Si frange* [is broken] here means struck, and the poet means struck with her hands, etc. The sense is clear [...]. But the chance arrangement of the words is such that I wager that many who read Chiabrera's canzone, with their minds on the description, first of all imagine Florence personified [...] who strikes her head and dashes her hair against Zanchini's tombstone [...]. Now, leaving aside whether or not the image that I cite is appropriate, it is certainly not intended by the poet, and therefore he must avoid such illusion, even if it's only momentary [...], except where it might please him, which could perhaps be the case. But this must not occur except where the illusory image does not detract from the true one and there is no need to think again before seeing the latter, since two images cannot be seen at the same time, but rather one after the other; and, if this occurs, the poet could also allow and even seek to obtain this illusion, providing that it doesn't harm the remaining context, because it causes no damage, [...] awakening images whose reason is not obvious, but almost hidden, and such that they seem accidental and not sought after by the poet in any way, but as though inspired by something invisible and incomprehensible.] (*Zib.* 25–26)

The mind, suggests Leopardi, organizes thought along linear sequences. In the moment in which he concentrates on a part of this sequence, other unsuspected combinations can emerge to inform secondary representations, in which case it is the word itself, on its own, without the mind guarding it, which inspires an illusory image. But the moment the illusory image is born, it uses the body, the oblivious mind of the poet, and his means of communication, to express itself to the reader or listener. In that particular creative instant, the relationship between person and thing is turned on its head: the poet becomes the means appropriated by the word for the production of images 'quasi ispirate da *cosa* invisibile e incomprensibile'. Only later does the mind of the poet regain control over writing and re-personalize the image, or once again reduce the language to object, and decide whether or not to leave on the page what language has produced. Far from representing the outcome of a truth already obtained, the independent development of thought is for Leopardi a danger to the basic identity of the person. Therefore in the performativity intrinsic to language reside risks of loss innate to the appropriative structure of the image, against which constant vigilance is required through the use of attenuation. This game of re-appropriation of fugitive senses between the mind and the word is essential and fruitful for creative purposes, because the poet can later satisfyingly perceive a combination that produces unexpected outcomes, yet such a (magical) process based largely on the event, on the surprise, and on unpredictability, also hides the risk that the poet will never realize that a certain illusory image exists and therefore never manage to reappropriate the creative product entirely. The danger of the thing is thus not only hidden in exceptionally changed states, such as those of mourning previously described, but is constitutive of an ordinary creative condition of production and externalization of thought. It is not simply a question of attention or distraction in communication, but of the awareness that the 'linguistic person' has a degree of freedom from the mind. It is in this light that we must consider Leopardi's compulsive use of metaphorical attenuation, and interpret it not as a mitigation that weakens his images, but rather as the residue of an operation of watchfulness over the text so as to prevent the mind from being subjected to the prevaricating autonomy of the word. By this logic we can explain those cases in which Leopardi, having created images, takes the time to elucidate them: 'se Virgilio senz'arte non sarebbe stato Virgilio, se *in poesia un bel corpo con vesti di cencio, dico, bei sensi senza bello stile* [...] non si soffrono' ('if Virgil without art would not have been Virgil, if *in poetry a fine body clothed in rags, by which I mean fine meanings without fine style order choice* [...] is insufferable') (*Zib.* 20; my emphasis); 'si può dire che *da una stessa sorgente, da una stessa qualità dell'animo*, diversamente applicata [...] vennero i poemi di Omero e di Dante, e i Principii matematici della filosofia naturale di Newton' ('one could say that *from the same source, the same quality of spirit*, differently applied [...] came the poems of Homer and Dante and Newton's Mathematical principles of natural philosophy' (*Zib.* 2132–33; my emphasis, apart from Mathematical principles of natural philosophy), and:

> L'anima non si svelle come un membro, ma parte naturalmente quando non può più rimanere, nello stesso modo che una fiamma si estingue e parte da quel corpo dove non trova più alimento, *nel che, per dire un'immagine, noi non vediamo né ci figuriamo neanche astrattamente nessuna violenza e nessun dolore sia nel combustibile sia nella fiamma.*

> [The soul is not torn off like a limb but leaves naturally when it can no longer remain, in the same way that a flame goes out and leaves the matter that can no longer sustain it, *and in this, to use an image, we neither see nor remotely suppose that any violence or pain is involved for the combustible material or the flame.*] (*Zib.* 282; my emphasis)

In these examples Leopardi prefers 'dire un'immagine' (*Zib.* 282) (literally, 'to say an image') rather than leaving it free to transmit its own ideas, almost so as to prevent the danger that ulterior meanings might escape at the moment of writing or present themselves unexpectedly at a second reading. What is at stake is the very identity of being human, if it is true that what characterizes a person are precisely a 'facoltà del pensiero [...] indipendente dagli accidenti' ('faculty of thought, which is [...] independent of accidents'), without which it would be 'un altro essere ma non un uomo' ('another kind of being, but not a man'), and the inalienable exercise of the will, for which 'nessuna promessa, contratto, volontà propria e libera, lo può mai spogliare in minima parte del diritto di seguir[la]' ('no promise, contract, or free expression of his own will can ever divest him in the least of the right to abide fully by his own will') (*Zib.* 580–81). Rather, the illusory image as an idea 'che il poeta non pensa o anche non vorrebbe' (*Zib.* 26), undermines precisely the two principles that make a human being — thought and will. The origin of the danger is self-generated, and if one can in any way speak of an 'automatic' development of the idea, the outcomes, compared to Hegel, are the opposite. More than anything else, the moment of awareness is completely detached from the process, and in fact the 'automatism' coincides with the very loss of self and of the person. One pays attention only in the moment in which the 'automatism' is interrupted, as long as the poet manages to trace the mechanism. However, a residue of alteration that cannot be reabsorbed by the thought is always insinuated. This process, far from leading to truth, in fact represents the extreme limit of technique, namely the risk of reducing the work to a simulacrum. As Esposito states, concentrating on the meaning of technique in modern thought, even the technique, like a work of art, is founded on a 'vita di relazione' [life of relations]. Unlike in a work of art, however, the technique:

> Pare scaturire dal loro [degli oggetti] meccanismo interno, in forma indipendente da chi l'ha attivato. È proprio questa autonomia che sembra conferire alle cose il profilo delle persone, a produrre un effetto di depersonalizzazione in coloro che, non essendosene più soggetti, ne divengono oggetti passivi.[17]
>
> [Seems to be generated by the mechanism intrinsic to the objects, independently of the person who activated it. It is precisely this autonomy which seems to confer on the things the profile of a person, and to produce an effect of depersonalization in those who, from being subjects, become passive objects].

Leopardi's illusory image, which slips from the grasp of the poet, embodies this risk of person and thing being reversed and a resulting loss of function. By guarding and attenuating, he protects his identity and poetic properties from the incantation of the simulacrum.

Notes to Chapter 16

1. See Angela Esterhammer, 'Philosophies of Identity and Impersonation from Locke to Charles Mathews', in *Romanticism and Philosophy*, ed. by Sophie Laniel-Musitelli and Thomas Constantinesco (New York: Routledge, 2015), pp. 147–65.
2. Cf. Ibid., p. 151.

3. Klaus Hölker, '"Diciamo" come mitigatore', in *Aspetti dell'italiano parlato*, ed. by Klaus Hölker and Cristiane Maaß (Münster: Lit Verlag, 2005), pp. 53–79 (p. 76).
4. Cf. Claudia Caffi, *La mitigazione: un approccio pragmatico alla comunicazione nei contesti terapeutici* (Münster: Lit Verlag, 2001).
5. See Franco D'Intino, 'Oralità e dialogicità nello "Zibaldone"', in *Lo 'Zibaldone' di Leopardi come ipertesto*, ed. by Muñiz, pp. 221–43.
6. See Roberto Esposito, *Le persone e le cose* (Turin: Einaudi, 2014), and *Due: la macchina della teologia politica e il posto del pensiero* (Turin: Einaudi, 2013), Kindle edition.
7. Cf. Esposito, *Due*, location 2269.
8. Cf. Esposito, *Le persone e le cose*, p. 8.
9. See also the already quoted *Zib.* 778–79.
10. '*per manus*' is in italics in the text.
11. Remo Bodei writes: '"Oggetto" [...] sembra ricalcare teoricamente il greco *problema* [...] inteso dapprima quale ostacolo che si mette davanti per difesa, un impedimento che interponendosi e ostruendo la strada sbarra il cammino e provoca un arresto. [...] Implica quindi una sfida, una contrapposizione con quanto vieta al soggetto la sua immediata affermazione, con quanto, appunto, "obietta" alle sue pretese di dominio. Pre-suppone un confronto che si conclude con una definitiva sopraffazione dell'oggetto, il quale, dopo posto agone, viene reso disponibile al possesso e alla manipolazione da parte del soggetto' (*La vita delle cose* (Rome: Laterza, 2014), Kindle edition, location 278); '"Object" [...] seems to derive theoretically from the Greek term *problema*, where "problem" is understood as an obstacle put forward as a form of defense, an impediment that blocks the way and causes something to stop. [...] [It] implies a challenge, a contraposition that prevents the subject's immediate affirmation precisely because it "objects" to the subject's pretensions to dominance. It presupposes a confrontation that concludes with a definitive overpowering of the object, which, after the struggle between subject and object, is made available to be possessed and manipulated by the subject' (*The Life of Things, the Love of Things*, trans. by Murtha Baca (New York: Fordham University Press, 2015), p. 17).
12. Cf. *Zib.* 1702.
13. Elizabeth A. Meyer, *Legitimacy and Law in the Roman World: Tabulae in Roman Belief* (Cambridge: Cambridge University Press, 2004), p. 10. See also Giacomo Viggiani, 'Diritto, magia e performatività', in *Linguaggio e istituzioni: discorsi, monete e riti*, ed. by Marco Carapezza and Francesca Piazza, special issue of *Rivista italiana di filosofia del linguaggio*, (2013), 325–38, <http://www.rifl.unical.it/index.php/rifl/article/view/216> [accessed 20 March 2017].
14. Michele Prandi and Elisa Raschini, 'La similitudine tra le forme di attenuazione dell'interazione concettuale', in *Euphémismes et stratégies d'atténuation du dire*, ed. by Paola Paissa and Ruggero Druetta, special issue of *Synergies Italie* (2009), 21–30 (p. 22), <https://gerflint.fr/Base/Italie-special/prandi.pdf> [accessed 20 March 2017].
15. Cf. *Zib.* 597: '*Stupeo, o stupesco, stupefacio, stupefio, stupidus*, ec. coi composti, non solo si sono conservati materialmente nel verbo *stupire, stupefare, stupidire* ec. ec. ma se ben questi sono restati nella nostra lingua seccamente e nudamente, e senza il significato etimologico (che vuol dire, diventar di stoppa), come infinite altre parole delle quali resta quasi il corpo e non l'anima, tuttavia la nostra lingua conserva ancora per altra parte quella prima metafora, *diventar di stoppa*, e l'usa familiarmente per *istupire* ec. sebbene non sia registrata nella Crusca' ('*Stupeo* [to be struck senseless], or *stupesco, stupefacio, stupefio, stupidus*, etc., with their compounds, are not only materially preserved in the verb *stupire, stupefare, stupidire*, etc. etc., but, even if these are now bare, dry words and, like countless other words whose body in effect remains without a soul, have lost their etymological sense (which means "turn into tow"), nonetheless our language does still retain that original metaphor *diventar di stoppa*, and uses it informally for *istupire* [to be dazed], etc., even though it is not recorded in the Crusca').
16. Esposito, *Le persone e le cose*, p. 13.
17. Ibid., p. 61.

PART III

Everyday Life

CHAPTER 17

The Practice of Everyday Life

In shielding the image from the risk of becoming one with the real, which he performs through attenuation, Leopardi mourns the death of the Muse, who, by speaking only through the poet, protected the common listener from the unsustainable impact of truth at the origin of Western poetry. For Homer, the Muse was the sole witness and receiver of history as it presented itself in its integral reality. The real was remembered and recounted by the Muse in its total temporal and spatial development and her tale had the power to recreate the full unfolding of visual events in the form of voice. In the Muse's story, the verbal and the visual merge, with her version the perfect replica of the facts. If the Muse's story were to be heard directly, the telling of the story would take as long to unfold as the events themselves, and convey equal force and sensations as the experience of the real. This extreme actuality of the real in the Muse's words made her tale overwhelming and inaudible to human ears, and only communicable to poets, who were gifted with super-human powers and could in turn reproduce a filtered version of the story.[1] Their voice could now refer to the real through omissions, attracting the spirit of the listeners through the embellishment of poetic imagination.[2] In Leopardi's use of attenuation, the primordial creative filtering role of the poet remains, but at the same time his relationship with the image is the sign of the collapse of the a priori assurance that the receiver of the creative discourse will be spared the full impact of the real. As we have seen, the replica is now a self-generating production, potentially arising by chance or by mistake at any time in the poet's or reader's mind, as the internalized and psychologized equivalent of an integral reality which previously only the memory of the Muse could approach. The power of the word, which was once ordered and transmitted safely through the reins of the poet, is now independently activated in the solitary experience of the reader.

The spectators of an oral performance once shared the divine message in a commonality of values and feelings. The tale had a powerful transporting impact, but one which would require the most immediate responses of the body rather than the mind. By contrast, in the experience of the writerly subject, which is the cultural and psychological condition of reference for Leopardi's reflection on modernity, there are no filters to protect the mind of the reader from contact with truth. While creative fruition has moved from the vital and dynamic realm of the body to the static inner shelter of the mind, and while the written word has lost the immediacy which characterized the ancient experience of poetic songs, objectified truth can insinuate itself, annihilate hopes and positive beliefs, and fatally paralyze action. This finds close correspondence in a dual idea of verbal enchantment conceived by Plato. Not only is there the magnetic poetic transport derived from the Muse and emitted by poets and rhapsodists, as described in the *Ion* and in other dialogues such as *Gorgias*, in which enchantment is linked to dynamics of desire and pleasure, but there is also enchantment intended as a form of intellectual possession enacted by dialectic reason.[3] For example, Socrates in the *Meno* is described as an enchanter who, through his dialectics, undermines the eloquence of his interlocutors. In particular, Meno remarks how Socrates is always perplexed about everything, and how he drags everyone else down to the same view: 'you are casting your spells over me, and I am simply getting bewitched and enchanted, and am at my wits' end [...] you seem to me both in your appearance and in your power over others to be very like the flat torpedo fish, who torpifies those who come near him and touch him, as you have now torpified me'.[4] After interacting with Socrates, Meno feels that his rhetorical skills have been paralyzed, his tongue and mind rendered numb. His long experience in giving speeches about virtue is of no avail now that his personal gift of eloquence has been deactivated by Socrates's reasoning. Because of this, Meno continues, Socrates is right not to leave Athens for some foreign city, as this would certainly lead him to be expelled from it as an evil enchanter. However, the same effect that his words have on others, Socrates responds, also applies to himself. He accepts the comparison with the fish but provided that 'the torpedo is itself torpid as well as the cause of torpidity in others, [...] for I perplex others, not because I am clear, but because I am utterly perplexed myself'.[5] The effect of cognition, Socrates implies, is universal, nobody is excluded, and his personal experience corresponds to the general. In a foreign city he would be no exception, and like anybody else he himself would have to suffer the consequences of dialectics. Thus already in Plato the metaphorical ground of magnetic imagery is shared between the domain of the body and that of the mind. The energy of vocal expression is challenged by the immobility brought about by intellectual realization. There is a moment when the exceptionality or peculiarity of one's own vocal story is overwhelmed and silenced by an absolute universal recognition enlightened by reason. Words capable of magnetic effects carry the risk of crossing the threshold of safety and balance which originally characterized the poetic medium, when it reached a collective audience more given to spontaneous excitement and commotion, and who responded only through vital physical impulses.

Leopardi's interest in electricity and animal magnetism and his own practice of 'hypnotic writing', while mirroring a timely philosophical concern with the relationship between the real and the mind and a genuine scientific interest in mesmeric discoveries of the eighteenth and nineteenth centuries, is therefore also the response to a cultural shift pertaining to a different system of signification, that of the passage between orality and literacy, which also employs the image of magnetic enchantment as its constituent form. Leopardi witnessed and sensed the most radical consequences of the fracture intrinsic to the passage from the stability of shared morality and worldview enhanced by the fleeting voice, to the ephemerality of values entrusted to the fixity and reproducibility of the written text, which in the course of the nineteenth century had reached the climax of its affirmation and diffusion through an unprecedented abundance in the quantity and circulation of printed materials. Leopardi is aware of the irreversibility of the shift which led to the loss of the oral world and to a process of abstraction which characterized the development of the modern intellect. His relationship with Plato, the philosopher who marked the first hiatus between the two psychological and cultural universes, is telling of a broader operation of simultaneous intellectual acceptance and creative reaction to the loss of the fugitive voice. Leopardi never ceased to admire the eloquent and poetic Plato, with poetic here being used in the sense of 'orale, epico, se per epica intendiamo [...] una enciclopedia del sapere trasmessa non attraverso la ragione, ma invece attraverso le emozioni, l'immaginazione e il piacere di cedere all'autorità di una parola musicale' [oral and epic, if by epic poetry one means an encyclopaedia of knowledge transmitted through emotion, imagination, and the pleasure to yield to the authority of a musical word, rather than reason].[6] However, he held Plato responsible for having for the first time irreversibly established a rational ethics based on intellectual rather than emotional persuasion.

Leopardi's creative work can be read as an attempt to recreate and re-enliven the oral voice through the mute fixity of the written sign. Writing assumes a twofold meaning as both the graveyard of the oral voice but also as its only means of resurrection. This, as we have seen, for Leopardi can be achieved through a kind of ultra-philosophical forgetfulness which allows the poet-turned-philosopher to abandon a close adherence to reality, to forget the truth if only for a moment and give up the need for absolute, abstract thinking in order to return to a praxis of everyday life. This is a way of conceiving of writing as a partial but salvific remedy, as a beneficial magic tool capable of transforming and recreating the lost world of sound, performance, and example, and thus enriching the lived life of the writer day by day, entry by entry. It is also a way for the philosopher to step back and return to being a poet for a moment, to return the power of reason to that of a measured influence and thus to restore a middle ground for action and imagination. The *Zibaldone* is precisely the field where daily writing becomes a practice of everyday survival, in a relationship with the text which is primarily one of intermittence and distraction from thought and immediate scope for creative expression.

In what follows we shall investigate in detail the way in which Leopardi's everyday relationship with his notebook develops forms of thinking that restore the idea of writing as action and as vital fruition. This focus will be on two modalities which characterize Leopardi's daily practice of note-taking, namely writing as recreation of oral performance, and writing as wandering, with the latter image corresponding to Michel de Certeau's parallel between the act of writing and that of walking. Certeau makes a distinction between the act of walking meant as an 'operation', or 'the act itself of passing by', and the route as it may be drawn or seen on a map.[7] The former contains elements of unpredictability, blindness, and otherness which struggle to find expression in organized sequences and linear representations. In the practice of walking, perceptions originate from sources which are often out of focus and compounded in that unique, and gradual, spatial and temporal coming-forth of the visual prospect to the moving subject. It is a combination of all sensory elements in that particular moving visual frame, with walking conceived as a mode of being immersed in the landscape or cityscape. When certain perceptions hit the subject, they have already started to fade into a set of other immediately subsequent perceptions. This lived experience of space is different from the same space described through precise waymarkers on a map, which is instead totalizing and reversible, and deriving from aerial observation. These points of a map, writes Certeau, 'allow us to grasp only a relic set in the nowhen of a surface of projection. Itself visible, it has the effect of making invisible the operation that made it possible'.[8] I believe that Certeau's model can be employed to understand the difference between two kinds of relationship that Leopardi built with his own *Zibaldone*, in that the everyday writing as a form of 'pedestrian enunciation' is distinct from the reading and organizing task that Leopardi completed with the 1827 'Index'.[9] While the former develops through unpredictable outcomes which are generated by writing itself, and makes abundant use of examples and dialogical modalities of expression which convey a sense of contingent urban communication between implicit interlocutors, the latter represents the attempt to trace linear pathways and thematic waymarkers synthetizing the intricate geography of the diary from above, through organized routes which make topics retrievable but at the same time remove the sense of passing by from one entry to the next, and make invisible the specific contingent reasons which lead Leopardi to consult already-written materials and adopt intra-textual references. These constituent forms of pedestrian and aerial writing bear structural analogies to elements of the complex universe of signification generated by the passage from orality to literacy as well as from the ancient to the modern worlds. An idea of *disappearance of visibility* associated with rationalization for Leopardi is at the basis of the evolution of language, which helps us understand how the written text of the *Zibaldone* embodies experiences that the subject normally undergoes in the everyday physical and material world, and which in turn reflect broader cultural shifts in the history of civilization.

In order to show how the micro-structures of the text reflect wider cultural systems which have been assimilated as generative forms, it is important to highlight how an original tension between appearance and disappearance regulates for Leopardi the very essence of language, that is, the relationship between consonants and vowels in the formation of words. Despite the fact that vowels were the original sounds that the human voice produced and the first sounds that the human mind perceived, in the initial stages of alphabets languages lacked vowel signs, which are 'suoni più sottili [...], più difficili a separarsi dal resto de' suoni di quello che sieno le consonanti' ('thinner sounds [...], harder to distinguish from the remaining sounds, than consonants are') (*Zib.* 1286), and by presenting consonants only the first written languages were similar to stenographic writing. The predominance of consonant signs was at the origin of much confusion and diversification within idioms once writing started to be employed more systematically. The greatest impact of these consonant-only types of writing was a divergence between the way in which words were pronounced and the way in which they were written. Indeed, the identicalness of words written with the same consonants would only be illusory, each evoking instead a different ensemble of vowel-sounds.[10] As far as pronunciation is concerned, vowels are rather the sounds on which our voice eventually wants to rest. Leopardi observes our difficulty in maintaining the prolonged release of consonants and expresses the relationship between consonants and vowels in terms of gravitational *fall*: 'provatevi a pronunziar sola una consonante p. e. l'f, o l'n: [...] vedrete che la pronunzia non potendo star sospesa e finita nella pura consonante, e dove [sic] cascare in vocale vi casca nell'e' ('try to pronounce only a consonant, e.g., the f or the n [...] and you will see that, because the pronunciation cannot be suspended and completed in a simple consonant, and must fall onto a vowel, it falls on the e') (*Zib.* 30). Vowels perform a relieving function in discharging tension and alleviating the voice's efforts by representing a 'riposo momentaneo e passeggero alla pronunzia' ('a momentary and passing support and pause in the pronunciation') (*Zib.* 3872). The fact that vowels 'formano la sostanza [delle] lingue, ma non della loro gramatica' ('form the substance of [...] languages, but not of their grammar') (*Zib.* 1289), explains the gap between orality and literacy, namely between the spontaneous *use* of language and the process of rationalization and codification which is at the origin of written culture. In the alphabet, vowels initially tended to hide themselves, as it were, and to escape being grasped as a means to safeguard language momentarily from its inevitable consumption by the written code. Indeed, once all the vowels were discovered and classified, once they made it possible to reveal and complete the final form of words, their employment in written form started to trigger the need for their *sacrifice*:

> Il concorso delle vocali suol essere accetto generalmente alle lingue [...] tanto più, quanto elle sono più vicine ai loro principii, [...] e quanto più la loro formazione si dovè a tempi vicini alla naturalezza de' costumi e de' gusti. Per lo più vanno perdendo questa inclinazione col tempo, e col ripulimento, e si considera come duro e sgradevole il concorso delle vocali che da principio s'aveva per fonte di dolcezza e di leggiadria. [...] Ed è che nella poesia latina se una parola finita per vocale è seguita da un' altra che incominci per vocale, l'ultima vocale della parola precedente *è mangiata dalla seguente, si perde*, e non si conta fra le sillabe del verso. All'opposto nella poesia greca non è mangiata, nè si perde o altera in verun modo.
>
> [The closer languages are to their beginnings, [...] and the more their formation occurred at a time when customs and tastes were natural, the more they tend [...] generally to accept the concurrence of vowels. For the most part, they go on losing this propensity as time passes and the cleansing goes on, and the running together of vowels which at the beginning was regarded as a source of sweetness and grace is now regarded as harsh and grating. [...] And it is that in Latin poetry if a word ending in a vowel is followed by another beginning with a vowel, the final vowel of the preceding word *is swallowed by the following one, it is lost*, and does not count as one of the syllables in the verse. Conversely, in Greek poetry it is not swallowed, nor is it lost or altered in any way.] (*Zib.* 1157–58; my emphasis)

The salvific role of vowels made it possible for languages to achieve clarity and systematization, but this operation at the same time led to their consumption. The development of the linguistic structure seems to reflect the outcomes of the history of civilization, that is, a gain in knowledge in parallel to the loss of nature, including the religious and messianic connotations which are echoed by the idea of the 'fall' of consonants and 'sacrifice' of vowels. Furthermore, the other essential concept at the root of these reflections — the importance of action (or use) for the conservation of life and at the same time the constitutive risk of dissipation to which it is exposed in dynamics of excess — is at the core of Leopardi's analysis of modernity, and it clearly also crucially informs the dialectic between orality and literacy.

It is interesting to note how Leopardi's analysis of the development of the alphabet anticipates the later interpretation provided by Eric A. Havelock in his *Origins of Western Literacy* (1976). Leopardi notes that while in the Hebrew language the names of the letters referred to specific *things* of the material world, for instance 'alèf' signified 'dottrina' ('doctrine') and 'beth', 'casa' ('house') (*Zib.* 2956), progressively alphabets became self-reflexive; the names of the letters started to coincide with their sound (for example in Italian we use *a*, *bi*, *ci* (or *be*, *ce*) as names for the sounds 'a', 'b', 'c'), thus losing any reference to concrete meaning.[11] Havelock observes how the advent of Greek script had a psychological impact which changed the way the human mind processed thought. Because the names of the letters no longer referred to objective and factual reality, once the letter was learned 'you did not have to think about it'. The word, 'though a visible thing, a series of marks, [...] ceased to interpose itself as an object of thought between the reader and its recollection of the spoken tongue'. The alphabet became better able to convey external meaning thanks to the loss of its own meaning, that is, its specific properties or intrinsic value in their names, which the Hebrew letters still possessed when their names signified 'house' or 'camel'. Thanks to the fact that they 'were robbed of any independent meaning', the Greek letters became a true alphabet, or in other words, 'convertible into a mechanical mnemonic device'. For this reason Havelock uses the comparison between the Greek script and 'an electric current communicating a recollection of the sounds of the spoken word directly to the brain so that the meaning resounded as it were in the consciousness without reference to the properties of the letters used'.[12] The increased visibility and clarity of Greek signs — the fact that all the phonetic elements were now covered by the graphic signs — in fact made them invisible to the mind. Through the polyphonic image of the refreshing breeze depicting the effect of Anacreon's odes, Leopardi seems to suggest a metaphorical allusion revolving around similar dynamics of concealment: the composition of verbal signs in a poem hits our mind, generating imaginative senses, but only as a condition of their invisibility, as long as their trick (phonic, syntactical, and lexical) remains unexplored and unrevealed. If instead the words are examined, their effect vanishes, and the more we try to see, the blinder we become. This is also, I believe, the process that Leopardi faced when in 1827 he reread and revised his *Zibaldone* materials for the preparation of the 'Index': by tracing a detailed orientational map he suffered the sacrifice of the spontaneous emergence of thought, which was consumed by its fixation through precise coordinates of page and paragraph numbers.

In the following chapters we shall investigate the meaning of writing as a salvific practice, bearing in mind that for Leopardi language itself contains in its most essential letter structure the potential to rescue the subject from the unbalanced domain of reason. When dissipation finally reaches the notebook, as in any experience of use turned into consumption, Leopardi's aims will be projected outside the book and into life as it is lived. The *Zibaldone* will then be the embodiment of the final, most radical performance.

Notes to Chapter 17

1. Cf. Adriana Cavarero, *For More Than One Voice: Toward a Philosophy of Vocal Expression*, trans. by Paul A. Kottman (Stanford, CA: Stanford University Press, 2005), particularly pp. 95–102. See also Michael Caesar, 'Voice, Vision and Orality: Notes on Reading Adriana Cavarero', in *Orality and Literacy in Modern Italian Culture*, ed. by Michael Caesar and Marina Spunta (Oxford: Legenda, 2006), pp. 7–17.
2. On omission and lacuna in the construction of literary and philosophical sense see Nicola Gardini, *Lacuna: saggio sul non detto* (Turin: Einaudi, 2014).
3. Cf. D'Intino, *L'immagine della voce*, p. 80.
4. Plato, 'Meno', in *The Dialogues of Plato*, trans. by Benjamin Jowett, 4th edn, 4 vols (Oxford: Oxford University Press, 1967), I, 249–301 (p. 276).
5. Ibid., p. 277.
6. D'Intino, *L'immagine della voce*, p. 188.
7. Michel de Certeau, *The Practice of Everyday Life*, trans. by Steven Rendall (Berkeley, Los Angeles, & London: University of California Press, 1988), p. 97.
8. Ibid.
9. Ibid., p. 99.
10. Cf. *Zib.* 1283–91.
11. Cf. *Zib.* 30.
12. Eric A. Havelock, *Origins of Western Literacy* (Toronto: Ontario Institute for Studies in Education, 1976), pp. 46, 47.

CHAPTER 18

Leopardi as Master and Student in the *Zibaldone*

Leopardi's tendency to retrieve past thoughts in order to investigate further their possible application is frequently marked by repetition and rephrasing, demonstrating great efforts to revise or memorize certain passages. This practice, which at times appears obsessive, resembles a mode of study in which the subject matter must be repeated and learnt by heart; in fact, it is almost possible to catch a glimpse of Leopardi the student in the pages of the *Zibaldone*, revising a lesson, memorizing its parts, and even testing the correctness of his ideas through a kind of self-assessment. But the role of the student is only one side of a reflexive perspective in which Leopardi plays also the role of the teacher, giving instructions, eliciting dialogue between different points of view, monitoring the learning process, and assessing the student's findings. Because both figures, student and teacher, coincide in the binary perspective of the writer, Leopardi's process of education is in fact self-education, marked by self-checking and self-examination. When referring to Leopardi's self-education in the *Zibaldone* it is important to specify that the idea of education as a process of learning — involving rote, of course, but also skills and habits — differs from mere acquisition of knowledge. As Richard S. Peters explains, education involves also the orientation of knowledge towards certain standards and outcomes of achievement. Moreover, education establishes principles of knowledge and develops structures or *formae mentis* which can be adopted when dealing with different fields of inquiry.[1] Leopardi's theory and practice of education reflect a certain religious symbolism that functions as a structure and imparts deeper meaning. When we consider the idea of education in Leopardi there are two main antithetical models that shape our understanding: on the one hand, as we have seen, the model of Christian and Jesuit instruction, which informed Leopardi's own upbringing and education;[2] and, on the other hand, the model of ancient Greek education.[3] The model provided by Christianity is founded on an ideal of cultivation of the spirit rather than the body, rationalism, fixed rules, and prescriptions, as well as a need to elucidate and punish sin.[4] The model of ancient Greek education, which was based on an immediate acknowledgement of virtue and talent without the need to refer to divine judgement, is characterized by vitality, corporeality, and dialogical and oral modalities of communication.[5] In the *Zibaldone* Leopardi's own voice frequently gives way to those of other authors who animate the notebook by introducing other or similar points of view. Moreover, there are non-literary voices that echo throughout the text; for example, the popular songs he heard in his youth or the voices of passers-by which burst into the *Zibaldone* as the voices of everyday life, and which also allude to a model of education based on direct experience rather than study.[6]

The first question to be addressed is what kind of learning outcome Leopardi aims to achieve through writing, and my first observation again stems from Leopardi's insistence on the importance of clarity of expression, which is reached when writing renders 'lo stato preciso della nostra mente, o ch'ella veda chiaro, o veda scuro' ('the precise state of our mind, whether it sees clearly or sees obscurely') (*Zib.* 1372). As we have seen in the first part of this book, expression may be clear even when the idea remains obscure, if the writer is humble and honest enough to confess ('confessare [o] dare a vedere' ('admit and let it be seen'), *Zib.* 1372) that what he sees is still unclear, and if he conveys an exact radiograph of his mind and captures the most minuscule parts of his thought. When Leopardi writes that he 'piglier[à] sempre buonissima speranza di un fanciullo o di un giovane, il quale ponendosi a scrivere e comporre, vada sempre dietro alle idee proprie, e voglia a ogni costo esprimerele' ('will [...] place the highest hopes in, a child or youth who, when setting out to write and compose, always follows his own ideas, and seeks at all costs to express them') (*Zib.* 1544–45), we imagine the voice of a teacher giving good advice to a student by referring to his own experience and example. This advice is clearly put into practice in the *Zibaldone*, as Leopardi applies his own ideas as well as those of other authors to a variety of topics as in the following examples:

> I piaceri [...] non sono piaceri, se non in quanto noi ci siamo fatti delle ragioni e delle abitudini, perchè lo sieno. [...] Applicate il sopraddetto ai piaceri che recano le altre arti belle, e i vari generi di letteratura ec. [...] Ed alle forme umane delicate [...], e ad altri tali generi e fonti e ragioni di bellezze.
>
> [Pleasures are [...] only pleasures insofar as we have formed reasons and habits for them to be so. [...] Apply the above to the pleasures that the other fine arts, and the various genres of literature, etc., procure [...]. And to delicate human forms [...], and to other such kinds and sources and causes of beauty.] (*Zib.* 1758–59)

Leopardi extends one observation and applies it to all the possible areas for which it might be valid, indicating his impulse to group together all new aspects of the analysis so that the evidence for the full extent of the concept become present and visible. The same can be said for Leopardi's frequent practice of addressing ideas of other authors in support of his own, thereby giving new validity to a particular idea by expanding its range of influence and by supporting an opinion with reference to literary authorities such as, for example, Rousseau and Goethe:

> Non [...] siamo più capaci di [...] felicità da che abbiamo conosciuto [...] il niente di questi stessi piaceri naturali del che non dovevamo neppur sospettare: tout homme qui pense est un être corrompu, dice il Rousseau [...]. E pure vediamo che questi piccoli diletti non ostante che noi siamo già guasti pur ci appagano meglio che qualunque altro come dice Verter ec.

> [We are no longer capable of [...] happiness from the moment we have experienced [...] the nothingness of these same natural pleasures, which we ought not even to suspect: 'Tout homme qui pense est un être corrompu' ["Every man who thinks is a corrupted being"], as Rousseau says [...]. And yet [...], we see that these small pleasures reward us better than any other, in the words of Werther, etc.] (*Zib.* 56)

Here his own ideas become part of a wider picture comprising other voices, almost like an assemblage or a puzzle in which different presences and sources seem to fit together into one whole.

In other cases Leopardi's own experience becomes paradigmatic, and his practice of addressing a virtual audience resembles that of a master giving an assignment to a student:

> Un uomo diviene eloquente a forza di legger libri eloquenti; [...] pensatore, matematico, ragionatore, poeta [...]. Sviluppate questo pensiero, applicandovi l'esempio mio, e distinguendolo secondi [*sic*] i gradi di adattabilità, e formabilità naturale o acquisita degli' individui.
>
> [A man becomes eloquent by dint of reading eloquent books; he becomes [...] a thinker, a mathematician, a reasoner, a poet [...]. Develop this thought, applying it to my own case, and differentiate between degrees of adaptability and conformability, natural or acquired, in individuals.] (*Zib.* 1541)

Compare the first sentence to an essay title that a master asks a student to write and reflect upon by following specific guidelines and requirements. Leopardi first provides the general title or topic, 'A man becomes eloquent by dint of reading eloquent books', then asks a virtual listener to develop this statement, and then provides a clear example, which he uses as a concrete starting-point, namely his own experience, which is of course well-known to the virtual student and to himself, as teacher and student are one and the same person. Similarly, in the following entry Leopardi seems to be assessing himself, checking his own deductions: 'Gli argomenti ch'io tiro dalla considerazione della grazia, in ordine al bello, sono giusti, e giustamente dedotti' ('The proofs I draw from a consideration of grace, with respect to beauty, are correct, and correctly deduced') (*Zib.* 1522), which may be interpreted as a practice of self-assessment by a student who is going through his research once again and is happy with his achievements.

A further, more complex example shows how Leopardi attempts to keep a certain reflection present in his mind by repeating and revising all the steps of his reasoning, thus transforming the separate parts of the discourse into a continuous flow, in an operation which resembles an exercise in rote learning:

> [1a] Siccome la memoria [...] è una pura abitudine, [2a] così ciascun'altra abitudine è una Memoria. [3a] Di memoria son provveduti tutti i sensi, tutti gli organi, tutte le parti fisiche o morali dell'uomo, che son capaci di avvezzarsi, e di abilitarsi, e di *acquistare* qualunque facoltà. La memoria è da principio una disposizione, poi una facoltà di assuefarsi che ha l'intelletto umano; [...] [1b] La memoria è un' abito [*sic*], [2b] gli abiti altrettante memorie, [3b] attribuite dalla natura a ciascuna parte assuefabile del vivente, in quanto disposizioni, ed acquistate in quanto facoltà ed assuefazioni. Questo pensiero si può

molto stendere, e cavarne delle belle conseguenze, intorno alla natura della memoria.

> [[1a] Since memory [...] is a pure habit, [2a] so every other habit is a memory. [3a] All the senses, all the organs, all the moral or physical parts of man, which can become habituated and capable, and can *acquire* any faculty, are provided with memory. Memory is first a disposition, then a faculty of habituation which the human intellect possesses. [...] [1b] Memory is a habit, [2b] habits are likewise memories, [3b] assigned by nature to each part of the living thing that is able to become habituated as dispositions, and acquired as faculties and habits. This thought could be greatly expanded, and obtain some good results concerning the nature of memory.] (*Zib.* 2047–48)

All the essential elements of the first part, from 'since memory is a pure habit' to 'the human intellect possesses', are repeated in a more synthetic way in the part that immediately follows. We see in fact that: 'Memory is [...] a pure habit' corresponds to 'Memory is a habit', 'so every other habit is a memory' corresponds to 'habits are likewise memories'. The same applies to section three, where elements are summarized in the second portion of the text: 'All the senses, all the organs, all the moral or physical parts of man' becomes 'each part of the living thing'; and all the key words ('disposition' and 'faculty') and concepts (to 'become habituated', to 'acquire') recur. It seems that Leopardi is using writing to rehearse the passages and commit them to memory, as we may do for instance when we prepare a speech and repeat it again and again until all the words flow. After completing this process of synthesis, Leopardi feels he has mastered the thought, and possesses a clear vision of its elements, and now can 'greatly expand it', which shows how his way of exercising memory serves as a technique for developing his reflection without allowing anything to disappear from his mind. In Leopardi's practice of revision, which has been examined already as a form of 'elastic writing', one also detects the persistence of the Jesuit pedagogical model emphasizing rhetorical skills and refined eloquence. Specific sessions of the school day and days of the week were devoted exclusively to revising learnt notions, and the range of materials covered also spanned different intervals of time, from the follow-up repetition of a class which has just been delivered or the previous day's lesson, to weekly and monthly revisions taking place according to designated schedules (normally on Saturdays), and to the final revision of the whole academic year.[7] Repetition was a means of reinforcing in the students the sense of the systematic nature of knowledge; it was conceived as a way of perceiving the logical sequentiality between one class and the next, thus locating each new element of learning in a harmonic ensemble of interconnected thought. The fundamental objectives of the repetition at the root of Jesuit education, highlighted by Allan P. Farrell, are a 'drill in vocabulary and syntax in the lower grammar classes', and the 'accuracy in stating and exemplifying rules'.[8] Leopardi's independent self-learning strategies through annotation are a residue of this training, as is more specifically his constant attempt to refine his terminology, to study etymologies and the diachronic changes of linguistic senses, and to appeal to foreign languages to provide shades of meaning corresponding as accurately as possible to the devised idea. As for the other three objectives of repetition underlined by Farrell, namely the 'detection of student weaknesses', the 'organization of material already studied', and the 'suggestion of questions or topics for further study', they also find correspondence in the general scopes of eighteenth- and nineteenth-century notebook-writing and, more specifically, in the correcting and refining impulses of the kind of self-examining thought that is found in the *Zibaldone*.[9] Leopardi's wide use of examples and similes which derive from reading and from his own experience to corroborate his arguments corresponds to the Jesuit vision of learning as not merely superficial abstract knowledge but as knowledge applicable to and effective in the praxis of living. The aims of reading were meant to show the pupil that they were not 'examining a dead series of words, but a living organism with life and feeling in it', and that they were studying 'the actual expression of real human feelings', according to the vivifying imagery which, as we have seen, has many religious and aesthetic echoes, but also scientific resonances.[10]

What we have seen so far reinforces the idea that Leopardi's standard that distinguishes education from mere knowledge is clarity, and this is the state that he endeavours to attain in the *Zibaldone*. To that end, and in line with his confessional inclination, he gives instructions and advice to the hypothetical reader and to himself. Clarity consists in '[lo] stato preciso della nostra mente' ('the precise state of our mind') (*Zib.* 1372) not as inert form, but as action, process, and application. Clarity is achieved by a natural operation of composition and decomposition of the language we already possess: 'Nè altri è per l'ordinario mai una nuova idea, 1. che una porzione d'idea già posseduta, nuovamente separata dalle altre porzioni della medesima, e nuovamente determinata in modo ch'ella sussista da se, e sia idea da se, e da se si concepisca' ('A new idea is ordinarily thus simply but a portion of an idea already possessed, and newly separated from the other portion of the same, and newly determined in such a way that it subsists by itself') (*Zib.* 2950). Finally, an essential principle, clarity must always be present, and it must be of a balanced intensity: 'la chiarezza e la semplicità [...] denno [...] esser [...] sempre della medesima quantità, [...] e sempre uguali a se stesse nell'esser di chiarezza e semplicità, e nell'intensione di questo essere' ('clarity and simplicity [...] must be of the same quantity [...], and always the same to themselves in their essence of clarity and simplicity, and in the intensity of this essence').] (*Zib.* 3050)

I believe that Leopardi recommends this balanced use of clarity because he could not escape the idea of a different form of clarity, a very unbalanced kind with potentially dangerous effects; namely, the hyper-clarity experienced by Adam and Eve as a result of original sin. Leopardi devotes many pages of the *Zibaldone* to interpreting the passage in Genesis which describes the Fall, and, as discussed earlier, suggests that what Adam and Eve experienced was an increase of reason to the point that, through hyper-clarity of the intellect, they acquired cognition of the structuring principles of life.[11] The Fall, Leopardi explains, revealed a contradiction between the relative essence of man and the absolute essence of life, destroying the harmony which man previously possessed, and transforming the essence and outcomes of his desires: the fulfilment of happiness, which in the state of innocence was granted by a self-sufficient human nature, became perpetual dissatisfaction. It is important to look closely at the specific terminology of Leopardi's reflection on sin and its consequences, as the lexicon and semantics employed correspond to those used in his observations on clarity. Leopardi writes that with original sin began: 'questo squilibrio, questo contrasto di due qualità [ragione e natura] [...]. Anzi dopo il peccato, e *mediante* il peccato l'uomo ebbe l'intelletto rischiaratissimo, acquistò la scienza del bene e del male, e divenne effettivamente per questa, quasi unus ex nobis, disse Iddio' ('this imbalance, this clash of two qualities [reason and nature] [...;] the intellect of man was greatly illuminated after this sin, and *by way of* his sin. He acquired the knowledge of good and evil, and became effectively in this way "quasi unus ex nobis" [as one of us], in the words of God') (*Zib.* 434). Before original sin Adam possessed only *credenze*, or primitive beliefs, fuelled by imagination, which functioned as a positive energy that would have driven the first man towards the satisfaction of everything he desired, through constant action, spontaneously and without the need to be taught:

> Il fanciullo, bambino, applicategli le labbra alla mammella, ne succhia il latte senza maestro. [...] Perciò è un vero acciecamento il dire che il bruto ha dalla natura tutta quella istruzione che gli bisogna per esistere: l'uomo no: e dedurne ch'egli dunque ha bisogno di ammaestramento, di società ec. [...] l'uomo aveva naturalmente tutto il necessario.
>
> [The baby, for example, putting its lips to the breast, sucks milk from it without being taught [...]. Therefore it is real blindness to suggest that nature teaches the brute everything it needs to exist, but not man, and to deduce from this that man therefore needs teaching, society, etc. [...] Man [...] had all that he needed naturally.] (*Zib.* 440–41)

In the same way, Leopardi alludes to the language of clarity as language that intrinsically possesses all the necessary sources for new ideas, which are created through a process, by composition and decomposition of words already contained in the language. The parallel between the corresponding but also contrasting features of these two states, sin and clarity, can be extended. With original sin man acquired cognition of the immobilizing essence of truth:

> Dove alla determinazione dell'uomo, non è necessario [...] altro che la credenza; la cognizione [...] viene a esser nemica della credenza, e però della determinazione. E in vece che l'ignoranza, tal qual è in natura [...] conduca l'uomo o l'animale all' indifferenza [...] ve lo conduce anzi il sapere (e l'eterna esperienza lo prova). E l'uomo tanto meno, tanto più difficilmente, lentamente, e dubbiamente si determina, quanto più sa. Tanto minore è la determinazione, quanto maggiore è il sapere.
>
> [Whereas nothing but belief is needed [...] for the determination of man, knowledge [...] is the enemy of belief, and therefore of determination. And rather than ignorance, such as is found in nature [...] leading men or animals to indifference, [...] it is knowledge that leads them there (and eternal experience proves it). And the more man knows, the more difficulty, hesitation, and doubt he has in forming a decision. The greater the knowledge, the less the determination.] (*Zib.* 450)

Notice that the consequences of sin are diametrically opposed to the principles of clarity previously outlined. Sin imparted a destabilizing hyper-clarity ('[With original sin began] this imbalance, this clash of two qualities [reason and nature] [...;] the intellect of man was greatly illuminated ['ebbe l'intelletto rischiaratissimo'] after this sin', *Zib.* 434) that caused a loss of instinctual drive towards action (determination), dissatisfaction with humankind's extant knowledge and tools, which were no longer sufficient for happiness, and a need to seek new forms of rational education, whereas no education or instruction had been necessary before. As a result, humankind became almost immobilized in a kind of 'heat death', in which the vision of truth, of the real and essential principles of life, paralyzed action.[12] The following table highlights the various correspondences and antitheses between Leopardi's ideal of clarity and his conceptualization of the Fall:

Clarity in writing	Hyper-clarity (consequence of sin)
Balance	Imbalance
Action	Immobility
Language is already naturally possessed (to form new ideas)	Natural happiness is lost
Energy: connecting, composing and deconstructing ideas	Heat death: elimination of tension from the relative to the general, as the process has exhausted itself in a sudden illumination
Natural, easy	Rational, through instruction

As anticipated in the first part of this book, it is in response to this model, which represents a strong inner, sometimes unconscious, driving force, that Leopardi continues to prescribe for himself a balanced use of clarity as a form of 'veridiction', insisting on the importance of confessing that a certain thought is unclear and on the fact that language already naturally possesses all that a writer needs to express a new idea. Of course from the point of view of modernity, Leopardi knows that cognition is irreversible and that it is impossible to return to the primordial state of innocence as if nothing had happened. Modernity as a whole cannot escape — indeed it actively subsists on — Adam's sinful abuse of reason, as is evident from the presence of key concepts connoting the antithesis of action and immobility in Leopardi's analysis of modern man:

> Un amico o persona desiderata che ritorni dopo lungo tempo, o che vediate per la prima volta. Il fanciullo e l'uomo selvaggio l'abbraccerà, lo carezzerà, salterà, darà mille segni esterni di quella gioia che l'anima veram. e vivamente; [...] L'uomo ordinario, o l'uomo di sentimento affievolito e intorpidito dall'esperienza del mondo, e dalla misera cognizione delle cose, insomma l'uomo moderno, conserverà di dentro e di fuori il suo stato giornaliero, non proverà emozione se non piccola, minore ancora di quello che forse si aspettava, ed o che lo prevedesse o no, quello sarà per lui un avvenimento ordinario della vita, uno di quei piaceri che si gustano con indifferenza, e che appena arrivati, quando anche voi lo desideraste, ansiosamente, vi par freddo e ordinario e incapace di riempiervi o di scuotervi.
>
> [A friend or much longed-for person who returns after a long absence or that

you see for the first time. A child or a savage will embrace and caress him and jump for joy, and give a thousand different signs of the true and lively joy that animates him. [...] The average man, or the man whose feelings have been dulled and enfeebled by his experience of the world and wretched knowledge of things, in other words modern man, will maintain his everyday state inside and out, he will feel only slight emotions, even less than he perhaps expects. And whether he foresaw it or not, that will be for him just an ordinary event in life, one of those pleasures which you sample with indifference, and which, as soon as they arrive, even if you had been anxiously awaiting them, seem ordinary and unable to satisfy you or stir you.] (*Zib.* 267–68)

Lack of action, indifference (or lack of determination), and dissatisfaction all distinguish the condition that modernity shares with Adam. What is most important is that Leopardi has Adam in mind when he describes the effects of education on the child. Childhood, 'la più bella e fortunata età dell'uomo' ('the finest and most fortunate age of man') — note the Edenic connotation — is tormented by upbringing and education (*Zib.* 3078–79), as the child is forced to relinquish his naturalness and spontaneity in order to acquire knowledge and perfection, that is, culture and civilization, thus losing the 'felicità della fanciullezza, quella che la natura avea destinato e preparato siccome a questa, così a ciascun' altra età dell'uomo' ('happiness which nature had destined and prepared both for childhood and for every other age of man') (*Zib.* 3079), in the same way that original sin changed the lot of Adam and the entire human race.

The insistence on clarity as a property whose characteristics oppose those of sin suggests that Leopardi, as a poet, teacher, and student, conceived of writing as the only possible way of recreating the illusions of that primordial stage by eliciting action and escaping the immobility of pure cognition. I believe that it fell to the *Zibaldone* itself to accomplish this, as it were, redemptive role by offering the possibility, albeit only intermittently, of distraction from truth (cf. *Zib.* 104). This operation could only be accomplished through a different system of thought than that of Christianity, namely, the Greek model of education, corresponding to Leopardi's belief that one never fully learns 'dai soli libri' ('from books alone') (*Zib.* 58), for exposure to life (namely to oral, physical, or practical impulses) is as important as exposure to books. The focus here will be on an idea of education based on a dialogical model, which corresponds to Leopardi's practice of addressing a virtual reader, or better a listener, to clarify all the passages of a certain thought. The dialogical form is in itself a modality which resists uniformity because it is based on questioning and on the living voice; that is, on a kind of stimulus which catches the attention of the listener with different degrees of unpredictability, and is therefore the most effective technique to activate a spontaneous response. Of course, besides the phenomenological value of the question and answer, the Socratic dialogue is the specific cultural and educational model which Leopardi had in mind, representing a system of values antithetical to Christianity and based on the harmony between mental and physical exercise.

In the following entries one can see how Leopardi gives voice to experience by developing his thought through dialogue and by assuming the point of view of each interlocutor, often simulating a lively discussion. It is a kind of conversation which might occur on meeting someone by chance:

> Osservate quell'uomo disperatissimo di tutta quanta la vita, [...] e sul punto di uccidersi. Che cosa credete voi ch'egli pensi? pensa che la sua morte sarà o compianta, o ammirata, o desterà spavento [...]; che si discorrerà di lui, se non altro per qualche istante con un sentimento straordinario; [....] Credete voi ch'egli non tema? Egli teme [...] che queste speranze non abbiano effetto.
>
> [Observe that man, who despairs completely of all that life has to offer, [...] and is about to kill himself. What do you suppose he is thinking about? He thinks that his death will either be regretted, or admired, or will arouse fear [...]; that he will be talked about, at least for a few moments, with deep emotion [...]. Do you suppose that he is not fearful? He fears [...] that these hopes might not come true.] (*Zib.* 1547–48)

We could almost imagine these lines being exchanged between two friends in response to an encounter with a third person while walking in the street. In other cases the conversation becomes very animated and the two contrasting points of view develop into a heated argument:

> Dirò: la materia può pensare e sentire; pensa e sente. — Signor no; anzi voi direte: la materia non può, in nessun modo mai, nè pensare nè sentire. — Oh perchè? — Perchè noi non intendiamo come lo faccia. — Bellissima: intendiamo noi come attiri i corpi, come faccia quei mirabili effetti dell'elettricità, come l'aria faccia il suono? [...] E se non l'intendiamo, nè potremo intenderlo mai, neghiamo noi per questo che la materia non sia capace di queste cose, quando noi vediamo che lo è? — Provatemi che la materia possa pensare e sentire. — Che ho io da provarlo? Il fatto lo prova. [...] Non ho bisogno di altre prove.
>
> [I say: matter can think and feel; it does think and feel. — 'No, Sir, rather you should say: matter can never think or feel in any way.' — Oh but why? — 'Because we do not understand how it can.' — That's fine! Do we understand how matter attracts bodies, how it makes those wonderful effects of electricity, how air makes sound? [...] And if we do not understand it, and never shall, do we therefore deny that matter is capable of doing these things, when we see that it is? — 'Prove to me that matter can think and feel.' — Why should I have to prove it? It is proven by fact. [...] I need no other proof.] (*Zib.* 4252)

This urban and dialogical dimension is important because it informs Leopardi's writing also when there seems to be only one voice.

A dialogical dimension is present but implicit, for instance, in an image that Leopardi adopts to explain why a teacher should put himself in the shoes of the student, especially when the teacher is very knowledgeable about a certain subject, when he masters the matter so well that his intellect 'spazia [...] a piacer suo, o almeno vi passeggia per entro con franchezza [...]: allora ha bisogno di una particolare e continua avvertenza per riuscir chiaro [...] perchè intendendosi egli subito, crede che subito sarà inteso, misura l'altrui mente dalla sua' ('roams through it at will, or strolls freely at least [...] then he needs to take special and constant care to be clear, [...] because his own immediate understanding of himself leads him to believe that he will be understood immediately, because he measures the other person's mind on the basis of his own') (*Zib.* 1374). In using the image of a stroll Leopardi here has both a general and a particular reference in mind; the general being the ancient mode of education, where master and pupil would discuss philosophy on a walk, combining physical and mental exercise.[13] More particularly, the reference is to Plato's *Phaedrus*, when Phaedrus tells Socrates that he has been learning Lysias's discourse but wonders whether he will be able to remember and recite it adequately, at which point Socrates states that Phaedrus would never have decided to go for a walk if he had not already learnt the discourse by heart: 'when he [Phaedrus] was tired with sitting, he went out to take a walk, not until, by the dog, as I believe, he had simply learned by heart the entire discourse'.[14] D'Intino suggests that the *Phaedrus* had a latent influence in certain entries of the *Zibaldone* written at the same period as Leopardi's reflection on clarity and the confident master.[15] Thus D'Intino's hypothesis strengthens the plausibility of my Socratic interpretation of Leopardi's reflection, and, in turn, my interpretation of Leopardi's reflection on clarity and the confident master adds weight to the explanatory scope of D'Intino's hypothesis. Whereas Phaedrus's walk belongs to the content of the narrative, in Leopardi's reflection the text itself is the field that the philosopher's intellect 'roams through at will'. The text constitutes a world animated by different characters, friends and opponents with whom the writer and reader can interact, in the same way as in the natural world, and therefore the text becomes a kind of living organism where action can take place.

Another suitable image for the *Zibaldone* refers to the model of ancient education in the form of a symposium or, better, a kind of merrymaking. On 27 February 1827 (*Zib.* 4248) Leopardi describes his habit of eating alone, and reconnects with a previous entry (*Zib.* 4184) in which he had praised the ancient custom of maintaining a division between eating and making conversation, since he prefers to engage in conversation only after the meal has finished.[16] This is immediately followed by a quotation from Lord Chesterfield, whose voice appears in the *Zibaldone* without introduction or mediation, and to whom Leopardi replies, 'Begging pardon of his Lordship, I do not believe that the last remark is true', as if engaging in direct conversation:

> Alla p. 4184[17] [...] *Giuoco di mano, giuoco di villano, is a very true saying, among the few true sayings of the Italians*. Chesterfield Letters to his son [...]. *Petrarca is, in my mind, a sing-song love-sick Poet; [...] he deserved his Laura better than his Lauro [...] and that wretched quibble would be reckoned an excellent piece of Italian wit.* [...] Io, con licenza di Milord, non credo che sia vera quest'ultima cosa.

> [For p. 4184 [...] '*Giuoco di mano, giuoco di villano* [magic trick low trick], is a very true saying, among the few true sayings of the Italians.' Chesterfield, *Letters to His Son* [...] 'Petrarca is, in my mind, a sing-song lovesick Poet; [...] he deserved his *Laura* better than his *Lauro* [...]; and that wretched quibble would be reckoned an excellent piece of Italian wit'". Begging pardon of his Lordship, I do not believe that the last remark is true.] (*Zib.* 4248–49)

It seems clear that the conversational tone and the form of this remark are influenced by the reference to the practice of conversing after eating, momentarily transforming the text itself into the scene of an after-dinner conversation, another typical ancient mode of education, as in Plato's *Symposium*. How highly Leopardi must have valued these performative moments in his notebook is shown by an entry on the following page (28 February 1827), which unfolds as an afterthought to the performance which had taken place in the text the day before. Leopardi refers to 'Desiderio naturale [...] nell'uomo, di un futuro miglior del presente' ('Man's natural [...] desire [...] for a future which is better than the present'), and alludes to the:

> Importanza del sapersi fare, comporre e propor da se stesso tal prospettiva. [...] Utilità somma del sapersi proporre di giorno in giorno un futuro facile, o anche certo, ad ottenere; dei beni che avvengono d'ora in ora; godimenti giornalieri, di cui non v'ha condizione che non sia fornita o capace: il tutto sta sapersene pascere, e formarne la propria espettativa, prospettiva e speranza, ora per ora.
>
> [Importance of knowing how to make, compose, propose such a prospect for oneself. [...] The great benefit of knowing how to propose day by day a future that can be obtained easily or with certainty, or benefits that arrive hour by hour, daily pleasures that are provided or attainable unconditionally: all is to be found in knowing how to nurture, form one's own expectations, prospects, and hopes, hour by hour.] (*Zib.* 4249–50)

To what is Leopardi referring here if not his own *Zibaldone*? Just as in the entry where the *Zibaldone* becomes a virtual urban setting for a stroll in which education takes the form of a conversation, similarly here Leopardi conjures a scene of merrymaking, and then reflects on his own diary as a means of keeping himself active through constant application, by proposing and facing new challenges from day to day. This is the main function of the *Zibaldone*, and this is how Leopardi, through clarity and through writing as performance, tries to escape the immobilizing effect of cognition. The image of the *Zibaldone* as a daily stroll, a conversation, or form of nourishment should also invite us to reflect on whether the high degree of project-planning, which in Cacciapuoti's view characterizes the *Zibaldone*, is the only force shaping the manuscript, or whether there is not also another impulse that resisted the realization of these plans; namely, Leopardi's fascination with the immediacy of the *Zibaldone* and perhaps even the unpredictability of what reading and writing could produce in the moment of performance.[18] Leopardi's practice of addressing an implicit reader, or listener, and of treating his sources as animated interlocutors is telling of his admiration for pre-Platonic modalities of learning. However, as Socrates realizes in the course of his dialogue with Meno, it is difficult to establish whether virtue can really be taught, or if it remains an illusion constantly threatened by abstract reason. Leopardi is unable to reach the same conclusions as Plato, namely that there is virtue of divine origin instilled in the soul of man. Nevertheless, similarly to Socrates, Leopardi also envisions a concept of virtue dissociated from the exclusive striving for knowledge, and combined with the positive beliefs which instinctually and imaginatively enrich one's everyday life. Leopardi's awareness of the importance of positive beliefs was so radical that paradoxically it led to the interruption of the very same intellectual diary that had constantly attempted to recreate them. We know that Leopardi's productive energy for some reason at a certain point exhausted itself, and on 4 December 1832 (*Zib.* 4526), Leopardi ended his notebook. This outcome was accelerated by his work on the 1827 'Index'. The function of the *Zibaldone* up to that point had been to propose and re-propose impulses for action which transformed the lack of real personal life into the enlivened life of writing. But the 'Index' somehow forced Leopardi to change the nature of the text for purposes of notebook organization. Instead of inhabiting and wandering through his reflections 'from the inside', he had to move to a detached aerial perspective in order to trace a map of thematic entries. At the end of this cartographical operation Leopardi sensed the impossibility of retrieving the original, authentic, methodical, and at the same time familiar and comforting relationship with his entries. His *Zibaldone* became the world 'figurato [...] in breve carta' ('described on one brief page') to which he refers in the poem 'Ad Angelo Mai' (l. 98; *C*, pp. 34 & 41), where knowledge is described as a tool which does not increase but diminishes a sense of curiosity towards vastness. The habit of memory brought about by the indexing process is not dissimilar to the experience that Leopardi describes in relation to poetic models which cannot be forgotten, acting as a secure road from which the writer never deviates: 'con tanti usi con tanti esempi, con tante nozioni, definizioni, regole, forme, con tante letture ec. per quanto un poeta si voglia allontanare dalla strada segnata a ogni poco ci ritorna' ('with so many customs and so many examples, with so many notions, definitions, rules, forms, with so much to read, etc., however much a poet might want to leave the beaten track, he keeps coming back to it') (*Zib.* 40). The 'Index' created an unavoidable precedent in terms of intra-connections established in the revision process, which, in Leopardi's experience of re-reading his manuscript, risked turning the pleasure of episodic rediscoveries into the mechanical exercise of immediately visualizing the fixed path indicated by the headings to which a note belongs.

Before reaching the end of the *Zibaldone*, in the next chapter I will look at the pages immediately prior and subsequent to the completion of the 1827 'Index' as revealing of Leopardi's changed relationship with his sources. In the post-'Index' phase, Leopardi transforms his notebook from the status of a community village, where inhabitants (sources), routes (linking patterns between entries), and landscapes (poetic and philosophical horizons of certain speculations) are frequented by the author in order to engage with them and derive creative and evocative inspiration, to that of a metropolis crowded with casual encounters. Here, places and acquaintances filled with Leopardi's own personal and intellectual history give way to the pathos-free *flânerie* of the modern wanderer.

Notes to Chapter 18

1. Richard S. Peters, 'What is an Educational Process?', in *The Concept of Education*, ed. by Richard S. Peters (London: Routledge, 1967), pp. 1–23.
2. On the dual character of the Christian model absorbed by Leopardi and corresponding to the views of 'i suoi primi veri maestri, in fatto di religione, ovvero il padre Monaldo e la madre Adelaide Antici' [his first true instructors, for what concerns religion, that is, his father Monaldo and his mother Adelaide Antici], see Colaiacomo, '*Zibaldone di pensieri* di Giacomo Leopardi', pp. 256–58.

3. For a general historical and cultural reconstruction of ancient education see Henri-Irénée Marrou, *A History of Education in Antiquity*, trans. by George Lamb (Madison & London: University of Wisconsin Press, 1956).
4. On the relationship between writing (grammar), error, and religious structures in Leopardi see D'Intino, 'Errore, ortografia e autobiografia in Leopardi e Stendhal'.
5. Cf. D'Intino, *L'immagine della voce*, p. 95.
6. See *Zib*. 29, 50.
7. See *The Jesuit 'Ratio Studiorum' of 1599*.
8. Allan P. Farrell, 'Notes to the Translation', in *The Jesuit 'Ratio Studiorum' of 1599*, p. 129.
9. Ibid.
10. Robert Schwickerath, *Jesuit Education, its History and Principles, Viewed in the Light of Modern Educational Problems* (St. Louis, MO: B. Herder, 1903), p. 460.
11. Leopardi's reflection on Christianity and original sin occupies more than sixty pages (*Zib*. 393–455). I discuss the Leopardian motif of sin and guilt in my '"Di temenza è sciolto"'. For an in-depth analysis of Leopardi's relationship with religion see Girolami, *L'antiteodicea*, and Alfredo Bonadeo, 'Leopardi e la religione della vita', *Italica*, 87.4 (2010), 554–81.
12. The term 'heat death' is derived from thermodynamics, designating conditions of exhaustion of the free energy necessary for processes of work production. I employ this image metaphorically, referring to cognition as exhaustion of 'determination' (and therefore of action and process). For a more detailed reflection on Leopardi's proto-entropic thought see my '"Time-image" in Poetry and Cinema', pp. 194–203.
13. On the significance of walking in ancient cultures see Silvia Montiglio, *Wandering in Ancient Greek Culture* (Chicago, IL: University of Chicago Press, 2005), and Timothy M. O'Sullivan, *Walking in Roman Culture* (Cambridge: Cambridge University Press, 2011).
14. Plato, *Phaedrus*, in *The Dialogues of Plato*, III, 107–89 (p. 134).
15. D'Intino, 'Oralità e dialogicità nello *Zibaldone*', pp. 235–36. D'Intino also believes that the quoted passage from 'Phaedrus' is essential for the understanding of Leopardi's 'Elogio degli uccelli' (*L'immagine della voce*, p. 28).
16. Stefano Jossa explores the general links between language and food imagery in 'Il cibo della mente: appunti per una metafora', in *La sapida eloquenza: retorica del cibo e cibo retorico*, ed. by Cristiano Spila (Rome: Bulzoni, 2004), pp. 35–41.
17. The relevant passage begins on *Zib*. 4183: 'Gli antichi [...] avevano ragione, perchè essi non conversavano insieme a tavola, se non dopo mangiato, e nel tempo del simposio propriamente detto, cioè della comessazione' ('The ancients [...] were right, because they did not converse with one another at table, until they had eaten, when the symposium in the true sense of the word began, that is the merrymaking').
18. Cf. Cacciapuoti, *Dentro lo 'Zibaldone'*.

CHAPTER 19

Metropolitan Encounters: Quotations and the *Zibaldone* 'Index'

In modern times the only way for an author to benefit from a productive relationship with his or her own sources is through study and application; yet reading a lot, says Leopardi, is not enough to produce original writing and in order to detach oneself from excessive imitation, and in order to develop the ability to think, one needs to put into practice what one studies, thus acquiring a certain stylistic feature.[1] Study, Leopardi believes, moulds the mind so that it becomes not only receptive to the sources of literature to which it applies itself but also capable of using certain features of style and content as a starting-point for an original creation. New ideas, Leopardi believes, are not those which appear brand new for the first time but rather those which are newly composed from pre-existing ideas.[2] As we see from *Zib.* 64, Leopardi's own experience as a reader serves this creative function. The productive and conservative pattern described by Leopardi with regards to the composition of ideas is similar to the one previously discussed in relation to both Adam's original beliefs (he had everything he needed from the outset) and the evolution of languages through new forms assumed by an existing linguistic matrix, which sustains positive influences and contaminations. Indeed, Leopardi writes that:

> La lettura de' libri non ha veramente prodotto un [*sic*] me nè affetti o sentimenti che non avessi, nè anche verun effetto di questi, che senza esse letture non avesse dovuto nascer da se: ma pure gli ha accelerati, e fatti sviluppare più presto, in somma sapendo io dove quel tale affetto moto sentimento ch'io provava, doveva andare a finire, quantunque lasciassi intieramente fare alla natura, nondimeno trovando la strada come aperta, correvo per quella più speditamente.
>
> [Reading books has not produced in [him] any affects or feelings that [he] did not previously have, or any outcome from these that would not have arisen by itself without reading. But [reading] has accelerated such feelings and made them develop more quickly. In short, knowing where such an affect, impulse, feeling would take me, though allowing nature to run its course freely, nevertheless [he] found the path open before [him] and moved along it more swiftly.] (*Zib.* 64)

Further on he recognizes that the feature that distinguishes his own intellect from other intellects is his:

> Facilità di assuefarlo a quello ch'io volessi, e quando io volessi, e di fargli contrarre abitudine forte e radicata, in poco tempo. Leggendo una poesia, divenir facilmente poeta; un logico, logico; un pensatore, acquistar subito l'abito di pensare nella giornata; uno stile, saperlo subito o ben presto imitare.
>
> [Ability to accustom it with ease to whatever I wished, and when I wished, and for it to contract a sturdy, well-rooted habit in not much time. So that if I read a poem, I easily become a poet; if I read a logician, a logician. If I am reading a thinker I acquire the habit of thinking straight away in the space of a day; if I am reading a particular style, I can imitate it immediately or very quickly.]
> (*Zib.* 1254–55)

These reflections are important not only because they provide a clear spectrum of Leopardi's interest in the phenomenology of reading, and of his method of study, but also because they offer a further insight into Leopardi's performative writing. They stress an effect of reading which is capable of modifying Leopardi's own personality, projecting it into different kinds of 'lives'.[3] The effect of reading is therefore not only directed from the source text to the style of the notebook but also to Leopardi's own material life. In *Zib.* 2821, Leopardi stresses the derivation of the verb *citare* [to quote] from the Latin verb *cieo*, which also means 'to move', 'to produce', 'to raise', and is the root of verbs such as *excitare, incitare, concitare*, all denoting pathos and presupposing a kind of effect or reaction on behalf of the interlocutor. The act of quoting in the *Zibaldone* is never just a function of memory intended as a sole means to preserve ideas and passages that would otherwise be lost, but can be seen above all as an action which produces something in the text and in the physical senses of the writer. The following few examples show that often the quoted texts in the *Zibaldone* are made to incarnate the etymological sense of *citare* as 'calling someone (or something) for an appeal', and actively influence Leopardi's own writing. His text effectively 'responds to the call' by letting itself be influenced by the quotation and assuming specific thematic and stylistic aspects of it.

Leopardi quotes a text from Madame Lambert and adds comments revealing that he is not satisfied with the way the author applies her own ideas:

> *On aime à savoir les foiblesses des personnes estimables*, non già solamente di quelle che si odiano o invidiano, ma di quelle che si amano [...] e ci giovano coi loro benefizi, consigli ec. e in questo senso lo dice Mad. Lambert, *La Femme Hermite. Nouvelle Nouvelle.* dans ses œuvres complètes citées ci-dessus (p. 633.), p. 229. Tu puoi però applicarti questo pensiero, e renderlo proprio, giacchè Mad. lo stende, lo spiega, e l'applica in maniera ordinaria, così che il pensiero sembra comune, e non fa gran colpo e non se ne osserva l'originalità. Essa lo applica principalmente alla confidenza che ne deriva verso quelle tali persone: *et j'étois trop heureuse de trouver en elle, non-seulement des conseils, mais de ces foiblesses aimables qui nous rendent plus indulgens pour celles d'autrui.* Ma si può considerare questa verità molto più in grande, dilatarla, osservarne i rapporti, applicarla anche al teatro, alla poesia, a' romanzi ec. ed alle arti imitatrici, e confermarne quella regola di Aristotele, che il protagonista non sia perfetto. (15. Feb. 1821).
>
> ['On aime à savoir les foiblesses des personnes estimables' ["We like learning about the frailties of estimable persons"], and not indeed only of those whom we hate or envy but of those whom we love, [...] and who benefit us with

their kindness and advice, etc., and this is how Mme. Lambert puts it, in *La femme hermite. Nouvelle nouvelle* in her *Œuvres complètes* quoted above (p. 633), p. 229. You can, however, apply this thought to yourself and make it your own, since Madame extends, develops, and applies it in a routine fashion, so that the thought seems commonplace, has no great impact, and its originality cannot be seen. She applies it chiefly to the trust that it produces in relation to those particular people: 'et j'étois trop heureuse de trouver en elle, non-seulement des conseils, mais de ces foiblesses aimables qui nous rendent plus indulgens pour celles d'autrui' ["and I was only too glad to find in her, not only advice, but some of those endearing frailties which make it easier for us to forgive those of others"]. But one may consider this truth on a much larger scale, expand it, note how it relates to others, and even apply it to the theater, poetry, novels, etc., and the mimetic arts, and so confirm Aristotle's rule, namely, that the hero should not be perfect. (15. Feb. 1821.).] (*Zib.* 661–62)

The next day Leopardi returns to this source by adding further quoted lines and reflections which would help him to reconnect with the full sense of the quotation, if he wished to return to it a second time. Hence from pp. 661–63 Leopardi directs his thought exclusively to the quoted text to which he is applying his own comments and expanding the hints offered always in strict relation to the quoted passage. On p. 663 he suddenly switches topic producing a creative piece on the image of life as a comedy which emerges as a leap out of his previously focused concentration as a form of distraction from study: 'Messer tale sentendo dire che la vita è una commedia, disse che oggidì è piuttosto una prova di commedia, ovvero una di quelle rappresentazioni, che talvolta i collegiali, o simili fanno per loro soli' ('A certain gentleman, hearing it said that life is a comedy, remarked that today it is more like a rehearsal of a comedy, or one of those performances that schoolboys or the like sometimes put on for their own amusement'). This image and its philosophical implications occupy Leopardi's attention until p. 666 (6 February 1821), where he adds the date to the page presumably before closing his diary. His focus has leapt from the world of the quoted text to that of his own imagination; and this, although not directly linked to the content of the quoted text, nevertheless is a spontaneous *reaction* to it. His own image has been 'excited' by the quotation in precisely the same way that Leopardi describes in his own notebook. Then, at a later moment in the day, Leopardi returns to study and continues to quote the French text, in a dialogue between the source and his own reflections, which extends until p. 674.

In other cases the influence of a quotation on Leopardi's prose produces a more direct effect on his writing, as for instance:

La grazia non può venire altro che dalla natura, e la natura non ista mai secondo il compasso [...] della geometria [...]. Quindi la scarsezza di grazia nella lingua francese tutta analitica [...] e diremo angolare, [...] se bene se ne compensano col nominar la grazia 20. volte per pagina, e non c'è un libro francese dove non troviate a ogni occhiata grace, grace massime parlando dei libri della loro nazione, encomiandoli ec. Grace grace, mi viene allora in bocca, et non erat grace (pax pax et non erat pax, ma non so se così veram. dica S. Paolo,) o qual altro Scrittor sacro).

> [Grace cannot come except from nature, and nature never works according to the compass of [...] geometry [...]. Hence the scarcity of grace in the French language, all analytical [...] and shall we say angular [...] even if they do compensate for it by referring to grace 20 times a page, and there is not a single French book where you do not find it, wherever you look, 'grace, grace' especially when speaking of their nation's books, praising them, etc. 'Grace, grace' makes me then want to say, 'et non erat grace' ('pax pax et non erat pax,' but I don't really know whether St. Paul says this, or some other sacred writer).]
> (*Zib.* 46–47)

In fact the quotation 'pax pax et non erat pax' does not come from Paul but from Jeremiah (6:14), and Leopardi is here referring to it from memory, without having the text in front of him.[4] I believe that there are two specific, intertwined reasons why he confuses Jeremiah with Paul, the first related to a certain semantic suggestion of the concept of grace, which is a typically messianic term and which by simple association could have been attributed to Paul, who incarnates the messianic Revelation. But there is also a more pragmatic reason for this confusion, and this is the fact that the quotation probably derives from a book which Leopardi had in his library in Recanati, namely the *Esercizio di perfezione* [Exercise in Perfection] by the Jesuit Alfonso Rodriguez, who mentions the quoted passage on *pax* by Jeremiah immediately before another reference to Paul, and therefore Leopardi's confusion might have resulted from a kind of inaccurate 'memory of the page' of that book. What is worth insisting upon, though, is that even in this most mechanical confusion of sources, which Leopardi himself suspects might have taken place, there is an active interplay between Leopardi's own writing and the reference: Leopardi's own mocking of the French use of *grâce* leads him to remember the passage on *pax*, which he found written next to another reference to Paul; and because it is now used in the *Zibaldone* in a discourse on grace, and grace is a Pauline concept, this leads him to suppose initially that the quotation might in fact be from Paul.

Another interesting passage providing us with evidence of how Leopardi transforms his quotations into action is on p. 222. First Leopardi notes how 'la lettura per l'arte dello scrivere è come l'esperienza per l'arte di viver nel mondo, e di conoscer gli uomini e le cose' ('Reading is to the art of writing as experience is to the art of living in the world and knowing about other people and other things'), in which study appears as an image of life and a vital process of growth and acquisition of experience. Following this entry Leopardi adds direct and indirect quotations from Machiavelli, Montesquieu, and Giordani who are introduced almost as offstage characters in a play, as immediately afterwards Leopardi, stimulated by their views, transforms his writing into passages of imaginary dialogue:

> Dice Macchiavelli che a voler conservare un regno una repubblica o una setta, è necessario ritirarli spesso verso i loro principii. Così tutti i politici. V. Montesquieu, Grandeur etc. Ch. 8. dalla metà in poi, dove parla dei Censori. Giordani *sulle poesie del M. di Montrone* applica questo detto alle *arti imitatrici*. Ai principii s'intende, non quando erano bambine, ma a quel primo tempo in cui ebbero consistenza. (Così anche si potrebbe applicare alle lingue.). Ed io dico nello stesso senso; a voler conservare gli uomini, cioè farli felici, bisogna richiamarli ai loro principii, vale a dire alla natura. — Oh pazzia. Tu non sai

che la perfettibilità dell'uomo è dimostrata. — Io vedo che di tutte le altre opere della natura è dimostrato tutto l'opposto, cioè che non si possono perfezionare, ma alterandole, si può solamente corromperle, e questo principalmente per nostra mano. Ma l'uomo si considera quasi come fuori della natura, e non sottomesso alle leggi naturali che governano tutti gli esseri, e appena si riguarda come opera della natura. — Frattanto l'uomo è più perfetto di prima. — Tanto perfetto che, tolta la religione, gli è più spediente il morire di propria mano che il vivere. Se la perfezione degli esseri viventi si misura dall'infelicità, va bene. Ma che altro indica il grado della loro perfez. se non la felicità? E qual altro è il fine, anzi la perfezione dell'esistenza? Il fatto sta che oggidì pare assurdo il richiamare gli uomini alla natura, e lo scopo vero e costante anche dei più savi e profondi filosofi, è di allontanarneli sempre più, quantunque alle volte credano il contrario, confondendo la natura colla ragione.

[Machiavelli says that if you want to preserve a kingdom, a republic, or a sect, it is often necessary to draw it back to its beginnings. Likewise all political writers. See Montesquieu, *Grandeur*, etc., from the middle of ch. 8 onward, where he talks about the Censors. Giordani on the poems of the Marquis of Montrone applies this saying to the *imitative arts*. By beginnings, I mean not when the arts were in their infancy but the early stage when they began to have some consistency. (The same could be applied to language.) And I mean in the same sense; in order to preserve men, that is, to make them happy, it is necessary to call them back to their beginnings, which means nature. — 'What madness. Don't you know that man's perfectibility is demonstrated?' — 'I see that all the other works of nature demonstrate the opposite, that they cannot be perfected, but, rather, being altered they can only be corrupted, mainly by our own hand. But man thinks of himself as somehow outside nature, and not subject to the natural laws that govern all living things, and hardly regards himself as a work of nature.' — 'Meanwhile man is more perfect than before.' — 'So perfect that, without religion, he finds it preferable to die by his own hand than to go on living.' If the perfection of living beings is measured in terms of unhappiness, so be it. But what indication of their level of perfection is there other than happiness? And what else is the purpose of existence, if not its perfection? The fact is that today it seems absurd to call men back to nature, and the real and constant aim of the wisest and most profound philosophers is to distance us ever more from it, though at times they believe the opposite, confusing nature with reason.] (*Zib.* 222–23)

It is not by chance that at the end of p. 223 Leopardi mentions Lord Byron, criticizing his way of conveying passions by description and by providing historical examples, when instead the reader 'deve sentire e non imparare la verita conformità che ha la tua descriz. ec. colla verità e colla natura' ('should feel and not be told that your description, etc. conforms to reality and nature'). The use of references and quotations as a means to populate the pages of the *Zibaldone* and transform it into a familiar local environment is a constant feature of the diary and a means by which Leopardi is able to counterbalance the immobilizing effect of cognition and of study, which, without this device, would lead him into a kind of intellectual implosion. But this interaction, which takes place between Leopardi's own voice and the voices of other authors, is subject to a change after the completion of the 'Index' in 1827, as quotations continue to be very frequent and are in fact predominant in the notebook, together with linguistic analyses, but they progressively cease to be accompanied by developed comments and expansions. It is as if in the last pages of the *Zibaldone* Leopardi's own voice withdraws to leave room for other authors who are often referred to without further engagement. As already discussed, we could compare the changed use of others' voices in the pre- and post-'Index' *Zibaldone* to the difference that exists between a close community of friends hosting people with whom one might interact in an intimate, relaxed neighbourhood context, and the multiplicity of voices and sounds of a busy metropolitan environment that are heard without the need for active participation. I would like to focus on the moment of transition between the pre- and post-indexing phases in the *Zibaldone* by looking at the entries written at the time of the indexing, 11 July to 14 October 1827. There seems to be an encrypted message in these pages, as if Leopardi were looking back to his own relationship with the diary to acknowledge the completion of a specific stage of writing and at the same time the beginning of a new phase.

The penultimate note written on 14 October 1827 (*Zib.* 4294–95), before the completion of the 'Index', is an internal cross-reference to p. 4238. We find references to Greek authors who had 'degl'Itinerari, delle Descrizioni di città e di provincie, anche con dettagli appartenenti a storia, arti, monumenti, costumi, prodotti, statistica [...]; delle Relazioni di Viaggi p. mare e p. terra' ('Itineraries, Descriptions of cities and provinces, together with details relating to history, art, monuments, customs, products, statistics [...] they had Reports of Travels by sea and land') (*Zib.* 4294). The text on p. 4295 reads 'fin qui si stende l'Indice di questo *Zibaldone*' ('here ends the Index of this Zibaldone of Thoughts'), which suggests a sense of territorial extension as well as of limits and divisions. Here, Leopardi also uses a graphic device to mark the completion of the 'Index', which is similar to the graphic layout used on both the first page and the last page of the 'Index', consisting of two rules framing the relevant inscription.[5] As in the 'Index' itself, the graphic framing on p. 4295, together with the content it expresses, suggests a kind of signpost or waymarker that one might find placed at the boundaries of a territory. These lexical choices, as well as the graphic form of the label (which is uniquely associated with the 'Index' in the *Zibaldone*) in conjunction with the reference to Greek travel literature, operate as a kind of 'territorialization' of the notebook. In the pages written during the preparation of the 'Index' and preceding the page analyzed here, frequent references to voice and pronunciation as well as use of direct quotations without comment by Leopardi seem to reveal Leopardi's urge to counterbalance with the lightness of oral expression the rigid operation of reading and rereading that he was undertaking during the preparation of the 'Index'. It seems as if now that he is re-reading his manuscript he also accepts a kind of dissipation of the mental energy that has been required for the obsessive analysis of his own and other authors' thought. On 14 October 1827, immediately after the reference to itineraries that we have just analyzed, Leopardi wrote the last note before the signpost, testifying to a change of attitude in his treatment of quotations. The last lines before the territorial boundary registering the completion of the 'Index' read:

> Persone la cui compagnia e conversazione ci piaccia durevolmente, e si usi volentieri con frequenza e lunghezza, non sono in sostanza, e non possono essere altre che quelle dalle quali giudichiamo che vaglia la pena di sforzarci e adoperarci d'essere stimate, e stimate ogni giorno più.
>
> [Those whose enduring company and conversation we enjoy, and whom we are willing to visit frequently and for long periods, are and can only be those in relation to whom we consider it worth striving and labouring in order to be respected, and to be respected more each day.] (*Zib.* 4294–95)

Leopardi is here implicitly talking about his *Zibaldone*, as the reference to a daily habit ('ogni giorno') suggests. He is thinking of his friends in the *Zibaldone*, of people with whom he keeps company, namely the authors he approaches and interacts with, and he offers a kind of declaration of a new conduct that he is going to adopt in his own *Zibaldone*. He somehow abandons the attitude of the scholarly student obsessed with demonstration and application — he does so because this approach has been excessive during the indexing process — and he makes clear that not all authors deserve compulsive attention. At the same time, he also tells us that it is now time to choose our own company and friends because there are too many of them who would potentially offer themselves for conversation and only a few of them worthy of being selected from the crowd, which is also an important change of perspective, from the familiarity of 'the village', as it were, to the challenges and chance-encounters of the metropolis.

This idea is supported by another hidden presence in this final section of the *Zibaldone*, which acts as a virtual interlocutor for Leopardi, that is, Ariosto's *Orlando Furioso*. Leopardi refers to Ariosto's work in words similar to those employed to praise the lack of a rigid plan in Homer's writing:

> Il Furioso è una successione di argom. diversi, e quasi di div. poesie; non è fatto sopra un piano concepito e coordinato in principio; il poeta si sentiva libero di terminare quando voleva; continuava di spontanea volontà, e con una elez., impulso, ὁρμὴ primitiva ad ogni canto; e certo in princip. non ebbe punto d'intenz. a quella lunghezza.
>
> [The Furioso is a succession of different topics, almost of different poems; it is not created on a plan which is conceived and arranged from the beginning; the poet felt free to stop when he wished; he continued each canto of his own free will, from choice, impulse, primitive ὁρμὴ [impetus]; and at the beginning he certainly did not intend it to be so long.] (*Zib.* 4356)

It is likely that Leopardi felt that Ariosto's verse shared the spontaneous and performative character of Homer's and believed that Ariosto continued a literary tradition founded on unprogrammatic writing, which also extended to his own *Zibaldone*.[6] Looking closely at the words employed by Leopardi to signpost the completion of the 'Index', one notes that the line 'Fin qui si stende l'Indice di questo Zibaldone di Pensieri' recalls a specific passage of *Orlando Furioso*:

> Signor, qui presso una città difende
> il Po fra minacciose e fiere corna;
> la cui iuridizion di *qui si stende*

> *fin* dove il mar fugge dal lito e torna.
> Cede d'antiquità, ma ben contende
> con le vicine in esser ricca e adorna.
> Le reliquie troiane la fondaro,
> che dal flagello d'Attila camparo.
> (XLIII, 32; my emphasis)

[There is a city close by, sir, protected between the horns of the Po, full of menace. Its jurisdiction reaches from here to where the sea washes back and forth across the shore. This city, Ferrara, yields to its neighbours in antiquity, but not in wealth or beauty. It was founded by the survivors of Troy who escaped Attila's scourge.][7]

These verses are part of the story recounted by the paladin whom Rinaldo meets in Canto XLII. He tells Rinaldo how he accepted the test posed by the sorceress Melissa, who was determined to prove that the paladin's wife (like all other wives) was unfaithful. The sorceress invited him to drink from a magic goblet. If the paladin was able to drink, this signified that the woman was faithful; if instead the liquid refused to pass his lips and spilled all over his body, this would mean his wife was unfaithful. When the paladin first tried he was able to drink, but Melissa assured him that this would not happen again were he to leave his wife alone for some time. He recounts how he was convinced to seduce his wife under the guise of a gentleman of Ferrara; how his wife (who could not resist his courtship and was unfaithful in the end) finally discovered the trick and left her husband for the real Ferrarese nobleman; and how the paladin regretted having decided to undertake the test in the first instance. The lines that I have quoted above refer to the city of Ferrara (and his lord, the gentleman in question), which is mentioned again later on in the canto with respect to Rinaldo's own journey in search for Orlando, which will lead him to Ravenna, Rome, and finally to Trapani and Lampedusa. Looking at the city from a distance, from the boat in which he is sailing, Rinaldo associates that sight with the prophecy of his cousin Malagigi, who had foreseen that that small swampy town would flourish to become one of the wealthiest and most cultured cities:

> Così venia Rinaldo [...]
> [...]
> [...] l' umil città mirando:
>
> — Come esser può ch' anchor (seco dicea)
> debban così fiorir questa paludi
> de tutti i liberali e degni studi?
> e crescer abbia di sì piccol borgo
> ampla cittade e di sì gran bellezza? (XLIII, 60–61)

[Thus Rinaldo, [...] [a]s he gazed upon the humble town he observed: 'How can it be that these marshes shall one day blossom with every humane study? | How shall a city so extensive and so beautiful grow out of so modest a village?'][8]

These verses describe the transformation of a small village into a city, and the flourishing of study from originally formless matter. I aim to show how they can be applied to interpret the *Zibaldone* with regards to its pre and post-'Index' status and how they resonate in this area of the diary precisely because of their metaphorical meaning. In order to do so, it is essential to allow the full potential of the source text to be evoked as its significance subtly permeates the *Zibaldone*. The last entry before the signpost signalling the completion of the 'Index' contains further echoes of Ariosto. As we have seen, just after completing his revision and rereading his diary and just before sealing this achievement with the reference to the completed 'Index', Leopardi salutes the friends and companions (books, authors, and characters) who have frequently and for a long time inhabited his diary. At the end of Canto XLII, Rinaldo has been invited by the paladin to follow him to his castle to drink from the magic goblet in order to discover whether his wife is unfaithful. Canto XLIII opens with the reference to Rinaldo's indecisiveness, as he is tempted to try the goblet but cannot resolve to do so. Then we learn that he prefers not to take the test. He already knows that women are constitutionally unfaithful, but proving that his own wife confirms the rule would bring him only sorrow:

> [...] folle
> chi quel che non vorria trovar, cercasse.
> Mia donna è donna, et ogni donna è molle:
> lascián star mia credenza come stasse.
> Sin qui m'ha il creder mio giovato, e giova:
> che poss'io megliorar per farne prova?
>
> Potria poco giovare e nuocer molto;
> che 'l tentar qualche volta Idio disdegna.
> Non so s'in questo io mi sia saggio o stolto;
> ma non vo' piu saper, che mi convegna. (XLIII, 6–7)

[He would be an utter fool who sought for what he had no wish to find. My wife is a woman, and every woman is pliant. Let my faith remain undisturbed: it has stood me in good stead hitherto — what am I to gain by putting it to the test? | Little good and much harm could result, for sometimes God objects to being tested. Whether in this I am being wise or foolish I know not, but I desire no further knowledge than is suitable.]⁹

So far, Rinaldo's positive beliefs have benefitted him and he is satisfied with a general awareness of the conduct of women, which does not cause him particular trouble as the rule is still untested in his own personal case. Converting his beliefs into truth, a truth which confirms the validity of his personal circumstances over the norm, would be to stray into a dangerous grey area in which wisdom might turn to confusion ('Non so s'in questo io mi sia saggio o stolto'). It is no surprise, given the religious imagery with which these stanzas are laden, that Adam, the atavistic model of breaking limits and suffering the consequences, appears as an object of comparison:

> Or questo vin dinanzi mi sia tolto:
> sete non n'ho, né vo' che me ne vegna;
> che tal certezza ha Dio piu proibita,
> ch'al primo padre l'arbor de la vita.

> Che come Adam, poi che gustò del pomo
> che Dio con propria bocca gl'interdisse,
> da la letizia al pianto fece un tomo,
> onde in miseria poi sempre s'afflisse;
> cosi, se de la moglie sua vuol l'uomo
> tutto saper quanto ella fece e disse,
> cade de l'allegrezze in pianti e in guai,
> onde non puo piu rilevarsi mai. (XLIII, 7–8)

Have this wine removed: I do not, and prefer not to, thirst for it. God has proscribed this kind of certainty even more than he proscribed the Tree of Life to our first father. | For just as Adam, after tasting the apple which God had with His own lips forbidden him, fell from happiness to tears, and lived in affliction for ever after; so if a man wants to know everything his wife has said and done, he falls from bliss to tears and despondency, and out of this he can never drag himself.[10]

The paladin is moved by Rinaldo's reasoning and regrets not having met him before — ten years earlier — because on his advice he would not have drunk from the goblet and his conversation would have spared him so much suffering:

> Perche non ti conobbi gia dieci anni,
> sì che io mi fossi consigliato teco,
> prima che cominciassero gli affanni. (XLIII, 10)

[Why did I not know you ten years sooner, so as to have sought your advice before the onset of my misery.][11]

Returning to Leopardi's entry, one might hypothesize that Leopardi is making an analysis of his long-term companionship with his diary now that, like for the paladin in *Orlando Furioso*, exactly ten years have passed since the beginning of the notebook. The fact that Cantos XLII and XLIII might have been in Leopardi's mind at this specific moment in his relationship with his diary is also suggested by his reference to women, which stands out from the familiar and retrospective tone of the entry: 'Perciò la compagnia e conversazione delle donne non può esser durevolmente piacevole, se esse non sono o non si rendono tali da rendere durevolmente pregiabile e desiderabile la loro stima' ('Therefore the company and conversation of women cannot be of lasting pleasure unless they are or render themselves such as to make their respect lastingly valuable and desirable') (*Zib.* 4295). Cantos XLII and XLIII of *Orlando Furioso* are permeated by reflection on the character of women and, despite and in addition to the stereotype of their unfaithfulness, Canto XLII ends with a list of exemplary female figures engraved on the columns of the fountain of the palace, who distinguished themselves by their virtue and genius, from Lucrezia Borgia to Isabella D'Este, among others. The influence of Ariosto is subtle but clearly discernible. These echoes from the source suggest that Leopardi perceives of his text as an inhabited land which has grown in time, flourished in study, and been populated by heartening presences. As we have already seen, Leopardi consistently refers to writing or to the influence of other sources through the image of walking. Moreover, in a letter to his brother Carlo dated 12 March 1823, Giacomo tells him that his German friend Niebuhr commented on his philological achievements by making reference to the fact that he is 'nella vera strada' [on the true path] and that instead 'tutti gli italiani sono fuor di strada' [all Italians are off track] (*E*, I, 668). Leopardi's model of clarity is that of a philosopher who has been able to master his subject to the point that his intellect 'vi passeggia per entro con franchezza' ('roams through it at will') (*Zib.* 1374), and clarity itself is compared to civil law, or the law of the city (cf. *Zib.* 119). Leopardi praises Isocrates's writing because 'par di sentirvi quel gusto che si prova quando in buona disposizione di corpo, e volontà di far moto, si cammina speditamente p. una strada, non pur piana, ma lastricata' ('we seem to experience the same pleasure we sense when our bodies feel right, and we want to move, and we walk briskly along a road that is not only level but paved') (*Zib.* 4251); and Montaigne, who was a point of reference for Leopardi, also refers to the relationship between master and student as one of walking at the right pace, as well as employing a metaphor that might also describe Leopardi's relationship with his notebook:

> I would have a tutor [...] taking up a subject [...] according to the child's capacity [...]; sometimes opening for him the way, at other times leaving him to open it for himself. I would not have the tutor do all the talking, but allow the pupil to speak when his turn comes. Socrates, and after him Arcesilaus, made their pupils speak first, and then would speak themselves. [...] The tutor should make his pupil, like a young horse, trot before him in order that he may the better judge of his pace, determine how long he will hold out, and accordingly, what may fit his strength. [...] I can more easily walk up than down a hill.[12]

Among Leopardi's *Disegni letterari* there is a 'Storia di una passeggiata' [Story of a Walk], with the title clearly remarking on the value of wandering as a practice. Wandering here forms not just the background to a certain experience, but the actual subject matter. The landscape or cityscape is here intended, in Certeau's terms, as a 'place of transformations and appropriations, the object of various kinds of interference but also a subject that is constantly enriched by new attributes'.[13] This also applies to Leopardi's daily relationship with his text, with each entry behaving like a footstep:

> They are myriad, but do not compose a series. They cannot be counted because each unit has a qualitative character: a style of tactile apprehension and kinaesthetic appropriation. Their intertwined paths give their shape to spaces. They weave places together.[14]

The image of walking not only stresses the bodily action of the mind, but links Leopardi's interest in the psychology and physiology of the mind with a reference to the ancient world, where philosophy was a form of conversation held while walking. This also shapes the form of the *Zibaldone* as a territory (landscape and cityscape) to be explored and lived through writing in the most physical possible way. As Foucault explains, walking has traditionally been associated with a form of self-analysis and self-control. For Epictetus, walking every morning should afford the opportunity to assess whether an encounter has the power to impress or whether the subject can remain indifferent.[15] For Rousseau, who was influenced by Epictetus and who devoted his last unfinished work *Rêveries d'un promeneur solitaire*

[Meditations of a Solitary Walker] to walking and meditation, walking assumes a therapeutic function, as a way to master his obsession with conspiracies. His walks are solitary and secluded, hidden from the sight of his persecutors. His wandering is an exercise in wisdom and in the practice of an 'ethic of mastery'.[16] For Leopardi, wandering through the pages of the *Zibaldone* as a scholar is also a therapeutic means to practice intellectual clarity; yet the search for the self cannot take place in isolation but is elicited by constant comparison with others. In the Christian tradition, a similar exercise serves to test one's dependence on God, and the ability to appreciate his providential intervention in everything one sees, and we have seen how the idea of a subconscious confessional practice also applies to Leopardi. However, in the early-modern tradition, since Boccaccio, walking in the city is also associated with an idea of perdition and disorder as opposed to the safer and more secluded setting of the countryside.[17] Leopardi is constantly on the verge of 'falling' as he is frequently tempted by the 'piacer dell'inaspettato' ('pleasure of the unexpected') (*Zib.* 4508), and through his subtle dialogue with Rinaldo on p. 4295, he communicates a certain disquietude about an ongoing transition. It is essential to point out that Rinaldo has been interpreted as 'un eroe della transizione' [a hero of transition], one who represents the 'superamento del passato, identificato con la tradizione bretone, a favore di un ingresso nella modernità' [overcoming of the past, which is identified with the Breton tradition, in favour of his entry into modernity], with his 'funzione di passaggio' [function of transition] being manifest specifically between Cantos XLII and LII, narrating his journey along the River Po.[18] The post-'Index' phase opens up a new, wider cityscape dimension in which Leopardi is a *flâneur* among his readings and quotations.

One of the characteristics of this area of the diary is that Leopardi continues to intervene and comment on his sources, but mostly by privileging specific recurrent themes to which he devotes more attention and more lengthy reflections, such as the previously mentioned Homeric question and the issue of oral memory. Otherwise, quotations are often left to speak for themselves or with only brief comments. The first entry after the reference to the completion of the 'Index' is telling of this more detached attitude. Immediately after the horizontal rules containing the reference to the completed 'Index', which I have likened to a city 'boundary', a quotation from Benjamin Franklin appears with no preliminary introduction and no direct reference in the following comment:

> Peut-être que, si l'on examinait avec impartialité les mœurs de toutes les nations de la terre, on trouverait qu'il n'y a point de peuple si grossier qui n'ait quelques règles de politesse, et point de peuple si poli qui ne conserve quelque reste de barbarie. Franklin. Traduit de l'anglais. (Mélanges de Morale, d'Économie et de Politique, extraits des ouvrages de Benjamin Franklin. 2.e édition. Paris, chez Jules Renouard. 1826. tom. 2. p. 1–2. Observations sur les Sauvages de l'Amérique du Nord. 1784.). (Firenze. 1827. 25. Ottobre.).
>
> Bisogna guardarsi dal giudicare dell'ingegno, dello spirito, e soprattutto delle cognizioni di un forestiere, da' discorsi che si udranno da lui ne' primi abboccamenti. Ogni uomo, per comune e mediocre che sia il suo spirito e il suo intendimento, ha qualche cosa di proprio suo, e per conseguenza di

originale, ne' suoi pensieri, nelle sue maniere, nel modo di discorrere e di trattare. Massime poi uno straniere, voglio dire uno d'altra nazione; [...] Così è avvenuto a me più volte: trovandomi con persone nuove, specialm. con letterati, sono rimasto spaventato del gran numero degli aneddoti, delle novelle, delle cognizioni d'ogni sorta, delle osservazioni, dei tratti, ch'esse mettevano fuori [...]. Un viaggiatore, per poco capitale ch'egli abbia di spirito e di sapere, dev'essere ben povero d'arte *conversativa*, se dovunque egli passa, non si fa *passare* per un grand'uomo.

['Peut-être que, si l'on examinait avec impartialité les mœurs de toutes les nations de la terre, on trouverait qu'il n'y a point de peuple si grossier qui n'ait quelques règles de politesse, et point de peuple si poli qui ne conserve quelque reste de barbarie' ["Perhaps, if we could examine the manners of different nations from ours, which we think the perfection of civility, we should find no People so rude, as to be without any Rules of Politeness; nor any so polite, as not to have some remains of Rudeness"]. Franklin. Translated from English. (Mélanges de Morale, d'Économie et de Politique, from Benjamin Franklin's works, 2nd edition, Paris, Jules Renouard, 1826, tome 2, pp. 1–2: 'Remarks concerning the Savages of North America,' 1784.) (Florence, 1827, 25 October.)

We should be cautious about judging the intelligence, wit, and above all the knowledge of someone whom we do not know, from his conversation upon first contact. Any man, however ordinary and mediocre his wit and understanding might be, has something personal, and therefore original, in his thoughts, in his manner, in his way of speaking and behaving. This is especially true of a foreigner, by which I mean a person from another nation [...]. This has happened to me several times. Finding myself with new people, especially men of letters, I have been intimidated by the great number of anecdotes, stories, knowledge of every kind, observations, witticisms that they laid out. [...] A traveler with even only a small amount of wit and knowledge must be truly poor in the art of *conversation* if, wherever he passes, he does not *pass* for being a great man.] (*Zib.* 4295–97)

Franklin's 'voice' appears suddenly, with no paraphrasing or translation, as if it were a voice heard by a passenger who has just reached a new populated territory after crossing the border. Leopardi, now in Florence, leaves it undiscussed and dates the entry 25 October 1827. The following entry, on the theme of foreignness, is dated 13 November 1827, and this time is from Pisa. Leopardi must have reopened his notebook and read the last notes: the French of the previous quotation and its reference to the customs of different people opens the path to the new content, but the way Leopardi 'uses' Franklin's words is precisely in the form of some 'primi abboccamenti' ('conversation upon first contact') with a foreign person, which he discusses in this entry. Leopardi does not engage specifically in a reflection on Franklin's ideas, but treats Franklin as a casual encounter who provides hints for reflection which Leopardi prefers to project onto his personal experience, rather than addressing his source directly. A similar treatment of the source takes place for instance on pp. 4302–04, where Leopardi quotes from D'Alembert's *Éloge de M. Jean Bernoulli*. Instead of engaging directly with the content of the source (a comparison between poetry and geometry), Leopardi uses his ideas as a cue to discuss a comparison between geometry and metaphysics. Once again, there is a sense of adjacency between the topics quoted and discussed, and this proximity could be represented as one's actual 'physical' vicinity to a speaker who is heard, and whose words open the way to more personal considerations, which Leopardi prefers to share with his selected friends (his implicit readers or himself) rather than gazing back at the source. The text demonstrates a growing attention to worldliness (visible in Leopardi's frequent notes on city life, urbanity, and conversations in the post-'Index' area), as it transforms itself into a modern city. And indeed, another characteristic of this part of the notebook (which Leopardi wrote mostly in Pisa and Florence, where he stayed before returning to Recanati in November 1828) is Leopardi's frequent accounts of his experience as a wanderer, such as for instance, 'Nelle mie passeggiate solitarie per la città, suol destarmi piacevolissime sensazioni e bellissime immagini la vista dell'interno delle stanze che io guardo di sotto dalla strada per le loro finestre aperte' ('In my solitary walks around cities, the view into the rooms which I see from the street below, through their open windows, arouses within me very pleasurable sensations and beautiful images') (*Zib.* 4421), or in the recurring references to the 'crosses' depicted on the streets of Florence and Pisa to avoid 'brutture' ('all indecency') and 'profanazioni' ('profanations') (*Zib.* 4298).[19] On p. 4520 he notes that '*Amicizia non può essere che in città grandi*, o pur fra persone lontane' ('*Friendship can only be found in large cities*, or between people living far away from each other'), and reiterates the concept soon after:

> Chi non è mai uscito da luoghi piccoli [...] nel particolare dell'amicizia, la crede uno di quei nomi e non cose, di quelle idee proprie della poesia o della storia, che nella vita reale e giornaliera non s'incontrano mai [...]. E s'inganna. Non dico Piladi e Piritoi, ma amicizia sincera e cordiale si trova effettivam. nel mondo, e non è rara.

> [Someone who has never been out of small towns, [...] as far as friendship is concerned, he believes it to be one of those names that are not things, one of those ideas belonging to poetry and history which are never to be found in real daily life [...]. And he is mistaken. I am not talking about Pylades or Pirithous, but sincere and cordial friendship actually exists in the world, and it is not rare.] (*Zib.* 4523)

Compared to his account of his first experience outside Recanati (in Rome, from November 1822 to April 1823), when, in a letter to his brother Carlo of 18 January 1823, he described Rome as a 'letamaio di letteratura, di opinioni e di costumi (o piuttosto d'usanze, perchè I Romani [...] non hanno costumi)' [dunghill of literature, opinions and customs (or, rather, practices, because Romans [...] do not have customs)] (*E*, I, 603), Leopardi here articulates a new and more hopeful conception of social life rooted in everyday praxis, which also implies a shift in his own attitude towards human interaction. On 1 December 1828 he had remembered the time spent in Rome as a shocking experience, when his interior and exterior abilities to gain stimulus and entertainment from conversation were frozen in unproductive immobility:

Andato a Roma, la necessità di conviver cogli uomini, di versarmi al di fuori, di agire, di vivere esternamente, mi rese stupido, inetto, morto internamente. Divenni affatto privo e incapace di azione e di vita interna, senza perciò divenir più atto all'esterna.

[When I went to Rome, the need to live with other people, to pour forth, to act, to live externally, made me stupid, inept, dead internally. I became completely devoid and incapable of internal action and life, without thereby becoming more adapted to external life.] (*Zib.* 4420)

He was then of the opinion that other people who were more comfortable in interacting externally lacked inner life, but later experience, he states in the following notes, proved him wrong. Cities, Leopardi tells us, are frequented by strangers who might present themselves as figures of erudition and shock us with our own feelings of inadequacy: 'trovandomi con persone nuove, specialm. con letterati, sono rimasto *spaventato* del gran numero degli aneddoti, delle novelle, delle cognizioni d'ogni sorta, delle osservazioni, dei tratti, ch'egli esse mettevano fuori. Paragonandomi a loro, io m'avviliva nel mio animo' (*Zib.* 4296; my emphasis). However, sooner or later it becomes clear that their knowledge is in fact very limited, and we become more able to assess their learning compared to our own. In cities we feel estranged because of their vastness and lack of points of reference and usually we are able to acquire familiarity only when we can associate personal remembrances with the places we visit.[20] Living and operating in a city requires constant refocusing and re-personalization. When Leopardi writes that true friendship is possible in cities, he is addressing, from a pragmatic social point of view, the same practice of circumscribing which he values as the most important gift in the art of writing. On close inspection, the conceptual lens through which Leopardi looks to describe social life in a city is similar to the one through which he depicts the activity of an author:

In questo secolo, stante la filosofia, e stante la liaison che hanno acquistata tutte le cognizioni tra loro, ogni menomo soggetto facilissimam. diviene vastissimo. Tanto più è necessario, volendo pur fare un libro, che uno sappia limitarsi, che attenda diligentem. a circoscrivere il proprio argomento [...]; e *che si faccia un dovere di non trapassare i termini stabilitisi*. [...] Altrimenti seguirà o che ogni libero sopra ogni tenuiss. argom. divenga un'enciclopedia, o più facilm. e più spesso, che un autore, *spaventato e confuso* dalla vastità di ogni soggetto che gli si presenti, dalla moltitud. delle idee che gli occorrano sopra ciascuno, si perda d'animo, e non ardisca più mettersi a niuna impresa. Il che tanto più facilm. accadrà, quanto la persona avrà più cogniz. e più ingegno.

[In this century, because of philosophy, and because of the *liaison* [linkage] which all areas of knowledge have developed between themselves, every tiny subject becomes vast with the greatest of ease. When a writer intends to produce a book, it is all the more necessary that he must know how to limit himself, that he take diligent care to circumscribe the argument, [...] and that *he impose on himself an obligation not to exceed the terms established*. [...] Otherwise it follows either that every book on every tenuous argument becomes an encyclopedia, or more easily and more frequently, that an author, *frightened and confused* by the vastness of every subject that arises, by the multitude of ideas which emerge from each of them, loses heart, and no longer has the courage to undertake any project. This is all the more likely to happen the more knowledgeable and more intelligent the person is, that is, the more capable he is of writing books.] (*Zib.* 4484; my emphasis, apart from *liaison*)

Leopardi here applies to writing the same selective and 'trimming' attitude that a worldly man requires in his social interaction. It is necessary to limit and to exclude from our intentions any totalizing perspective. The risk — which becomes greater in proportion to the level of cognition — is to be overcome, stupefied, and reduced to silence. Any author, the more sensitive he or she is, is exposed to the danger of being transformed into a new Adam, excessively enlightened and thus in a state of deadly stupefaction. The first man is a constant presence in the *Zibaldone*, and continues to haunt Leopardi until the end of the notebook.

Leopardi moves towards an ideal of action which he gradually puts more and more consistently into practice and which will ultimately find its place outside the pages of the *Zibaldone* and in the unwritten life of its author. The exposure to life has become more and more attractive, writing is gradually giving way to lived experience, and the real is advancing to devour his writing. For fifteen years Leopardi has constantly been trying to circumscribe 'life', while at the same time gazing at and leaning towards the 'openness' of infinite possibilities. As with his use of et ceteras, which are 'eaten' by the indeterminate they come into contact with and which by necessity is left unsaid, and similarly to the understanding reached by Socrates before his death, Leopardi's intuition of his notebook's 'lacunosità irriducibile' [unreducible lacunosity] compared to pure life, does not come without sacrifice.[21] Leopardi's ending of his notebook is the last unwritten et cetera which leaves it suspended in the indeterminacy of life.

Shortly before silencing his notebook for ever, and just before the declaration of the three most radical truths of existence, 'non saper nulla, [...] non esser nulla [...] non aver nulla a sperare dopo la morte' ('we know nothing, [...] we are nothing [...] there is nothing to hope for after death') (*Zib.* 4525), Leopardi writes:

> Gli uomini verso la vita sono come i mariti in Italia verso le mogli: bisognosi di crederle fedeli benchè sappiano il contrario. Così chi dee vivere in un paese, ha bisogno di crederlo bello e buono; così gli uomini di credere la vita una bella cosa. Ridicoli agli occhi miei, come un marito becco, e tenero della sua moglie. (Firenze 23 maggio. 1832).

> [Men approach life in the same way as Italian husbands do their wives: they need to believe they are faithful even though they know otherwise. The same way someone who has to live in a place needs to think it is lovely and good; the same way men believe life is a lovely thing. Ridiculous in my view, like a cuckold who's tender with his wife. (Florence, 23 May 1832.)] (*Zib.* 4525)

The literary reference here is again to Rinaldo, who chose precisely not to uncover the truth of his wife's infidelity and preferred to believe or pretend that she might be honest. In doing so, he escaped the sin of Adam. Leopardi, instead, is about to take the last audacious step which the pre-modern Rinaldo decided not to take.

Notes to Chapter 19

1. See *Zib*. 1541–44.
2. See *Zib*. 2950.
3. See also the 'Discorso sopra lo stato presente dei costumi degli italiani' [Discourse on the Present State of the Customs of the Italians], where Leopardi says that it is impossible that one, after reading a book, 'non pensi, almeno per una mezz'ora, *anche suo malgrado*, in maniera [...] conforme allo scrittore del libro, non prenda il suo spirito, non sia mosso dalla sua autorità, e non le dia qualche peso' ('does not think, at least for half an hour and *in spite of himself*, in a manner similar to the writer of the book; that he does not embody his spirit, or that he is not moved by his authority and does not give weight to it') (*TPP*, p. 1016, n. 20; my emphasis).
4. Cf. Michael Caesar and Franco D'Intino, 'Editorial Notes', in *EZ*, p. 2120.
5. The beginning of the 'Index' is signalled in the index manuscript by the following title: 'Indice del mio Zibaldone di Pensieri' ('Index to my Zibaldone di pensieri'). Below, between two parallel rules, is the specification 'cominciato agli undici di Luglio del 1827, in Firenze' ('begun on the eleventh of June 1827 in Florence'). Below the second line Leopardi explains his indexing convention: 'I primi numeri indicano le pagine del Zibaldone: gli altri i capoversi delle pagine' ('The first numbers indicate the pages of the Zibaldone: the others refer to the paragraphs on each page'). Two parallel rules at the end of the 'Index' contain the following: 'Finito questo dì quattordici Ottobre del 1827, in Firenze' ('Finished this fourteenth day of October 1827, in Florence'), and underneath the lower line Leopardi added 'N.B. Questo Indice si stende dalla pagina 1. del Zibaldone di Pensieri, fino alla pagina 4295' ('N.B. This Index goes from page 1 of the *Zibaldone di Pensieri* up to page 4295').
6. See *Zib*. 4322: 'io ammetto assai volentieri che Omero, non avendo nessuna idea di quello che fu poi chiamato poema epico, nè anche avesse alcun piano o intenzione di comporne uno' ('I am quite willing to accept that Homer, having no idea about what was later to be called the epic poem, did not have any plan or intention to compose one either'); and pp. 4324–25: 'non è egli verisimile che [...] dopo aver cominciato dove il caso volle, andasse avanti immaginando e narrando, aggiungendo oggi al racconto di ieri, senza [...] mirar mai ad altro, che a tirare innanzi la narrazione?' ('is it not likely [...] that after having begun where chance would have it, he would have gone ahead imagining and narrating, adding today onto yesterday's story, without [...] ever aiming at anything other than proceeding onward with the narration?').
7. Ludovico Ariosto, *Orlando Furioso, An English Prose Translation*, trans. by Guido Waldman (Oxford: Oxford University Press, 1974), p. 512.
8. Ibid., p. 516.
9. Ibid., p. 510.
10. Ibid.
11. Ibid.
12. Michel de Montaigne, *The Education of Children*, ed. and trans. by L. E. Rector (New York: Appleton, 1899), pp. 28–29.
13. Certeau, *The Practice of Everyday Life*, p. 95.
14. Ibid., p. 97.
15. Cf. Michel Foucault, 'On the Genealogy of Ethics: An Overview of Work in Progress', in *Ethics, Subjectivity and Truth: The Essential Works of Michel Foucault (1954–1984)*, ed. by Paul Rabinow, 3 vols (New York: New Press, 1997), I, 253–80.
16. See Carole Dornier, 'Writing the Inner Citadel: The Therapeutics of the Soul in Rousseau's *Rêveries d'un promeneur solitaire*', in *Subject Matters: Subject and Self in French Literature from Descartes to the Present*, ed. by Paul Gifford and Johnnie Gratton (Amsterdam: Rodopi, 2000), pp. 60–74 (p. 73).
17. See Stefano Jossa, *L'Italia letteraria* (Bologna: Il Mulino, 2006), pp. 82–83.
18. Stefano Jossa, 'Oltre la tradizione romanzesca: Rinaldo e "l'aspra legge di Scozia" (*Orlando Furioso*, IV–VI)', *Chroniques Italiennes*, 19.1 (2011), 1–20 (pp. 2–3).
19. See also *Zib*. 4305, 4307.
20. See *Zib*. 4286

21. Gardini, *Lacuna*, p. 144.

CHAPTER 20

The End of the *Zibaldone*: Conclusions

From the paralyzing enchantment of Socratic dialectics to the myth of the Fall, and from the aesthetic and scientific implications of the image of the spark to the loss of identity in the magnetic and hypnotized subject, recurrent forms of thought trace a history of the human mind which continues to propose the motif of a risky interplay between positive distraction and excessive totalizing exposure. As we have seen, Leopardi responds to this awareness by maintaining a dual attitude throughout his notebook: on the one hand, the adherence to the principle of 'confessional clarity' which allows him to monitor any single development of his reasoning, as well as a cautious use of attenuation to curtail the uncontrolled effects of writing; on the other, the return to a pre-Platonic ideal of performance transforming the text into a lively setting for encounters and dialogical exchange.

I would like to conclude by suggesting that in the last entry of the *Zibaldone*, the tension between the ancient Greek and the Adamic poles is resolved in the creation of an alternative model of life, a model that is distinctively Leopardian and purely modern. The final entry of the *Zibaldone* reads:

> La cosa più inaspettata che accada a chi entra nella vita sociale, e spessiss. a chi v'è invecchiato, è di trovare il mondo quale gli è stato descritto, e quale egli lo conosce già e lo crede in teoria. L'uomo resta attonito di vedere verificata nel caso proprio la regola [4526] generale. (Firenze. 4. Dic. 1832.)

> [The most unexpected thing for someone who is entering social life, and very often for someone who has grown old there, is to find that the world is as it has been described to him, and as he already knows and believes it to be in theory. Man is stupefied to see in his own case that the general rule is shown to be true. (Florence, 4 Dec. 1832.)] (*Zib.* 4525–26)

Man is 'attonito'. This expression encapsulates the sense of being overwhelmed by a visual shock, and recalls the impact of hyper-clarity when a particular case is first discovered to correspond to the general. Unlike Rinaldo, who is introduced at the end of the *Zibaldone* as the last subject of cultural and philosophical comparison, Leopardi decides to drink from the goblet and learn the truth. He accepts all the incendiary effects of cognition, but at the same time finds a way to continue coherently along the path of his performative philosophy, which transforms words into action, and thought into life. Clement of Alexandria had taught Leopardi that a text always finds a reader willing to learn, and writing can point the reader in the right direction, but 'after this they must walk and find out the rest for themselves'.[1] Having applied both a pedestrian and an aerial viewpoint to his *Zibaldone*, having discovered the corrosion brought about by excessive thought, and nevertheless having prolonged the redemptive mission of the notebook through vital dialogical interaction, Leopardi proceeds now to a further level of exposure. He pushes experience beyond the word and fully into life. He acknowledges that his is not a state of exception, which, as we have seen, also signifies the supreme form of grace in allowing for a revocation of the law. Instead, Leopardi recognizes himself as a sort of modern Adam in abandoning local beliefs to embrace a universal rule. The only difference — and this is not a minor one — is that this experience and passage belong now to the dimension of praxis, the practice of dealing with society, and no longer to the realm of abstract metaphysics illuminating ontological principles. As the Adamic model resurfaces at the very last moment, it does so with characteristics that pertain to an ancient Greek way of life and education; namely, life as action in society. However, the characteristics of modern society, Leopardi's society, dominated by selfishness and ephemeral values, had very little in common with the ancient models. This is why the end of the *Zibaldone* also seals the moment when Leopardi definitively projects himself into modernity rather than into the past. Leopardi here also attempts to answer, at the end of his journey, the question that Plato's Socrates had been unable to resolve, when in the *Meno* Anytus asks him: 'have there not been many good men in this city?'.[2] Socrates replies that indeed, 'many good statesmen also there have been and there are still, in the city of Athens. But the question is whether they were also good teachers of their own virtue'.[3]

Leopardi has been wondering all his life whether virtue can be taught. He has engaged in conversation with the worthiest literary and philosophical models and drawn vital energy from them for his own, original production. But he has also pushed his intellect beyond the limits and thus unveiled the most destructive consequences of truth. The last implicit reference to Rinaldo through the anecdote of the self-deceived husband seals the departure of Leopardi's choice from that of Rinaldo. Leopardi has discovered that the world of reading and thinking is insufficient as a teacher if what is learnt is not applied to the everyday praxis of living. Meno was right to tell Socrates that because of his perplexing dialectics he had been 'wise in not voyaging and going away from home', for in some foreign city he would be cast into prison as an evil enchanter.[4] Leopardi, who has already experienced all possible forms of magnetic spell — he has been both immobilized by the fixed gaze of reason and transported by unpredictable poetic outcomes — has progressively learned to inhabit the city, he has understood that it is now time to return to praxis. Leopardi is very careful to leave a reasoning forwhy his notebook ends, suggesting that his move must not be interpreted as a defeat, as was the case with his lack of conversational skills in his Roman experience and the final outcome of Adam's intellectual presumption.

The end of the *Zibaldone* is foreshadowed on the previous page, where Leopardi, before declaring that 'there is nothing to hope for after death' — a thought at odds with Christian doctrine — quotes Plato's *Apology of Socrates*, and in particular the passage 'avrete *nome* di avere ucciso Socrate' ('you will have the *name* of having killed Socrates') (*Zib.* 4525). The text refers to the moment when Socrates, shortly before his death, addresses the Athenian people who had condemned him to death. He tells them that it was not a lack of words that defeated his defence: 'You think that I was convicted because I had no words of the sort which would have procured my acquittal — I mean, if I had thought fit to leave nothing undone or unsaid. Not so'; and he affirms that 'the difficulty [...] is not to avoid death', but to escape from doing wrong, 'to avoid unrighteousness'.[5] And this, in Leopardi's case, meant ceasing trying to escape death (or the dangers of cognition) through writing, and to start living.[6]

This merging of the particular into the general which Leopardi discusses in his last note occurs also in the form of the writing. The last page of the original manuscript is occupied only by the word 'generale', which thus appears to be the only isolated word in the whole notebook. The word 'generale' is the most particular of all, and this contradiction enacts the content of the entry to which it belongs; that is, the merging of the particular and the general. If Leopardi wanted to preserve the coexistence but also the transcendence of both models, the symbolic Adamic model, which reappears as a modern experience of hyper-clarity, and the performative model of the Greeks, embodied in this last isolated word, he would have to preserve this word — and thus the integrity of the seal — in isolation, and end his *Zibaldone*.

Notes to Chapter 20

1. Clement of Alexandria, *Stromateis*, 4.2.5.1, quoted in Osborn, *Clement of Alexandria*, p. 41.
2. Plato, 'Meno', p. 292.
3. Ibid.
4. Ibid., p. 277.
5. Plato, 'Apology', in *The Dialogues of Plato*, I, 329–66 (pp. 363–64).
6. As Caesar and D'Intino comment in their note to *Zib.* 4526: 'In this last entry, the Book and the World become one — in the end' (*EZ*, p. 2365).

BIBLIOGRAPHY

ACCADEMIA DELLA CRUSCA, *Vocabolario degli accademici della Crusca*, 4th edn, 6 vols (Florence: Manni, 1729–38), <http://www.lessicografia.it>

AGAMBEN, GIORGIO, *The Open: Man and Animal*, trans. by Kevin Attell (Stanford, CA: Stanford University Press, 2004)

—— *State of Exception*, trans. by Kevin Attell (Chicago, IL, & London: University of Chicago Press, 2005)

—— *The Time That Remains: A Commentary on the Letter to the Romans*, trans. by Patricia Dailey (Stanford, CA: Stanford University Press, 2005)

ALEXANDER, AMIR, *Infinitesimal: How a Dangerous Mathematical Theory Shaped the Modern World* (New York: Farrar, Straus & Giroux, 2014)

ALIGHIERI, DANTE, *The Divine Comedy: Paradiso*, trans. by Robin Kirkpatrick (New York: Penguin, 2012)

ALOISI, ALESSANDRA, *Desiderio e assuefazione studio sul pensiero di Leopardi* (Pisa: ETS, 2014)

—— 'Elogio dell'inoperosità: Agamben e Leopardi', *Italian Studies*, 72.3 (2017), 282–91

ANDERSON, OWEN, *The Clarity of God's Existence: The Ethics of Belief After the Enlightenment* (Eugene, OR: Wipf & Stock, 2009)

ANDRIA, MARCELLO, 'Dallo schedario all'indice', in Giacomo Leopardi, *Zibaldone di pensieri*, photographic edition of the *Zibaldone*, ed. by Emilio Peruzzi, 10 vols (Pisa: Scuola Normale Superiore, 1989–94), x, 49–61

ANSALDI, CASTO INNOCENTE, *Della necessità e verità della religione naturale rivelata* (Venice: Valvasense, 1755)

ARGAN, GIULIO C., 'Preface', in Paul Klee, *Notebooks. Vol. 1. The Thinking Eye*, trans. by Ralph Manheim (London: Lund Humphries, 1973), pp. 11–18

ARIEMMA, TOMMASO, 'Dell'esposizione: contro l'integralismo', *Kainos*, 8 (2008), <http://www.kainos.it/numero8/ricerche/ariemma-esposizione.html>

—— *Il nudo e l'animale: filosofia dell'esposizione* (Rome: Editori Riuniti, 2006)

—— *Il senso del nudo* (Milan: Mimesis, 2007)

ARIOSTO, LUDOVICO, *Orlando Furioso, An English Prose Translation*, trans. by Guido Waldman (Oxford: Oxford University Press, 1974)

ARMANDO, DAVID, 'Ignaro, ignoto, inconoscibile... metamorfosi di una parola', in *L'Africa interiore: l'inconscio nella cultura tedesca dell'Ottocento*, ed. by Ludger Lütkehaus, trans. by Antonio Marinelli (Rome: L'asino d'oro, 2015), pp. 271–316

ATHANASIUS, Saint, *The Life of Antony and the Letter to Marcellinus*, trans. by Robert C. Gregg, (New York: Paulist Press, 1980)

BACHELARD, GASTON, *L'Activité rationaliste de la physique contemporaine* (Paris: PuF, 1951)

BACON, FRANCIS, *Novum Organum*, in *The Works of Francis Bacon*, IV, *Translations of the Philosophical Works 1* (1858), ed. by James Spedding, Robert Leslie Ellis, and Douglas Denon Heath (Cambridge: Cambridge University Press, 2011)

BAPTANDIER, BRIGITTE, 'Le Texte en filigrane', in *Du corps au texte: approches comparatives*, ed. by Brigitte Baptandier and Giordana Charuty (Nanterre: Société d'ethnologie, 2008), pp. 7–24

BARAD, KAREN, *Meeting the Universe Half-way: Quantum Physics and the Entanglement of Matter and Meaning* (Durham, NC: Duke University Press, 2007)

BAUDRILLARD, JEAN, *The Consumer Society*, trans. by Chris Turner (Los Angeles, CA, London, New Delhi & Singapore: Sage, 2008)

—— 'Symbolic Exchange and Death', in *Selected Writings*, ed. by Mark Poster (Stanford, CA: Stanford University Press, 1988), pp. 119–48

BECCARIA, CESARE, *Ricerche intorno alla natura dello stile* (Milan: Galeazzi, 1770)

BENJAMIN, WALTER, *The Arcades Project*, trans. by Howard Eiland and Kevin McLaughlin (Cambridge, MA, & London: Harvard University Press, 1999)

—— 'G. Leopardi, *Gedanken*', in *Critiche e recensioni*, ed. by Giorgio Agamben (Turin: Einaudi, 1979)

BERGSON, HENRI, *Matter and Memory*, trans. by Nancy Margaret Paul and W. Scott Palmer (London: Allen & Unwin, 1919)

BERTUCCI, PAOLA, and GIULIANO PANCALDI (eds), 'Introduction', in *Electric Bodies: Episodes in the History of Medical Electricity* (Bologna: University of Bologna Press, 2001), pp. 5–15

BIANCHI, ANGELA, *Pensieri sull'etimo: riflessioni linguistiche nello 'Zibaldone' di Giacomo Leopardi* (Rome: Carocci, 2012)

BIGI, EMILIO, 'La teoria del piacere e la poetica del Leopardi', in *Lo 'Zibaldone' cento anni dopo: composizione, edizioni, temi*, ed. by Ronaldo Garbuglia (Florence: Olschki, 2001), pp. 1–15

BLAIR, ANN M., *Too Much to Know: Managing Scholarly Information Before the Modern Age* (New Haven, CT, & London: Yale University Press, 2010)

BLASUCCI, LUIGI, 'I registri della prosa: Zibaldone, Operette, Pensieri', in *Lo 'Zibaldone' cento anni dopo, composizione, edizioni, temi*, ed. by Ronaldo Garbuglia (Florence: Olschki, 2001), pp. 17–35

—— 'Su una famosa pagina dello *Zibaldone*: il giardino malato (4174–77)', in *Lo 'Zibaldone' di Leopardi come ipertesto* ed. by Maria de las Nieves Muñiz Muñiz (Florence: Olschki, 2013), pp. 41–53

BODEI, REMO, *La vita delle cose* (Rome: Laterza, 2014), Kindle edition

—— *The Life of Things, the Love of Things*, trans. by Murtha Baca (New York: Fordham University Press, 2015)

BOLOGNA, CORRADO, 'I ghiribizzi di Guicciardini', in *Francesco Guicciardini tra ragione e inquietudine*, ed. by Paola Moreno and Giovanni Palumbo (Liege: Faculté de Philosophie et Lettres de l'Université de Liege, 2005), pp. 75–107

BOLZONI, LINA, *La rete delle immagini: predicazione in volgare dalle origini a Bernardino da Siena* (Turin: Einaudi, 2009)

—— *La stanza della memoria* (Turin: Einaudi, 1995)

—— *Il teatro della memoria: studi su Giulio Camillo* (Padua: Liviana, 1984)

BONADEO, ALFREDO, 'Leopardi e la religione della vita', *Italica*, 87.4 (2010), 554–81

BOTTURI, FRANCESCO, 'Ingegno verità storia: filosofia dell'immaginaio vichiano', in *Simbolo e conoscenza*, ed. by Virgilio Melchiorre (Milan: Vita e pensiero, 1988), pp. 127–68

BOURGUET, MARIE-NOËLLE, 'A Portable World: The Notebooks of European Travellers (Eighteenth to Nineteenth Centuries)', *Intellectual History Review*, 20.3 (2010), 377–400

BROZZI, ELISABETTA, 'Le note filologiche dello *Zibaldone*', in *Lo 'Zibaldone' di Leopardi come ipertesto*, ed. by Maria de las Nieves Muñiz Muñiz (Florence: Olschki, 2013), pp. 183–89

BRUSOTTI, MARCO, 'Figure della caducità: Nietzsche e Leopardi', in *Leopardi: poeta e pensatore / Dichter und denker*, ed. by Sebastian Neumeister and Raffaele Sirri (Naples: Guida, 1997), pp. 319–35

CACCIAPUOTI, FABIANA, *Dentro lo 'Zibaldone': il tempo circolare della scrittura di Leopardi* (Rome: Donzelli, 2010)

―― 'La forma della scrittura nello *Zibaldone* di Giacomo Leopardi: dalla circolarità al progetto', in *Lo 'Zibaldone' di Leopardi come ipertesto*, ed. by Maria de las Nieves Muñiz Muñiz (Florence: Olschki, 2013), pp. 73–85

―― 'Polizzine richiamate e non richiamate', in Giacomo Leopardi, *Zibaldone di pensieri*, photographic edition of the *Zibaldone*, ed. by Emilio Peruzzi, 10 vols (Pisa: Scuola Normale Superiore, 1989—94), x, 63–68

―― 'La scrittura dello 'Zibaldone' tra sistema filosofico ed opera aperta', in *Lo 'Zibaldone' cento anni dopo. Composizione, edizioni, temi*, ed. by Ronaldo Garbuglia (Florence: Olschki, 2001), pp. 249–56

CAESAR, MICHAEL, '"Mezz'ora di nobiltà": Leopardi e i suo lettori', in *Leopardi a Firenze*, ed. by Laura Melosi (Florence: Olschki, 2002), pp. 461–71

―― 'On the Indexing of the *Zibaldone*', in *Lo 'Zibaldone' di Leopardi come ipertesto*, ed. by Maria de las Nieves Muñiz Muñiz (Florence: Olschki, 2013), pp. 287–300

―― 'Poet and Audience in the Young Leopardi', *The Modern Language Review*, 77.2 (1982), 310–24

―― 'Voice, Vision and Orality: Notes on Reading Adriana Cavarero', in *Orality and Literacy in Modern Italian Culture*, ed. by Michael Caesar and Marina Spunta (Oxford: Legenda, 2006), pp. 7–17

CAFFI, CLAUDIA, *La mitigazione: un approccio pragmatico alla comunicazione nei contesti terapeutici* (Münster: Lit Verlag, 2001)

CAMILLETTI, FABIO A., 'Leopardi *avec* Sade: Impotence and *Jouissance* in "La ginestra"', in *Ten Steps: Critical Inquiries on Leopardi*, ed. by Fabio A. Camilletti and Paola Cori (Oxford: Peter Lang, 2015), pp. 205–25

―― *Leopardi's Nymphs: Grace, Melancholy, and the Uncanny* (Oxford: Legenda, 2013)

CAMPANA, ANDREA, *Leopardi e le metafore scientifiche* (Bologna: Bononia University Press, 2008)

CARRERA, ALESSANDRO, 'Nietzsche e Leopardi: per una critica della modernità', in *Giacomo Leopardi: estetica e poesia*, ed. by Emilio Speciale (Ravenna: Longo, 1992), pp. 11–36

CARRUTHERS, MARY, *The Book of Memory: A Study of Memory in Medieval Culture* (Cambridge & New York: Cambridge University Press, 1990)

―― *The Craft of Thought: Meditation, Rhetoric, and the Making of Images, 400–1200* (Cambridge: Cambridge University Press, 1998)

CASINI, PAOLO, 'L'iniziazione di Leopardi: filosofia dei lumi e scienza newtoniana', in *Giacomo Leopardi e il pensiero scientifico*, ed. by Giorgio Stabile (Rome: Fahrenheit 451, 2001), pp. 59–77

Catechismo cioè istruzione secondo il Decreto del Concilio di Trento a' parrochi, trans. by Alessio Figliucci (Lucca: Giuntini, 1791)

CAVAGNA, ANDREA, 'Information Transfer and Behavioural Inertia in Starling Flocks', *Nature Physics*, 10 (2014), 691–96

―― 'Interaction Ruling Animal Collective Behavior Depends on Topological Rather than Metric Distance: Evidence from a Field Study', *Proceedings of the National Academy of Sciences of the United States of America*, 105 (2008), 1232–37

CAVARERO, ADRIANA, *For More Than One Voice: Toward a Philosophy of Vocal Expression*, trans. by Paul A. Kottman (Stanford, CA: Stanford University Press, 2005)

CERTEAU, MICHEL DE, *The Practice of Everyday Life*, trans. by Steven Rendall (Berkeley, Los Angeles, & London: University of California Press, 1988)

CERVATO, EMANUELA, *A System that Excludes All Systems: Giacomo Leopardi's 'Zibaldone di Pensieri'* (Bern: Peter Lang, 2017)

―― 'Lo *Zibaldone* come ipertesto: limiti e possibilità', in *Lo 'Zibaldone' di Leopardi come ipertesto*, ed. by Maria de las Nieves Muñiz Muñiz (Florence: Olschki, 2013), pp. 313–32

CHAMBERS, EPHRAIM, 'Common-Place-Books', in *Cyclopaedia: or, An Universal Dictionary of Arts and Sciences*, 2 vols (London: J. & J. Knapton, 1741), I

—— *Dizionario universale delle arti e delle scienze di Efraimo Chambers*, 9 vols (Venice: Pasquali, 1747)
CHARUTY, GIORDANA, 'Somnambules à la lettre', in *Du corps au texte: approches comparatives*, ed. by Brigitte Baptandier and Giordana Charuty (Nanterre: Société d'ethnologie, 2008), pp. 151–84
CICERO, MARCUS TULLIUS, *On the Republic and On the Laws*, trans. by David Fott (Ithaca, NY, & London: Cornell University Press, 2014)
CITATI, PIETRO, 'Così Leopardi ha scritto il libro infinito', *La Repubblica*, 6 August 2009, <http://ricerca.repubblica.it/repubblica/archivio/repubblica/2009/08/06/zibaldone-cosi-leopardi-ha-scritto-il-libro.html>
COLAIACOMO, CLAUDIO, 'Al di qua del Paradiso (Su autorità e religione nello sviluppo intellettuale leopardiano)', in *Letteratura e critica: studi in onore di N. Sapegno*, ed. by Walter Binni and others, 5 vols (Rome: Bulzoni, 1975), II, 537–74
—— *Camera obscura: studio di due canti leopardiani* (Naples: Liguori, 1992)
—— 'Crisi dell' "ancient regime": dall'uomo di lettere al letterato borghese', in *Letteratura italiana*, ed. by Alberto Asor Rosa, 16 vols (Turin: Einaudi, 1982), II, 363–412
—— *Il poeta della vita moderna: Leopardi e il romanticismo* (Rome: Sossella, 2013)
—— '*Zibaldone di pensieri* di Giacomo Leopardi', in *Letteratura italiana*, ed. by Alberto Asor Rosa, 16 vols (Turin: Einaudi, 1995), III, 217–301
CORI, PAOLA, 'L'attenuazione in Leopardi: lingua, diritto e storia delle idee', in *La metafora da Leopardi ai contemporanei*, ed. by Antonella Del Gatto, special issue of *Studi Medievali e Moderni*, 1 (2016), 43–62
—— '"Di temenza è sciolto": pensiero e poesia della soglia', *Rivista Internazionale di Studi Leopardiani*, 7 (2011), 41–68
—— '"ec. ec. ec.": modi e forme della sospensione nello *Zibaldone*', in *Lo 'Zibaldone' di Leopardi come ipertesto*, ed. by Maria de las Nieves Muñiz Muñiz (Florence: Olschki, 2013), pp. 93–107
—— 'Ephemera: The Feeling of Time in Leopardi's *Canto notturno*', *Italian Studies*, 67.1 (2012), 70–91
—— 'Intelletto', in *Lessico leopardiano 2016*, ed. by Novella Bellucci, Franco D'Intino and Stefano Gensini (Rome: Sapienza Università Editrice, 2016), pp. 57–63
—— 'Ipnotismo e iperrealtà: spunti per un dialogo tra Leopardi e il postmoderno', *Italian Studies*, 74. 3(2019)
—— 'Italian Mesmerism, Religion and the Unconscious: Irresistible Analogies from Muratori to Morselli', in *Archaeology of the Unconscious: Italian Perspectives*, ed. by Alessandra Aloisi and Fabio A. Camilletti (London: Routledge, forthcoming), pp. 113–40
—— 'Reflections on Leopardi, Borges, Deleuze and the Rhizome', *Appunti leopardiani*, 1.1 (2011), 20–25, <http://www.appuntileopardiani.cce.ufsc.br/edition012011/artigosphp/paola.php>
—— '"Tensione" nello *Zibaldone*', in *Per un lessico leopardiano*, ed. by Novella Bellucci and Franco D'Intino (Rome: Palombi, 2011), pp. 133–49
—— '"Time-image" in Poetry and Cinema: Leopardi and Antonioni', in *Ten Steps: Critical Inquiries on Leopardi*, ed. by Fabio A. Camilletti and Paola Cori (Oxford: Peter Lang, 2015), pp. 175–203
—— 'The *Zibaldone* as Leopardi's Self-education', *Italica*, 93.1 (2016), 77–91
COSTA, PAOLO, *Della elocuzione* (Bologna: Riccardo Masi, 1827)
—— *Del modo di comporre le idee e di contrassegnarle con vocaboli precisi*, 3rd edn (Parma: Fiaccadori, 1838)
CRARY, JONATHAN, *Suspension of Perception: Attention, Spectacle and Modern Culture* (Cambridge, MA, & London: MIT Press, 2001)
—— *Techniques of the Observer: On Vision and Modernity in the Nineteenth Century* (Cambridge, MA, & London: MIT Press, 1992)

DARNTON, ROBERT, *Mesmerism and the End of the Enlightenment in France* (Cambridge, MA, & London: Harvard University Press, 1968)

DAVIDSON, LUKE ANTONY FRANCIS, 'Raising Up Humanity: A Cultural History of Resuscitation and the Royal Humane Society of London, 1774–1808' (unpublished doctoral thesis, University of York, 2001)

DE FRENZA, LUCIA, 'La morte e l'elettricità: esperienze di elettrofisiologia tra XVIII e XIX secolo', in *Storia della definizione di morte*, ed. by Francesco Paolo de Ceglia (Milan: Franco Angeli, 2014), pp. 251–74

DELEUZE, GILLES, *Difference and Repetition*, trans. by Paul Patton (New York: Columbia University Press, 1994)

—— *Francis Bacon: The Logic of Sensation*, trans. by Daniel W. Smith (London & New York: Continuum, 2002)

DEL GATTO, ANTONELLA, *Aspetti della mimesi nella modernità letteraria: premesse petrarchesche e realizzazione romantica* (Sesto Fiorentino: Apice, 2015)

—— '*Quel punto acerbo*': temporalità e conoscenza metaforica in Leopardi (Florence: Olschki, 2012)

DELIEGIS, GIOVANNI, *Dottrina cristiana, ovvero catechismo polemico* (Venice: Occhi, 1764)

DE LUCA PICIONE, RAFFAELE, *La mente come forma, la mente come testo: una indagine semiotico-psicologica dei processi di significazione* (Milan: Mimesis, 2015)

DE LUCA PICIONE, RAFFAELE, and MARIA FRANCESCA FREDA, 'The Processes of Meaning Making, Starting from the Morphogenetic Theories of René Thom', *Culture & Psychology*, 22.1 (2016), 139–57

DESCARTES, RENÉ, *The Philosophical Writings of Descartes*, trans. by John Cottingham, Robert Stoothoff, and Dugald Murdoch, 2 vols (Cambridge: Cambridge University Press, 1999)

DESTUTT DE TRACY, ANTOINE-LOUIS-CLAUDE, *Elementi d'ideologia*, ed. by Giuseppe Compagnoni (Milan: Stellam 1817)

DIDEROT, DENIS, 'Léibnitzianisme ou philosophie de Léibnitz', in *Encyclopédie méthodique: philosophie ancienne et moderne*, ed. by Jacques-André Naigeon, 3 vols (Paris: Panckoucke, 1791–94), III, 109–27

DIHLE, ALBRECHT, *The Theory of Will in Classical Antiquity* (Berkeley & Los Angeles: University of California Press, 1982)

DI NAPOLI, GIUSEPPE, *I principi della forma: natura, percezione e arte* (Turin: Einaudi, 2011)

D'INTINO, FRANCO, 'Errore, ortografia e autobiografia in Leopardi e Stendhal', in *Memoria e infanzia tra Alfieri e Leopardi*, ed. by Marco Dondero and Laura Melosi (Macerata: Quodlibet, 2004), pp. 167–83

—— *L'immagine della voce* (Venice: Marsilio, 2009)

—— 'I misteri di Silvia: motivo persefoneo e mistica eleusina in Leopardi', *Filologia e critica*, 19 (1994), 211–71

—— 'Il monaco indiavolato: Lo *Zibaldone* e la tentazione faustiana di Leopardi', in *Lo 'Zibaldone' cento anni dopo, composizione, edizioni, temi*, ed. by Rolando Garbuglia (Florence: Olschki, 2001), pp. 467–512

—— 'Oralità e dialogicità nello "Zibaldone"', in *Lo 'Zibaldone' di Leopardi come ipertesto*, ed. by Maria de Las Nieves Muñiz Muñiz (Florence: Olschki, 2013), pp. 221–43

D'INTINO, FRANCO, and LUCA MACCIONI, *Leopardi: guida allo 'Zibaldone'* (Rome: Carocci, 2016)

DI STEFANO, MARIA DONATA, *Per ragionar da poeta: il linguaggio poetico nello 'Zibaldone' di Giacomo Leopardi*, (Florence: Atheneum, 2007)

DOLFI, ANNA, 'Da l'"intime" al "philosophique": le strutture cognitive dello *Zibaldone*', in *'Journal intime' e letteratura moderna*, ed. by Anna Dolfi (Rome: Bulzoni, 1989), pp. 109–39

—— *Le verità necessarie: Leopardi e lo 'Zibaldone'* (Modena: Mucchi, 1995)

DORNIER, CAROLE, 'Writing the Inner Citadel: The Therapeutics of the Soul in Rousseau's *Rêveries d'un promeneur solitaire*', in *Subject Matters: Subject and Self in French Literature from Descartes to the Present*, ed. by Paul Gifford and Johnnie Gratton (Amsterdam: Rodopi, 2000), pp. 60–74

DU BOIS, PHILIPPE GOIBAUT, sieur, 'Discours sur les "Pensées" de M. Pascal', in Blaise Pascal, *Pensées sur la religion, et sur quelques autres sujets* (Amsterdam: Henry Wetstein, 1701), pp. 5–65

DUC, KHANH DAO, 'Leibniz dans l'*Encyclopédie*', *Recherches sur Diderot et sur l'"Encyclopédie"*, 48 (2013), 123–42

ELLENBERGER, HENRI, *The Discovery of the Unconscious: True History and Evolution of Dynamic Psychiatry* (New York: Basic Books, 1970)

—— 'The Unconscious Before Freud', *Bulletin of the Menninger Clinic*, 21.1 (1957), 3–15

ESPOSITO, ROBERTO, *Due: la macchina della teologia politica e il posto del pensiero* (Turin: Einaudi, 2013), Kindle

—— *Le persone e le cose* (Turin: Einaudi, 2014)

—— *Pensiero vivente: origine e attualità della filosofia italiana* (Turin: Einaudi, 2010)

—— *Living Thought: The Origins and Actuality of Italian Philosophy*, trans. by Zakiya Hanafi (Stanford, CA: Stanford University Press, 2012)

ESTERHAMMER, ANGELA, 'Philosophies of Identity and Impersonation from Locke to Charles Mathews', in *Romanticism and Philosophy*, ed. by Sophie Laniel-Musitelli and Thomas Constantinesco (New York: Routledge, 2015), pp. 147–65

FARRELL, ALLAN P., 'Notes to the Translation', in *The Jesuit 'Ratio Studiorum' of 1599*, trans. by Allan P. Farrell (Washington, DC: Conference of the Major Superiors of Jesuits, 1970)

FERRERI, PIETRO MARIA, *Istruzioni in forma di catechismo per la pratica della dottrina cristiana* (Venice: Baglioni, 1790)

FERRUCCI, CARLO, 'Leopardi e l'esperienza estetica della verità', in *Leopardi e il pensiero moderno*, ed. by Carlo Ferrucci (Milan: Feltrinelli, 1989), pp. 199–213

—— *Leopardi filosofo e le ragioni della poesia* (Venice: Marsilio, 1987)

—— 'Il "sistema" dello *Zibaldone*', in *Leopardi e la cultura europea*, ed. by Franco Musarra and Serge Vanvolsem (Rome: Bulzoni, 1989), pp. 227–34

FONTANA, FELICE, *Ricerche filosofiche sopra la fisica animale*, 5 vols (Florence: Cambiagi, 1775)

FOUCAULT, MICHEL, 'On the Genealogy of Ethics: An Overview of Work in Progress in Ethics', in *Subjectivity and Truth: The Essential Works of Michel Foucault (1954–1984)*, ed. by Paul Rabinow, 3 vols (New York: New Press, 1997)

—— *Wrong-doing, Truth-telling: The Function of Avowal in Justice*, ed. by Fabienne Brion and Bernard E. Harcourt, trans. by Stephen W. Sawyer (Chicago, IL: University of Chicago Press, 2014)

FRATTINI, ALBERTO, 'Leopardi e gli ideologi francesi del Settecento', in *Leopardi e il Settecento*, ed. by Salvatore Battaglia and others (Florence: Olschki, 1964), pp. 253–82

GALLIFUOCO, SILVANA, 'Pensieri di varia filosofia e di bella letteratura', in Giacomo Leopardi, *Zibaldone di pensieri*, photographic edition of the *Zibaldone*, ed. by Emilio Peruzzi, 10 vols (Pisa: Scuola Normale Superiore, 1989–94), X, 9–18

GALVANI, LUIGI, 'From *De Viribus Electricitatis* (1791)', in *Literature and Science in the Nineteenth Century: An Anthology*, ed. by Laura Otis (Oxford: Oxford University Press, 2002), pp. 135–39

GARDINI, NICOLA, *Lacuna: saggio sul non detto* (Turin: Einaudi, 2014)

GAZZERI, CECILIA 'Pensiero, parola, corporeità: un nesso ideologico-sensista nella filosofia del linguaggi di Giacomo Leopardi', *Segni e comprensione*, 19.56 (2005), 113–23

GENSINI, STEFANO, *Linguistica leopardiana* (Bologna: Il Mulino, 1984)

―――'Manzoni, Leopardi e lo scacco della lingua', *Bollettino di Italianistica*, 11.2 (2012), 66–81

GHIRLANDA, GIANFRANCO, *Il diritto nella chiesa, mistero di comunione: compendio di diritto ecclesiale* (Rome: G & B Press, 2014)

GIORDANI, PIETRO, 'Ode del Monti (Per le nozze dell'egregia donzella Adelaide Calderaia col signor Giacomo Butti)', *Antologia*, 18 (1825), 77–78

GIROLAMI, PATRIZIA, *L'antiteodicea: Dio, dei, religione nello 'Zibaldone' di Giacomo Leopardi* (Florence: Olschki, 1995)

GÖDDE, GÜNTER, 'Freud and Nineteenth-century Philosophical Sources on the Unconscious', in *Thinking the Unconscious: Nineteenth-century German Thought*, ed. by Angus Nicholls and Martin Liebscher (Cambridge: Cambridge University Press, 2010), pp. 261–86

GOLDSTEIN, JAN, 'The Advent of Psychological Modernism in France: An Alternate Narrative', in *Modernist Impulses in the Human Sciences, 1870–1930*, ed. by Dorothy Ross (Baltimore, MA: John Hopkins University Press, 1994), pp. 190–209

―――*The Post-revolutionary Self: Politics and Psyche in France, 1750–1850* (Cambridge, MA, & London: Harvard University Press, 2008)

GRATTON, PETER, and MARIE-EVE MORIN (eds), 'Introduction', in *Jean-Luc Nancy and Plural Thinking: Expositions of World, Ontology, Politics and Sense* (Albany: State University of New York Press, 2012), pp. 1–10

GUIDI, FRANCESCO, *Trattato teorico-pratico di magnetismo animale considerato sotto il punto di vista fisiologico e psicologico* (Milan: Turati, 1854)

HARAWAY, DONNA, *Modest_Witness@Second_Millennium: FemaleMan[(c)]_Meets_OncoMouse(tm)* (New York & London: Routledge, 1997)

HARTMANN, EDUARD VON, *Philosophie des Unbewussten: Versuch einer Weltanschauung* (Berlin: Duncker, 1869)

HAVELOCK, ERIC A., *Origins of Western Literacy* (Toronto: Ontario Institute for Studies in Education, 1976)

HAWTHORNE, NATHANIEL, *Selected Stories*, ed. by Brenda Wineapple (Cambridge, MA, & London: Harvard University Press, 2011)

HEBSGAARD, MARK, 'Giacomo Leopardi's 'Zibaldone' and Hypertext', in *Storia e multimedia*, ed. by Francesca Bocchi and Peter Denley (Bologna: Grafis, 1994), pp. 647–53

HEILBRON, J. L., *Electricity in the 17th and 18th Centuries: A Study of Early Modern Physics* (Berkeley: University of California Press, 1979)

HÖLKER, KLAUS, '"Diciamo" come mitigatore', in *Aspetti dell'italiano parlato*, ed. by Klaus Hölker and Cristiane Maaß (Münster: Lit Verlag, 2005), pp. 53–79

HUFELAND, CHRISTOPH WILHELM, *The Art of Prolonging Life*, 2 vols (London: Bell, 1797)

JESUITS, *The Jesuit 'Ratio Studiorum' of 1599*, trans. by Allan P. Farrell (Washington, DC: Conference of the Major Superiors of Jesuits, 1970)

JOHNSON, LAURIE RUTH, *The Art of Recollection in Jena Romanticism: Memory, History, Fiction, and Fragmentation in Texts by Friedrich Schlegel and Novalis* (Tübingen: Max Niemeyer, 2002)

JORDANOVA, LUDMILLA, *Nature Displayed: Gender, Science and Medicine 1760–1820* (London & New York: Routledge, 1999)

JOSSA, STEFANO, 'Il cibo della mente: appunti per una metafora', in *La sapida eloquenza: retorica del cibo e cibo retorico*, ed. by Cristiano Spila (Rome: Bulzoni, 2004), pp. 35–41

―――*L'Italia letteraria* (Bologna: Il Mulino, 2006)

―――'Oltre la tradizione romanzesca: Rinaldo e "l'aspra legge di Scozia" (*Orlando Furioso*, IV–VI)', *Chroniques Italiennes*, 19.1 (2011), 1–20

JOYCE, MICHAEL, *Of Two Minds: Hypertext Pedagogy and Poetics* (Ann Arbor: University of Michigan Press, 1995)

JULLIEN, VINCENT (ed.), *Seventeenth-century Indivisibles Revisited*, special issue of *Science Networks: Historical Studies*, 49 (2015)
JUVENAL, *The Sixteen Satires*, trans. by Peter Green (London: Penguin, 1998)
KANT, IMMANUEL, *Critique of Pure Reason*, trans. and ed. by Paul Guyer and Allen W. Wood (Cambridge: Cambridge University Press, 1998)
KLEE, PAUL, *Notebooks. Vol. 1. The Thinking Eye*, trans. by Ralph Manheim (London: Lund Humphries, 1973)
KOELB, CLAYTON, *The Revivifying Word: Literature, Philosophy, and the Theory of Life in Europe's Romantic Age* (Rochester, NY: Camden House, 2008)
LACOUE-LABARTHE, PHILIPPE, and JEAN-LUC NANCY, *The Literary Absolute: The Theory of Literature in German Romanticism*, trans. by Philip Barnard and Cheryl Lester (Albany: State University of New York Press, 1988)
LAURO, ROBERTO, 'Le idee e le parole: il lessico straniero nello *Zibaldone*', in *Ten Steps: Critical Inquiries on Leopardi*, ed. by Fabio A. Camilletti and Paola Cori (Oxford: Peter Lang, 2015), pp. 87–119
LAUXTERMANN, P. F. H., 'Five Decisive Years: Schopenhauer's Epistemology as Reflected in His Theory of Colour', *Studies in History and Philosophy of Science*, 18.3 (1987), 271–91
LEIBNIZ, GOTTFRIED WILHELM VON, 'Preface', in *New Essays of Human Understanding*, ed. by Peter Remnant and Jonathan Bennet (Cambridge: Cambridge University Press, 2000)
LEJEUNE, GUILLAUME, 'Early Romantic Hopes of Dialogue: Friedrich Schlegel's Fragments', in *Literature as Dialogue: Invitations Offered and Negotiated*, ed. by Roger D. Sell, special issue of *Dialogue Studies*, 22 (2014), 251–70
LEOPARDI, GIACOMO, *Canti*, trans. by Jonathan Galassi (New York: Farrar, Straus & Giroux, 2010)
—— *Dissertazioni filosofiche*, ed. by Tatiana Crivelli (Padua: Antenore, 1995)
—— *Epistolario*, ed. by Franco Brioschi and Patrizia Landi, 2 vols (Turin: Bollati Boringhieri, 1998)
—— *The Letters of Giacomo Leopardi 1817–1837*, trans. by Prue Shaw (Leeds: Northern Universities Press)
—— *Moral Tales*, trans. by Patrick Creagh (Manchester: Carcanet New Press, 1983)
—— *Pensieri di varia filosofia e di bella letteratura*, ed. by Giosuè Carducci, 7 vols (Florence: Successori Le Monnier, 1898–1900)
—— *Scritti e frammenti autobiografici*, ed. by Franco D'Intino (Rome: Salerno, 1995)
—— *Storia dell'astronomia dalla sua origine fino all'anno MDCCCXI*, in Giacomo Leopardi and Margherita Hack, *Storia dell'astronomia dalle origini al 2000 e oltre* (Rome: Edizioni dell'Altana, 2002)
—— *Tutte le poesie e tutte le prose*, ed. by Lucio Felici and Emanuele Trevi (Roma: Newton Compton, 2007)
—— *Volgarizzamenti in prosa (1822–1827)*, ed. by Franco D'Intino (Venice: Marsilio, 2012)
—— *Zibaldone di pensieri*, ed. by Anna Maria Moroni, 2 vols (Milan: Mondadori 1997)
—— *Zibaldone di pensieri*, ed. by Fiorenza Ceragioli and Monica Ballerini (Bologna: Zanichelli, 2009) (CD-ROM)
—— *Zibaldone di pensieri*, photographic edition, ed. by Emilio Peruzzi, 10 vols (Pisa: Scuola Normale Superiore, 1989–94)
—— *Zibaldone di pensieri: nuova edizione tematica condotta sugli indici leopardiani*, ed. by Fabiana Cacciapuoti (Rome: Donzelli, 2014)
—— *Zibaldone di pensieri*, Hypertext Research Platform by Silvia Stoyanova, Princeton University, <http://digitalzibaldone.net/entry>
—— *Zibaldone: The Notebooks of Leopardi*, ed. by Michael Caesar and Franco D'Intino, trans. by Kathleen Baldwin and others (London: Penguin, 2013)
LIOY, PAOLO, *Lo studio della storia naturale* (Florence: Le Monnier, 1857)

LOCKE, JOHN, *An Essay Concerning Human Understanding*, ed. by Kenneth P. Winkler (Indianapolis, IN: Hackett, 1996)

LONGO, ODDONE, *Volatilia: animali dell'aria nella storia della scienza da Aristotele ai giorni nostri*, ed. by Oddone Longo (Naples: Procaccini, 1999)

LOTMAN, JURI, 'On the Semiosphere' [1984], trans. by Wilma Clark, *Sign Systems Studies*, 33.1 (2005), 205–29

LUCAN, *The Civil War (Pharsalia)*, trans. by J. D. Duff (Cambridge, MA: Harvard University Press, 1977)

LUPTON, JULIA REINHARD, 'Creature Caliban', *Shakespeare Quarterly*, 51.1 (2000), 1–23

MCLUHAN, MARSHALL, *Understanding Media: The Extensions of Man* (Cambridge, MA, & London: MIT, 2002)

MAFFEI, SCIPIONE, *Istoria teologica delle dottrine e delle opinioni corse ne' cinque primi secoli della Chiesa in proposito della divina Grazia, del libero arbitrio, e della Predestinazione* (Trent: Parone, 1742)

MAPELLI, ROBERTO, 'Nichilismo attivo e rigenerazione di civiltà: Leopardi e Freud interpreti della crisi', in *Il Contributo*, 31.2 (2009), 19–30

MARCON, LORETTA, *Kant e Leopardi* (Naples: Guida, 2010)

—— 'La ragione, il corpo, la vita: Kant, Hufeland, Leopardi', *Rivista di letteratura italiana*, 25.2 (2007), 49–70

—— *Vita ed esistenza nello 'Zibaldone' di Giacomo Leopardi* (Rome: Stango, 2001)

MARROU, HENRI-IRÉNÉE, *A History of Education in Antiquity*, trans. by George Lamb (Madison & London: University of Wisconsin Press, 1956)

MARTINELLI, BORTOLO, *Leopardi tra Leibniz e Locke: alla ricerca di un orientamento e di un fondamento* (Rome: Carocci, 2003)

MEYER, ELIZABETH A., *Legitimacy and Law in the Roman World: Tabulae in Roman Belief* (Cambridge: Cambridge University Press, 2004)

MILDER, ROBERT, *Hawthorne's Habitations: A Literary Life* (Oxford: Oxford University Press, 2013)

MILLS, CHARLES WRIGHT, *White Collar: The American Middle Classes* (New York: Oxford University Press, 1956)

MONETA, MARCO, *L'officina della aporie: Leopardi e la riflessione sul male negli anni dello 'Zibaldone'* (Milan: Franco Angeli, 2006)

MONNO, OLGA, '"Migrazioni" della gru: da Omero ai simboli medievali', *Vetera Christianorum*, 45 (2008), 91–111

MONTAIGNE, MICHEL DE, *The Education of Children*, ed. and trans. by L. E. Rector (New York: Appleton, 1899)

MONTESPERELLI, FRANCESCA, *Flussi e scintille: l'immaginario elettromagnetico nella letteratura dell'Ottocento* (Naples: Liguori, 2002)

MONTIGLIO, SILVIA, *Wandering in Ancient Greek Culture* (Chicago, IL: University of Chicago Press, 2005)

MORAVIA, SERGIO, *Il pensiero degli idéologues: scienza e filosofia in Francia, 1780–1815* (Florence: La Nuova Italia, 1974)

MUELLNER, LEONARD, 'The Simile of the Cranes and Pygmies: A Study of Homeric Metaphor', *Harvard Studies in Classical Philology*, 93 (1990), 59–101

MURATORI, LUDOVICO ANTONIO, *Della forza della fantasia umana* (Venice, Pasquali: 1745)

NANCY, JEAN-LUC, *Being Singular Plural*, trans. by Robert D. Richardson and Anne E. O'Byrne (Stanford, CA: Stanford University Press, 2000)

NEGRI, ANTIMO, 'Leopardi e la filosofia di Kant', *Trimestre*, 4 (1971), 479–91

NICHOLLS, ANGUS and MARTIN LIEBSCHER, 'Introduction: Thinking the Unconscious', in *Thinking the Unconscious: Nineteenth-Century German Thought*, ed. by Angus Nicholls and Martin Liebscher (Cambridge: Cambridge University Press, 2010), pp. 1–25

NIETZSCHE, FRIEDRICH, *Beyond Good and Evil*, ed. by Rolf-Peter Horstmann and Judith Norman, trans. by Judith Norman (Cambridge: Cambridge University Press, 2002)
—— *Intorno a Leopardi*, ed. by Cesare Galimberti (Genoa: Il melangolo, 1992)
—— *Untimely Meditations* ed. by Daniel Breazeale, trans. by R. J. Hollingdale (Cambridge: Cambridge University Press, 2007)
NOBILI, LEOPOLDO, and VINCENZO ANTINORI, 'Sopra la forza elettromotrice del magnetismo', *Antologia*, 131.11 (1831), 149–61
ORIOLI, FRANCESCO, *Fatti relativi a mesmerismo e cure mesmeriche* (Corfù: Tipografia del governo, 1842)
—— 'Lettera II. Mesmerismo nella sua maggior semplicità. Definizione del medesimo. Forza del desiderio, della volontà, della speranza, della fiducia, del timore, dell'attenzione nel produrre o nel togliere i morbi e generalmente nel perturbare il corpo: riflessioni generali e particolari', *Opuscoli scientifici*, 1.2 (1817), 117–40
OSBORN, ERIC, *Clement of Alexandria* (Cambridge: Cambridge University Press, 2008)
O'SULLIVAN, TIMOTHY M., *Walking in Roman Culture* (Cambridge: Cambridge University Press, 2011)
PAUL, SAINT, 'Epistle to the Romans', in *The King James Version of the Holy Bible*, ed. by Dan Cogliano, 2004, p. 647, <http://www.davince.com/download/kjvbiblea.pdf>
PASCAL, BLAISE, *Pensées sur la religion, et sur quelques autres sujets* (Amsterdam: Henry Wetstein, 1701)
—— *Thoughts*, trans. by Edward Craig (Andover: Allen, Morrill & Wardwell, 1846)
PASSERIN D'ENTRÈVES, ALEXANDER, *Natural Law: An Introduction to Legal Philosophy* (New Brunswick, NJ, & London: Transaction, 2009)
PEDRETTI, CARLO, '*Eccetera perché la minestra si fredda' (Codice Arundel, fol. 245 recto)*, XV Lettura Vinciana (Florence: Giunti Barbera, 1975)
PELLEREY, ROBERTO, 'Significato e comunicazione: il ruolo della grammatica negli "idéologues"', *Belfagor*, 45 (1990), 369–84
PERUZZI, EMILIO, 'Presunti antecedenti', in Giacomo Leopardi, *Zibaldone di pensieri*, photographic edition of the *Zibaldone*, ed. by Emilio Peruzzi, 10 vols (Pisa: Scuola Normale Superiore, 1989–94), I, XIX–XXIII
—— 'Stesura e stile', in Giacomo Leopardi, *Zibaldone di pensieri*, photographic edition of the *Zibaldone*, ed. by Emilio Peruzzi, 10 vols (Pisa: Scuola Normale Superiore, 1989–94), I, LVI–LXI
PETERS, RICHARD S., 'What is an Educational Process?', in *The Concept of Education*, ed. by Richard S. Peters (London: Routledge, 1967), pp. 1–23
PICK, DANIEL, *Svengali's Web: The Alien Enchanter in Modern Culture* (New Haven, CT, & London: Yale University Press, 2000)
PINTO, RAFFAELE, 'L'archeologia delle emozioni: le pulsioni di morte nello *Zibaldone*', in *Lo 'Zibaldone' di Leopardi come ipertesto*, ed. by Maria de las Nieves Muñiz Muñiz (Florence: Olschki, 2013), pp. 245–56
PIPERNO, MARTINA, *Rebuilding Post-revolutionary Italy: Leopardi and Vico's 'New Science'* (Oxford: Voltaire Foundation, 2018)
PLATO, *The Dialogues of Plato*, trans. by Benjamin Jowett, 4th edn, 4 vols (Oxford: Oxford University Press, 1967)
PLINY THE YOUNGER, *The Letters of the Younger Pliny*, trans. by Betty Radice (Harmondsworth: Penguin, 1969)
POLETTI, GEMINIANO, 'Considerazioni sopra l'uso del calcolo nella fisica', *Antologia*, 18 (1825), 44–57
POLIZZI, GASPARE, 'Alla ricerca dello "specioso" e dell' "insolito": Francesco Orioli e Giacomo Leopardi', *Lettere italiane*, 60.3 (2008), 394–419

—— *Galileo in Leopardi* (Florence: Le Lettere, 2007)
—— *Leopardi e 'le ragioni della verità': scienze e filosofia della natura negli scritti leopardiani* (Rome: Carocci, 2003)
PRANDI, MICHELE, and ELISA RASCHINI, 'La similitudine tra le forme di attenuazione dell'interazione concettuale', in *Euphémismes et stratégies d'atténuation du dire*, ed. by Paola Paissa and Ruggero Druetta, special issue of *Synergies Italie* (2009), 21–30, <https://gerflint.fr/Base/Italie-special/prandi.pdf>
PRETE, ANTONIO, *Il pensiero poetante* (Milan: Feltrinelli, 1980)
—— 'Sulla scrittura dello *Zibaldone*: la forma dell' essai e i modi del preludio', in *Lo 'Zibaldone' cento anni dopo: composizione, edizioni, temi*, ed. by Ronaldo Garbuglia (Florence: Olschki, 2001), pp. 387–93
PUYSÉGUR, ARMAND-MARIE-JACQUES DE CHASTENET, MARQUIS DE, *An Essay of Instruction: Teaching the Method of Magnetizing*, trans. by John King (New York: J. C. Kelley, 1837)
REGENBOGEN, ARNIM, and HOLGER BRANDES, 'Unbewußte, das', in *Europäische Enzyklopädie zu Philosophie und Wissenschaften*, ed. by Hans Jörg Sandkühler, 4 vols (Hamburg: Felix Meiner, 1990), IV, 647–61
RENNIE, NICHOLAS, *Speculating on the Moment: The Poetics of Time and Recurrence in Goethe, Leopardi and Nietzsche* (Göttingen: Wallstein, 2005)
RICCI, ALESSIO, 'Sintassi e testualità dello *Zibaldone di pensieri* di Giacomo Leopardi, parte I', *Studi linguistici italiani*, 27.2 (2001), 172–213
—— 'Sintassi e testualità dello "Zibaldone di pensieri" di Giacomo Leopardi, parte II', *Studi linguistici italiani*, 28.1 (2002), 33–59
RICCINI, MARCO, 'Lo *Zibaldone di pensieri*: progettualità e organizzazione del testo', in *Leopardi e il libro nell'età romantica*, ed. by Michael Caesar and Franco D'Intino (Rome: Bulzoni, 2000), pp. 81–104
RICHARDS, I. A., *The Philosophy of Rhetoric* (Oxford: Oxford University Press, 1965)
—— *Practical Criticism: A Study of Literary Judgement* (London: Kegan Paul, 1930)
RICŒUR, PAUL, *The Rule of Metaphor: The Creation of Meaning in Language*, trans. by Robert Czerny, Kathleen McLaughlin, and John Costello (London & New York: Routledge, 2003)
RIESMAN, DAVID, *The Lonely Crowd: A Study of the Changing American Character* (New Haven, CT, & London: Yale University Press, 2001)
ROSA, GIULIO, *Gli infiniti disordini delle cose: sullo 'Zibaldone' di Leopardi* (Salerno: Edisud, 2012)
ROSENZWEIG, FRANZ, *The Star of Redemption*, trans. by William W. Hallo (New York: Holt, Rinehart & Winston, 1971)
ROSSI, PAOLO, *Clavis universalis: arti della memoria e logica combinatoria da Lullo a Leibniz* (Bologna: Il Mulino, 2000)
—— *Il passato, la memoria, l'oblio: otto saggi di storia delle idee* (Bologna: Il Mulino, 2013)
ROSSI MONTI, MARTINO, *Il cielo in terra: la grazia fra teologia ed estetica* (Turin: UTET, 2008)
SABATINI, ANGELO G., 'Nietzsche e Leopardi', in *Leopardi e il pensiero moderno*, ed. by. Carlo Ferrucci (Milan: Feltrinelli, 1989), pp. 173–81
SANTNER, ERIC L., *On Creaturely Life: Rilke, Benjamin, Sebald* (Chicago, IL, & London: Chicago University Press, 2006)
SAPIENZA UNIVERSITÀ DI ROMA, 'Lo Zibaldone parla l'inglese', 29 July 2013, <http://www.uniroma1.it/archivionotizie/lo-zibaldone-parla-inglese>
SCHLEGEL, FRIEDERICH, 'Critical Fragments', in *German Aesthetic and Literary Criticism: The Romantic Ironists and Goethe*, ed. by Kathleen Wheeler (Cambridge: Cambridge University Press, 1984)

SCHLUN VAN, BETSY, *Science and the Imagination: Mesmerism, Media and the Mind in Nineteenth-century English and American Literature* (Berlin: Galda & Wilch, 2007)
SCHWICKERATH, ROBERT, *Jesuit Education, its History and Principles, Viewed in the Light of Modern Educational Problems* (St. Louis, MO: B. Herder, 1903)
SECONDULFO, DOMENICO, 'Introduzione', in *I volti del simulacro: realtà della finzione e finzione della realtà*, ed. by Domenico Secondulfo (Verona: Quiedit, 2007), pp. 9–34
SHELLEY, MARY, *Frankenstein*, ed. by David H. Guston, Ed Finn, and Jason Scott Robert (Cambridge, MA, & London: MIT Press, 2017
SOLMI, SERGIO, 'Il pensiero in movimento di Leopardi', in Giacomo Leopardi, *Zibaldone di pensieri*, ed. by Anna Maria Moroni, 2 vols (Milan: Mondadori, 1997), I, IX–XXVI
—— *Studi leopardiani* (Milan: Adelphi, 1987)
SPENCER, HERBERT, *Principles of Sociology* (London: Macmillan, 1969)
SPEYR, ADRIENNE VON, *La confessione*, ed. by H. U. von Balthasar (Milan: Jaca Book, 2002)
STAUM, MARTIN S., *Minerva's Message: Stabilizing the French Revolution* (Montreal & Kingston: McGill-Queen's University Press, 1996)
STOYANOVA, SILVIA, 'Lo *Zibaldone di pensieri* di Leopardi: un'edizione ipertestuale e una piattaforma di ricerca (http://zibaldone.princeton.edu)', in *Lo 'Zibaldone' di Leopardi come ipertesto*, ed. by Maria de las Nieves Muñiz Muñiz (Florence: Olschki, 2013), pp. 333–42
STRONATI, MONICA, *Il governo della 'grazia': giustizia sovrana e ordine giuridico nell'esperienza italiana (1848–1943)* (Macerata: Giuffrè, 2009)
TALAMONTI, ADELINA, 'Prefazione', in Clara Gallini, *La sonnambula meravigliosa: magnetismo e ipnotismo nell'Ottocento italiano* (Rome: L'Asino d'oro, 2012), Kindle edition
TARDE, GABRIEL, *The Laws of Imitation* [1890], trans. by E. C. Parsons (New York: Henry Holt, 1903)
TATAR, MARIA M., *Spellbound: Studies on Mesmerism and Literature* (Princeton, NJ: Princeton University Press, 1978)
TERDIMAN, RICHARD, *Present Past: Modernity and the Memory Crisis* (New York: Cornell University Press, 1993)
THOMAS AQUINAS, *Summa theologiae*, ed. by Liam G. Walsh, 61 vols (Cambridge: Cambridge University Press, 2006)
TIMPANARO, SEBASTIANO, *Classicismo e illuminismo nell'ottocento italiano* (Pisa: Nistri-Lischi, 1969)
TOMMASEO, NICCOLÒ, and BERNARDO BELLINI, *Dizionario della lingua italiana*, 8 vols (Turin: Unione tipografico-editrice, 1861–79), <http://www.tommaseobellini.it/#/items>
TORALDO DI FRANCIA, GIULIANO, 'L'infinito in una scienza finita', in *Le dimensioni dell'infinito/ Les Dimensions de l'infini*, ed. by Umberto Eco, Claudio Chiuderi, and Fernando Caruso, 50 Rue de Varenne: supplemento italo-francese di Nuovi argomenti, 29 (Paris: Istituto italiano di cultura, 1989), pp. 63–70
TRZECIAK, MALGORZATA EWA, *L'esperienza estetica nello 'Zibaldone' di Giacomo Leopardi* (Rome: Aracne, 2013)
UGNIEWSKA, JOANNA, 'Strutture saggistiche e strutture diaristiche nello *Zibaldone* leopardiano', *La rassegna della letteratura italiana*, 91.1 (1987), 325–38
UNIVERSITY OF BIRMINGHAM, 'Promoting the Zibaldone', 2013, <http://www.birmingham.ac.uk/research/activity/leopardi/projects/promoting.aspx>
VAN DER TUIN, IRIS, 'A Different Starting Point, a Different Metaphysics: Reading Bergson and Barad Diffractively', *Hypatia*, 26.1 (2001), 22–42
VECCE, CARLO, 'Appendice: "Una voce chiamantemi a cena"', in *Tre letture leopardiane* (Recanati: Edizioni CNSL, 2000), pp. 85–106
—— 'Leonardo da Vinci', in *Letteratura italiana*, ed. by Alberto Asor Rosa, 16 vols (Turin: Einaudi, 1993), II, 95–124

VERATI, LISIMACO, *Sulla storia teoria e pratica del magnetismo animale*, 4 vols (Florence: Bellagambi, 1845)

VERDENELLI, MARCELLO, 'Cronistoria dell'idea leopardiana di *Zibaldone*', *Il Veltro*, 5–6.31 (1987), 591–621

VERONESE, COSETTA, 'Leopardi and the "Zibaldone" into the New Millennium', in *Ten Steps: Critical Inquiries on Leopardi*, ed. by Fabio A. Camilletti and Paola Cori (Oxford: Peter Lang, 2015), pp. 57–83

—— *The Reception of Giacomo Leopardi in the Nineteenth Century: Italy's Greatest Poet After Dante?* (Lewiston, NY: Edwin Mellen Press, 2008)

—— 'Il sistema dello *Zibaldone* e i suoi lettori: Solmi e Timpanaro a confronto', in *Lo 'Zibaldone' di Leopardi come ipertesto*, ed. by Maria de las Nieves Muñiz Muñiz (Florence: Olschki, 2013), pp. 451–60

VERONESE, COSETTA, and PAMELA WILLIAMS, *The Atheism of Giacomo Leopardi* (Leicester: Troubador, 2013)

VERRI, PIETRO, *Discorsi* (Milan: Marelli, 1781)

VETRANO, FLAVIO, 'Giacomo e la scienza: suggestioni dell'infinito, riflessioni sull'eternità', in *Giacomo Leopardi e il pensiero scientifico*, ed. by Giorgio Stabile (Rome: Fahrenheit 451, 2001), pp. 169–75

VICO, GIAMBATTISTA, *Institutiones oratoriae*, ed. by Giuliano Crifò (Naples: Istituto Suor Orsola Benincasa, 1989)

—— *The Art of Rhetoric (Institutiones oratoriae 1711–1741)*, ed. by Giorgio A. Pinton and Arthur W. Shippee (Amsterdam: Rodopi, 1996)

—— *La scienza nuova 1744*, Laboratorio dell'ISPF, XII, 2015, digital ed. by Centro di Umanistica Digitale dell'ISPF-CNR and based on the critical ed. by Paolo Cristofolini and Manuela Sanna (Rome: Edizioni di Storia e Letteratura, 2013)

—— *The New Science*, trans. by Thomas Goddard Bergin and Max Harold Fisch (Ithaca, NY, & London: Cornell University Press, 1970)

VIGGIANI, GIACOMO, 'Diritto, magia e performatività', in *Linguaggio e istituzioni: discorsi, monete e riti*, ed. by Marco Carapezza and Francesca Piazza, special issue of *Rivista italiana di filosofia del linguaggio*, (2013), 325–38, <http://www.rifl.unical.it/index.php/rifl/article/view/216>

VIGORELLI, AMEDEO, *Il disgusto del tempo: la noia come tonalità affettiva* (Milan & Udine: Mimesis, 2009)

VOGEL, JOSEPH ANTON, *Epistolario*, ed. by Marcello Verdenelli (Ancona: Transeuropa, 1993)

VOLTA, ALESSANDRO, 'Continuazione delle osservazioni sulla capacità de' conduttori elettrici e sulla commozione che anche un semplice conduttore è atto a dare eguale a quella di una boccia di Leyden. Del signor Alessandro Volta in una lettera al signor De Saussure', in *Opuscoli scelti sulle scienze e sulle arti*, 22 vols (Milan: Marelli, 1778), I, 289–312

—— *On the Method of Rendering Very Sensible the Weakest Natural or Artificial Electricity* (*Del modo di rendere sensibile la più debole elettricità sia naturale, sia artificiale*) (London: Nichols, 1782)

WEBER, MAX, *Economy and Society: An Outline of Interpretive Sociology*, ed. by Guenther Roth and Claus Wittich (Berkeley: University of California Press, 1978)

WHYTE, LANCELOT LAW, *The Unconscious Before Freud* (London: Tavistock, 1960)

YATES, FRANCES A., *The Art of Memory* (London: Routledge & Kegan Paul, 1966)

YEO, RICHARD, *Encyclopaedic Visions: Scientific Dictionaries and Enlightenment Culture* (Cambridge: Cambridge University Press, 2001)

—— *Notebook, English Virtuosi, and Early Modern Science* (Chicago, IL, & London: The University of Chicago Press, 2014)

Zito, Paola, 'Danno del conoscere la propria età', in Giacomo Leopardi, *Zibaldone di pensieri*, photographic edition of the *Zibaldone*, ed. by Emilio Peruzzi, 10 vols (Pisa: Scuola Normale Superiore, 1989–94), x, 31–42

Zimmer, Nina, and Bodil Holst, 'Representations of Electricity: The Development of a Visual Language for Electrical Phenomena', *Interdisciplinary Science Review*, 27.4 (2002), 257–70

Zumbini, Bonaventura, *Studi sul Leopardi*, 2 vols (Florence: Le Monnier, 1902–04)

INDEX

Accademia della Crusca 97
   Vocabolario degli accademici della Crusca 97
Adam 8, 24, 26, 78, 89, 108, 118, 142, 155, 181, 182, 218, 219, 220, 221, 227, 235–36, 242, 243, 246
Aelian 136
   De natura animalium 136
Agamben, Giorgio 101–03
Alexander the Great 159
Alighieri, Dante 26, 110, 112, 136–37, 171, 202
   Divina Commedia. Paradiso 137
Aloisi, Alessandra and Fabio A. Camilletti x, 60 n. 4
Anacreon 52, 102, 154, 156, 212
Andrès, Juan 66
Antici, Adelaide 225 n. 2
Antologia 76 n. 14, 157
Arcesilaus 237
Ariosto, Ludovico 233, 235, 236
   Orlando Furioso 233, 236
Aristotle 136, 160, 184, 228
art of memory 14, 164
Athens 208, 246
Attila the Hun 234

Bacon, Francis 15, 16
Baudelaire, Charles 21, 28
Baudrillard, Jean 18, 169–70
Bayle, Pierre 147
Beccaria, Cesare 24, 57
Benjamin, Walter 21, 28, 35 n. 78, 44–45
Bergson, Henri 129, 165
   Matter and Memory 129
Biblioteca Italiana 60, n. 9
Biran, Maine de 30 n. 7, 165
Blair, Ann 14
Boccaccio, Giovanni 238
Bodei, Remo 204 n. 11
Boios 136
Bologna 34 n. 61, 175
Bologna, Corrado 74 n. 7
Braid, James 177
Brozzi, Elisabetta 139
Buffon, Georges Louis Leclerc de 128, 135
   Histoire naturelle des oiseaux 135
Buonarroti, Michelangelo 155, 182
   Creation of Adam 155, 182
Byron, George Gordon Noel 231

Cabanis, Pierre Jean Georges 30 n. 7, 46 n. 6
Cacciapuoti, Fabiana 32 n. 34, 33 n. 47, 34 n. 59, 132, 224
Caesar, Michael x, 16
Caesar, Michael and Franco D'Intino 247 n. 6
Caffi, Claudia 188
camera obscura 22–23, 172
Campana, Andrea 128
Carducci, Giosuè 28
Careno, Luigi 177
Cato the Elder 70
Cavagna, Andrea 134
Cavalieri, Bonaventura 49
Certeau, Michel de 209, 210, 237
Cervato, Emanuela x, 12, 16, 17, 29 n. 6
Chambers, Ephraim 13
   Cyclopaedia: or, An Universal Dictionary of Arts and Science 13
Charuty, Giordana 179
Chesterfield, Philip Dormer Stanhope Lord of 223
   Letters to His Son 223
Christianity:
   Christian catechism 91
   Christian faith 94, 95, 180
   Christian tradition 88, 89, 96, 238
   early Christianity 79–80, 94, 98–99
   post-Christian thought 81, 95, 96, 97, 108, 109
Cicero, Marcus Tullius 88, 92 n. 2, 106, 136
   De natura animalium 136
   De oratore 106
Citati, Pietro 29
Clement of Alexandria 97–100, 245
   Cohortatio ad gentes 97
   Stromateis 98
Colaiacomo, Claudio 48 n. 26, 94, 102–03, 225 n. 2
Coleridge, Samuel Taylor 28
Condillac, Etienne Bonnot de 43, 152
Costa, Paolo 69–70, 160
   Della elocuzione 160
   Del modo di comporre le idee 183
Council of Trent 84
   Catechismo cioè istruzione secondo il Decreto del Concilio di Trento a' parrochi 84
Crary, Jonathan 170, 172–73
Crivelli, Tatiana 61 n. 12

Index

D'Alembert, Jean Baptiste Le Rond 60 n. 11, 239
   Éloge de M. Jean Bernoulli 239
Darius III 159
Da Vinci, Leonardo 66
Degli Uberti, Fazio 142
   Dittamondo 142
Deleuze, Gilles 55
Descartes, René 41, 43, 55, 58, 62 n. 21, 77, 128, 192
   Principia philosophiae 62 n. 21
Destutt de Tracy, Antoine-Louis-Claude 61 n. 14
   Éléments d'idéologie 46 n. 6
Dihle, Albrecht 96
D'Holbach, Paul Henri Thiry baron 90
Diderot, Denis 56, 57, 58
Di Napoli, Giuseppe 10–11
D'Intino, Franco x, 78, 79, 100 n. 12, 223, 226 n. 15
Drexel, Jeremias 15
Du Bois, Philippe Goibaut 77
   Discours sur les Pensées de M. Pascal 77
Duc, Khanh Dao 60 n. 10
Du Maurier, George 178
   Trilby 178

elastic force 128–29
electricity 11, 5, 21, 23, 26, 39, 119, 150–57, 163 n. 16, 168 n. 18 177, 188, 212, 222
Ellenberger, Henri 55
Encyclopédie 56, 60 n. 10 and n. 11
Encyclopédie méthodique 56
Ennius 70
entropy 22, 23, 24, 43–44, 48 n. 26, 119–20
Epictetus 237
Esposito, Roberto 42, 112, 192, 200, 203
Esterhammer, Angela 187
examination:
   examination of conscience 82–84
   self-examination 40, 120, 192, 214, 218
exception (state of) 7–8, 25, 31 n. 21, 112–13, 144–46, 246
excess 63–73, 75 n. 10, 112, 113, 185, 189, 191, 199, 212
   of attention 21, 129, 233
   of imagination 188
   of intellectual power, rationality and thought 26, 98, 100, 177, 242, 246
   of sensitivity 22
   of vividness 183
   thought in excess 8, 13
exposure 1, 2, 6–8, 12, 20–27, 30 n. 16, 118–19, 134, 143, 148, 155, 166, 170, 174, 187–203, 221, 242, 245, 246

Farrell, Allan P. 217, 218
Ferrara 234
Ferreri, Pietro Maria 81
   Istruzioni in forma di catechismo per la pratica della dottrina cristiana 81
Ferrucci, Carlo 29
Fichte, Johann Gottlieb 108
   Über Geist und Buchstab in der Philosophie 108
Financial Times 27–28
Florence, 27, 34 n. 61, 201, 239, 240, 243 n. 5
Fontana, Felice 155
   Ricerche filosofiche sopra la fisica animale 155
Foucault, Michel 79–82, 237
Franklin, Benjamin 238, 239
   Mélanges de Morale, d'Économie et de Politique 239
   'Remarks concerning the Savages of North America' 239
French Idéologues 2, 43, 46 n. 6, 56, 61 n. 14, 90
Freud, Sigmund 40, 41, 177

Gaius the jurist 88
Galilei, Galileo 49
Galvani, Luigi 154, 155
generative forms 3–6, 9–11, 13, 23, 24, 117, 210
   everyday life 2, 18–21, 23, 111–12, 207–13, 215, 224, 246
   mathematics 5, 50, 51, 52 n. 5, 55, 89, 164
      actual infinity 71, 73
      calculus 15, 73, 76 n. 14
      divisibility 5, 49, 51, 53, 72, 73, 153–54
      indivisibles (theory of the) 49–52
      limits 5, 73
   religion, 2, 3, 4, 5, 6, 14, 24–25, 45, 46 n. 8, 49, 51, 77–85, 87–92, 94–100, 101–03, 105–13, 118, 148, 150, 154, 179, 180, 181–83, 194, 198, 211–12, 214, 225 n. 2, 230–31, 235–36
   science 2, 3, 5, 6, 21–23, 117–20, 152, 153
Genesis 218
Giordani, Pietro 76 n. 14, 140, 230, 231
   'Ode del Monti (Per le nozze dell'egregia donzella Adelaide Calderaia col signor Giacomo Butti)' 76 n. 14
Gödde, Günter 41, 43
Goethe, Johann Wolfgang 9, 28, 41, 173, 215–16
   Metamorphosis of Plants 9
   Theory of Colours 173
Goldstein, Jan 30 n. 7 and n. 10, 40
grace 5, 25, 97, 106, 109, 109–10, 112, 113, 117, 154, 156, 159, 160, 229–30, 246
   theological Grace 88, 97, 98, 101, 105–13, 229–30
Gratton, Peter and Marie-Eve Morin 8
gravitational force 21, 117, 119, 151, 152, 153, 164, 211
Gray, John 28
Guidi, Francesco 180

Hardy, Thomas 35 n. 70
   'The withered Arm' 35 n. 70
Harrison, Robert Pogue 28
Hartmann, Eduard von 41, 42
Havelock, Eric A. 212
   Origins of Western Literacy 212

Hawthorne, Nathaniel 35 n. 70, 180
  Berkshire notebook 180
  Ethan Brand 35 n. 70
Hazlitt, William 187
Hebsgaard, Mark 29
Heilbron, J. L. 151
Herder, Johann Gottfried von 41
Hoffmann, Friedrich 128
Homer 110, 136, 148 n. 6, 202, 207, 233, 238
  Iliad 136
Hufeland, Christoph Wilhelm 177
  Die Kunst, das menschliche Leben zu verlängern 177
Hume, David 187
hyper-clarity 26, 184, 218, 220, 221, 223, 224, 237, 245, 247
hypertext 16–17
  The *Zibaldone* as a hypertext, *see Zibaldone*
  The Hypertext Research Platform 29 n. 4

Isocrates 237
Issus, battle of 159

Jeremiah 230
Jerome 137
Jesuit instruction 5, 14–15, 16, 117, 120 n. 2, 127, 214, 217, 218, 230
  Ratio studiorum 127
Jesus Christ 84, 97, 108, 109, 110, 182
Jordanova, Ludmilla 91
Joyce, Michael 17
Justinian 88
  Digest 88
  Institutes 88
Juvenal 136

Kant, Immanuel 41, 43, 129, 192, 196
Kite, Charles 155
  Essay on the Recovery of the Apparently Dead 155
Klee, Paul 9–10
Köbell, Wilhelm von 184
Koelb, Clayton 107

Lacoue-Labarthe, Philippe and Jean-Luc Nancy 43
Lambert, Anne-Thérèse de Marguenat de Courcelles Madame de 228
  La Femme Hermite. Nouvelle Nouvelle 228
Lampedusa 234
Landow, George 16
Leibniz, Gottfried Wilhelm von 41, 43, 45, 54–59, 60 n. 2 and n. 9, 77, 84
  Leibnizian tradition 50, 60 n. 11
  New Essays, 56
Leopardi, Carlo 34 n. 61, 236, 240
Leopardi, Monaldo 34 n. 61, 225 n. 2
Leopardi, Paolina 34 n. 61
Leopardi's early scientific instruction 120 n. 2

Leopardi's philosophy of language 6, 57, 120, 191–95, 200–03
Leopardi's reflections on walking 20, 34 n. 61, 240
Leopardi's work:
  Canti:
    'Ad Angelo Mai' 225
    'Inno ai patriarchi' 118
    'Palinodia al marchese Gino Capponi' 138, 139, 142, 143
  'Discorso sopra lo stato presente dei costumi degli italiani' 243 n. 3
  Disegni letterari 32 n. 35, 178, 237
  Dissertazioni filosofiche 21
    'Dissertazione sopra i fluidi elastici' 128
    'Dissertazione sopra la luce' 173
    'Dissertazione sopra la percezione, il giudizio, e il raziocinio' 56
    'Dissertazione sopra la virtù morale in generale' 89
    'Dissertazione sopra l'elettricismo' 156
  Dissertazioni fisiche 117, 153, 154
  Operette morali:
    'Cantico del gallo silvestre' 189
    'Dialogo della Natura e di un Islandese' 7, 25–27
    'Dialogo di Federico Ruysch e delle sue mummie' 103
    'Dialogo di Timandro e di Eleandro' 104
    'Dialogo di Torquato Tasso e del suo genio familiare' 113
    'Elogio degli uccelli' 135, 148
    'Il Copernico' 117
    'Parini, ovvero della gloria' 140
    'Proposta di premi fatta dall'accademia dei sillografi' 175
  'Saggio sopra gli errori popolari degli antichi' 136, 141
  Storia dell'astronomia 117
  Zibaldone:
    attenuation (significance and use of) 187–203
    the confessional character of the *Zibaldone* 24, 45, 77–85, 111, 112, 113, 215, 218, 220, 238, 245
    cross-references in the *Zibaldone* 19, 20, 34 n. 60, 39, 63, 65, 66, 68, 121, 122–23, 131, 132, 169
    the demonstrative speculations of the *Zibaldone* 6, 13, 121–32, 143–48
    the dialogical character of the *Zibaldone* 2, 85, 98–99, 179, 188, 210, 214–43
    the elastic character of the *Zibaldone* 130–32
    the electric character of the *Zibaldone* 158–62
    the encyclopaedic character of the *Zibaldone* 2, 16, 43
    the end of the *Zibaldone* 20–21, 245–47
    et cetera (use of) 17, 55, 63–76, 113, 143, 148, 242
    the hypertextual character of the *Zibaldone* 17–18, 29 n. 4
    the 1827 *Index* 6, 8, 12, 16, 18, 19–20, 21, 25, 26, 29 n. 4, 32 n. 35, 33 n. 47, 34 n. 59,

34 n. 60, 39, 140, 210, 212, 225, 231–33, 235, 238, 240, 243 n. 5
The 1827 *Index* heading 'Assuefazione. Assuefattibilità e conformabilità dell'uomo. Attenzione. Imparare. Ingegno. Disposizioni naturali. Facoltà umane' 127
The 1827 *Index* heading 'Filologia. Passi d'autori, spiegati, corretti, ec. ec.' 139
The 1827 *Index* heading 'Piacere (Teoria del)' 121
The 1827 *Index* heading 'Vitalità, Sensibilità: il grado dell'amor proprio e dell'infelicità del vivente, è in proporzione di esse' 13, 121–32, 134–48
key motifs of Leopardi's philosophy:
   action 218, 219, 220, 221, 223, 225, 226 n. 12, 228, 230, 237, 241, 242, 245, 246
   antiquity 4, 5, 14, 24, 68
      vs modernity 6, 22, 24, 48 n. 26, 65–66, 99, 144, 158, 207–08, 210, 246
   attention 2, 5, 16, 21–22, 41, 58, 63, 68, 83, 129–30, 150, 154, 161, 169, 176, 177, 191, 202, 203, 221, 233
   clarity 4, 6, 24, 41, 43, 46, 53–59, 65, 66, 68, 69, 74 n. 5, 87, 108, 109, 111, 113, 120, 131, 146, 147, 148, 175, 183, 195, 215, 218, 219, 220, 238
   distraction 12, 21, 124, 129, 202, 209, 221, 229, 245
   error 17, 44, 53, 79, 80, 84, 108, 111, 147, 179, 185
   the Fall 24, 89, 108, 118, 180, 181, 182, 218, 220, 245
   habituation 64, 127, 165, 166, 174, 217
   imagination 2, 3, 7–8, 27, 40, 55–57, 78, 99, 102, 106, 110–13, 152, 153, 155, 158, 165, 175, 176, 187–88, 190, 201, 207, 209, 219
   indifference 22, 24, 128, 131, 219, 220, 221
      human indifference 128, 130, 237
      indifferent Nature 7, 31 n. 20
      modern indifference 22, 219, 220, 221
   modernity 4, 5, 21, 22, 24, 44, 90, 96, 97, 99, 103, 108, 138, 140, 143, 148, 170, 181, 207, 212, 220–21, 238, 246
   naturalness 24, 45–46, 75, 221
      and natural law 87–92, 96, 97, 101
      as the style of grace 105–13
   reason 25, 51, 55, 88, 89, 95, 98, 147, 153, 157, 161, 178, 181, 213
      dialectic reason 199, 208, 209
      excess of reason, *see* excess and hyperclarity
   theory of pleasure 91–92, 121, 124–27, 129, 130–31, 152, 190
   ultra-philosophy 6, 25, 95 97–100, 102, 108, 109, 113, 148, 209
metaphors used to describe the *Zibaldone* 2
mnemotechnics 11, 120, 164–70

the performative character of the *Zibaldone* 4, 9, 12, 21, 40, 64–65, 69, 70, 131, 148, 168, 169, 187–88, 198–99, 202, 209, 223–24, 227–28, 233, 245, 247
the private character of the *Zibaldone* 2, 139
reception of the English *Zibaldone* 27–28
revision (significance and practice of), 4, 8, 39, 121, 127–28, 129, 143, 195, 212, 214, 216, 217, 225, 235
the start of the *Zibaldone* 13
suspension of thinking and writing 17, 66
the systematic character of the *Zibaldone* 2, 3, 12, 13, 22, 39
unconscious thought and writing 13, 39–48, 79
the un-programmatic character of the *Zibaldone* 2, 12–25
variety of contents and forms 2
wandering in the *Zibaldone* 4, 18, 19–20, 21, 25–26, 27, 34 n. 59, 209–10, 222, 225, 236–40
Lioy, Paolo 135, 137
Locke, John 22, 30 n. 7, 43, 46 n. 6, 47 n. 9, 61 n. 14, 152, 192
Lotman, Juri 32 n. 30
Lucan 136
Lupton, J. 6–7

Machiavelli, Niccolò 230
Mai, Angelo 140
Manet, Édouard 184
McLuhan, Marshall 160, 161
Mesmer, Franz Anton 174, 175
mesmerism (or animal magnetism), hypnotic and magnetic imagery 5, 21, 23, 26, 35 n. 70, 150, 151, 152, 172–85, 188, 191, 196, 208, 245, 246
messianic thought 97, 98, 101–03
Milder, Robert 179, 180
Moneta, Marco 31 n. 20
Monno, Olga 137
Montesperelli, Francesca 153
Montesquieu, Charles-Louis de Secondat 105, 230
   Esprit des lois 128
   Grandeur et décadence des Romains 230
Monti, Vincenzo 140, 194
Muratori, Ludovico Antonio 175
   Della forza della fantasia umana 175

Nakedness, nudity 1
Nancy, Jean-Luc 1, 3, 8
Newton, 22, 118, 128, 202
   Newtonian geometry, optics and physics 21, 23, 117, 119, 173
   Newtonian revolution 23
   post-Newtonian science 73, 128
New York Review of Books 28
Nicholls, Angus and Martin Liebscher 47 n. 9

Nietzsche, Friedrich 28, 35 n. 78, 41, 42, 161
   On the Uses and Disadvantages of History for Life 42
   Untimely Meditations 42
Nobili, Leopoldo and Vincenzo Antinori 157
   'Sopra la forza elettromotrice del magnetismo' 157
Noto wind 136

Ohm, Georg Simon 151
Old Testament 96, 107
Opuscoli scientifici 176
Orioli, Francesco 175, 176, 183
Ovid 136

Pascal, Blaise 45, 77, 78, 109, 110
   Pensées 77
Pavel, Thomas 28
Pellerey, Roberto 62 n. 17
Peruzzi, Emilio 33 n. 37
Peters, Richard S. 214
Petrarch 97
Pisa 239, 240
Platner, Ernst 41
Plato 98, 209, 224
   Apology of Socrates 246
   Gorgias 208
   Ion 208
   Meno 208, 246
   Phaedrus 107, 223
   Protagoras 1
   Symposium 224
Pliny the Elder 14
Pliny the Younger 14
Plutarch 130
   De sollertia animalium 136
Poletti, Geminiano 76 n. 14
   'Considerazioni sopra l'uso del calcolo nella fisica' 76 n. 14
Polizzi, Gaspare 175
Puységur, Armand-Marie-Jacques de Chastenet marquis de 175

Rabanus Maurus 137
Ravenna 234
Recanati 18, 20, 21, 34 n. 61, 123 n. 2, 140, 230, 240
Ricci, Alessio 46 n. 1, 149 n. 20, 163 n. 24
Ricoeur, Paul 160
Rodriguez, Alfonso 230
   Esercizio di perfezione 230
Rome 7, 27, 34 n. 61, 234, 240
   ancient Rome 200
Rosenzweig, Franz 6
Rousseau, Jean-Jacques 215, 237
   Rêveries d'un promeneur solitaire 237
Royal Human Society of London 155

Sacchini, Francesco 15

Santner, Eric L. 6
   On Creaturely Life 6
Sawyer, Stephen W. 85 n. 6
Schelling, Friedrich Wilhelm Joseph von 41
Schlegel, Friedrich 103, 161
Schopenhauer, Arthur 41, 42, 173
scientific revolution 15
Secondulfo, Domenico 3–4
Seth, Vikram 28
Seurat, Georges 184
Shelley, Mary 35 n. 70
   Frankenstein 35 n. 70
simulacrum 11, 21, 120, 148, 169–70, 203
Sinner, Louis de 139, 140, 141
Sistine Chapel 155
Smith, Adam 187
Soave, Francesco 46 n. 6
   Saggio filosofico di Gio. Locke su l'umano intelletto, compendiato dal Dr. Winne, tradotto, e commentato 46 n. 6
Socrates 237
   Plato's Socrates 107, 208, 223, 224, 242, 246, 247
Solari, Filippo 13
Solmi, Sergio 31 n. 20, 86 n. 13
Spettatore 60, n. 9
Speyr, Adrienne von 82–83
Staël, Germaine de 60 n. 9
Stoyanova, Silvia 29, 34 n. 60
St. Paul 94, 107, 108, 230
   Epistle to the Romans 96
   Second Epistle to the Corinthians 107
Stronati, Monica 25

Tercier, Jean-Pierre 66
Terdiman, Richard 39–40
Testament of the Twelve Patriarchs 96
The New Republic 28
Theon 139, 141, 142
   Progymnasmata 139, 142
Thomas Aquinas 88, 89, 105
   Summa theologiae 88
Timpanaro, Sebastiano 31 n. 20
Tommaseo, Niccolo and Bernardo Bellini 163 n. 18
   Dizionario della lingua italiana 163 n. 18
Toraldo di Francia, Giuliano 72
tradition of notebook writing 13–16, 18–19, 68, 217–18
Trapani 234
Turner, J. M. W. 184
   Light and Colour (Goethe's Theory) — The Morning After the Deluge 184
   The Angel Standing in the Sun 184

Ulpian the jurist 88

Vecce, Carlo 66, 74 n. 6

Verati, Lisimaco 181, 182, 183
Veronese Cosetta and Pamela Williams 94
Verri, Pietro 128, 129
 'Discorso sull'indole del piacere e del dolore' 128
Vico, Giambattista 106, 107
 Institutio oratoriae 106
 New Science 107
Virgil 136, 70, 202
Vogel, Joseph Anton 13
Volney, Constantin François de Chasseboeuf 90, 91
 La Loi naturelle, ou catechisme du citoyen Français 90, 91
 Les Ruines ou Méditation sur les Révolutions des Empires 91

Volta, Alessandro 151, 152

walking in the Western philosophical tradition 4, 223, 237, 238, 246
Western philosophical reflections on the unconscious 30 n. 7, 30 n. 10, 40–44, 55, 179–80
White, Hayden 28
Wolff, Christian 41

Zumbini, Bonaventura 31 n. 20

www.ingramcontent.com/pod-product-compliance
Lightning Source LLC
Chambersburg PA
CBHW050453110426
42743CB00017B/3341